The Essential Ayurvedic Cookbook

The Essential Ayurvedic Cookbook

200 Recipes for Health, Wellness & Balance

Lois A. Leonhardi

Robert
ROSE

May this book be of benefit to all those
seeking to make positive change in their lives.
May that change bring harmony and balance
to body, mind and spirit, reverberating and
reaching all sentient beings.

Contents

Preface

I was first introduced to ayurveda in 2001 while living in Portsmouth, New Hampshire. At that time, I was running my own investment advisory firm and mastering the art of multitasking. I considered myself healthy but was keenly aware of the need to actively manage my stress levels. To deal with the type-A financial world energy that dominated my waking hours, I had taken up the practice of yoga six years earlier. Occasionally, I would experience an undiagnosable ailment (bloating, headaches, insomnia), but generally I felt that all was well.

The summer of 2001 changed my perspective on health and my life forever. Ed Danaher, a visiting doctor from Dr. Vasant Lad's Ayurvedic Institute in New Mexico, was seeing new clients for wellness consultations. I had never heard of ayurveda, even though it is the sister science to yoga. There was a lot of buzz around Dr. Danaher's visit and the famous Dr. Lad under whom he had trained extensively. I felt compelled to see what the fuss was all about, so I scheduled an appointment.

The consultation included a comprehensive intake interview. Dr. Danaher reviewed my diet, elimination, exercise, lifestyle and emotional stressors, and performed pulse diagnosis and tongue diagnosis. After a half-hour, he concluded, "You're vata. And your vata is high." Then he recommended an ayurvedic wellness plan: herbs and dietary changes that would bring me back to a state of balance.

I was a bit overwhelmed by the magnitude of the recommendations, but nonetheless intrigued; I wanted to learn more. Dr. Danaher directed me to a table of books. My eyes lit up when I saw the cookbook *Ayurvedic Cooking for Self-Healing*. Always on the lookout for new recipes, I grabbed that first. Then he suggested *Ayurveda: The Science of Self-Healing* as a good primer on ayurveda, so I purchased that one too. Both books were written by Dr. Vasant Lad.

That was the beginning of my ayurvedic journey. I read those books over and over and continued to purchase more of Dr. Lad's books over the next 10 years.

I found the concepts and terminology in ayurveda to be very similar to and symbiotic with my yoga studies. Ayurveda sees each individual as having a unique constitution. These unique constitutions are predisposed to certain imbalances. The imbalances may be precursors to disease if left unchecked. By understanding your constitution, you can take preventive measures to maintain balance and good health.

Reading about my constitution (vata), I quickly discovered links to my long-standing issues with dehydration, asthma, dry and cracked skin, a bloated belly and elimination issues. But what was more enlightening was the solution: I simply needed to adjust my diet and incorporate some meditation and other calming influences into my frenetic lifestyle.

As I began to implement the prescribed lifestyle and dietary changes — gradually, as time permitted — I noticed profound physical and emotional changes. My dry, chapped skin healed; my asthma subsided; my elimination became regular; my bloated belly slimmed down; my mind felt more focused and calm; my relationships with others became more balanced; I was more productive at work; I slept better and had more energy. I developed an awareness of the connection between what I ate and how I felt. Food was more than fuel. It was medicine and nourishment on many levels.

With the notable improvements to my physical and emotional health, it was easy to make the ayurvedic way of living my priority. I made a commitment to managing my investment career around my ayurvedic lifestyle. As I learned more about the other constitutions (pitta and kapha), I started informally offering advice based on ayurvedic principles. I cooked ayurvedic meals for guests and delighted in their enjoyment. During this time, I also began to teach private and group yoga classes in my spare time. In these classes, I integrated ayurvedic concepts to work more effectively with the various imbalances I observed in the students.

Curiously, the more immersed in ayurveda I became, the more I found myself encountering people who had sworn off ayurveda. They had been unsuccessful in their attempt to quickly integrate their doctor-prescribed wellness plan into their life, so they quit. Their objections to ayurveda were the same: "I'm not a vegetarian"; "I don't understand the Sanskrit words"; "I don't know how to cook for my family, since we are all different constitutions"; "I don't like Indian food"; "I don't have time for all these rules"; "No eating leftovers — are you serious?"

So I would try to get them back on track. I guided them through the maze of rules and helped them prioritize and streamline the recommendations. Cooking was a major obstacle, so I started creating recipes that would be balancing to their constitution and their family members' constitutions. Sometimes I taught them how to shop for and prepare ayurvedic meals. My recipes used fresh whole foods and were easy to prepare. I was frequently told I should write a book to explain all this, so I began recording my recipes. In the meantime, ayurveda wellness coaching was becoming a full-time hobby.

In 2010, I received a newsletter from the Ayurvedic Institute, offering summer courses taught by Dr. Lad. I immediately signed up for his intensive classes on marma therapy and pulse reading. Those classes were life-changing. Dr. Lad opened my eyes to the magnitude of ayurveda. I realized that, up until then, I had been exposed to a very small part of the vast system.

I decided to take a sabbatical and study ayurveda full time. I bolstered this decision with a visit to my astrologer, the world-renowned Chakrapani Ullal. He confirmed that I was predisposed to a career in natural medicine, yoga, cooking, writing and consulting. That marked the end of my investing career and the beginning of a holistic medicine career in alignment with my ayurvedic lifestyle.

After researching schools, I enrolled in Dr. Lad's Ayurvedic Studies Program Level 1 course, graduating in May 2012. I then traveled to Pune, India, to attend Dr. Lad's 6-week clinical application program. I spent 5 months traveling in India and met informally with ayurvedic doctors in Dharamsala, Pune, Varkala and Thodupuzha. It was interesting to note regional differences and approaches. I experienced firsthand the ayurvedic remedies for anemia, malnutrition, lung infections and dysentery. The herbal formulations were tailored to my constitution and imbalance, and the doctors worked closely with me to tweak the dosage and formulas as my condition changed. I enjoyed learning about herbs in this organic manner and noting the changes in my tongue as my condition improved.

I noticed a direct correlation between my attitude and my health. When I was feeling healthy and energetic, I enjoyed everyone I met and laughed about communication challenges and travel disruptions; when I felt sick and exhausted, I was extremely irritable and easily became impatient or angry when dealing with routine travel hassles. This made me think about all the cranky people in the world: perhaps they, too, have underlying physical health issues related to inadequate nutrition that keep them from optimal wellness and a feeling of joy.

After India, I traveled to Thailand and New Zealand, where I began writing this book. I sought out native doctors in each country I visited, informally gathering information on the local traditions, researching them online and comparing them to ayurveda.

I lived at a Buddhist monastery in Australia while studying Buddhism for two and a half months. While there, I was fortunate to meet a Tibetan doctor who accurately diagnosed the root cause of my "frozen shoulder" as severe anemia. Protein, iron and vitamin B_{12} deficiencies, along with depleted reserves, were confirmed with blood tests. As a yoga practitioner/instructor, I was relieved it was not arthritis. Things began to make sense as I connected this shoulder pain with my experimentation with vegetarianism at various times over the past 20-plus years. Each time I tried to follow this diet, I experienced symptoms such as clumps of hair falling out, loose teeth, an inability to focus, memory loss, deteriorating vision and fatigue that led me to sleep 10 or more hours per day. With my allergies to wheat, dairy, soy and nuts, a diet that is completely vegetarian is difficult at best. I have concluded that, for me, including meat in my diet brings balance. But I'm particular about the animal protein I ingest. At a minimum, it is organic. Ideally, it's from a local farm where the animals are grass-fed and treated humanely.

Armed with all this information, I returned to the U.S. to finish the book. My goal was to provide a general introduction to the principles of ayurveda that was accessible to people in a modern society. I designed the book to help people get started on their journey. It is by no means the final destination; rather, it is the first step on the path — developing an awareness of how food affects us physically and emotionally. With that awareness, we can make conscious and profound shifts in our lives, our relationships and our health. Ayurveda is about finding balance.

To address the chief complaints I have heard about implementing an ayurvedic approach, I followed these guidelines:

+ minimal use of Sanskrit
+ recipes suited to a Western palate
+ recipes designed to be balancing to all constitutions — tridoshic recipes — to make cooking for a family easier, with dosha-specific condiment tables for those who want to target specific constitutions
+ well-organized charts and time-saving tips to help readers prioritize and implement important concepts
+ dairy-free, gluten-free and soy-free alternatives with most recipes to address digestive sensitivities
+ some recipes containing animal protein for the carnivores
+ easy-to-digest, tasty bean and lentil recipes for aspiring vegetarians

Looking ahead, I intend to continue studying and creating new recipes (especially gluten-free and non-inflammatory dishes). There are various ways you can stay connected with me, to be notified of new recipes and learn about upcoming classes:

1. My blog: www.yogawithlois.com
2. Facebook: www.facebook.com/LoisALeonhardi
3. Twitter: http://twitter.com/yogawithlois
4. Instagram: http://instagram.com/yogawithlois
5. Pinterest: www.pinterest.com/yogawithlois
6. Author Central: www.amazon.com/author/loisaleonhardi
7. Sign up for my newsletter: http://yogawithlois.com/yoga/contact

Namaste,

Lois A. Leonhardi

Acknowledgments

My gratitude to Ed Danaher, my ayurvedic counselor, who first introduced me to ayurveda and the healing cookbooks of Dr. Vasant Lad.

Heartfelt appreciation to Dr. Lad for his prolific teachings (textbooks, classroom lectures and clinics), generosity and compassion, through which I continue to learn the vast wisdom of ayurveda. My recipes were created using information from Dr. Lad's "Qualities of Food Substances" and "Food Combining" tables, which are found in his book *Ayurvedic Cooking for Self-Healing*.

Thanks to Raj Chattergoon and the many reviewers, classmates, neighbors, family and taste-testers who helped with candid feedback, recommendations and support. And to Jiwan Shakti Khalsa, whose words of inspiration ("May your way to a smooth, graceful finish be shown to you with ease") magically helped me stay focused and meet my deadlines.

Gratitude to Coleen O'Shea for getting this book to a publisher; Robert Rose Inc. for their faith in my work; PageWave Graphics for the beautiful layout; and Sue Sumeraj and Jennifer MacKenzie for their thoughtfulness and patience throughout the editing process.

Thanks to everyone who has supported me on this journey. Without their feedback on the recipes, cooking supplies, help with proofing, places to stay, moral support and anything else I needed along the way, this book would not have been possible.

- ✦ Diana Adams, RN and gourmet
- ✦ Shawn Padulo, carpenter, chef and gastronomist
- ✦ Jeanie Kane, office manager and resource extraordinaire
- ✦ Heather Armishaw, teacher, chorister and foodie
- ✦ the cheery staff at A-Market
- ✦ Paula Scarborough, ayurveda goddess
- ✦ Laure Lacroix
- ✦ Erik Smith
- ✦ Hannah Goldblatt
- ✦ Dan Schmidt
- ✦ Iain Grysak
- ✦ Hayden Hernandez
- ✦ MaryBeth Ball-Nerone
- ✦ Shannon McCall
- ✦ Sue Duncan
- ✦ Michael Richard
- ✦ Christy Forbes

Introduction

Would you like to be healthier? Would you like to be able to better cope with the daily stresses of life? Would you like to have more happiness and balance in your life? The solution can be as simple as modifying your food choices to be in sync with your unique constitution.

The Essential Ayurvedic Cookbook is a wellness cookbook — a holistic approach to cooking that integrates the energetics of your body and your emotions to bring about a balanced state of health. I have taken the time-honored principles of ayurveda and interpreted them for use in a modern, Western society. My goal is to help you to understand and implement the theory so that you can immediately experience the benefits.

I have used ancient dietary guidelines to develop recipes designed for busy professionals, families and empty-nesters with discriminating taste and tight time schedules. The recommended ingredients are fresh, organic whole foods. Many of the recipes can be prepared in a multitude of ways (dairy-free, gluten-free, soy-free, with meat, vegetarian or vegan) to accommodate various preferences. I also suggest variations so you can modify the base recipe to create fresh new dishes. Once you start, you will see the endless possibilities.

To get started, it will be helpful to take a look at the big picture of the guiding philosophy of wellness called ayurveda.

Who Will Benefit from This Book?

✦ **People seeking to improve their dietary habits:**
This book provides an introduction to the key concepts of ayurveda. These principles have been successfully used in India to provide overall wellness for thousands of years. I have adapted ancient dietary principles to suit a Western lifestyle and palate, making healthy living accessible to all.

+ People who are new to ayurveda may feel overwhelmed and unsure about how to implement the food recommendations for themselves and their family. This book will provide answers. +

+ **Clients of ayurvedic practitioners:** People who are new to ayurveda may feel overwhelmed and unsure about how to implement the food recommendations for themselves and their family. This book will provide answers when their practitioner is not available, empowering them to understand the concepts and easily assimilate them into their life.

+ **Ayurvedic practitioners:** Practitioners will find this a valuable resource to give to clients. It will reinforce key concepts they have explained during the consultation. The amount of material presented at the first consultation can be overwhelming, so this book will serve as a handy reference guide — it is the notes clients wish they had taken during the consultation! Most important, this book will help their clients to easily implement their customized ayurvedic plan. With ease of implementation, client retention rates are much higher.

The goal is to spread wellness (and happiness) to everyone!

Part 1

———— ∽ ————

Understanding Ayurveda

What Is Ayurveda?

✦ Investing time
and money to stay
healthy makes sense,
especially if you consider
the alternative of
getting sick. ✦

Ayurveda is an ancient system of natural healing that has been used successfully in India for thousands of years. It is rooted in nature and was developed during a time when people lived in sync with the natural rhythms of their bodies, the days and the seasons. They had great respect for the environment and wanted to preserve the ecological balance for the welfare of humankind. During this time, the four aims of life were virtue, wealth, gratification and spiritual fulfillment. A long, disease-free life was necessary to achieve these goals.

The ancients believed in an interconnectedness of the body, mind and consciousness — a whole-body approach to well-being. To maintain a sustained state of well-being, ayurveda recommended diet and lifestyle choices designed to purify the physical and energetic channels of the body and promote longevity. These purifying measures were largely preventive, as the ancients knew that an ounce of prevention was worth a pound of cure. Ayurveda was more than a healing science; it was a way of life.

Unlike most holistic healing systems, ayurveda recognized that each person has a unique physical, spiritual and mental constitution. As such, diet and lifestyle recommendations were tailored to the individual — this was not a one-size-fits-all approach. Likewise, if a person fell ill, the physicians would custom-design a remedy so as to achieve optimal results. The ayurvedic healer would look for the root cause of an illness and advise the individual on how best to remedy the problem. The recommendations were tailored to the client and could consist of herbal formulations, cleansing therapies, rejuvenation therapies, dietary changes and lifestyle changes. The client was expected to actively participate in the healing process. Reversing the disease process took precious amounts of time, which is why there was so much emphasis on avoiding sickness in the first place.

The human body works the same today as it did then. Investing time and money to stay healthy makes sense, especially if you consider the alternative of getting sick. The costs of doctor visits, medicine, surgery and time away from your life and work are enormous in comparison to the costs (in time and money) to stay healthy with a preventive approach. Some insurance companies have done the math and are now reimbursing for preventive programs for their policy-holders. The time is ripe for a return to the time-honored practice of whole-body wellness.

The Five Elements and the Twenty Qualities

The wisdom of ayurveda is based on the theory that everything in the universe is derived from various combinations of five elements: ether (or space), air, fire, water and earth. Ayurveda does not define these elements in the literal sense that is used today; rather, the elements can be seen as metaphors that encompass physical qualities, energetic properties and biological functions.

Each of the five elements encompasses twenty different energies, or qualities, in varying amounts. The twenty qualities are grouped into ten pairs of opposites:

The Twenty Qualities in Pairs of Opposites

Heavy	Light
Slow/dull	Sharp/penetrating
Cold/cool	Hot
Oily	Dry
Slimy/smooth	Rough
Dense	Liquid
Soft	Hard
Static	Mobile/spreading
Subtle	Gross
Clear	Cloudy/sticky

Although all twenty qualities are present in every element, each element has dominant qualities that express themselves more strongly than others.

Every individual embodies the five elements in a unique combination that influences our constitutional makeup. Typically, one or two of the elements express themselves more strongly. When our elements are in balance, energy flows smoothly, we are in harmony with our true nature, and we are healthy and happy — our physical, mental and spiritual bodies are in sync. When our elements are out of balance, energy stagnates and channels become blocked; we become prone to diseases of the body and mind, which can bring physical and emotional distress.

Listed below are the dominant qualities associated with each of the elements, along with examples of how these qualities may manifest physically and emotionally in an individual; how they might express themselves as personality traits; and how an excess of an element can affect the individual's health.

Ether

Like the mind of Albert Einstein, the ether element is expressed in an individual as creativity, a vivid imagination and vivid dreams or daydreaming. When the ether element is elevated, individuals easily pick up on subtleties: they can enter a room and, without speaking to anyone, can immediately sense the mood of the people within. The default mood for someone with predominant ether is joy and lightheartedness. The individual may also have a delicate, "willowy" frame.

A person with etheric qualities may be the "life of the party," a child joyfully playing in the park with his imaginary friend or an office manager who proposes a grandiose vision of expanding into new territories but leaves the task of completing the details for implementation and execution up to others.

In the body, the ether element physically manifests as all the spaces, such as the spaces between organs. An excess of ether in the body can lead to insomnia, fear and memory loss.

Air

Like a cool breeze, the air element is expressed in an individual as movement (quick thinking, rapid speech and fast walking), coldness (in body temperature) and perhaps an aloof attitude. The air element can create a tendency toward dryness (flaky skin, constipation), roughness (cracked heels and elbows) or dry speech (choppy sentences). An "airy" person may also be very light in weight.

Dominant Ether Qualities

+ light
+ subtle
+ clear
+ spreading

Dominant Air Qualities

+ light
+ cold
+ dry
+ rough
+ mobile
+ clear

Examples of individuals with an abundance of the air element include the person who is always cold and is constantly requesting a warmer temperature setting, the nonstop talker who switches topics without taking a breath, the consummate multitasker and the person who fidgets in his seat and taps fingers, pens or toes to release nervous energy.

In the body, the air element manifests as all movement but has an affinity for the nervous system. An excess of air in the body can lead to stress, anxiety, bloating, gas, constipation and dehydration.

Fire

Like a blazing fire, a person with dominant fire qualities is easy to spot; they often stand out, whether for great accomplishments or raging tempers. They are hotheaded and may blow off steam on a regular basis. With laser-sharp intelligence and focus, they can solve complex problems that require determined effort. They can make you cry with a sharp tongue-lashing or laugh hysterically at their sarcastic wit. They can be intense, like the sun on a hot summer day. While they may be light in weight, the light quality here is more precisely associated with the light of intelligence or luminosity. Their eyes and skin may be sensitive to sunlight.

Individuals with an abundance of the fire element may look red (red hair, flushed face, sunburned skin). You are likely to find them giving a motivational speech to a captivated audience or working on a spreadsheet of their life plan, plotting how to achieve their lofty goals, then popping antacids because they have given themselves heartburn trying to reach those goals. These are the overachievers. They are well-read and are so intelligent that their idea of conversation often feels more like a debate as they expertly counter every comment with a statistic or a penetrating question; they are expert at cross-examining a witness. Regardless of the season, these people are always warm. You can spot them wearing a T-shirt or sandals even after the weather has turned cool, and they will most likely be arguing with an air individual about the optimal thermostat setting.

In the body, the fire element manifests as vision, digestive enzymes and metabolism. An excess of fire in the body can lead to inflammation, rashes, heartburn, acid indigestion and migraines.

Dominant Fire Qualities

- ✦ hot
- ✦ sharp
- ✦ light
- ✦ dry
- ✦ subtle
- ✦ spreading

Water

Dominant Water Qualities
✦ dull
✦ cool
✦ oily
✦ slimy
✦ liquid
✦ soft

Like a glacier-fed lake, people with predominant water qualities have a cool and calm personality. They have a tendency to retain water, and a roundness to their body shape. Their skin will generally be smooth, cool and clammy, but they are often the first to break a sweat playing team sports. At the end of a competition, they are most likely to say with sincerity, "It's not whether you win or lose, but how you play." They tend to "go with the flow," and they have a loving disposition.

Examples of individuals with a dominant water element include the "chill" surfer dude and the enlightened monk — they don't sweat the small stuff (or the big stuff) in life. This is the person you want in the exit row if your plane crashes, to calmly assist passengers off the plane.

In the body, the water element manifests as all bodily fluids: plasma, urine, synovial fluid and mucus. An excess of the water element can lead to phlegm, mucus, swelling and profuse sweating.

Earth

Dominant Earth Qualities
✦ heavy
✦ dull
✦ dense
✦ hard
✦ static
✦ gross

Like the earth, which supports human life, the earth element manifests as someone who is very strong (physically and emotionally), stable (a steady mind with unwavering thoughts) and heavy (large, heavy bones and weight, and a tendency for feeling heavyhearted, gloomy or moody). They remind me of a turtle — slow and steady with a hard protective shell. They talk and walk slowly and are slow to take action, make decisions or grasp new concepts; they are immovable (in their faith, ideas and opinions) and can be stubborn. Because of the dense quality, subtleties elude them: they will not perceive that you are upset with them; you will have to tell them quite directly.

People with an abundance of the earth element make strong, supportive friends. If you have been close friends with someone for many years, that person likely has a lot of earth qualities; if most of your friends are long-term close friends, then *you* are likely an earth person!

Examples of individuals with a predominant earth element include the college professor who puts her students to sleep with her slow, dull speech; the child who resists his mother's request to leave the playground by firmly rooting his bottom to the ground, defiantly folding his arms across his chest, pursing his lips and stubbornly refusing to move; and the employee who "hunkers down" in his cubicle for the evening to meet a project deadline. (Note that the energy is slower and duller as compared to a fire person, who would be blazing through the project with intensity.)

In the body, the earth element serves as our foundation and manifests primarily as our bones and cartilage. An excess of the earth element can lead to depression, obesity, lethargy and tumors.

The Elements and Emotions

Our moods and emotions also have an energetic makeup that can be linked back to the elements. Joy is related to the ether element and the quality of light (think of the expression "lightheartedness"). Sadness is related to the earth element and the quality of heavy (think of the heavy feeling of depression or moodiness). Anger is related to the fire element (picture a cartoon character with a red face and smoke coming out of the ears to represent the inferno inside). Calm is related to the water element (imagine the sense of calm you feel when seated next to a lake or listening to a waterfall).

Diet and the Five Elements

Ayurveda teaches us that the five elements are found in everything, including the food we eat. As with the elemental makeup of an individual, each food tends to have one or two dominating elements, along with the corresponding energetic qualities. For example, chile peppers are related to the fire element, which has hot, sharp, light, dry, subtle and spreading qualities. When you eat a chile, you can taste the heat on your tongue. Then, as the chile enters your digestive system, the heat spreads and you may begin to feel warm. If the chile is really hot (or you are ultrasensitive), you may feel an intense, sharp burning sensation and may even begin to perspire. Likewise, when you eat ice cream, you immediately feel the coolness of the water element flow to your core — you may even feel goosebumps on your skin.

If we understand the elements that rule our constitution and the elemental makeup of our food, we can shift to a diet that keeps those elements in balance. Consider the example of an individual with a predominant fire element. Fiery individuals are prone to acid indigestion, heartburn and fits of anger. To cool down the flames, such a person should eat foods with an abundance of the water element — foods that are cooling — and avoid foods with a dominant fire

Become Familiar with the Elements

As an exercise to help you become more familiar with the elements, observe how each element is expressed in your body and personality, then identify which elements dominate. Expand the exercise to evaluating how the elements display themselves in friends, family and coworkers.

element. If that person instead ignores a fiery symptom, such as heartburn, and proceeds to eat a bowl of chili, she is adding heat to the fire.

This leads us to an intuitive formula for balancing the energetic qualities: opposites balance, while like increases like, creating or perpetuating imbalance.

Looking back at the list of twenty qualities on page 17, we can see that most of the pairs of opposites are intuitive; however, a few are not. For instance, the opposite of dry is oily, not wet. So if you are experiencing symptoms of dryness (dry skin, constipation), you will want to include more healthy oils in your diet and minimize dry foods, such as beans. Applying this principle to cooking, it is important even for people without symptoms of dryness to add liberal amounts of ghee or oil to bean dishes; this reduces the likelihood of digestive disturbance by balancing the dryness of the beans.

As another example, the opposite of rough is slimy or smooth. Rough can be seen as a more extreme version of dry. It can manifest as chapped or cracked skin or a sore throat. A slimy food such as honey would be soothing to that hoarse throat.

Creating Balance

We are constantly bombarded with elements that can create imbalance in our lives: a stressful, fast-paced job can gradually increase the ether, air and fire elements in your body; a diet rich in cheese, meat or beer accompanied by a lifestyle lacking vigorous exercise can lead to an excess of the earth element; living in a hot desert environment and/or eating spicy foods can create an excess of the fire element.

If we do not bring in healthy opposites to balance these influences, our bodies eventually adapt to the new state of imbalance, acclimating to the new "normal." But eventually, the body will protest. First, it will give you a warning sign (indigestion, insomnia, heartburn, diarrhea, constipation, bloating, lethargy, headaches). If you don't heed the warning, your body will respond with an alarm bell (inflammation, acid reflux, migraines, sciatic pain, low back pain, depression). And if you ignore the distress signal, your body will put up a roadblock in the form of a serious disease requiring medical intervention to force you to contemplate the origin of your suffering (and hopefully discontinue its cause).

Did You Know?
A Balanced Lifestyle

While this book focuses on dietary changes for optimal health, ayurveda is not all about diet; balance also comes from other types of lifestyle changes. For example, someone with an excess of the fire element might practice meditation to cool themselves down, and someone experiencing symptoms of dryness would benefit from an oil massage.

Ayurveda explains that disease can be avoided by understanding your starting point of balance — your prakruti — and then modifying your diet and lifestyle so that you are consistently working toward maintaining that state of balance. Your prakruti is determined using a logical classification system in which the elements are combined into three main categories, known as doshas.

The Three Doshas

The Sanskrit term "dosha" is used to broadly classify individuals into three unique combinations of elements: vata, pitta and kapha. These Sanskrit words have no direct translation in English, but are generally understood as follows: vata primarily represents the qualities of the ether and air elements; pitta primarily represents the qualities of the fire and water elements; and kapha primarily represent the qualities of the water and earth elements. As you read through the following descriptions of how these qualities manifest in our bodies, relate them back to the metaphorical qualities of the elements described on pages 18–21.

Vata: The Air Dosha

Vata is primarily influenced by the elements of air and ether. For simplicity, it is called the air dosha. The wind embodies the qualities of vata. Visualize a clear, crisp, autumn day in New England, with leaves blowing off the trees, and think of the drying effect that cold air has on your exposed skin.

Vata governs all movement in the body — respiration, circulation, the nervous system, the musculoskeletal system, digestion, absorption, assimilation and elimination. Nothing in the body moves without vata. Vata is typically involved with degenerative functions, such as those of sickness or old age.

The vata qualities translate into physical and physiological characteristics that include a small frame, irregular features, a thin, angular face, small eyes, wiry hair, cold, dry skin, brittle nails, quick, clipped speech, quick movements, an erratic metabolism and an erratic appetite. Vatas typically are light sleepers, are joyful and creative, have an active imagination, have an ability to perceive subtleties (clairvoyance or extrasensory perception), have an eclectic fashion sense,

Vata Qualities

+ light
+ cold
+ dry
+ rough
+ mobile
+ subtle
+ clear

have a tendency to be loners, are noncommittal in their relationships, and are adaptable and flexible in the face of change.

People whose vata is out of balance may be fearful, lonely, insecure, nervous or anxious. They may daydream excessively, be forgetful, be unable to concentrate or have racing thoughts. Excess vata can manifest as constipation, dehydration, flaking skin, rough, cracking skin (especially at the heels or elbows), external hemorrhoids, popping joints, difficulty with speech (such as stuttering), emaciation, black circles under the eyes, gas, bloating, vague abdominal pain and distention, neuromuscular disorders (tremors, spasms, numbness, tingling), sciatic pain, heart palpitations, breathlessness, hiccups, wheezing, asthma, nightmares, fatigue or insomnia.

Pitta: The Fire Dosha

Pitta is primarily influenced by the elements of fire and water. For simplicity, it is called the fire dosha, and it governs transformation. Cooking over a campfire is a useful analogy for understanding pitta's fire. Just as the campfire transforms our food into something edible, the fire of pitta transforms food (so it can be digested on the cellular level) and feelings (so they can be digested on the subtle energetic level). The light of pitta symbolizes knowledge and facilitates understanding and compassion to help us transform feelings (such as anger, grief or stress) into higher intelligence or love.

Pitta regulates our body temperature and is responsible for metabolic activities. To understand how pitta works in the body, think of the interplay of fire with water. A large quantity of water can put out a fire, but if the fire gets too hot, its heat scorches everything in its path, drying up all the water. When the fire element of pitta is balanced, laser-sharp intelligence burns inside, while the exterior disposition is cool, calm and collected.

The pitta qualities translate into physical and physiological characteristics that include a medium frame, a heart-shaped face with a straight, sharp nose and chin, almond-shaped eyes that are sensitive to bright light, shiny pink fingernails, shiny thin hair that is often red or with red highlights, a tendency for premature balding or gray hair, oily skin, sensitive skin, a yellow undertone to the skin, skin that feels hot to the touch, fleshy-smelling perspiration and a voracious appetite. Pittas generally

Pitta Qualities

- light
- penetrating
- hot
- oily
- liquid
- spreading

are avid readers and love to read at night before sleep, are highly intelligent, brave and passionate, are fashion-conscious dressers, are proud of possessions and family, are predisposed to intellectual work, and have a strong desire to be in control and to be famous.

Like vatas, pittas have the ability to grasp subtleties in a situation, but pitta's understanding is based on laser-sharp intelligence and logical analysis that combine to formulate an instantaneous conclusion, whereas vata's understanding is based on intuition and subtle feelings.

People whose pitta is out of balance may be angry, hateful, overly critical, judgmental, egotistical, mistrusting or fiercely competitive. Excess pitta can manifest as heartburn, indigestion, inflammation, acid reflux, rashes, jaundice, mononucleosis, depression, suicidal thoughts, dizziness, nausea, fever, diarrhea, migraines, a sour taste in the mouth or bleeding disorders (such as bloodshot eyes or a bleeding rectum or gums).

Kapha: The Water Dosha

Kapha is primarily influenced by the elements of water and earth. For simplicity, it is called the water dosha, and its role is to support and nourish. To understand kapha's earth qualities, think of a mighty oak tree. Oak trees are hardy, strong, unwavering and long-lived; they tend to retain water and can produce a lot of fruit (acorns). Likewise, kapha is considered the heartiest of the three constitutions. Kaphas are likely to have long, healthy lives and bear many offspring. They have a tendency to retain water and can be unwavering in their views.

In the body, kapha provides lubrication to prevent wear and tear on the joints and their ligaments, and releases serotonin and tryptophan to bring on a peaceful sleep. It brings people together, creating peace through compromise and understanding. Kapha builds in the body and is especially active during childhood and preadolescence, when the body is growing. Its loving and nurturing qualities can manifest as a desire to be liked by everyone, a need to connect with people and a temperament that is compassionate and friendly.

The kapha qualities translate into physical and physiological characteristics that include a large frame, big, strong bones, a soft, curvaceous figure, a tendency to carry several extra pounds, a round face, large round eyes with thick eyelashes, a large, spreading nose, cool,

Kapha Qualities

+ heavy
+ slow
+ cool
+ oily
+ slimy
+ dense
+ soft
+ static

clammy, pale white skin, thick, wavy hair, hairy bodies (especially the backs and chests of men) and large, developed chests or breasts. Kapha babies often have very chubby cheeks, legs and arms. Kaphas tend to have a sweet, loving temperament. They are typically slow-talking, slow-moving and slow to make decisions but have a great memory (like an elephant, they never forget!). They are generally relaxed and content with the way things are and love to sleep. They tend to sweat — a lot. They often have a living/work space that is cluttered and untidy; have a preference for loose-fitting, casual attire; can sleep anywhere, through any amount of noise; thrive in relationships; and love working with a coach or partner to accomplish goals.

People whose kapha is out of balance may be stubborn, selfish, moody, depressed, greedy, miserly or overly attached to possessions and relationships. Excess kapha can manifest as obesity (from emotional eating), congestion, phlegm, mucus, swelling/water retention, excess salivation, lethargy, diabetes, lipomas (benign tumors composed of fatty tissue), cysts, tumors and high cholesterol. Like vatas, kaphas are prone to constipation, but kapha's constipation is caused by an excess of the slow quality (earth element), whereas vata's constipation is typically due to an excess of the dry quality (air element).

Weight Loss

Some people come to ayurveda looking to lose weight. That may happen, but it is more important that you gain an accurate understanding of the optimal weight for your body type. It is futile to compare your body to someone else's; you are unique.

Vatas generally have smaller bones and are light in weight and angular in shape. They should not envy the beautifully curvaceous kapha bodies.

Pittas usually have moderate-size bones and are of average weight, with a muscular shape. They should not try to emulate the willowy body structure of vatas by constant dieting — that would be the equivalent of emaciation for pitta and would not be healthy.

Kaphas typically have the largest bones and, thanks to their tendency to retain water, generally weigh the most. Kaphas should love their curves and be grateful that there is "more to love," but should not let this be an excuse to be sedentary or to eat in excess.

Doshas in Action

You may have read the descriptions of the three doshas and identified with aspects of each one. Of course! That is because you are a combination of all the elements and all the underlying qualities. The key is to determine which doshas, or combinations of elements, are expressed most strongly in your constitution. Most people find that they are best represented by one or two doshas, though it is possible for all three doshas to have an equal presence.

My family provides a useful example of the dosha qualities in action. My older sister is kapha-predominant. As a child, she was content to play in her crib, she was always happy and rarely cried, she loved food and sleep, and she ate and napped on schedule. And then I came along. As a vata, I had trouble digesting many foods and was a colicky baby with a tendency to become dehydrated. I needed more space, was unable to sit still and never wanted to nap. I figured out how to escape from the confines of the crib — then became an instigator, encouraging my content kapha sister to move beyond the borders of the playpen.

My mother's head was spinning from the contrast between her first and second child! I was a picky eater and hated broccoli, beans and salads (perhaps an instinctive reaction to my constitution's inability to handle these rough, cold foods). Gaining weight was a struggle for me. My sister, on the other hand, liked everything and would often eat the leftovers on my dinner plate. As she grew older, she had to be mindful of her diet and benefited greatly from vigorous exercise.

I was a light sleeper, and movies with a scary plotline gave me nightmares. I assimilated the energy of my surroundings and at times felt unbalanced by the hubbub of my boisterous Italian family. As a young adult, I was a multitasker and made quick decisions. My speech was fast and clipped, and I often finished people's sentences because I perceived what they were going to say. I could quickly analyze a situation and make a decision, but I was reluctant to commit and would often change my mind. (Discovering yoga helped to finally ground and balance my life.)

Did You Know?
Dosha Colors

The colors associated with vata are blue, indigo and brown. The colors associated with pitta are red and yellow. The color associated with kapha is white.

Did You Know?
The Yoga-Ayurveda Connection

Traditionally studied together, yoga and ayurveda are intimately connected via their premise of the energetic constitution of our bodies, with the heart being the center of intelligence. They teach us to develop our awareness of the mind–body connection, which helps to prevent diseases and increase longevity.

As for my pitta mother, she had a fiery constitution and loved to keep things under control. When she set an intention, things would get done. She, too, would finish others' sentences, but in her case it was because she couldn't wait for them to get the information out. She had a stomach of steel and could easily digest beans and cabbage. She loved pungent and sour foods and ate them in spite of the acid reflux they often caused. (These foods increased the oily quality of her pitta constitution and perhaps led to her gallstones.) She was an avid reader and always had a book (or two or three) going. She was intelligent and liked to analyze things and come to her own conclusion.

I have relayed these details about the three doshas at work in my family to help you figure out how they may come into play in your life. These examples can help you determine which doshas have the strongest influences on you, your family and friends.

Determining Your Doshas

Your prakruti — your starting point of balance — is defined as your unique physical and psychological composition at birth. Your vikruti — your current energetic state — may or may not be the same as your prakruti. Comparing your prakruti to your vikruti tells you which doshas are out of balance. It is best to consult an ayurvedic practitioner to determine your prakruti and vikruti. But you can approximate it on your own by filling in the Dosha Evaluation (pages 29–32).

Once you understand the energetics of your prakruti, you can follow dietary and lifestyle habits designed to keep those energetics — your doshas — in balance. When you learn to recognize what balance feels like (joy, proper weight, mental clarity, energy, sound sleep, etc.), you will immediately recognize when you are veering off track and can take action to return to optimal health.

Dosha Evaluation

To determine your prakruti (your state of balance), review each characteristic in the left-hand column and place a checkmark next to the description(s) in the other three columns that *best* describe you. When making your selections, consider the characteristics in the context of your life in general, with emphasis on your childhood. It may be helpful to get unbiased input from family members or longtime friends. Compare their observations to yours and try to be completely honest. When you have completed the evaluation, tally the checkmarks in each column to see which dosha predominates.

To determine your vikruti (your current energetic state), review the characteristics a second time, but this time make your choices based on how the characteristics apply to you today. Again, it is helpful to get someone who knows you well (a close friend or coworker) to complete the survey with you, or on your behalf, for the most unbiased results. Tally the checkmarks and compare your prakruti to your vikruti to determine which doshas are out of balance.

If you are unsure of which boxes to check for a particular characteristic, just skip that characteristic. You will still be able to get a good approximation of your prakruti and vikruti by answering the remaining questions. Of course, the best results are obtained from a consultation with a qualified ayurvedic practitioner.

Note: The questions on skin tone, hair and eyes must be considered relative to others with your ethnic background. For instance, Asians should compare their skin tone to other Asians.

Characteristic	Vata	Pitta	Kapha
Frame size/ body type	☐ small, thin frame ☐ small bones ☐ delicate or lanky ☐ finds it difficult to develop muscles	☐ medium frame ☐ moderate-size bones ☐ athletic build ☐ develops muscles easily	☐ large, heavy frame ☐ large bones ☐ well-developed chest ☐ curvaceous or round body
Skin	☐ thin (veins are easily seen) and cold ☐ dry, rough, chapped (a tendency for cracked heels, fingertips and elbows) ☐ rashes tend to be dry and itchy ☐ sometimes blackheads	☐ thin or medium ☐ hot, oily (a tendency toward hives and eczema) ☐ rashes tend to be red and burning ☐ sometimes red pimples	☐ thick and smooth ☐ cool and clammy ☐ rashes tend to be wet and oozing ☐ sometimes whiteheads
Skin tone	☐ dark, brown	☐ red, yellow, freckled	☐ white, smooth, porcelain
Nails	☐ dry, brittle, cracked	☐ shiny, pink	☐ shiny, thick, white
Hair	☐ wiry, dry ☐ dark	☐ shiny, thin, oily ☐ red, auburn highlights, premature gray or bald	☐ wavy, thick, lustrous ☐ sometimes blond or light brown

Characteristic	Vata	Pitta	Kapha
Face	☐ angular, thin face, sunken cheeks ☐ asymmetrical features ☐ crowded teeth ☐ thin lips	☐ heart-shaped face ☐ straight, pointy nose and chin ☐ medium-size teeth ☐ medium lips	☐ round or rectangular face ☐ broad nose ☐ large white teeth ☐ full lips
Eyes	☐ small ☐ dark ☐ darting	☐ medium, almond-shaped ☐ hazel ☐ sensitive to bright light (needs sunglasses outside/ prefers dark rooms inside)	☐ large, round ☐ sometimes blue ☐ thick eyelashes
Appetite	☐ variable (even when very hungry, appetite may be satiated after a few bites) ☐ often forgets to eat ☐ becomes light-headed or cranky when meals are missed	☐ voracious ☐ rarely skips meals ☐ can become angry if food is not available when hunger strikes	☐ emotional eating ☐ tends to eat large amounts even when not hungry ☐ does not experience discomfort when skipping a meal
Digestion	☐ flatulence, bloating, abdominal distention after eating	☐ heartburn, acid reflux, sour stomach after eating	☐ heavy, sleepy feeling after eating
Elimination	☐ dry stools with a small "rabbit pellet" shape ☐ irregular elimination times, with a tendency toward constipation ☐ at times may have to strain and "push" to eliminate	☐ hot, oily stools that may be loosely shaped like a cow patty ☐ tendency toward diarrhea ☐ at times stools may burn	☐ regular morning elimination ☐ well-formed banana-shaped stool ☐ sometimes constipated
Weight	☐ finds it difficult to gain weight	☐ weight is moderate	☐ finds it difficult to lose weight and tends to carry a few extra pounds
Circulation	☐ cold hands and feet	☐ hot body temperature	☐ cold hands and feet but warm at the core
Perspiration	☐ scanty	☐ fleshy smell	☐ profuse
Mind	☐ learn quickly but forget quickly	☐ intelligent, brilliant	☐ slow to learn, but never forget
Disposition — in balance	☐ joyful, happy, friendly ☐ flexible views ☐ free-spirited	☐ brave, courageous, a leader ☐ passionate ☐ structured	☐ a team player ☐ loving, compassionate ☐ stable, dependable

Characteristic	Vata	Pitta	Kapha
Disposition — out of balance	☐ forgetful, with scattered thoughts ☐ anxious, fearful ☐ afraid of the dark ☐ lonely	☐ angers easily ☐ cutthroat competitiveness ☐ judgmental, critical, sarcastic, egotistical ☐ has suicidal thoughts	☐ moody, feeling sorry for oneself ☐ slow to change (mind and habits), stubborn ☐ greedy, overly attached (a tendency to stay in relationships even if they are ill-serving) ☐ depressed and lethargic
Perception	☐ subtle, almost clairvoyant, perceives the feelings of others; may absorb the energy of people or situations	☐ understands the feelings of others using logical analysis	☐ subtleties are elusive; may be unaware of the feelings of others
Relationships	☐ loner ☐ noncommittal, short-term relationships ☐ can easily terminate relationships	☐ wants to be highly regarded in prestigious circles ☐ likes relationships that bring prestige and status ☐ may abruptly terminate a relationship that is ill-serving	☐ desire to be liked by everyone; keeps friends for a long time ☐ prefers doing things (exercise, travel) with a partner or friend ☐ has difficulty terminating relationships (even if they are ill-serving)
Energy levels	☐ tires easily ☐ suited for artistic, creative jobs	☐ tends to work beyond physical capacity ☐ suited for intellectual jobs	☐ strong as an ox ☐ a good laborer
Attire	☐ eclectic, trendy fashion	☐ polished designer fashion	☐ disregards fashion; loose-fitting, relaxed clothing that is never discarded
Monetary attitudes	☐ money comes and goes ☐ inconsistent savings	☐ tends to save ☐ spends on luxury items	☐ a consistent saver ☐ frugal spending habits
Speech	☐ high-pitched, fast, clipped, stuttering ☐ off-topic, run-on sentences; chatty	☐ quick-witted, clear, precise ☐ sarcastic	☐ deep, slow, dull, monosyllabic answers to questions ☐ melodious singing voice
Organization	☐ nonlinear, creative	☐ organized, logical and methodical	☐ untidy, "pack rat," saves everything, but can find everything

Characteristic	Vata	Pitta	Kapha
Reaction to high stress	☐ anxiety, worry, fear	☐ acid indigestion, anger	☐ calm and cool, no worries
Environmental influences	☐ does not tolerate cold weather; prefers sun	☐ prefers cool weather and shade	☐ prefers moderate weather
Sleep	☐ light sleeper, easily awoken, has difficulty getting back to sleep ☐ irregular sleep makes it difficult to rise in the morning ☐ tendency for nightmares	☐ moderate sleeper, likes to read before bed ☐ finds it easy to rise in the morning ☐ tendency for dreams about being in control or leading people	☐ sound sleeper, can sleep anywhere ☐ slow to rise in the morning ☐ tendency for dreams about water
Disease proneness	☐ dehydration ☐ constipation ☐ anxiety, breathlessness, heart palpitations ☐ wheezing, asthma, fatigue ☐ insomnia ☐ sciatic pain, low back pain ☐ dry, itchy external hemorrhoids	☐ heartburn, indigestion, acid reflux ☐ inflammation ("-itis" diseases), bleeding disorders (bleeding in gums, bloodshot eyes, internal hemorrhoids) ☐ rashes, hives, acne ☐ dizziness, nausea ☐ migraines ☐ high fevers ☐ sour taste in mouth	☐ sinus/lung congestion, phlegm, mucus ☐ swelling/water retention ☐ excess salivation, drooling ☐ obesity ☐ diabetes ☐ high cholesterol ☐ lipomas, cysts, tumors
Total: Prakruti			
Total: Vikruti			

Source: Adapted with permission from Dr. Vasant Lad. *Ayurvedic Cooking for Self-Healing.* The Ayurvedic Press, Albuquerque, NM: 1994. All rights reserved.

Doshic Times

Ayurveda also applies the concept of dosha to time by correlating the qualities of vata, pitta and kapha to the time of day, the season and time of life.

Doshic Times

	Vata	Pitta	Kapha
Time of day	2–6 a.m. and p.m.	10–2 a.m. and p.m.	6–10 a.m. and p.m.
Season	fall	summer	winter and spring
Time of life	old age	adult	child (birth to age 16)

Source: Adapted with permission from Vasant Lad, M.A.Sc. *Textbook of Ayurveda: A Complete Guide to Clinical Assessment*, Volume Two. The Ayurvedic Press, Albuquerque, NM: 2006. All rights reserved.

Time of Day

Ayurvedic diet and lifestyle recommendations are synchronized with doshic times of day. For instance, meditating before sunrise and at dusk is considered auspicious because of the vata/etheric qualities predominant at those hours; the subtle energies are more easily perceived.

Midday, when the sun is strongest, correlates to peak pitta/digestive capacity and is thus recommended as the optimal time for the main meal of the day. Manual labor or vigorous exercise is considered unbalancing during this fiery time.

It is best to be in bed before 10 p.m. to take advantage of slow, sleepy kapha time. At 10 p.m., pitta energy kicks in and provides a burst of energy that could keep you awake until 2 a.m.!

Season

The correspondence of dosha classifications to the seasons epitomizes how the ancients lived in symbiotic harmony with nature.

During the fall, root vegetable crops mature and the cool, windy weather causes people to experience a little more vata than normal; eating the grounding seasonal vegetables can help balance the effects of vata from the external environment on your body, as can daily oil massage.

Did You Know?

Circadian Rhythms

We are wired to live in sync with the sun and seasons. Our bodies flow on circadian rhythms (physical, mental and behavioral changes) on a roughly 24-hour cycle, responding primarily to light and darkness. These rhythms influence sleep-wake cycles, hormone release, body temperature and other important body functions. Internal clocks throughout the body regulate these functions, which are, in turn, synchronized by a "master clock." Abnormal circadian rhythms have been linked to insomnia, obesity, diabetes, depression, bipolar disorder and seasonal affective disorder.

In the heat of summer, emphasizing the cooling seasonal crops, such as sweet, juicy fruits and cooling, bitter green leafy vegetables, helps to balance out the heat of the scorching sun and the corresponding pitta flames.

In the dead of winter, kapha's earth element is dominant; eating warming, hearty stews and exercising regularly will help us avoid stagnation and limit mucus buildup, which can lead to illness.

In the cool, damp spring, the water element of kapha dominates, leaving us vulnerable to colds and runny noses. During this season, we need to stay warm and dry and emphasize foods that are balancing to kapha dosha, such as mushrooms and barley. Avoiding mucus-forming dairy products is also beneficial.

Time of Life

Kapha age is birth to about age sixteen, when we are young and growing. During this developmental growth stage, we need nutritious, energizing foods to help create a healthy body.

The pitta time of life is the young adult stage, the period during which we have the fire to progress at school, advance in our careers and raise children. During the pitta time of life, we benefit from pitta-pacifying foods and drinks that are cooling in nature. It is very important to make time for adequate rest so you don't burn out.

As we get older, we tend to dry out and experience vata imbalances such as dry skin, popping joints, scattered thoughts and memory loss. These symptoms are associated with the degenerative vata forces in our body. During the vata time of life, we benefit from vata-balancing foods that are moist, oily, warm and grounding.

The Six Tastes

As mentioned earlier, food is made up of the five elements. All of these elements (and all of their qualities) are contained within each of six tastes: sweet, sour, salty, pungent, bitter and astringent. However, two elements typically dominate each taste. The energetics of a taste are based on the qualities of its dominating elements.

Since the elements are forms of energy, the food we consume correspondingly impacts the energetics in our bodies — our state of balance. In general, people with dominant vata dosha (which has a light, dry, cool nature) will benefit from heavy, moist, oily, warming foods; people with dominant pitta dosha (which has a fiery nature) will do best with cooling foods; and people with dominant kapha dosha (which has a slow, dull, cool nature) will do best with heating, sharp (spicy) foods.

We can determine the physical and emotional effects of food by understanding the underlying elements. With practice, you will be able to discern the energetic effect of a food by simply tasting it and observing your reaction to it. For now, you can rely on ayurveda's designations of underlying characteristics, as outlined in the next few pages.

Rasa, Virya and Vipak

For simplicity in understanding the six tastes, I have omitted the Sanskrit terms "rasa," "virya" and "vipak." "Rasa" refers to taste. It is the first experience when the food hits the tongue, and you can intuit a food's properties from its taste. "Virya" refers to the energetic effect of the food on the dosha and on the digestive fire. Generally, the virya is defined as being heating or cooling, but it could also be heavy, light, slow, sharp, oily or dry. "Vipak" refers to the post-digestive effect — the effect of food on the urine, feces and sweat. The sweet and salty tastes generally have a sweet vipak; the sour taste generally has a sour vipak; and the pungent, bitter and astringent tastes generally have a pungent vipak.

In classifying the energetic effects of tastes that have multiple conflicting energetics, I have categorized them under the taste that displays the most powerful energetic and added the lesser tastes in parentheses. So if an herb has a sweet and pungent taste, with a heating virya and a pungent vipak, it would be classified as pungent, not sweet, because the pungent/heating energetic dominates.

Sweet: Earth and Water

The sweet taste comprises the elements earth and water. Its dominant energetics are cooling, moist and heavy. Its general effects on the dosha are to balance (or reduce) vata and pitta and increase kapha.

The sweet taste is nourishing and provides energy. It is related to the emotions of love, joy and bliss. In excess, it can create a sluggish thyroid, thick blood, diabetes, greed and attachment.

Foods that have a sweet taste include:

✦ almonds, peeled and soaked	✦ cucumbers
✦ amaranth (*also astringent*)	✦ fennel (*also astringent*)
	✦ maple syrup
✦ asparagus	✦ milk
✦ barley	✦ oats
✦ beets, cooked	✦ rabbit
✦ cilantro (*also astringent*)	✦ sugar
	✦ tarragon
✦ coconut	✦ vanilla (*also astringent*)
	✦ white basmati rice

Foods that have a sweet taste but a heating energetic include:

✦ buffalo	✦ lamb/mutton
✦ carrots, cooked	✦ millet
✦ corn	✦ molasses
✦ honey	✦ pork
✦ jaggery	✦ salmon

Sour: Earth and Fire

The sour taste comprises the elements earth and fire. Its dominant energetics are heating, sharp and not too heavy. Its general effects on the dosha are to balance (or reduce) vata and increase pitta and kapha.

The sour taste can overpower all the other tastes and should be used in moderation. It creates moistness, reduces gas and stimulates the appetite and purgation. It heightens the mind's alertness. Something very sour will prompt the reflex action to close your eyes. In excess, the sour taste can create dampness and cold in the lungs, skin eruptions of acne and rashes, sensitive teeth, gastritis and diarrhea. Emotionally, an excess of the sour taste can influence you to be judgmental and overly critical. When such harsh thoughts are brought into a relationship, they can destroy it, leaving a "sour taste in your mouth."

Foods that have a sour taste include:

✦ butter	✦ tomatoes (*also sweet*)
✦ cheese	✦ umeboshi plums (*also salty*)
✦ fermented foods	
✦ grapefruit	✦ vinegar
✦ lemons	✦ yogurt older than 3 days from manufacture date
✦ sour cream	
✦ tamarinds	

Salty: Fire and Water

The salty taste comprises the elements fire and water. Its dominant energetics are heating, heavy and oily. Its general effects on the dosha are to balance (or reduce) vata and increase pitta and kapha.

The salty taste is an appetizer, a digestive, an antiflatulent and an antispasmodic, and it provides energy. Emotionally, it supplies courage and enthusiasm. In excess, the salty taste will cause water and sodium retention, leading to swelling. It can also result in premature graying of the hair, hair loss and wrinkling, and it can induce vomiting. Salt is an addictive taste, and attachment, greed and possessiveness are exacerbated when the salty taste is in excess.

Foods that have a salty taste include:

- rock salt
- sea salt
- seaweed
- Vegemite (yeast extract)

✦ Salt is an addictive taste, and attachment, greed and possessiveness are exacerbated when the salty taste is in excess. ✦

Pungent: Fire and Air

The pungent taste comprises the elements fire and air. Its dominant energetic is heating, but it is also sharp, light, drying and rough. Its general effects on the dosha are to increase vata and pitta and balance (or reduce) kapha.

The pungent taste is antispasmodic and stimulates circulation, digestion, absorption and assimilation of nutrients. It thins the blood and removes clots, fat and worms. It can cleanse the sinuses by stimulating nasal secretions and dissolving kapha. Its sharp, penetrating qualities generate enthusiasm and dynamism. In excess, the pungent taste can create dryness, kill sperm and ova, and cause irritation and ulceration. Emotionally, an excess can lead to anger, competitiveness and aggressiveness.

Foods that have a pungent taste include:

- ajwain
- anise
- asafoetida (hing)
- basil (*also sweet*)
- beets, raw
- black pepper
- cayenne pepper
- chile peppers
- cinnamon (*also sweet*)
- cumin (*also bitter*)
- fenugreek (*also bitter*)
- garlic
- ginger
- horseradish (*also astringent*)
- mustard seeds
- onion, raw
- paprika
- star anise

> **Did You Know?**
> **Bloat Be Gone**
>
>
> Cumin seeds, ajwain seeds, ginger, oregano and asafoetida are carminatives, which means they dispel gas and prevent bloating. They are warming in nature and stoke the digestive fire.

Bitter: Ether and Air

The bitter taste comprises the elements ether and air. Its dominant energetic is cooling, but it is also light and drying. Its general effects on the dosha are to increase vata and balance (or reduce) pitta and kapha.

The bitter taste is anti-inflammatory, antipyretic (it reduces fever) and laxative. It is balancing to blood sugar levels and benefits the liver, pancreas and spleen. It is beneficial for introspection. In excess, the bitter taste can cause nausea and osteoporosis. It can deplete plasma, blood, muscle, bone marrow, fat, semen and sex drive. Emotionally, an excess of the bitter taste can create aversion, cynicism (the expression of a "bitter person" is an appropriate image), detachment, loneliness and depression.

Foods that have a bitter taste include:

+ aloe vera
+ bitter gourd
+ broccoli
+ coffee
+ endive
+ most leafy greens, including arugula, chicory, collard greens, dandelion greens and kale
+ neem juice (*also pungent and astringent*)
+ radicchio
+ rhubarb
+ turmeric

Astringent: Earth and Air

The astringent taste comprises the elements earth and air. Its dominant energetics are cooling and drying. Its general effects on the dosha are to increase vata and balance (or reduce) pitta and kapha.

The astringent taste is anti-inflammatory, improves absorption, stops bleeding, binds stool, heals ulcers and scrapes excess fat. In excess, it can create spasms, constipation, emaciation and a dry choking sensation in the mouth (so don't eat or drink something with an astringent taste before giving a speech!). Emotionally, it is related to sensitivity or, in excess, hypersensitivity.

Foods that have an astringent taste include:

- amaranth (*also sweet*)
- apple pulp, cooked
- avocados
- basil (*also sweet*)
- Brussels sprouts
- cabbage
- cauliflower
- celery
- cranberries
- green beans
- legumes
- lettuce
- pomegranates
- popcorn
- potatoes
- quinoa (*also sweet*)
- rice cakes
- savi seeds
- spinach, raw
- sprouts
- tofu (*also sweet*)
- tea
- venison
- wheat pasta
- zucchini

Foods that have an astringent taste but a heating energetic include:

- oregano (*also sweet*)
- parsley (*also pungent*)
- poppy seeds (*also sweet*)
- rosemary (*also sweet*)
- rye

+ **Your goal should be to eat with awareness and observe how the food is affecting you physically and emotionally – just as the ancients did.** +

Dosha-Balancing Foods

Most of the recipes in this book are tridoshic — designed to be balancing to all constitutions. Those that are not tridoshic include recommendations for condiments and spices to balance for specific doshas.

If you want to create your own dosha-specific recipes, refer to the appendices on pages 328–339, which outline the foods and spices that are balancing to each dosha. But please consider these lists to be a general reference and not a mandate. The energetic impact of foods will vary depending on your unique energetic makeup, your present state of balance, the environment in which you are living, the environment in which the food was grown and so forth. Use the lists as a compass to point you in the right direction. Over time, as you work with this system, your awareness will increase and you will be able to determine which tastes and foods are most beneficial for your constitution.

Your goal should be to eat with awareness and observe how the food is affecting you physically and emotionally — just as the ancients did.

WHAT IS AYURVEDA?   **39**

Ayurvedic Cooking

Ayurveda was not intended to be a rigid approach. In fact, the original teachings of ayurveda consisted of broad general guidance, like recommending that people eat wholesome foods and avoid unwholesome foods. There is a lot of flexibility in how these teachings are interpreted and applied — flexibility that is necessary to accommodate an individual's unique needs and current circumstances.

Ayurveda is all about balance, and happiness is essential to balance. The ancients also said that one should not suddenly avoid wholesome foods, as that could lead to unhappiness. So, if you love beets, don't suddenly remove them from your diet because your predominant dosha is pitta and a list says beets are warming and unbalancing to pitta. That would decrease your happiness. Instead, observe how you feel after eating beets. If you experience symptoms of imbalance (heat, anger, rashes, diarrhea, heartburn), consider adding cooling spices (such as coriander), peeling the beets, cooking them or reducing the quantity you eat gradually, over the course of several months. Eventually, you may find a new favorite to replace them with — perhaps steamed kale or escarole.

This chapter teaches you how to use ayurvedic principles to balance your doshas by reviewing and changing your eating habits. I describe the fundamentals of ayurvedic food combining to give you an understanding of how certain food combinations can improve your digestion and bring balance to your doshas. I have also shared my ten essential ayurvedic wellness tips. These ten tips, like ayurvedic food combining, are simple changes that provide instant results. These positive changes will give you the motivation necessary to continue to modify long-standing habits. But even when you start seeing the immediate positive effects, attempting to incorporate all of ayurveda's beneficial changes at once can be daunting. I recommend you go at a pace that suits your lifestyle to ensure that the end result is sustainable.

I conclude the chapter with specific examples of how to balance each of the three doshas, and offer guidance on how to cook within the ayurvedic framework for your entire family.

Bread First, Salad Last

Ayurveda recommends that the foods in a meal be eaten in sequential order according to their tastes and that all six tastes be represented in the meal. The eating order corresponds to the digestive order (the order in which the energetic effects of the underlying elements of the taste are processed into cellular nutrition). Specifically, sweet foods should be eaten first, then sour foods, salty foods, pungent foods, bitter foods and finally astringent foods. This is easy to do when you are eating off a thali plate in India, with rice at the center and breads and other sweet foods at one o'clock, followed by a clockwise succession of small dishes containing each of the remaining tastes. But Westerners don't generally prepare meals this way. A simple way to adapt this principle to Western-style meals is to eat your bread, rice and other sweets first, followed by a sour-tasting appetizer, then the main meal and then an astringent salad.

Food Combination Principles

Using their understanding of the tastes and energetics of foods, the ancients established fundamental principles for efficient food combinations. The intent of these guidelines was to optimize digestion, absorption, assimilation and elimination so as to promote health and longevity. The immediate effect of ayurveda's lighter food combinations was (and is) an alert mind and an energetic body.

The Food Combining table (page 42) lists some common Western combinations that cause the most digestive torment. It is not meant to be an exhaustive list of dos and don'ts — let's not go there. The energetic impact of foods varies depending on many factors, including your unique energetic makeup, your present state of balance and the environment in which you are living. You will be well served simply to understand the following basic principles:

✦ Animal protein (meat and fish), which is generally heating and heavy, is best eaten in a soup or stew. On occasion, if your digestive system is strong, animal protein can be combined with light foods such as vegetables or salads. Most of the common food combinations in Western society — steak and potatoes, chicken and bean burritos, spaghetti and meatballs, Philly cheesesteak — are excessively heavy and taxing on the system.

> ✦ The immediate effect of ayurveda's lighter food combinations is an alert mind and an energetic body. ✦

+ Fruits, which are light and liquid, are best eaten alone. They combine well only with other fruits. Raw fruits tend to be watery, so they move quickly through the digestive system, but their movement is slowed down when the gut is full of other foods, resulting in fermentation, gas and bloating. An exception to the general rule is cooked or dried fruits; their basic characteristic is altered by the cooking or drying process, so they are suitable for combination with other foods.

+ Cheese, which is cold and heavy, is best eaten alone, as it does not combine well with many other ingredients. Cheese and crackers, cheese and apples, macaroni and cheese, cheese with sandwiches and cheese pizza are all combinations that would be considered too heavy and therefore incompatible.

+ Honey should never be cooked. Ayurveda states that cooked honey can produce toxins at the cellular level that can manifest into disease. Whenever you prepare a cup of tea, let it cool to lukewarm before adding honey.

Food Combining

Food	Combines Well With	Avoid Eating With	Additional Advice
Fruit (fresh)	Other fruit (except melons)	Any other foods	Eat as a snack or for breakfast. Wait 1 hour before or after a meal to eat.
Melons	Other melons	Any other foods	Eat as a snack. Wait 1 hour before or after a meal to eat.
Fruit (dried)	Salads, grains, yogurt (in moderation, due to high sugar)	Milk, eggs, meat, fish, beans and lentils	
Lemons	Vegetables (except tomatoes and cucumbers), grains	Fruit, tomatoes, cucumbers, milk, yogurt	
Tomatoes	Vegetables (except cucumbers), grains	Fruit, cucumbers, cheese, milk, yogurt	Try unsalted organic corn chips and salsa with cilantro.

Food	Combines Well With	Avoid Eating With	Additional Advice
Cheese	Vegetables (except nightshades, such as eggplant, tomatoes, potatoes, peppers), leafy greens	Fruit, nightshade vegetables (eggplant, tomatoes, potatoes, peppers), yogurt, eggs, meat, beans and lentils, wheat, bread	Eat in small quantities, such as for a snack.
Milk (raw)	Dates	Anything with a sour energetic (such as bananas, sour fruits, radishes, yogurt and yeast breads), meat, fish, beans and lentils	It's best to boil and drink milk on its own or with warming spices (cinnamon, cardamom, turmeric, cloves, nutmeg, etc.); boiling reduces mucus formation.
Yogurt (fresh within 3 days of manufacture date)	Dried fruit, honey	Fruit, nightshade vegetables (eggplant, tomatoes, potatoes, peppers), cheese, milk, eggs, meat, fish, hot drinks	Avoid after sunset.
Eggs	Vegetables, grains	Fruit, cheese, milk, yogurt, meat, fish, beans and lentils	
Meat and fish	Vegetables (except radishes and nightshades, such as eggplant, tomatoes, potatoes, peppers), rice	Fruit, nightshade vegetables (eggplant, tomatoes, potatoes, peppers), radishes, milk, cheese, yogurt, eggs, other meats (e.g., bacon cheeseburgers), grains other than rice, honey	Animal protein is heavy and generally heating; for easiest digestion, add it to a soup or broth.
Beans and lentils	Vegetables, grains	Fruit, cheese, milk, yogurt, eggs, meat, fish	
Wheat and pasta	Pesto sauce, vegetables	Fruit, tomato sauces, cheese, fish, meat	Try pesto sauce variations made with spinach, arugula or cilantro.
Honey (raw)	Yogurt, tea	Ghee in equal quantities by weight, meat	Never cook honey. Before adding honey to tea, allow the tea to cool until you can comfortably hold it in your mouth without burning your tongue.

Source: Adapted with permission from Dr. Vasant Lad. *Ayurvedic Cooking for Self-Healing.* The Ayurvedic Press, Albuquerque, NM: 1994. All rights reserved.

The food combination principles account for the capacity of the digestive system to handle various quantities and qualities of food. The digestive system was not designed to handle nonstop large, heavy, complex meals, as are commonly eaten in Western societies. In addition, the Western habit of snacking places continual stress on the digestive system, with inadequate "downtime" for it to recuperate. Overworking the digestive system in this manner can cause blockages, resulting in undigested food that putrefies and ferments, which leads to gas, bloating and the potential accumulation of ama.

We can relate the ayurvedic principles of food combination to the modern scientific understanding of the biochemical digestion process, first introduced by Ivan Pavlov. Digestion begins when we smell the aroma of food and the salivary glands initiate secretions. As food enters the mouth, we begin to chew, which serves three main functions:

1. It breaks down food into small particles that enzymes can further process downstream (ideally, we should chew until the food is liquefied).
2. It mixes the amylase enzymes in saliva with the food particles to start digesting starches.
3. It alerts the stomach to begin secreting digestive enzymes in anticipation of incoming food.

Different foods require different enzymes to break them into tiny molecules suitable for assimilation into the bloodstream. These enzymes require a specific pH environment for proper functioning, and the enzymes will not be released until the pH has been regulated to the appropriate level. There must be the right amount of acid in the stomach and the right amount of alkali in the duodenum, and the right amount of time must be spent in each phase of digestion.

While there have been no comprehensive modern studies on the effects of specific food combinations on digestion, absorption and elimination, we do know the following:

✦ Poor digestion of starches results in fermentation, causing gas and bloating.
✦ Poor digestion of fats results in high levels of fat in the stool, which can lead to the loss of fat-soluble vitamins, such as A, D, E and K.

- Poor digestion of proteins results in short-chain polypeptides being absorbed into the bloodstream, where they can mimic the action of hormones and cytokines (chemical messengers). This interferes with normal biochemistry, potentially activating the immune system and leading to food allergies and/or autoimmunity.

- Poor digestion can result in malabsorption (food being eliminated as waste without proper assimilation of nutrients). This deprives the body of necessary nutrients and leads to anemia and other nutrient deficiencies.

Thus, we know that efficient digestion of food is vital for long-term health and prevention of disease. Based on what we know about the digestion process today, the food-combining rules prescribed by ayurvedic elders thousands of years ago do not seem so far-fetched.

Many of us routinely pass inefficient combinations of food through our digestive systems, with aftereffects that we have learned to live with (or perhaps we are unaware of what is causing our discomfort). If you have a very strong digestive fire — as is common among young adults, those with a pitta constitution and those who exercise regularly — then you may be able to eat inefficient combinations with few or no symptoms. But for most of us, inefficient food combinations create temporary discomforts (such as gas, bloating, acid indigestion, acid reflux, drowsiness, constipation or diarrhea) that over time can cause longer-lasting changes (including weight gain, food allergies or gastritis).

If you are accustomed to large, heavy combinations and would like to try the lighter ayurvedic approach, gradually introduce the food combination principles over a period of several months. Through this gradual approach, you will learn to identify when your desire to eat is based on true hunger, rather than eating to always feel full. Progressively eliminating inefficient combinations will help you to more clearly recognize the impact food has on your body.

To start, you can try eating one meal a day (breakfast, lunch or dinner) according to the food combination rules, or you can focus on one rule for the day (for example, always eating fruit on its own). A slow integration of the changes is the key to lasting success.

Did You Know?

Optimal Performance

The digestive process is a precisely designed mechanism comparable in its intricacy to a meticulously engineered automobile. BMW recommends premium fuel and regular maintenance for optimal performance. Similarly, ayurveda says optimal wellness can be achieved with high-quality food, regular exercise (in accordance with your specific constitution) and adequate rest (in the amounts recommended for your constitution).

Did You Know?

Healthy Satiety

Ideally, after eating a meal, you should feel satiated, clear, alert and happy. To feel otherwise is indicative of an improper quantity or quality of ingested food. Your goal is to find foods and food combinations that do not place undue stress on your digestive system.

Ama

Thanks to modern science, we know that ingested food is broken down into a form that is available for the body's cells, providing the nutrients for normal activity. According to ayurveda, the result of digestion is that food is transformed into vital life energy. But when food is not properly processed during digestion, the food instead becomes ama.

"Ama" is a Sanskrit word that can be translated to mean "toxic, morbid waste product." It can result from undigested food or unprocessed emotions (such as unresolved anger, fear, depression or insecurity). Ama clogs the channels of circulation in the body, and can prevent nutrients from flowing to the cells, organs and brain. It may also clog the channels that carry waste from the cells and tissues, resulting in toxic buildup that may irreversibly harm cells over long periods of time.

A major cause of improper metabolism of food is eating again before the previous meal has been completely digested. Portion control, proper food combinations and eliminating snacking can help reduce ama creation. Mental ama occurs when we have repressed or ignored our feelings. Taking time to contemplate that sinking feeling in your gut — discussing an issue with a friend or meditating quietly — will allow complete digestion of your emotions and promote a healthy mind and body.

The following signs indicate that you may have ama:

+ Your tongue has a white, black or brown coating.
+ Your urine, feces and/or sweat have a foul smell.
+ Your breath has a bad odor.
+ Your stool is sticky or gluey (it sticks to the toilet bowl).
+ You have a fever.
+ You have no appetite.
+ You have a heavy feeling in your body or mind.
+ Your joints are stiff.
+ You feel pain at your navel.
+ You feel dull and sleepy after eating.
+ Your mind is foggy.
+ You have trouble getting out of bed in the morning, even after many hours of sleep.
+ The roots of your hair hurt.

Health problems that may be caused by prolonged ama include:

+ Autoimmune diseases
+ Constipation
+ Diarrhea
+ Dullness and lethargy
+ Frequent colds and flu
+ Joint pain
+ Lowered immunity
+ Sadness and depression

If left unchecked, ama can be a precursor to disease. If you think you have ama, consult an ayurvedic practitioner, who can look for the root cause(s) and provide guidance on your options for addressing the problem.

Top Ten Essential Ayurvedic Tips for Wellness

At this point, you may be thinking you will never be happy without eating pepperoni pizza, apples with Brie or bacon double cheeseburgers. No worries. There are other places to begin, such as my top ten essential ayurvedic wellness tips. These tips will help minimize stress on your digestive system even if you are eating inefficient food combinations.

You have formed your eating habits over many years, so it is reasonable to expect that it might take three to six months (or more) to create lasting change — even for the most motivated individual. If you aren't accustomed to cooking or are constantly eating on the run, you will have additional hurdles. Keeping a balanced perspective and setting realistic goals will be key. To stay on track and avoid being overwhelmed, consider trying one tip a day (or week) and observing how you feel.

Eventually, you can start experimenting with some of the food combining principles. Remember, a gradual approach is the best way to ensure long-term success. Slowly eliminating inefficient food combinations from your diet, when combined with the ten wellness tips, will bring you to the next level of ayurvedic wellness. Incorporate daily exercise and adequate sleep into your routine, and your transformation to better health is well under way.

1 Eat only when you are truly hungry

Often, our desire for food is not related to true hunger. To determine whether your hunger is false, try sipping some warm water or herbal tea with honey. If that doesn't satisfy your hunger and mealtime is a long time off, try eating fruit.

Ideally, establish a daily eating schedule. Eating only at scheduled mealtimes (breakfast, lunch and dinner) will regulate your digestive system and minimize potential overload. If you often crave snacks between meals, try to identify the cause of your hunger. Are you prone to emotional eating out of loneliness, boredom or habit? Or are your meals too small or lacking in proper nourishment? If you can identify the root cause, it will be easier to find a solution that will ensure lasting change.

Did You Know?

Agni

Agni is a Sanskrit word that means "fire." It is often used metaphorically to refer to digestive strength, metabolic processes and innate intelligence. Located throughout the body, agni neutralizes toxins, processes ingested food into cellular nourishment and transforms emotions into pure awareness. Strong agni is the key to health and longevity. Strong agni can overcome occasional unsuitable food combinations, but habitual snacking and improper food combinations will eventually diminish agni and lead to ama (toxins).

Conversely, if you are not hungry when a scheduled mealtime arrives, give yourself permission to skip that meal. Lack of hunger may be your body's way of telling you that it is still processing a previous meal or attempting to purge some toxicity. Try drinking ginger tea to assist the cleansing process.

In general, ayurveda does not recommend snacks, but as modern practitioners, we need to be practical in our implementation. Let's say a meeting or another responsibility is going to overlap your scheduled mealtime. Rather than squeezing in a full meal before your meeting when you're not really hungry, you are better off carrying a snack with you to eat when you have a few minutes to yourself. The snack will help you postpone your mealtime until you are truly hungry and able to eat mindfully (see tip #3).

❷ Wait six hours between meals

It takes about six hours for an average Western-size meal to complete the digestion process as it is understood by ayurveda: 1 hour for each of the six tastes. It is best not to overload the digestive system with more food until it has properly absorbed and assimilated the previous meal. When you snack between meals, you are restarting your digestive cycle even though the previous cycle is incomplete — you are asking your system to work overtime with no breaks.

❸ Eat mindfully, in a harmonious environment

The ancients had an implicit understanding of the mind-body connection. They recommended eating in a harmonious environment, with good company, to aid digestion. Today we know that stress has an enormous impact on the gastrointestinal system, suppressing digestion and reducing blood flow, digestive muscle contractions and digestive secretions. So at mealtimes, set aside your obligations, stress and electronic devices and find a pleasant place to relax and enjoy your food. If you can find pleasant companions to share your meal, so much the better! Take a moment to reflect and give thanks for the meal you are about to eat. As you eat, consciously appreciate the taste and texture of the food, and embrace the nourishment entering your body.

The pace of your meals should be neither too slow nor too fast. Slow eating encourages overeating (as when we finish a large meal and feel full, but then find we have room for dessert a short time thereafter). Rapid eating and inadequate chewing impede optimal digestion (see box, below).

Chewing Food

It is important to chew food adequately. Chewing is the first stage of digestion and preps the food for further processing in the digestive tract. But how much chewing is enough? Ideally, you should chew your food until it becomes liquid. This could be anywhere from twenty to fifty bites, depending on the amount and type of food you put in your mouth (think of a bite of apple versus a bite of steak versus a bite of mashed potatoes).

That may seem like a lot of chewing, especially if you are trying to have a conversation during your meal. I encourage you to try it at least once and observe the effects. This will give you a baseline of how you feel when you chew your food properly.

A more manageable alternative may be to take smaller bites and wait until you have swallowed before taking another mouthful. This will slow down your eating rate and, as an added benefit, may keep you from mindlessly eating beyond your stomach's capacity.

❹ Drink warm water with your meals and upon rising

The ancients believed that water was sacred, and they had many methods of purification (boiling being one of the easiest to do in modern times). They believed that water was purifying and that, once consumed, it became auspicious and strengthening. Today we know that adequate water is vital for good health and that water is a reactant in many of the digestive processes. It is the ayurvedic drink of choice with meals. But exercise moderation: if you drink too much water, it can dilute the digestive enzymes, making your system work harder to process food.

Ayurvedic teachings suggest that everything, including water, should be cooked before entering the digestive system, for optimal functioning. Don't want to drink warm water? Then at least avoid iced drinks with meals, as extreme cold is less than ideal for the digestive process.

Another healthy practice is to drink a cup of warm water upon rising in the morning. This cleanses the gastrointestinal tract and stimulates the bodily processes for elimination.

Did You Know?

Damaging Beverages

Soft drinks, coffee, tea and alcohol tax the digestive system in general and the kidneys in particular. Excessive use of these beverages can damage the vital energy in your body over time.

⑤ Stop eating before you feel full

Ayurveda recommends eating the proper amount of food, broadly defined as "that which gets digested in the proper time." Food is more likely to be properly digested and absorbed if you don't overeat. A general guideline is to stop eating when you burp, a response that generally indicates your stomach is filled to capacity. Ayurveda also gives us the following practical guidance: your cupped hands approximate the size of your stomach, so that is the maximum amount of food you should consume at a meal.

What if you don't like to waste food by leaving it on your plate, even though you know you are full? I can still hear my mother lamenting, "There are children starving in the world; finish what's on your plate." But maybe there was too much on my plate. Try giving yourself smaller portions or save the leftovers for later (see box, page 52). When you overeat, the food ferments and putrefies — it is going to waste in your stomach. As one of my teachers, Jiwan Shakti, used to say: "Once you're full, you are going to waste the food whether you eat it or not. Do you want it to waste inside you, creating toxins, or waste outside where it could become beneficial compost?"

⑥ Eat your big meal at midday and lighter meals for breakfast and dinner

The ancients lived in harmony with the rhythms of the day and seasons. They believed digestion was strongest when the sun was strongest, and identified midday (11 a.m. to 2 p.m.) as the best time for the main meal. Breakfast should be a lighter meal, such as fruit, porridge, crêpes or a small veggie omelet. Dinner should be consumed before sunset and should be light and easy to digest (a warm lentil salad or soup rather than a T-bone steak).

Allow 1 hour after eating before physical exercise such as jogging or sex. Allow 3 hours after eating before going to bed.

⑦ Cook at home using whole foods

Commercially prepared foods are generally high in sugar, sodium, fat and chemical preservatives. Cooking your own food gives you control over the quality and type of ingredients that are used. In addition, you impart your energy into your home-cooked meals, which you will feel on a subliminal level, thereby helping to reinforce your commitment to health and well-being.

8 Emphasize local, organic foods in your diet

Vital energy and nutrients deteriorate quickly once food has been harvested. Food that has been shipped across the country (or world) has lost much of its vitality. Ideally, for optimal taste and nutritional content, eat food within a few hours of harvesting. Choose organic or pesticide-free foods whenever possible to maximize taste and minimize the potential long-term harmful effects of pesticide residue. Washing produce does not eliminate all pesticide residues. Organic or pesticide-free food is the best choice.

9 Minimize leftovers

Because of its focus on eating fresh foods, ayurveda does not encourage the use of leftovers. But realistically, eating leftovers will save you time and may keep you from resorting to commercially prepared food. Leftovers should be refrigerated in airtight containers, reheated only once and disposed of after 2 days. Freezing food is likewise not ayurvedic, but is a reality in a fast-paced modern society. Use freezer-grade, airtight, single-serving containers and eat the food within a month; defrost only the portion you are going to eat that same day. For tips on using up common leftovers, see the table on page 52.

10 Take a break with a mono-diet of kitchari

Give your digestive system an occasional rest (perhaps on a Sunday, after an indulgent weekend, or at the new moon to symbolize a healthy beginning) by eating a light, restorative mono-diet of kitchari for a day. This delicately spiced stew of mung beans and basmati rice is easily digested, absorbed, assimilated and eliminated. It helps to neutralize your gut's pH balance and provides a well-deserved vacation for your digestive system. See my recipe for kitchari on page 122.

Leftovers

Ayurveda recommends eating fresh foods and is not a proponent of leftovers. However, in today's society, where most people work at least forty hours a week and do not have someone at home cooking their meals, leftovers are a healthier alternative to most commercially prepared foods. Here are some tips on how to transform common leftovers into a delicious second meal, so you can move from one day to the next without wasting food or time.

Leftover Food	Transformation
Artichokes (packed in water)	✦ Broil, grill or lightly sauté and add to a salad of greens or white beans. ✦ Purée into an artichoke dip with some basil or arugula and lemon juice. ✦ Dilute the above artichoke dip with water or cream and use as a topping for pasta, as in Artichoke Lemon Cream Sauce (page 259).
Barley	✦ Add to Miso Soup (page 183) or vegetable soup.
Cabbage	✦ Make Asian-Style Vegetables (page 218). ✦ Make Borscht Lentil Soup (page 194).
Coconut milk	✦ Make Thai Lemongrass Vermicelli Soup (page 198). ✦ Make Vata Pitta Coconut Chai Shake (page 324) or add to smoothies. ✦ Add to hot chai. ✦ Make Okra with Ginger Lemongrass Sauce (page 214).
Dips	✦ Make a creamy dressing by combining dip with a few tablespoons (45 mL) of sunflower or olive oil, some lemon juice (or lime juice or cider vinegar) and some water to achieve the desired consistency.
Fennel (fresh)	✦ Chop and add to a salad of greens, lentils or beans. ✦ Add to soup.
Meat	✦ Chop or shred and add to soup. ✦ Slice and serve on a corn tortilla or wrap for lunch. ✦ Dice and add to a rice or vegetable salad for lunch.
Millet	✦ Combine with an egg and mashed sweet potato to make Millet Breakfast Patties (page 116). Serve with salad and avocado for lunch or with a poached egg for breakfast. ✦ Make Bison Meatloaf (page 174).
Puréed sweet potatoes, parsnips or kabocha	✦ Substitute for tomatoes in a soup when you're looking for something to cool pitta. ✦ Make Lime Tarragon Sweet Potato Breakfast Patties (page 114). ✦ Make Kabocha Cranberry Bread (page 296).
Quinoa or amaranth	✦ Make Moroccan Veggie Burgers (page 135). ✦ Add to soup. ✦ Combine with lentils in a salad. ✦ Add to quick breads or cookies as a substitute for nuts.
Rice (white or brown)	✦ Warm in a skillet with a few tablespoons (45 mL) of water; cover and gently steam over low heat. ✦ Stir-fry with a tablespoon (15 mL) of sunflower oil, sliced ginger, a minced garlic clove and some sliced fresh vegetables and/or meat. ✦ Make Baked Falafel Balls (page 136).
Risotto	✦ Combine with an egg and bread crumbs, then form into patties and fry in a small amount of ghee or sunflower oil. Serve with salad for lunch or with a poached egg for breakfast.

Balancing Foods for the Doshas

With our knowledge of the five elements, the three doshas, the six tastes and the food combination principles, we have a foundation for understanding dietary alternatives that can be balancing for specific doshas. The following examples reinforce how to work with the basic ayurvedic formula — opposites balance and like increases like — for each dosha.

Excess Vata

If you are feeling like a space cadet, are full of anxiety and fear, are frequently constipated or are experiencing itchy hemorrhoids, these symptoms indicate excess vata. Analyze your food and your lifestyle. Does your food have a preponderance of pungent, bitter and astringent tastes? Have you been eating a lot of raw, light, mobile, dry and/or rough foods, such as potato chips, crackers, beans, caffeinated drinks or raw salads? Has your life included a lot of activity — travel, running, gymnastics, nonstop talking at meetings — with no downtime?

Since the vata qualities are light, cold, dry, rough, mobile, subtle and clear, the opposite qualities of heavy, hot, oily, slimy/smooth, static, gross and cloudy/sticky will decrease excess vata. Emphasize the sweet, sour and salty tastes with warming foods and drinks such as a hearty root vegetable stew, beef broth, herbal tea, warm spiced milk, bananas and sweet oranges.

Excess Pitta

If you are feeling angry, irritable or judgmental, your skin is breaking out in hives, pimples or rashes, or your stomach is burning with acid, these symptoms indicate excess pitta. Analyze your food and your lifestyle. Does your food have a preponderance of pungent, salty and sour tastes? Have you been eating a lot of spicy foods, chile peppers, garlic, pickles, lemons, tomato sauce or fried foods? Have you been working long hours? Have you been in a hot climate? Have you been under pressure at work or in your relationships?

Since the pitta qualities are light, penetrating, hot, oily, liquid and spreading, the opposite qualities of heavy, slow/dull, cold/cool, dry, dense and static will decrease

> **Did You Know?**
>
> **Lifestyle Tips for Vata**
>
>
>
> To decrease excess vata, slow down, keep to a routine, stay hydrated and get plenty of rest. Try meditation, grounding yoga asana postures and daily oil massage (for self-massage, leave oil on for 15 to 20 minutes and follow with a warm shower).

> **Did You Know?**
>
> **Lifestyle Tips for Pitta**
>
>
>
> To decrease excess pitta, stop burning the midnight oil, meditate and "chill out." Relax near a calm, cool lake, and avoid sitting in the hot sun.

excess pitta. Emphasize the sweet, bitter and astringent tastes with cooling foods and drinks such as salads, bitter leafy green vegetables, organic ice cream or coconut ice cream, apples, avocados, cilantro, organic milk, coconut water and Pitta-Cooling Coriander Milk (page 320).

Excess Kapha

If you are feeling lethargic, sad or clingy, you are full of excess mucus or you can't fit into your skinny jeans, these symptoms indicate excess kapha. Analyze your food and your lifestyle. Does your food have a preponderance of sweet, sour and salty tastes? Have you been eating a lot of cheese, meat, dairy, wheat, fried foods, ice cream, bananas and chocolate?

Since the kapha qualities are heavy, slow, cool, oily, slimy, dense, soft and static, the opposite qualities of light, sharp/penetrating, warm, dry, rough, liquid, hard and mobile will decrease excess kapha. Emphasize the pungent, bitter and astringent tastes with cooked leafy green vegetables, liberal use of garlic, onion and ginger, spicy foods and drying foods such as beans, barley and corn.

Dosha Balancing Aids

I have provided more guidance on diet and lifestyle balancing for each of the doshas in Appendices A, B and C (page 328 for vata, 332 for pitta and 336 for kapha). Use these guidelines to help you get started on your ayurvedic journey. Remember, the ultimate determination of what foods are balancing is how you feel after eating. Relax, enjoy your food and be conscious of the effects the food has on your body, physically and emotionally.

Ayurvedic Cooking for the Family

Cooking within the ayurvedic framework for a family is not complicated, it simply requires a bit of forethought. When cooking for more than one person, you can either prepare recipes that are tridoshic (balancing to all doshas), or you can lay out suitable churnas (spice blends designed to balance specific doshas), garnishes, sauces or other accompaniments at the table so that each diner can adjust the meal to his or her specific needs. The recipes in this book are generally tridoshic, and many provide variations to target specific doshas.

You can also apply the general rules to prepare your own tridoshic meals for the family. For instance, let's say it is a sweltering summer day and you want to make a cool salad for lunch. Prepare a base salad using tridoshic ingredients (see Build Your Own Salad, page 247) and lay out dosha-specific dressings for added balance.

Now let's say you are serving that salad with brown rice and steamed vegetables. To make those dishes more balancing for vata, set out Basic Tahini (page 261) or tamari for grounding, moisture and warmth. For pitta, provide chopped fresh cilantro or shredded coconut for additional sweetness and cooling. For kapha, supply chili sauce for heat or green onions or sprouts for lightness.

In general, vata needs moisture (sauces, soups and dressings), pitta needs cooling (cilantro and coconut), and kapha needs movement and dryness (spices, garlic and raw onions; no sauces).

Dosha-Balancing Accompaniments

This table is your go-to reference for accompaniments to help balance each dosha. I've listed garnishes, sauces, chutneys and salad dressings that can be spread out at the table when you're cooking for a family or trying to accommodate more than one dosha. Here's how it works: Let's say a vata-predominant person wants to eat a salad but understands that lettuce is cold, dry and light — in other words, unbalancing for vata. The solution is to select some garnishes and a salad dressing from the Vata column to help warm, ground and moisten the salad. Or, if pittas want to indulge in some spicy Mexican food, they can peruse the Pitta column for suitable cooling garnishes.

Many of the accompaniments can be prepared in advance (or purchased) and stored in the refrigerator to make meal preparation easier.

	Vata	Pitta	Kapha
Garnishes	avocado chives cucumber dulse lemon lime nuts olives (black) salt seeds umeboshi paste/plums	avocado cilantro (fresh) coconut (dried shredded) cucumber dill jicama lime mint	chile peppers chives flax seeds ginger horseradish mushrooms mustard mustard seeds onion (raw) radish sprouts wasabi

	Vata	Pitta	Kapha
Sauces and chutneys	basil pesto Creamy Yogurt (page 117) Ginger Lemongrass Sauce (page 214) Spinach Pesto "Cream" Sauce (page 148) tamari Vata Lemon Cashew Cream Sauce (page 262) Vata Plum Compote (page 263) Vata Sweet Onion Chutney (page 267)	Cool Coconut Chutney (page 264) Cranberry Relish (page 269) Creamy Yogurt (page 117) Pitta-Cooling Date Chutney (page 265) tamari	basil pesto hot pepper sauce Kapha Hot Onion Chutney (page 268) Kapha Spicy Pear Chutney (page 266)
Salad dressings	Pomegranate and Sweet Balsamic Dressing (page 212) Basic Tahini (page 261) Vata Tamarind Honey Dressing (page 253)	freshly squeezed lime juice Pitta Kapha Pomegranate Vinaigrette (page 253) Pomegranate and Sweet Balsamic Dressing (page 212)	Kapha Wasabi Dressing (page 254) Pitta Kapha Pomegranate Vinaigrette (page 253)

The Ayurvedic Pantry

When making a recipe, the first step is to read the recipe all the way through and make a list of ingredients to purchase. But much to the chagrin of cookbook authors, this step is often skipped. I understand that your time and kitchen space may be limited, so this chapter is all about efficiently organizing your kitchen so you are ready to whip up most of the recipes in this book at a moment's notice.

You don't need a grand kitchen, expensive pans or exotic ingredients to cook healthy, nutritious meals. In my travels in Asia and the South Pacific, when I tired of spicy foods and craved some home-cooked meals, I made nutritious dinners from my hotel room using foods from the outdoor markets, a rice cooker, an electric kettle, an immersion blender and a sharp knife! On the other end of the spectrum, I have prepared meals in gourmet home kitchens using expensive pans and internationally sourced ingredients. Most of us exist somewhere between those two extremes, and our cooking skill set is likewise diverse.

This chapter includes two "essentials" tables, which are basically inventory lists of core ingredients that you will need to prepare the recipes in this book (or their variations). You likely already have many of these items on hand, so use the tables to create your shopping list and fill in any gaps.

The tables generally include only items that have a shelf life of two weeks or longer. Most perishable items (fresh fruits, vegetables, herbs and dairy) are not listed, except in a general manner. You can pick these up when you have extra time or are shopping for a specific recipe. I have also included detailed information on where to purchase, how to cook and/or how to store some lesser-known ingredients.

The focus of this chapter is to help you navigate the market and easily identify specific ingredients. Later on, in the individual recipes, I go into more detail about the ayurvedic energetics of particular ingredients and how they are used to balance out a meal.

The chapter concludes with some tips on time-saving kitchen tools that will help you prepare the recipes in this book.

> **Did You Know?**
> **Season with Love**
>
>
>
> Ayurvedic cooking doesn't have to be a time-consuming ordeal of shopping, prepping and cooking. The core of every meal should simply be fresh whole foods liberally seasoned with love.

Stocking Your Pantry

To ensure that you always have core ingredients on hand to make the recipes in this book, the Pantry Essentials table contains dry goods, canned and bottled items and bulk foods that typically have a shelf life of up to six months. I've expanded on each category in the paragraphs that follow.

Some of the lentils, beans, dals and grains are not staples in the Western diet, so I've included additional tables with prepping and cooking instructions, for easy reference. These tables provide general information; actual preparation methods and cooking times may vary in certain recipes. Soaking time (more soaking = less cooking), the freshness of the ingredients (old beans = longer cooking) and the stovetop temperature will also affect cooking times. The amount of water or broth used will, in many cases, vary depending on the recipe or your personal preferences. Use these tables as guidelines for experimenting on your own; for specific recipes, follow the method laid out in the recipe to achieve the desired results.

Pantry Essentials

Lentils, beans and dals	adzuki beans; black beans; cannellini (white kidney) beans; chana dal; chickpeas (garbanzo beans); heirloom scarlet runners; mung dal (split, hulled); Puy lentils; red lentils; toor dal; urad dal
Grains	amaranth; barley (hulled); couscous; farro; millet; oats (quick-cooking); polenta; quinoa (white, red or black); rice (basmati, brown or purple); wild rice
Seeds	flax seeds; green pumpkin seeds (pepitas); sesame seeds; sunflower seeds
Dried fruit	apricots; cherries; cranberries; currants; goji berries; raisins
Condiments	artichoke hearts (canned); rose water; tamari; tamarind paste; vinegar (apple cider, balsamic, rice, white balsamic)
Fats	coconut oil; ghee; olive oil; sesame oil; sunflower oil
Sweeteners	coconut sugar; honey (raw); maple syrup; pomegranate syrup
Dried herbs and spices	ajwain seeds; allspice (ground); asafoetida (hing); basil; bay leaves; black peppercorns (whole); cardamom (ground and seeds); cayenne pepper; chili powder; cinnamon (ground and sticks); cloves (ground and whole); coriander (ground and seeds); cumin (ground and seeds); dillweed; ginger (ground); nutmeg (ground); oregano; parsley; rosemary; saffron; salt (Himalayan rock); savory; star anise (pods); tarragon; thyme; turmeric (ground)
Asian ingredients	coconut milk (canned); curry leaves; glass noodles, kombu (dried kelp); lime leaves; miso; nori sheets; rice vermicelli noodles; shiitake mushrooms (dried); soba noodles; udon noodles; umeboshi paste; wakame; wasabi powder

Lentils, Beans and Dals

Lentils, beans and dals are a good source of protein and healthy carbohydrates, with a generally low glycemic load. They are rich in minerals and have no cholesterol, so they are a healthy addition to anyone's menu and an essential part of a vegetarian diet.

Growing up in Boston, for me beans were synonymous with canned, overly sweet Boston baked beans and the resultant embarrassing bloating and flatulence. I shied away from all legumes for many years. It wasn't until I started reading Dr. Lad's ayurvedic cookbook in my late thirties that I dared to venture into some culinary experiments, starting with dals, then moving into lentils and eventually embracing a few bean dishes. Wow, what a difference proper prepping, cooking and seasoning can make! I'm sure you will agree once you've tried a few of my recipes.

Dried lentils, beans and dals can be purchased from bulk containers at natural food stores or food cooperatives, allowing you to purchase small quantities to meet your immediate needs. They must be stored in airtight containers; otherwise, they will begin to dry out and become tough after about 6 months. To ensure freshness, purchase only as much as you will use within a few months.

For convenience, many lentils and beans are sold in cans, precooked and packed in water, sometimes with kombu (dried kelp that aids digestion). If time is of the essence and you find yourself in the canned beans aisle, read the labels and select a brand that is packed in a BPA-free (bisphenol-A-free) can and contains no added sugar, sodium or preservatives.

Adding Lentils, Beans and Dals to Your Diet

If you are new to lentils, beans and dals, I recommend the following guidelines, especially if you have dominant or excess vata or a challenged digestive system:

+ **Soak dried lentils, beans and dals overnight in water.** When you ingest lentils, beans and dals, they travel through your digestive system absorbing water like a sponge. This can create dryness and lead to constipation, gas and bloating in some constitutions. If you soak them in water before cooking them, they absorb much of the soaking water, reducing the amount of water they pull from your body. Use clean

---

Did You Know?

Glycemic Load vs. Glycemic Index

Glycemic load (GL) measures how carbohydrates impact post-meal blood sugar spikes — the lower the number, the lower the impact. The glycemic index (GI) measures sugar content. GI does not always correlate to blood sugar spikes, especially when it comes to healthy carbs such as fruits, beans, lentils and whole grains.

filtered water to soak beans. After soaking, if there is any remaining water, discard it and use fresh water for cooking.

+ **Try adding lentils to soup, with a bit of meat.** Lentils are easier to digest than beans. Cooking them in a soup or stew provides added moisture that will help your body acclimate to their dryness. Combine them with a small amount of meat to add warmth, grounding and a feeling of satiety. (Note: although meat is listed as incompatible with beans and lentils in the Food Combining table on pages 42–43, when they are prepared together in a soup, with only a small quantity of meat, the incompatibility lessens.)

+ **Add moisture, warmth and oil.** Lentils, beans and dals tend to be dry, light, rough and cold. To improve digestibility, they should be prepared with added moisture (water, broth), warmth (spices) and oil (ghee, coconut oil, sunflower oil). The oil is particularly important with beans, as it balances out their extreme dryness.

+ **Add digestive spices.** Most spices have a warming energetic that stokes the digestive fire so your body can fully process high-fiber, cool foods like beans and lentils. Some spices that are especially valued for combating bloating and flatulence include cumin, ajwain, ginger, asafoetida (hing) and oregano.

+ **Take it slow.** Start by incorporating a lentil dish into your diet 1 day a week for the first month. If you do not experience any digestive issues (constipation, gas, belching, bloating or malabsorption), then you can introduce another day of lentils, beans or dals the next month and continue until you are eating them as many days a week as you wish. If at any time you do experience digestive issues, try different recipes and a smaller amount of lentils, beans or dals. Consult your ayurvedic practitioner for assistance.

+ **Drink water throughout the day.** Lentils, beans and dals are drying, and it may take some time for your body to adjust.

Lentils

Lentils are part of the legume family. They are low in calories and very nutritious, providing dietary fiber, B vitamins and protein.

Lentils are available either dried or (in some cases) canned, but the recipes in this book use dried lentils. Dried lentils are sold packaged (in boxes or bags) or in bulk bins, where you can select exactly the amount you want. Packaged lentils should be in undamaged packaging with no signs of moisture damage. When buying in bulk, be sure that the bins are covered.

Lentils should be fairly uniform in size and color, and should be free of insect damage (no small pinholes or cracked or broken pieces). They can be stored in an airtight container, away from sunlight, in a cool, dry place for up to 6 months (a time period that assumes most lentils have already been in storage in a warehouse for up to 6 months). After a year, the color of lentils fades and they dry out and take longer to cook.

Dried lentils cook much faster than dried beans and do not require presoaking. However, if your digestion is sensitive or if you are new to lentils, you may want to presoak the lentils to aid digestion.

The recipes in this cookbook use Puy lentils and red lentils, which can be found in well-stocked grocery stores, health food stores, international grocery stores and specialty stores. I prefer these varieties because they seem to be the easiest to digest, they are super-easy to cook, and they have a nicely balanced flavor. They cook in 10 to 20 minutes, making them the perfect choice when time is tight and you need a quick meal. Start with the lentil recipes in this cookbook and I trust you will be a lentil lover in no time.

✦ **Puy lentils:** Puy lentils are grown in a region of France called Le Puy, which has mineral-rich volcanic soil. The lentils are nutrient-dense and have a mild, peppery smell. They retain their shape after cooking and are ideal in soups, stews, casseroles and cold salads. They are pricey, however, so a great alternative for the budget-conscious is French green lentils, which are a tad less earthy. You can use Puy and French lentils interchangeably in my recipes; the difference in taste is comparable to substituting a California sparkling wine for French Champagne. Note that French lentils are not the same as green lentils (or dried green peas), even

Did You Know?

Don't Mix Old and New

Do not mix newly purchased lentils with older lentils in your cupboard; the old lentils will be dryer, resulting in uneven cooking times.

Did You Know?

Reducing Foaming

When cooking lentils, beans and dals, add 1 tablespoon (15 mL) sunflower oil to the cooking water to reduce foaming. If the foam still rises to the top of the pan, you may skim it off.

though French lentils have some green in their coloring. When purchasing, look specifically for a label that says "French lentils" or "Puy lentils."

In terms of energetics, Puy lentils are a little dry, a little heavy and slightly heating. French Lentil Salad with Lemon Dressing (page 242) is a nicely balanced dish that is suitable for all the doshas (vata can apply liberal amounts of the dressing).

✦ **Red lentils:** Red lentils are actually salmon-colored. They cook in about 10 minutes. They are delicate and do not hold their shape or color when cooked — they turn to mush and become light yellow. That's how you know they are done, so don't be upset that your red lentils didn't stay round — or red! They are often added to soups to lend texture or add protein.

In spite of their mildly peppery flavor, red lentils are sweet, cooling and light. Check out the Moroccan Veggie Burgers with Tangy Tamarind Sauce (page 135) — gluten-free, dairy-free and soy-free, they will please everyone!

Cooking Lentils

To prepare dried lentils, sort them and remove any debris or stones, then rinse the lentils under cold water. (If desired, soak lentils for 1 to 2 hours in three times their volume of filtered water, then drain and rinse the lentils.) In a medium pan, combine the lentils, water and 1 tablespoon (15 mL) sunflower oil (and a digestive aid, if using; see sidebar, page 60). Bring to a boil over high heat. Reduce the heat and simmer, uncovered, until lentils are tender (for Puy lentils) or mushy (for red lentils). Drain and serve.

	Puy Lentils	**Red Lentils**
Best for	vata and kapha	pitta
Lentil measure	1 cup (250 mL)	1 cup (250 mL)
Soaking time	1–2 hours (if desired)	1–2 hours (if desired)
Water or broth measure	2 cups (500 mL)	2 cups (500 mL)
Simmering time*	20 minutes	10 minutes
Yield	2 cups (500 mL)	2 cups (500 mL)

* If cooking at a high altitude (above 3,500 feet/1,000 meters), lentils require a longer simmering time.

Beans

Beans tend to be hard, heavy, rough, dry and cooling — potential digestive misery for those who are new to beans or have a sensitive digestion. I find that the best introduction to beans is in a soup, where the added moisture and warmth of the broth will balance the dry, cold qualities of the beans. If you are new to beans or have a sensitive constitution, I recommend trying the Puréed Lemon Chickpea Soup (page 196).

Most of the beans used in this book (adzuki, black, cannellini and chickpeas) are readily available precooked and canned, which is a huge time-saver (see page 59 for advice on purchasing canned beans). If you opt to purchase dried beans, you must presoak them overnight and cook them for anywhere from 50 minutes to 2 hours, depending on the type of bean, so you'll need to plan ahead. (See the table on page 64 for recommended simmering times.)

Dried beans can be soaked up to 3 days in advance, then drained and stored in an airtight container in the refrigerator until you're ready to use them. They will absorb some of the soaking water and double in size, so be sure to use a container that is large enough to accommodate the expansion.

✦ **Adzuki beans:** Adzuki beans (also known as aduki beans or red beans) are astringent and cooling, with a pungent post-digestive effect. They are often sweetened and used in Asian desserts, or added to rice or Caribbean stews. Add them to vegetable soup for instant protein.

✦ **Black beans:** Black beans (also known as black turtle beans or Mexican beans) are astringent, cooling and difficult to digest. They are popular in the Caribbean (where they are often seasoned with allspice, cinnamon, nutmeg, cloves or ginger) and in Mexico (where the seasonings tend toward cilantro, oregano, chiles, cumin and lime) and are often used in burritos, salads and stews.

✦ **Cannellini beans:** Cannellini beans (also known as white kidney beans or Italian kidney beans) are astringent, cooling and difficult to digest. They are often flavored with Italian seasonings (basil, oregano, marjoram, garlic, sage, rosemary, thyme, parsley, bay leaves) and are nice additions to soups, stews and salads.

✦ **Chickpeas:** Chickpeas (also known as garbanzo beans) are astringent, cooling and difficult to digest. They are often flavored with Mediterranean seasonings

Did You Know?

Conserve Water

Instead of discarding the water your beans or grains soaked in, give it to your plants — they will benefit from the added nutrients!

Did You Know?

Old Beans

If your beans do not soften in the recommended cooking time, they are likely old.

(bay leaves, basil, cardamom, lemon, mint, cilantro, cloves, cumin, cinnamon, fennel, oregano, paprika, thyme) and are nice additions to soups, stews and salads. They are puréed with sesame seeds, lemon juice and garlic to make hummus.

+ **Heirloom scarlet runners:** Heirloom beans come from seeds that have been passed down through a family for several generations, preserving unique sizes, shapes, colors or textures. I have not seen them in cans, but the dried beans are available in the bulk food section or boxed in the specialty/gourmet aisle of the grocery store. Scarlet runners are large and colorful, and contain healthy compounds that may reduce inflammation and prevent chronic diseases such as cancer and heart disease. They have a nutty taste and a meaty consistency that satiates the appetite. Slightly cool and astringent, they are less dry and rough than other bean varieties, so most people can tolerate them — especially if they are seasoned with liberal amounts of oil and lemon juice.

Cooking Beans

To prepare dried beans, sort and rinse them, then soak them overnight in three times their volume of filtered water. The next day, drain and rinse the beans. In a medium pan, combine the beans, fresh water and 1 tablespoon (15 mL) sunflower oil (and a digestive aid, if using; see sidebar, page 60). Bring to a boil over high heat. Reduce the heat to low, cover and simmer until beans are fork-tender. Drain and serve.

	Adzuki	Black	Cannellini	Chickpeas	Heirloom Scarlet Runners
Best for	pitta and kapha	pitta and kapha	pitta and kapha	pitta and kapha	vata, pitta and kapha
Bean measure	1 cup (250 mL)	1 cup (250 mL)	1 cup (250 mL)	1 cup (250 mL)	1 cup (250 mL)
Soaking time	overnight	overnight	overnight	overnight	overnight
Water or broth measure	4 cups (1 L)	4 cups (1 L)	4 cups (1 L)	4 cups (1 L)	4 cups (1 L)
Simmering time*	50–60 minutes	75–90 minutes	60–90 minutes	90–120 minutes	75–90 minutes
Yield	3 cups (750 mL)	3 cups (750 mL)	4 cups (1 L)	3 cups (750 mL)	3 cups (750 mL)

* If cooking at a high altitude (above 3,500 feet/1,000 meters), beans require a longer simmering time.

Dosha-Balancing Foods

Vata

Pitta

Kapha

The Six Tastes

Sweet

Sour

Salty

Pungent

Bitter

Astringent

Lentil, Bean and Dal Varieties

Puy Lentils

Red Lentils

Adzuki Beans

Black Beans

Cannellini Beans

Chickpeas

Heirloom Scarlet Runners

Chana Dal

Mung Dal

Toor Dal

Urad Dal

Dals

"Dal" is a Sanskrit word meaning "splitting open." It is a general term used for beans or lentils that have been split and had their outer shells removed. This refining of the bean improves the digestibility and taste, but it decreases the nutritional benefits (especially the fiber content). In this book, I have included recipes that use chana dal, mung dal, toor dal and urad dal, which I find to be the most flavorful and easiest to digest for the aspiring vegetarians or those with sensitive digestion.

Dals generally cook more quickly than beans. They tend to lose their shape and become creamy after cooking. They are typically used in soups, stews and desserts.

Before cooking, dal must be soaked for a few hours or overnight. The dal will absorb the water and expand. It can then be drained and stored in an airtight container in the refrigerator for up to 3 days. Every Sunday night I soak some dal, and on Monday morning, I drain it and store it in an airtight container in the refrigerator. Later in the week, I am happy to have it on hand so I can whip up a tasty meal.

+ **Chana dal:** Chana dal (also known as Bengal gram dal or cholar dal) is very common in Indian cooking. It is essentially a younger, smaller, sweeter variation of chickpeas, and the two are often used interchangeably in recipes. Chana dal comes split, it doesn't lose its shape during cooking, and it has a lower glycemic index than chickpeas. Like chickpeas, chana dal can be a little heavy for delicate digestive systems. Indian recipes often call for a mixture of dals, which will provide depth of flavor while tempering the effects on the digestion. Chana dal is not common in the West, so you may need to visit an Indian market to find it. It requires presoaking and a little less cooking time than chickpeas.

+ **Mung dal:** Mung dal (or moong dal, also known as yellow dal or split hulled green gram) is very common in ayurvedic cooking. To find it, you may need to visit an Indian market, food cooperative or health food store, or you can purchase organic mung dal online at www.banyanbotanicals.com. It cooks relatively quickly with minimal soaking. However, if you are new to dal or have a fragile digestive system, you may want to soak it overnight.

Mung dal is used to kindle a weak digestive fire or to give the digestive system a rest. It is sweet, cooling, light and nutritious. Mung dal soup is often used as a

Did You Know?

Whole Mung Beans

Whole mung beans are green in color and are readily available in most supermarkets. If you decide to substitute mung beans in a recipe calling for mung dal, the beans will require overnight soaking and a longer cooking time. Mung beans are heavier than mung dal and are more difficult to digest for someone who is new to beans or who has a sensitive digestion. Mung dal, on the other hand, is much lighter and considered balancing for all constitutions.

Did You Know?

Alternative Dal and Bean Cooking Methods

Instead of the simmering method (see tables, below and on page 64), dal and beans can be cooked in a pressure cooker, which will reduce the cooking time. Or you can use a slow cooker and cook the dal overnight.

treatment to aid recovery from an acute illness. Kitchari, a traditional mung bean and rice dish that is delicately spiced according to your dosha, is eaten during restorative and cleansing therapies to rejuvenate the digestive system.

+ **Toor dal:** Toor dal (or tur dal, also known as split pigeon peas) is heavy, heating and astringent. It is yellow and is sometimes packaged with an oil coating (which is used as a preservative). It is generally found only at Indian markets.

+ **Urad dal:** Urad dal (or urid dal, also known as white dal or split hulled black matpe bean) is typically found at Indian markets. Rich in protein, iron and vitamins, it is creamy, heavy and grounding, with a distinct earthy taste.

In India, urad dal is used in curries, soups, idlis (steamed breakfast cakes) and dosa (a fermented, stuffed lentil pancake). I first experimented with urad dal when I was feeling exhausted on one of my vegetarian stints. A supportive friend from India recommended I eat urad dal, which he described as the food of Lord Hanuman — a vegetarian monkey-god with otherworldly strength. He shared with me his favorite recipe of Urad Dal with Tamarind, which I've adapted and included on page 127. I'm still not vegetarian, but I do love urad dal!

Cooking Dals

To prepare dal, sort and remove any debris or stones. Rinse the dal several times, until the water runs clear. Place the dal in a 4-cup (1 L) bowl and cover with filtered water; soak for at least 2 hours or overnight. The next day, drain the dal. In a heavy-bottomed pan, combine the dal, water and 1 tablespoon (15 mL) sunflower oil (and a digestive aid, if using; see sidebar, page 60). Bring to a boil over high heat. Reduce the heat and simmer, stirring occasionally, until dal is tender. Drain and serve.

	Chana Dal	Mung Dal	Toor Dal	Urad Dal
Best for	pitta and kapha	vata, pitta and kapha	vata and kapha	vata
Dal measure	1 cup (250 mL)	1 cup (250 mL)	1 cup (250 mL)	1 cup (250 mL)
Soaking time	2 hours or overnight	2 hours or overnight	2 hours or overnight	2 hours or overnight
Water or broth measure	3 cups (750 mL)	2 cups (500 mL)	3 cups (750 mL)	3 cups (750 mL)
Simmering time*	60–90 minutes	20–25 minutes	50–60 minutes	60–90 minutes
Yield	2 cups (500 mL)	2 cups (500 mL)	2 cups (500 mL)	2 cups (500 mL)

* If cooking at a high altitude (above 3,500 feet/1,000 meters), dals require a longer simmering time.

Grains

The recipes in this book venture beyond industrial-farmed, monoculture crops (wheat, soybeans, corn and rice) and introduce some lesser-appreciated grains that were commonly used by our ancestors, including amaranth, barley, farro, millet, oats and quinoa. The rise in gluten sensitivities over the past several years has placed a spotlight on these ancient grains. I personally have an intolerance to gluten, and since I must taste-test everything I cook, the recipes in this book are *mostly* gluten-free. There is a growing movement away from the processed foods of industrial farming, and the demand for unprocessed whole grains is booming.

In a vegetarian diet, healthy whole grains should be well represented in your meals. Whole grains are not just flavorful, but are also a good source of healthy carbohydrates (with a lower glycemic load), rich in nutrients and high in protein to provide lasting energy and satiety.

I prefer not to buy processed foods in general, so you will find only one or two recipes calling for wheat noodles. In some instances, I have modified traditionally wheat-based recipes to use ancient grains (like Quinoa Tabbouleh, page 149) or vegetables (like Summer Squash Pasta, page 217).

Whole grains are packed with nutrition, have rich flavors and are readily available in local supermarkets, either in the bulk bin section or with other packaged grains. Delicious, easy recipes and easy-to-source ingredients — there's no excuse not to experiment! Have a party and share the recipes with your friends. Let me know which recipes are your favorites!

Did You Know?

Healthy Carbs

Complex carbohydrates are a good source of energy. They slow digestion, moderate blood insulin and blood sugar levels, reduce cholesterol levels and help you feel satisfied and full for longer.

Storing Grains

Most grains should be stored in an airtight container in a cool, dry, dark location, though some (such as amaranth, millet and quinoa) are better stored in the refrigerator or freezer. A sealed container is very important for maintaining freshness and reducing the possibility of infestations.

Amaranth

Amaranth is an ancient plant that dates back to the Aztecs, who used it as a food staple and in religious ceremonies. It is a complete protein that contains all nine of the essential amino acids that our bodies do not produce, in the proportions necessary to support the repair of tissues and organs. Amaranth is also high in iron, calcium, vitamin B_6 and magnesium. It is gluten-free.

The slightly astringent and bitter seed must be cooked to obtain the nutritional benefits. It can be popped to make puffed amaranth for cereals or sweets; cooked as a breakfast porridge; added to soups; or used in salads. Store amaranth in an airtight container in the refrigerator or freezer for up to 6 months.

Barley

Barley is a cereal grain that is rich in fiber and selenium; it is a good source of phosphorus, copper and manganese. Barley is sweet, cooling and light, with diuretic properties. It has been labeled a "gluten grain," so keep this in mind if you are allergic or sensitive to gluten. Barley typically comes in one of three forms:

+ **Hulled barley** is a whole grain with only the inedible outer hull removed. It is brown in color. It requires longer soaking and cooking than the other forms, and is very chewy, but it has more nutrients.
+ **Pearl barley** has been "polished," which means most or all of the outer bran layer has been removed. It is white in color, has a lower cooking time and is less chewy, but it has a lower nutrient content.
+ **Pot (or scotch) barley** is lightly polished to remove only some of the outer bran layer, so while it is technically not a whole grain, it maintains more nutrients than pearl barley.

Hulled barley must be soaked overnight before cooking. For convenience, soak it on Sunday night, then on Monday morning, drain it, transfer it to an airtight container and store it in the refrigerator until you're ready to use it in a recipe sometime later in the week. Barley can be made into a breakfast porridge; added to a soup with root vegetables; or served as a warm salad, seasoned with heating spices.

Did You Know?

Adding Barley to Soup

Barley absorbs a lot of liquid, so if adding it to soup, use only a small handful; otherwise, you will end up with thick barley porridge.

Couscous

Couscous is tiny balls of rolled durum wheat or semolina that have been steamed and dried. Available in the pasta aisle or the bulk bin section of most grocery stores, it is labeled "instant" or "precooked" couscous, and it can be cooked in about 10 minutes by immersing it in boiled water. Its flavor is bland, making it a fun starting point from which to whip up a quick meal by adding a few fresh ingredients (herbs, spices and vegetables). It has a sweet and cool energetic.

Farro

Farro is an Old World heirloom wheat that is light and chewy, with a nutty taste. Whole-grain farro is high in fiber, protein and nutrients and has a low glycemic load. Its gluten content is lower than that of modern wheat. To me, the farro energetic feels dry and cold. It can be substituted for barley or brown rice in most dishes or served as a salad or breakfast porridge.

There are three varieties of farro: spelt (farro grande), emmer (farro medio, the parent of modern durum wheat) and einkorn (farro piccolo). In Italy, farro emmer cultivation is well established in the mountains of Tuscany; it is grown as an IGP (Indicazione Geografica Protetta) product, with its geographic identity protected by law. Farro emmer is what is typically sold in North America.

Millet

Millet is an ancient plant with origins in Africa and Asia. It is dry, light and heating. There are many varieties, but pearl millet is the one typically found in North American markets. It is rich in protein, calcium, iron and manganese, but must be cooked to obtain the nutritional benefits. It is gluten-free.

You can use millet to make porridge, soups and stews, or as a crunchy addition to muffins and breads. Store it in an airtight container in the refrigerator or freezer for up to 6 months.

Oats

Oats that have been harvested, cleaned and hulled are called whole oat groats. These can be cut into steel-cut oats, or they can be steamed and rolled into flakes to make large-flake (old-fashioned) rolled oats. The steaming and rolling process stabilizes the healthy oils in the oats, so they stay fresh longer, and the larger surface area helps

> **Did You Know?**
> **Ancient Grains**
>
>
> "Ancient grains" is a marketing term that applies to nutrient-dense crops that have been neglected by crop breeders. Booming in popularity, these great-tasting grains are successfully marketed with captivating stories about the ancient civilizations that first used them.

> **Did You Know?**
> **Millet and Thyroid Disease**
>
>
> People with thyroid disease should not consume millet in large quantities, as it is a mild thyroid peroxidase inhibitor.

them cook faster. Rolling the oat flakes thinner and/or steaming them longer creates quick-cooking oats and, ultimately, instant oats. The nutrition stays the same (all forms of oats are whole-grain), but the texture changes.

Heart-healthy oats are full of nutrients and have a low glycemic load (although the GL is lower the less processed the oats are, so steel-cut oats have the lowest GL and instant oats the highest). You can purchase oats in the bulk bin section or packaged cereal aisle of most grocery stores. If you purchase packaged oats, read the label to make sure there is no added sugar or salt.

Oats themselves are gluten-free, but they are subject to cross-contamination if processed with equipment that is also used to process gluten-containing grains (such as wheat). Oats may also become contaminated if they are grown in fields next to wheat. Look for the "certified gluten-free" label if gluten-free cooking is a priority for you.

Polenta

Polenta is made by combining cornmeal with water (or broth or sauce) and seasonings (such as fresh herbs, dried spices or vegetables) and cooking to a soupy consistency. Polenta's energetics are warm and dry, depending on how much liquid is added to the dish.

This is one item that I purchase precooked and packaged, because I can easily find organic, unadulterated polenta. I keep it on my shelf for those times when I'm in need of a quick warm meal. Look for organic polenta in an 18-ounce (511 g) tube at well-stocked supermarkets. Read the ingredients and choose a brand with no added preservatives or sweeteners.

Quinoa

Quinoa (pronounced "KEEN-wah") is a complete protein containing all nine essential amino acids in the proportions necessary to support the repair of tissues and organs. It is a good source of manganese, magnesium, iron, tryptophan, copper, phosphorus and riboflavin (vitamin B_2).

Quinoa is readily available in most supermarkets and comes in several different colors. All varieties have a light, nutty flavor, but I find the white to be the "lightest." Red quinoa is a little heavier (and warmer), and black is the densest (and warmest). The price of quinoa seems to increase with the color (white being the least expensive and black the most). If you are on a budget and want to try red or black quinoa, try using it in place of half of the white quinoa in your dish.

Due to its high oil content, quinoa should be stored in the refrigerator or freezer to prevent it from becoming rancid.

Cooking Grains

Rinse and soak the grain (if necessary). In a medium pan, bring the water to a boil over high heat. If desired, add salt and seasonings to the boiling water. Add the grain, reduce the heat to low, cover and simmer until tender and/or liquid is absorbed. Check occasionally and add more water if necessary. Let rest, covered, for the time indicated (if applicable), then fluff with a fork. (In the case of farro and barley, drain off excess liquid at the end of the simmering time; no rest time is required.)

	Amaranth	Barley (Hulled)	Couscous	Farro
Best for	vata, pitta and kapha	pitta and kapha	vata and pitta	pitta and kapha
Grain measure	1 cup (250 mL)	1 cup (250 mL)	1 cup (250 mL)	1 cup (250 mL)
Soaking time	10 minutes	overnight	none	overnight
Water or broth measure	2 cups (500 mL)	3 cups (750 mL)	1 cup (250 mL)	3 cups (750 mL)
Simmering time	20–25 minutes	60 minutes	none; add to boiling water, cover and remove from heat	20 minutes
Resting time	none	none; drain off excess water	5 minutes	none; drain off excess water
Yield	2 cups (500 mL)	2 cups (500 mL)	2 cups (500 mL)	2 cups (500 mL)

	Millet	Oats (Quick-Cooking)	Polenta (Precooked)	Quinoa
Best for	kapha	vata and pitta	kapha	vata, pitta and kapha
Grain measure	1 cup (250 mL)	1 cup (250 mL)	1 tube (18 oz/511 g)	1 cup (250 mL)
Soaking time	10 minutes	none	none	10 minutes
Water or broth measure	2 cups (500 mL)	1 1/2 cups (375 mL)	1 1/2 cups (375 mL)	2 cups (500 mL)
Simmering time	25 minutes	n/a	5 minutes	10–12 minutes
Resting time	10 minutes	1 minute	none	10 minutes
Yield	3 1/2 cups (875 mL)	1 1/2 cups (375 mL)	3 1/2 cups (875 mL)	3 1/2 cups (875 mL)

Rice and Wild Rice

White rice is sweet and cooling. Long-grain rice is drier, while short-grain rice is moister, starchier and softer. White basmati rice is considered tridoshic.

Brown rice, whether long- or short-grain, is heavy and heating. It is less processed than white rice and has higher nutritional content and a lower glycemic load.

Cooking Rice

Rinse and soak rice (if necessary). In a saucepan, combine the rice, water and any desired seasonings. Bring to a boil over high heat. Reduce the heat to low, cover with a tight-fitting lid (so steam does not escape) and simmer for the recommended cooking time. Remove from heat and check for doneness. If the rice is still crunchy, add 2 to 3 tablespoons (30 to 45 mL) of water and simmer for a few minutes or until the rice is the desired consistency. Remove from the heat, cover and let rest for the recommended resting time. Fluff and serve.

	Basmati Rice (White)	Bhutanese Red Rice	Brown Rice (Long-Grain)	Brown Rice (Short-Grain)
Best for	vata, pitta and kapha	vata	vata	vata
Rice measure	1/2 cup (125 mL)	1/2 cup (125 mL)	1/2 cup (125 mL)	1/2 cup (125 mL)
Soaking time	15 minutes*	none	none	none
Water or broth measure	1 cup (250 mL)	3/4 cup (175 mL)	1 cup + 2 tbsp (275 mL)	1 cup (250 mL)
Simmering time	12–15 minutes	20 minutes	35–40 minutes	40–45 minutes
Resting time	10 minutes	5 minutes	5 minutes	5 minutes
Yield	1 cup (250 mL)	1 cup (250 mL)	1 cup (250 mL)	1 cup (250 mL)
	Purple Rice	**White Rice (Long-Grain)**	**White Rice (Short-Grain)**	**Wild Rice**
Best for	vata	vata and pitta	vata and pitta	kapha
Rice measure	1/2 cup (125 mL)	1/2 cup (125 mL)	1/2 cup (125 mL)	1/2 cup (125 mL)
Soaking time	none	none	none	5 minutes*
Water or broth measure	3/4 cup + 2 tbsp (200 mL)	3/4 cup (175 mL)	1 cup (250 mL)	2 cups**
Simmering time	30 minutes	20–25 minutes	20–25 minutes	40–50 minutes
Resting time	5 minutes	5 minutes	5 minutes	none
Yield	1 cup (250 mL)	1 cup (250 mL)	1 cup (250 mL)	1 1/2 cups (375 mL)

* After soaking basmati or wild rice, drain the rice and discard the soaking water.
** Wild rice will not absorb all the cooking water; it will burst open when it is done. Drain after cooking.

Purple rice (also known as forbidden rice or black rice) and Bhutanese red rice are sweet and chewy, with a nutty flavor and a mildly warming energetic.

Wild rice is actually a grass. It is dark brown and very chewy. It is high in protein and has a warm and dry energetic. It is quite dense on its own, and is usually mixed with other varieties of rice for balance.

Using a Rice Cooker

Instead of the absorption method (see table, opposite), rice can be cooked in a rice cooker. First, rinse and soak the rice (if necessary). Using the same proportions of rice to water given in the table, combine the rice, water and any desired seasonings in the rice cooker. Cover and switch on. When the rice cooker switches to the Warm setting, check for doneness. If the rice is still crunchy, stir in 2 to 3 tablespoons (30 to 45 mL) of water; cover and steam on the Warm setting for 10 minutes or until the rice is the desired consistency. Fluff and serve.

Seeds

Seeds sprinkled on salads, baked goods and grains will add essential trace minerals, fiber, omega-3 and omega-6 fatty acids, amino acids and crunch. Additionally, seeds (like all foods) contain an energetic that combines with your constitution and can be used to positively affect your wellness.

Flax Seeds

Flax seeds (also called linseeds) have a hot, heavy energetic with purgative and strengthening properties. They can be used whole or ground, but it is best to buy them whole and use a mortar and pestle or a clean spice grinder or coffee grinder to grind them as needed. The seeds are high in fiber and help in binding and removing fats (when ground) and stimulating elimination (when whole), so I often add a few spoonfuls to baked goods.

Flax seeds have long been used in ayurveda to curb hunger, reduce cholesterol and reduce blood sugar. Seek the advice of an ayurvedic practitioner about the recommended amount for medical use, as they can generate a lot of heat in your body, especially with prolonged use.

Green Pumpkin Seeds

Also called pepitas, raw green pumpkin seeds are sweet, mildly heating and tridoshic (in moderation). They are loaded with zinc, iron, magnesium, phosphorus and the

Did You Know?

Egg Replacer

Flax seeds can be used successfully as an egg replacer in baked goods. For each egg you want to replace, combine 1 tablespoon (15 mL) ground flax seeds with 3 tablespoons (45 mL) water, then let stand for 5 minutes to thicken before using.

amino acid tryptophan. Studies have shown them to reduce anxiety and to be beneficial for the heart, bones, prostate and bladder. I like to sprinkle them on yogurt, salads and grains to add color, texture and taste. I also add them to trail mix.

Sesame Seeds

In Hindu legend, sesame seeds symbolize immortality. They are sweet and bitter, with a heating energetic. Unhulled brown or black sesame seeds are high in calcium and are a good dairy-free solution to supplement your calcium intake. I prefer the nutrient-dense brown sesame seeds over the hulled white seeds. When the raw unhulled seeds are crushed, as in tahini or sesame butter, their nutrients are more easily digested. Whole seeds tend to not break down as well during digestion (you may notice whole seeds being eliminated).

Sunflower Seeds

Sunflower seeds are sweet and a little astringent and cooling. They are considered tridoshic and can be sprinkled on salads, grains or yogurt or added to trail mix. They are a good source of vitamin E, vitamin B_1 and selenium and assist in cardiovascular health, repair of nerves and muscles and reducing inflammation.

Dried Fruit

When fruit is dried (or cooked), its energetics change and it becomes compatible with other foods. I like to sprinkle dried fruit on grains, salads and yogurts to add a bit of sweetness.

The dried fruits used in this book include apricots, cherries, cranberries, currants, goji berries and raisins. All of these are readily available in well-stocked supermarkets or specialty stores, either packaged or in the bulk bin section.

Look for unsweetened, unsulfured apricots. They will likely be brownish rather than bright orange, but the flavor will be fine. Cranberries and cherries should likewise be unsulfured — you can tell because they won't be bright red.

The natural sugars in fruit become concentrated after the drying process, making added sweeteners unnecessary. Read the label and make sure the only ingredient is fruit. Try to avoid dried fruit that has been coated with a low-quality vegetable oil (this is sometimes done to prevent clumping). If you are purchasing sour or tart fruits (such as cranberries or sour cherries), they will likely come presweetened. My sweetener of choice in this instance is fruit juice, rather than sugar or high-fructose corn syrup.

Eaten in small quantities, dried fruit can be a healthy and tasty addition to many dishes.

Condiments

In ayurveda, it is common to serve side dishes of condiments at the dinner table so that individual diners can balance out the energetics of their meal. In India, where the diet primarily comprises lentils, beans and dals, the condiments are typically churnas, spices, chutneys and relishes. But these options don't translate well to the types of foods Westerners tend to eat. So the recipes in this book include suggestions for condiments that are generally used in the West. I've included a few here that may not be in your pantry but will be useful to have on hand — this is by no means an exhaustive list.

Artichoke Hearts

Purchase artichoke hearts packed in water, ideally in a glass jar or a BPA-free can. Read the ingredients and look for a brand that is preservative-free and sodium-free. Artichokes packed in oil with spices are not suitable for the recipes in this book. Water-packed artichokes are available at most supermarkets and health food stores.

Rose Water

Rose water is made by boiling rose petals in distilled water, then straining the petals from the water. It is cooling and astringent, and only a drop or two is needed in most recipes. Look for certified pesticide-free rose water at international and gourmet markets, larger supermarkets and health food stores.

Tamari

Although soy sauce contains wheat, tamari is wheat-free; however, if you are allergic or sensitive to gluten, always read labels to make sure the manufacturer did not add wheat. Also check to make sure traditional brewing methods were used, as this ensures the highest quality. Tamari is brewed from whole soybeans, sea salt, water and koji (*Aspergillus hacho*). Since tamari contains fermented alcohol, it should be stored in the refrigerator after opening.

Did You Know?
Rose Water Spritz

Rose water can also be used externally — spritz a little on your face to freshen up on a hot day.

Because tamari is not diluted with sweet-tasting wheat, it has a stronger flavor than soy sauce. It is traditionally used to season longer-cooking dishes, such as soups, stews and casseroles. Tamari can also be used in marinades and salad dressings and as a condiment or dipping sauce.

Tamari is not as heating as salt, so pitta can use it to replace salt in many dishes. Kapha should avoid tamari; vata can benefit from it.

Tamarind Paste

Tamarind paste is made from the fruit of the tamarind tree, which was indigenous to Africa but now grows widely in Asia and Mexico. The fruit is contained in large brown pods that resemble bulbous snap peas. The fruit is extracted from the pods and boiled into a thick, sticky paste, then strained to remove the seeds. The remaining seedless paste is sticky, sour and heating. It is ideal for vata, as the sourness aids digestion. Pitta and kapha can use it in moderation.

Many Thai and Indian dishes use tamarind paste. You can find seedless tamarind pastes in most Asian markets, but they typically contain other unwanted ingredients. I recommend Neera's tamarind paste because it is not watered down and has no chemical preservatives or additives; a little goes a long way. Well-stocked supermarket chains carry Neera's, or you can order it online at cinnabarfoods.com.

Vinegars

Fermented foods in general are not recommended in ayurveda. However, small amounts of the sour taste aid digestion. The amount of vinegar used in the recipes in this book is minimal, and I feel the use of vinegar will help people transition from more offensive foods. Ayurvedically speaking, lemon or apple cider vinegar would be preferred over other vinegars, as they are both alkalizing (they help keep your gut's pH level balanced). They can generally be substituted in any recipe that calls for vinegar (unless otherwise stated in the recipe). In this book, I also use balsamic vinegar, white balsamic vinegar and rice vinegar, depending on the flavor profile of the recipe. All of these vinegars are available at large supermarkets, gourmet markets and international markets. When purchasing rice wine vinegar, make sure it is unseasoned.

Fats

Healthy fats are essential for the production of cell membranes, hormonal development, the absorption of vitamins, the production of the sheaths that surround our nerves, proper brain functioning and healthy skin. Ayurveda recommends healthy fats from naturally occurring sources, such as sesame oil, sunflower oil, coconut oil, ghee, nuts, milk and eggs.

Ayurveda views each individual as having a unique constitution. As such, the amount and type of fat that is suitable will vary from person to person. Other factors, such as the season and the individual's age, activity level and state of health will also influence the decision about which fats to choose.

The primary oils used in this book are ghee (a staple in ayurveda cooking), coconut oil (for its cooling properties) and sunflower oil (for its tridoshic qualities). The decision about which fat to use is recipe-specific based on the energetics I am trying to balance, the flavor the fat will impart and its smoke point. The recipes provide guidance on the energetics of the oils used and suitable substitutes, if appropriate.

Coconut Oil

Coconut is considered a divine plant in the Vedic tradition, and its ayurvedic healing properties are vast. It is sweet and cooling, nourishes the mind and provides balanced fatty lubrication. It is anti-inflammatory and antibacterial, aids digestion and absorption and promotes healthy skin, hair and bones. It is balancing to the immune system, the digestive system and nervous system.

Western science gives coconut oil similar accolades. It is a healthy fat that is rich in medium-chain fatty acids (MCFAs), including lauric acid. Virgin coconut oil has the highest concentration of MCFAs outside of human breast milk. MCFAs are more easily used by the body for energy than other fats. They do not circulate in the bloodstream to the degree that other fats do and thus do not clog artery walls or get packed away inside fat cells in healthy individuals.

Look for unrefined (virgin) coconut oil at your local grocery store. Store it in a cool, dark location. It does not need to be refrigerated and, in fact, will become a hard mass if you do so. It has a melting point of 76°F (24°C), so its consistency will vary from liquid to solid depending

Did You Know?

Smoke Point

The smoke point is the temperature at which a fat begins to break down. Above that temperature, the fat smokes or burns and gives food an unpleasant taste. Different fats have different smoke points, and it's important to be familiar with the smoke points of the fats you use before cooking with them. Of the fats used in this book, ghee and sunflower oil are suitable for high-heat cooking (up to 450°F/230°C). Coconut oil, extra virgin olive oil and sesame oil should only be used for low- to medium-heat cooking (up to 350°F/180°C).

on the season, the climate you live in and where you store it. In general, you can simply scoop out the amount you need for the recipe. If it is solid and you need it to be softer in order to measure it, place the jar in a bowl of hot water until the oil melts to the desired consistency. (It does not harm the oil to go back and forth between the liquid and solid states.)

Virgin coconut oil generally does not impart a coconut taste when used in small quantities, as in most recipes in this book.

Ghee

Ghee is a type of clarified butter that is common in Indian cooking because of its high melting point, its ability to be stored long-term without refrigeration and its amazing taste. The best ghee is said to come from cows that have been grazing in pastures. Expect seasonal variation in the color and taste if the cows switch to eating hay, legumes and silage (such as in the winter months).

The traditional method of ghee preparation in India entails fermenting the cream from whole milk into yogurt, churning the yogurt into butter, then cooking the butter over low heat until all the moisture evaporates and brown milk solids drop to the bottom. The golden liquid is strained through a fine-mesh strainer and stored in a dry glass jar.

Ghee is highly regarded in ayurveda and is considered to both detoxify and rejuvenate at the same time. It lubricates the joints and muscles and is generally indicated for vata conditions. It should be avoided in cases of high cholesterol or high ama (see box, page 46).

Olive Oil

I primarily use olive oil in salad dressings where I want to impart that unique olive flavor and smell. Look for the words "cold-pressed" (minimal processing at low temperatures) and "extra virgin" (the oil has passed a chemical analysis and a sensory analysis) on the label for the best quality. Avoid refined, or "light," olive oils, which have often been extracted with solvents, treated with heat or diluted with cheaper oils like soybean and canola.

✦ Ghee is highly regarded in ayurveda and is considered to both detoxify and rejuvenate at the same time. It lubricates the joints and muscles and is generally indicated for vata conditions. It should be avoided in cases of high cholesterol or high ama. ✦

Sesame Oil

Along with ghee, sesame oil is one of the most widely used products in ayurveda. The nutrient-rich sesame seed is a symbol of prosperity and health in ancient folklore. The benefits of sesame oil are highly touted in various ayurvedic regimens, the most popular use being for massage. Whether eaten or applied externally, sesame oil is used to support the nervous system, bones, muscles, skin, hair, digestive tract (specifically the colon) and reproductive system. It is considered nourishing, calming and warming.

I recommend purchasing organic, expeller-pressed, unrefined sesame oil, which can be found at most grocery stores. Asian markets tend to carry toasted sesame oil (even though the label may not indicate this), which has a much stronger flavor. In this book, sesame oil is mainly used in Asian-style salad dressings.

Sunflower Oil

If I could buy only one oil, it would be sunflower oil. Sure, I would miss ghee, but sunflower oil is more practical in many ways. It has a mild flavor that adapts to all recipes, it can be used in baking (as a substitute for vegetable oil), it is tridoshic, and it has a high smoke point. Enough said. Look for organic refined sunflower oil.

Sweeteners

The sweet taste is nourishing and gives us a feeling of being nurtured and loved. But this taste can easily be overused, with devastating health effects. I prefer sweeteners that have undergone minimal refining, because they retain some traces of minerals, but all sweeteners should be used in moderation.

Coconut Sugar

Coconut sugar (also known as coco sugar, coconut palm sugar, coco sap sugar or coconut crystals) is produced from the sap of cut flower buds of the coconut palm. The sap is boiled down to a syrup, then evaporated into crystals. The color, taste and sweetness vary depending on how long the sap was boiled. Coconut sugar is cooling and has a light caramel flavor. It offers trace amounts of calcium and potassium in each serving.

Coconut sugar is the only sugar I use. It is readily available in most supermarkets in the bulk food section

Did You Know?

Black Sesame Oil

Black sesame oil comes from black sesame seeds and has a very strong flavor. You can purchase black sesame oil at an Asian market.

Did You Know?

Palm Sugar

Coconut sugar is not the same as palm sugar, which is made from the sap in the stems of the date palm, boiled down to a sticky syrup, then whipped and poured into containers, where it crystallizes into a solid block as it cools.

or the sweetener aisle. Read labels carefully, as some brands may mix in cane sugar and other ingredients.

Coconut sugar is pricey; if you are on a budget, you can substitute brown sugar to achieve a similar flavor.

Honey

Ayurvedic practitioners believe raw honey has many benefits, including scraping fat and cholesterol from the body's tissues, making it the go-to sweetener for kapha or anyone trying to reduce kapha in their body. However, snacking on jars of honey will not lead to weight loss — ayurveda is about balance, so let moderation be your guide.

Ayurvedic wisdom cautions that heating honey above 108°F (42°C) renders it toxic at the cellular level, which could cause blockage of subtle energetic channels. Today we know that when honey is heated, its molecular structure changes: it coagulates and becomes sticky. This glue-like substance can clog mucous membranes and arteries — leading, just as the ancients cautioned, to cellular toxicity.

Maple Syrup

Maple syrup is cooling and light. It is made from the sap of sugar maple trees. During the spring, a pattern of freezing and thawing temperatures builds up pressure within the trees, causing the sap to flow. The color darkens and the flavor becomes more intense as the season progresses.

The sap is boiled down and thickens as the sugar caramelizes. It is then filtered, adjusted for density and graded for flavor and color. There is no difference in nutritional content, and the refining methods are all the same.

When purchasing maple syrup, read the label and look for pure maple syrup with no added sugars or corn syrup. Pancake syrup or maple-flavored syrup should not be used as a substitution. Maple syrup should be refrigerated after opening.

Pomegranate Syrup

Pomegranate syrup (also known as pomegranate molasses) is a sauce with a sweet and astringent taste. It is made from pomegranate juice concentrate that has been boiled with a sweetener (typically cane sugar) until it is reduced to a thick syrup. It is used frequently in Mediterranean cuisine and can be purchased at international grocery stores or in the international aisle of major grocery stores.

Did You Know?

Manuka Honey

Manuka honey is made by bees who feed on the flowers of the manuka tree (or tea tree) in New Zealand. It has long been used by the native Maori people for its medicinal properties and its unique earthy taste. The honey has grown in popularity, and there are several systems being used to rate its bioactive potency levels. It is said that honey with a rating over 10 has therapeutic value, while anything less does not. The price increases significantly with the potency rating. While the marketers quibble over ratings, I'm going to enjoy manuka honey that fits my budget.

Dried Herbs and Spices

To ensure optimal flavor, quality and freshness, dried herbs and spices should be purchased in small quantities and used within 6 months of purchase. Many stores now sell organic spices in bulk bins so you can purchase the quantity that meets your needs, often at a lower per-unit cost.

To help you set up your spice cabinet, I have included all of the dried herbs and spices that are used in *The Essential Ayurvedic Cookbook* in the table on page 58. In some cases, I have included the same spice in seed and powder form, for use in different types of recipes. In curries, soups and stews, I like to use coarsely ground or whole spices; in sauces, desserts and vegetable seasonings, I like to use a finely ground powder. Freshly ground seeds are the most flavorful and give you the flexibility of grinding them to your desired consistency (coarse or fine). But grinding adds a few extra minutes to meal prep. So I like to have both options available to suit my schedule.

Ajwain Seeds

Ajwain (also called ajowan, carom seeds or bishop's weed) has a sharp, pungent and bitter taste. It is heating and piercing, entering deep tissues. It is considered an extraordinary stomach tonic and is used extensively by ayurvedic physicians to improve digestive strength, relieve abdominal colic pain, expel gas and reduce bloating, clear deep-seated toxins (ama) and move congestion from the digestive tract. A small amount of ajwain seeds added to lentil or bean dishes will stimulate the appetite and aid digestion.

Asafoetida

Asafoetida (also called hing) is a dried resin notable for its sulfuric smell. Available in "rock" form or ground to a powder, pure asafoetida is light yellow and has a potent pungent taste. Commercially ground asafoetida is often cut with rice or wheat flour, so read labels before purchasing. In ayurveda, asafoetida is valued for having all six tastes (sweet, sour, salty, pungent, bitter and astringent). It is primarily used as a digestive aid to relieve gas and bloating. A pinch or two is all you need for most recipes. You can find it at Indian grocery stores.

Did You Know?

Tiny Seeds, Big Benefits!

Ajwain is a medicinal powerhouse used in ayurveda to treat many stomach disorders (colic, gas, bloating, worms, bacteria, germs). It is an expectorant (it clears mucus) and a strong decongestant for the digestive and respiratory tracts. It promotes kidney function and energizes the nerves. It is used for menstrual disorders, postnatal disorders and female infertility. Consult your ayurvedic practitioner for the proper quantities for medicinal uses — ajwain's heating properties are potent!

Salt

There is a wide variety of salts available to suit every taste and budget. The coarser salts are ideal for soups and stews, but a fine-textured salt is preferable for seasoning delicate dishes and dips. Rock salt, such as Himalayan pink salt, is tridoshic and an excellent choice. In comparison, table salt is heavily processed (which eliminates minerals), then supplemented with iodine and a chemical additive to resist clumping.

Asian Ingredients

The following ingredients can be found at grocery stores serving larger metropolitan areas or ethnically diverse communities. If that doesn't sound like your neighborhood, you may need to take a trip to an Asian, Indian or international market. But first check at your local supermarket: it may carry some of the products used in this book (such as the dals, fresh chile peppers, lemongrass and frozen coconut) or be able to special order them at no extra charge to you. Sometimes they will even start stocking a requested item. It never hurts to ask!

Coconut Milk

Coconut milk has a cooling energetic. It is readily available in the international food aisle of most grocery stores. It comes in 13.5- or 14-ounce (400 mL) cans and has a long shelf-life. The milk and cream tend to separate inside the can, so shake the can vigorously before opening it. Once opened, transfer unused coconut milk to an airtight container and store in the refrigerator for up to 1 week.

Coconut milk is a good alternative to cow's milk, cream or yogurt (with the addition of some lemon juice) in most recipes because of its smooth, creamy texture. When used in small amounts, the coconut taste is not noticeable. It is a great addition to quick baked goods, puréed vegetables, porridge and Asian soups.

Curry Leaves and Lime Leaves

Curry leaves and lime leaves are available at Indian and Asian markets, respectively. They can sometimes be difficult to find, so buy in bulk and freeze extras in a sealable freezer bag for up to 3 months. To use, remove the amount you need and return the rest to the freezer, being sure to seal tightly. Frozen curry leaves and lime leaves will thaw in 5 minutes at room temperature.

Curry leaves come from the curry tree (*Murraya koenigii* or *Bergera koenigii*). They are also called sweet neem leaves (but are not the same as ordinary neem leaves, which are very bitter). Curry leaves are cooling and have long been used to treat diabetes, eye diseases, liver problems, diarrhea, high cholesterol, hair loss, gastrointestinal problems, skin pigmentation and oral disorders. They are antidiabetic, antioxidant, antimicrobial, anti-inflammatory, anticarcinogenic and hepatoprotective (they protect the liver from damage). They are a good source of vitamins (A, E, K, B_6 and folate) and minerals (calcium, iron, magnesium, phosphorus, potassium, zinc, copper and manganese).

Lime leaves are popular in Thai cooking and impart a lime flavor to your dish. They are great to have on hand, especially when fresh limes are out of season or otherwise unavailable. Used whole to flavor curries, soups and stews, lime leaves are tough and are generally not eaten. They can be removed from the pot before serving (as with bay leaves), or they can be left on the serving dish as a garnish.

Did You Know?

Curry Powder

Curry leaves are not to be confused with curry powder. Curry powder was invented by the British. It's an all-in-one spice blend that greatly varies in preparation but generally includes ground coriander, cumin, fenugreek, mustard, turmeric and chile peppers.

Dried Shiitake Mushrooms

Shiitake mushrooms are astringent, dry and heating. They are highly regarded in traditional Chinese medicine for their ability to cleanse, improve circulation, prevent strokes and boost immunity. They provide a woodsy, meaty flavor and add depth to soups, sauces, broths and stews.

Fresh shiitakes perish quickly and are not always available, so I like to keep dried shiitakes on hand. They are more concentrated in flavor than the fresh mushrooms. To rehydrate them, soak them in 1 cup (250 mL) of boiling hot water for 30 minutes. I like to use a French coffee press for this: slide the plunger down to keep the mushrooms submerged during soaking.

Before using shiitake mushrooms in recipes, remove the stems, which are tough and woody. You can save the stems to make Vegetable Broth (page 182); store them in an airtight container in the freezer for up to 2 months (no need to defrost before use).

Kombu, Nori and Wakame

Kombu is a type of seaweed, or kelp, that is hand-harvested, sun-dried, then cut into wide strips and packaged. It is used in Japanese broths (such as dashi noodle broth) to provide flavor and nutrition. Kombu can also be added to beans and lentils during cooking to soften the beans and aid digestibility.

Nori is made by shredding edible seaweed and pressing it into paper-thin square sheets. It is mild and sweet-tasting, and is commonly used as a wrap for sushi rolls.

Wakame is an edible seaweed that is commonly used in Asian soups and salads. It comes dried in thin strips or as ready-to-use chopped strips. Only a small amount of dried wakame is needed, as it will expand when added to water — 1 tbsp (15 mL) ready-to-use wakame will expand to $\frac{1}{2}$ cup (125 mL) once hydrated.

Kombu and nori are rich in a wide range of trace minerals and calcium. Wakame is high in iodine and trace minerals. You can purchase these ingredients in the Asian food aisle of well-stocked supermarkets, health food stores and food cooperatives.

Miso

Miso is astringent, sour and heating. It is a traditional Japanese seasoning produced by fermenting soybeans with salt and the fungus kōjikin (rice and barley may also be used). During fermentation, the protein from the soybeans (and grain) is disassembled into amino acids, including all nine essential ones.

Miso preparation methods vary, resulting in a range of colors and tastes. White and yellow miso are also called sweet miso. They are prepared using less salt and more kōjikin, and have a shorter fermentation time (about 1 to 2 months in a warm temperature). Darker varieties, such as red and brown, use more soybeans and salt and are fermented longer (a minimum of 1 year in a cool temperature). The darker colors have a stronger, saltier taste.

To retain its health benefits, miso should not be boiled. When adding it to a dish, dissolve the required amount in a little water and add it after cooking is complete. It can be used in soups, sauces and dressings.

Rice Vermicelli, Glass Noodles, Soba and Udon Noodles

Rice vermicelli noodles are very thin rice noodles (about as thick as angel-hair pasta) that are commonly used in Asian soups. They cook very quickly and are great for a last-minute gluten-free meal. Glass noodles are likewise thin, gluten-free and used for Asian soups, but they are made from mung beans. They are sometimes served in cold salads. Both rice vermicelli and glass noodles can be substituted for angel-hair pasta in most recipes. Personally, I prefer glass noodles, as I don't get a blood-sugar crash after eating them. I don't notice a difference in flavor, but the texture of the glass noodles is more chewy.

Soba noodles are traditionally made with buckwheat flour, which is gluten-free, but if you are allergic or sensitive to gluten, always check the label to make sure wheat flour was not added. I have yet to find any soba noodles that do not have added wheat. The noodles are thin, are dark in color and have a nutty, firm texture. They are often served cold as salads.

Udon noodles are thicker white noodles made from wheat flour. They are often served in a warm soy-based broth with scallions and mushrooms.

Umeboshi Paste

Umeboshi paste is heating and salty, with a sour taste. It is a popular Japanese condiment that is made from dried pickled green umeboshi plums (a popular fruit in Japan). It is added to rice, veggie burgers or steamed vegetables for a burst of flavor. It has an alkalizing effect on the body, neutralizing fatigue, stimulating the digestion and promoting the elimination of toxins.

You can purchase umeboshi paste in the Asian food aisle of well-stocked supermarkets, health food stores and food cooperatives.

Wasabi Powder

The stem of the wasabi plant (*Wasabia japonica*, also called Japanese horseradish) is used to make wasabi powder and paste. Wasabi is heating, with a pungent flavor. Its strong vapors will enter your nasal passageways and clear your sinuses. This green condiment is frequently added sparingly to sushi and Japanese dishes. It is very strong, so use it in moderation.

Wasabi is generally sold as a stem, which must be very finely grated before use, as dried powder or as a ready-to-use paste in tubes. I recommend the powder because it is easiest to find. Look for it in the Asian aisle of most grocery stores. Pure wasabi is very expensive and is difficult to find outside of Japan. Read labels and look for a brand with the least amount of additives, colorings, preservatives and flavorings (typically mustard powder and horseradish).

> ### Did You Know?
> **Good Medicine**
>
>
>
> Umeboshi paste is reputed to be a potent hangover remedy, and many people consider eating one umeboshi plum a day to be the best preventive medicine available.

The volatile chemicals in wasabi powder will dissipate when exposed to air, so store it in an airtight container in a cool, dark place. You can use it as needed by mixing in some cold water. Adjust the water/powder ratio until the mixture is a paste consistency.

Stocking Your Refrigerator

The essential items you should have stocked in your refrigerator to prepare most of the recipes in this book include onions, leafy greens, fresh herbs and spices, nuts, seeds, butters and flours. Nuts have a high oil content and can go rancid quickly, so I recommend storing them in the refrigerator. I also store flours in the refrigerator or freezer in an airtight container or freezer bag to preserve freshness.

If you have a root cellar, that is the ideal place to store root vegetables. I live in an apartment that is sunny and warm, with limited storage space, so I store my root vegetables (even potatoes) in the crisper drawer in the refrigerator, as that is the only place that is cool and dark. I shop a few times a week, so my inventory is always rotating and stays fresh.

✦ The essential items you should have stocked in your refrigerator to prepare most of the recipes in this book include onions, leafy greens, fresh herbs and spices, nuts, seeds, butters and flours. ✦

Refrigerator Essentials

Fruits	cranberries; dried coconut (unsweetened shredded); lemons; limes
Vegetables	beets; Brussels sprouts; carrots; chile peppers; greens (kale, bok choy, Swiss chard, broccoli, escarole); kabocha; onions; potatoes (red, Yukon Gold or fingerling); pumpkin; squash; sweet potatoes
Fresh herbs and spices	basil; chives; cilantro; garlic; gingerroot; green onions; mint; oregano; parsley; rosemary; tarragon; thyme
Meat and fish*	bison; chicken; fish; lamb; mutton; rabbit; shrimp; turkey; venison
Dairy and dairy alternatives	butter (unsalted); milk (cow's, rice, soy or almond); yogurt (unsweetened plain)
Nuts and nut butters	almond butter; almonds (slivered, blanched, peeled); cashew butter; cashews; pecans; walnuts
Flours	almond flour; amaranth flour; arrowroot flour; brown rice flour; cornmeal
Asian ingredients	frozen shredded coconut; lemongrass; mizuna; tofu

* Recommended only in cases where the body is depleted or emaciated.

Fruits

✦ If you don't know your dosha, sweet berries are generally tridoshic. ✦

The essential fruits you will need are lemons and limes. In addition, you can stock seasonal and dosha-specific fruits as indicated in the dosha balancing aids in the appendices (page 328 for vata, 332 for pitta and 336 for kapha). If you don't know your dosha, sweet berries are generally tridoshic.

Dried Coconut

Coconut has a cooling energetic. In South Indian cooking, it is often added to curries (along with coconut milk). I like to sprinkle unsweetened shredded coconut on quinoa salad to add more bulk and fat, which I seem to miss when eating vegetarian. I also use it in gluten-free baking for added texture and taste. You can find it in most supermarkets in the bulk bin section or the baking aisle. Be sure to purchase unsweetened shredded coconut — the size of the shred is less important.

The Dirty Dozen and the Clean Fifteen

The Environmental Working Group publishes a yearly study that analyzes the pesticide content of a variety of fruits and vegetables and ranks the results to produce a "Dirty Dozen" list of the worst offenders and a "Clean Fifteen" list of the cleanest produce. Visit www.ewg.org/foodnews for the most up-to-date results, as the lists change yearly to reflect varying pesticide use. In general, apples, grapes, berries, celery and leafy greens fairly consistently make the Dirty Dozen list.

Although you would ideally purchase only organic foods, it can be pretty expensive to do so, and sometimes organic foods are not readily available. The lists give you a way to focus your priorities: limit your exposure to pesticides by purchasing the Dirty Dozen foods from organic producers (or avoiding them, if necessary); for foods on the Clean Fifteen list, the less expensive nonorganic option is likely pretty safe.

Vegetables

Fresh is best. Ideally, you would head to a farmers' market every week to pick up fresh vegetables and connect with the growers and your neighbors. At many points in my life, that has not been my reality. Instead, I seem to end up racing to the grocery store 30 minutes before the doors close. At that point, I find myself dashing through the produce section, looking for anything fresh and seasonal. To combat this tendency, I try to sit down on

Sunday to plan some meals for the week ahead. I jot down the ingredients on my smartphone calendar and set the reminder to go shopping after work.

Whether your shopping is focused on building community with farmers or fulfilling your minimum nutritional requirements, vegetables that are fresh and in season should be your starting point.

Understanding Labels

✦ **GMO-Free:** The term "genetically modified organisms" (GMOs), or genetically modified foods, refers to foods that use genetically modified seeds. Genetic modification is a laboratory technique that reprograms a plant with new and/or enhanced properties by inserting gene units into its DNA. These gene units are created by joining fragments of DNA, usually derived from multiple organisms. For example, the genetically modified gene in herbicide-resistant soybeans (grown since 1996) is pieced together from a plant virus, a soil bacterium and a petunia plant. Independent peer-reviewed studies designed to assess long-term and subtle health effects have not been conducted on GMOs. The United States and Canada currently have no labeling requirements for genetically modified foods; however, some companies are voluntarily adding "GMO-free" labels to their packaging. In addition, foods labeled "100% organic" in the U.S. cannot contain GMOs.

✦ **Organic:** Produce labeled "organic" must be grown in a manner that minimizes harm to the environment by emphasizing renewable (or sustainable) resources and the conservation of soil and water, thus protecting the environment for future generations. Synthetic fertilizers, sewage sludge, irradiation and genetic engineering may not be used. Meat, poultry, eggs and dairy products labeled "organic" must come from animals that have not been given antibiotics or growth hormones. Meat and dairy products labeled "organic" cannot have come from animals that have been fed genetically modified food (corn, hay, feed, etc.).

With the rise in consumer demand and the corresponding profits to be made, the right to use the "organic" label has become highly coveted. Corporate influence on government policy has resulted in modifications to the farmers' original rules, with complex lists and exceptions. When purchasing processed foods in the United States, look for the gold-standard label: "100% organic." A product cannot use this label unless 100% of its ingredients are certified organic. (Note that this designation is not available in Canada.) In both the United States and Canada, a product labeled "organic" must contain at least 95% certified organic ingredients.

✦ **Natural:** Beware of this label — it is a marketing term and is confusing and misleading to consumers. Any manufacturer can place it on a product, and there is no certifying or enforcing organization.

Fresh Herbs and Spices

Herbs and spices are generally heating in nature, with a few notable exceptions: coriander seeds, cilantro leaf, fennel seeds, cardamom, mint and tarragon. In ayurvedic cooking, herbs are used for flavoring and to aid digestion by altering the energetics. The recipes in this book are seasoned according to these principles.

Fresh herbs and spices are generally available year-round in large supermarkets and seasonally from local farmers' markets. But fresh herbs are best used right after they have been cut. So if you have the time and space and live in a suitable climate, consider starting an organic herb garden for year-round (or at least seasonal) fresh herbs. Mint, tarragon, thyme, chives, oregano, basil, cilantro, parsley and rosemary are relatively easy to grow in garden beds or pots and can liven up salads and most meals.

When purchasing fresh herbs, look for stems that have been freshly cut and leaves that are not brown or wilted. If they are fresh when you purchase them, they should last for a week or more. Most herbs should be stored in the refrigerator in a loose plastic bag to allow air circulation. For more delicate herbs, such as cilantro, rosemary, mint, parsley and basil, snip the ends and place the herbs in a small glass jar half-filled with water. Store cilantro, rosemary and mint in the refrigerator, covered with a plastic bag. Parsley and basil prefer room temperature. Change the water every few days as it becomes cloudy.

Gingerroot and garlic are pungent and heating. Both are used extensively in ayurvedic medicine.

Ginger is carminative (antiflatulent), aids digestion, thins blood, improves circulation and alleviates menstrual cramps. It is an expectorant (it liquefies and clears mucus) and burns ama. Fresh gingerroot is milder and less heating than ground ginger.

Garlic is pungent and heating, so it should be consumed in moderation. It contains five of the six tastes (sweet, salty, pungent, bitter and astringent). It is said to support the immune system and has many medicinal properties, including being antibacterial, antioxidant and anticarcinogenic. It stimulates the central nervous system and is an aphrodisiac (which is why many celibate yogis avoid it).

For tridoshic cooking, pressed garlic is more balancing than minced garlic, as it has a less pungent energetic. Whenever possible, use a garlic press to prepare garlic for your recipes.

Meat

According to ayurvedic doctrine, ingested animal flesh creates heaviness, dullness, depression and sleepiness — the very opposite of ayurveda's goals. Ayurvedic practitioners recommend a diet of light and easily digestible foods, which promote clarity and perception and are believed to unfold compassion and love.

Nonetheless, ayurveda is practical, and animal protein is recommended in certain cases where the body is depleted or emaciated. Specific meats are prescribed for specific conditions: rabbit for menstrual issues, mutton for anemia and so on. For medicinal purposes, meat is generally prepared in soups and stews that have been cooked for many hours (or sometimes days) with appropriate herbs for optimal assimilation of the nutrients and to balance the energetics. The recommended portion of meat in ayurveda is small relative to typical portions in America.

Cooked in stews and properly spiced, meats can be tolerated by all doshas. If you're feeling the need for meat, consider the following guidelines:

+ Lean, light meats (white turkey meat, white chicken meat, rabbit and venison) in small portions are more suitable for pitta and kapha. Darker meats tend to be oilier and more heating.

+ Bison is a lean alternative to beef and is easier to digest than other fatty meats. It promotes strength, so pitta can benefit from moderate intake. Vata will benefit from bison's warming and grounding effects. Bison is least suitable for kapha (due to its heavy quality), but all three doshas can try the Bison Meatloaf with Maple Tamarind Sauce (page 174), which includes quinoa to lighten and cool the overall energetic, providing balance.

+ Rabbit is cooling, drying and astringent, making it most suitable for pitta and kapha. Vata does well with rabbit in a stew.

+ Lamb (sheep less than 1 year old) and mutton (adult sheep) meat are heating, strengthening and heavy. Cooked in stews, they are ideal for regaining weight after an illness.

My Personal Struggle with Vegetarianism

It can be extremely difficult to convert to a vegetarian diet without experiencing major imbalances. I've been trying for years and always seem to become quite depleted if I abstain from meat for more than a week. I have yet to find a protein shake or supplement that does not upset my digestion and elimination, as they are generally highly concentrated and difficult for vata constitutions to digest. It took me many years to be able to digest lentils, and I am still unable to digest beans on a regular basis without experiencing some digestive discomfort.

I feel like I've tried everything. At one point, I even consulted with my astrologer, Chakrapani, in desperation. Perhaps out of compassion, he told me that my planetary positions predisposed me to eating meat and that I would have much difficulty with a vegetarian diet. Chakrapani explained that people who are raised vegetarian have no problem abstaining from meat. But if one is not raised vegetarian, then *some* people have difficulty adjusting to a 100% vegetarian diet.

Chakrapani is a strict vegetarian (no meat, fish or eggs), but he suggested that people who are trying to reduce meat intake but feel the need for extra protein can consume eggs as a transitional compromise. Fish and lighter meat, such as chicken, can also aid in the transition.

I hope you find my story helpful if you are also struggling to find a balance that will work for your body as you attempt to convert to a vegetarian diet. I continue my quest for supplements that my body will tolerate and will be happy when I am someday able to make the switch to 100% vegetarianism.

Fish

Most fish (especially saltwater fish) are heating. Shrimp and freshwater fish are generally tridoshic.

When purchasing fish, choose fillets that are firm and bright, with a fresh smell — fish should not smell "fishy." The skin should be firmly attached to the meat. Ask the vendor when it was caught; eating it the same day is ideal, but avoid eating fish that is more than 3 days old.

If using frozen fish, thaw it overnight by placing it (in its original packaging) in a dish in the refrigerator. Alternatively, you can thaw it in 10 minutes by placing the fish (in its original packaging) in a bowl of cold water. If you are not using it immediately, place the defrosted fish in the refrigerator. Once thawed, fish should be cooked the same day.

✦ Most fish (especially saltwater fish) are heating. Shrimp and freshwater fish are generally tridoshic. ✦

Dairy Products

In India, the cow is considered sacred and is symbolic of the bounty of Mother Earth, the giver of life. Traditionally, cows are not eaten; in fact, people go out of their way to avoid causing them harm. In small Indian towns today, thin cows can be seen roaming the streets eating garbage, but this reflects a lack of financial resources rather than a loss of respect. A cow taking a nap in the middle of a street will be left unharmed and undisturbed as rickshaws, pedestrians, cars and buses carefully navigate around it!

With an understanding of this aspect of Indian culture, one can appreciate why ayurveda praises dairy products in general and ghee in particular. The milk of a happy cow — one who is humanely treated and allowed to graze on grass — is considered light and easily digestible, as is everything made from its milk: yogurt, buttermilk, cheese, paneer, butter and ghee. (See page 78 for more information on ghee.)

In the West, however, the status of the cow is generally much lower. Many cows are kept in overcrowded feed stalls with inadequate space for resting and without access to pasture. The cows from these farms are not cherished, and the resultant mass-produced milk does not have a light, easily digestible energetic. In fact, we generally equate dairy products with high cholesterol and weight gain.

If you choose to consume dairy products, look for "organic" labels at a minimum, and ideally look for products labeled "certified humane raised and handled." Toxins tend to settle in body fat, and especially mammary glands; in organic dairy products, the impurities caused from pesticides, herbicides and toxins are minimized.

Dairy Alternatives

Many of the recipes in this book are nondairy or can be made with nondairy substitutions. The individual recipes list specific substitutions that will maintain the energetic and flavor of the recipe. If you have reason to avoid dairy products, review a recipe prior to making it to determine which nondairy alternative fits your needs.

Nuts and Nut Butters

The ancients favored almonds — soaked overnight and peeled to eliminate the heating qualities in the skin — for their digestibility and reputed value of building vitality. Today we know almonds are nutrient-dense and moderately alkalizing (helping to keep your gut's pH level balanced).

Most other nuts available in North America are oily and heavy. Pitta does best with coconuts (and almonds in moderation). Kapha should avoid nuts.

Nuts in general are nutritious and versatile. I have included some recipes that use nuts in place of dairy products, as they can mimic a smooth, creamy texture very convincingly. Nuts (and seeds) can be ground to a paste with the addition of a little oil and used in place of regular butter in many dishes. See Basic Nut or Seed Butter (page 280) for a detailed recipe. Cashews and almonds have a mild flavor and are good choices when you don't want to alter the taste of your recipe. You can also add water and seasonings to nut butter to make a creamy nondairy sauce, such as Vata Lemon Cashew Cream Sauce (page 262).

It is difficult to judge the quality of nuts in the shell, and some nuts are difficult to shell, so we tend to purchase shelled nuts for convenience and practicality. Nuts purchased from a health food store are typically stored in the refrigerated section and meet the store's standards of natural processing. Inquire at your local health food store for details. If you purchase commercially packaged nuts from a supermarket, be aware that they may have been processed using ethylene gas, methyl bromide fumigation, hot lye or a glycerin–sodium carbonate solution to loosen the skins, along with citric acid for rinsing.

Flours

The flours I typically use in my gluten-free baking recipes include amaranth flour, arrowroot flour, brown rice flour, cornmeal and nut flours. You can purchase all of these in the baking aisle or bulk bin section of your local grocery store. In general, look for organic brands and buy small quantities to ensure freshness.

> **Did You Know?**
> **Nut Nutrition**
>
>
> Tree nuts, such as almonds, walnuts and pecans, contain no cholesterol. Most of the calories in nuts come from fat, but mainly good fats necessary for essential functions in the body.

> **Did You Know?**
> **Chopping Nuts**
>
>
> When chopping small quantities of nuts, try using a clean coffee grinder or spice grinder; for larger quantities, use a food processor.

Amaranth Flour

Amaranth flour is cooling and light, with a bitter taste. It is generally used in combination with other flours in gluten-free baking.

Arrowroot Flour

Arrowroot flour is cooling, demulcent, mildly laxative and nutritive. I often add it to gluten-free baking recipes, as it is a "healthy" starch. It can also be used to thicken sauces. It relieves acidity, indigestion and colic, and has long been given to infants and used to treat convalescents, especially those with bowel complaints. Some studies have shown arrowroot flour to be beneficial in treating diarrhea.

✦ Arrowroot flour relieves acidity, indigestion and colic, and has long been given to infants and used to treat convalescents, especially those with bowel complaints. ✦

Brown Rice Flour

Brown rice flour is heating and heavy. It is generally used in combination with other flours in gluten-free baking.

Cornmeal

Cornmeal (sometimes called polenta) is heating and heavy. It is a gluten-free flour and tends to be very dry. It has a grainy texture and is generally used to make quick breads or breads with a cake-like texture.

The definition of cornmeal can vary by region. In this book, I am referring to whole corn that has been ground into a coarse flour. Cornmeal is not interchangeable with finely ground corn flour or cornstarch.

Nut Flours

Nut flours are becoming popular as gluten-free alternatives, but they don't rise, so they generally need to be mixed with other flours for baking.

Asian Ingredients

The following ingredients will be easiest to find at Asian grocery stores or supermarkets in ethnically diverse metropolitan areas.

Frozen Coconut

Frozen shredded coconut is available at Asian markets. As always, check the label to make sure the only ingredient is coconut — you definitely don't want any sweeteners or preservatives in your frozen coconut for the recipes in this book. I prefer frozen coconut for making coconut chutney, because it is moister than dried coconut and requires minimal preparation (as compared to cutting open and shredding a fresh coconut). To use it, remove the amount you need from the package and return the rest to the freezer, making sure to seal tightly. Frozen coconut will take 15 to 20 minutes to thaw at room temperature.

Lemongrass

Lemongrass has a warming energetic and is used in teas to clear the lymphatic system. It has several tightly wrapped layers surrounding a tender white core. Select firm lemongrass stalks that are pale yellow at the lower end and green at the upper end. Wrap them tightly in plastic wrap or place them in an airtight container and store in the refrigerator for up to 1 week or in the freezer for up to 2 months. Frozen lemongrass will thaw in 5 minutes at room temperature.

Before cooking lemongrass, remove the tough outer layers. To release the flavors and essential oils, lightly bruise the stalks by pounding them a few times with a mallet or the dull side of a knife blade.

✦ Lemongrass has a warming energetic and is used in teas to clear the lymphatic system. ✦

Mizuna

Mizuna is a Japanese green with a mildly peppery taste (less peppery than arugula). Its energetic is slightly warming, but it is generally suitable for all three doshas. It can be used raw in a salad; steamed with some noodles and an Asian dressing; or added to soup. I sometimes find mizuna at farmers' markets or local food cooperatives; more consistently, I find it at Asian markets. If you cannot find it, arugula is a good substitute.

Tofu

Tofu, or soybean curd, is cool and heavy. It is made by curdling fresh soy milk and pressing it into a solid block. On its own it has a bland flavor, but it readily absorbs the flavors of other ingredients. It is widely available in supermarkets, in a variety of textures that are suitable for different uses. Use extra-firm tofu for the recipes in this book.

Healthy Kitchen Equipment

You have chosen to improve your balance and well-being with ayurvedic recipes, so why take the risk of using unhealthy kitchen equipment to prepare and store your food? When choosing pots and pans, utensils and storage wraps and containers, select options that will not react or will react only minimally with your food. Reactivity is based on the item's composition, the cooking temperature (a higher temperature increases the rate of reactivity), the food's composition (acidic and fatty foods are more reactive) and time (cooking or storage time in the container).

Indispensable Tools

Having the proper equipment makes cooking easier. Three tools I cannot live without are an immersion blender, a yogurt maker and a food processor. All will greatly assist you with preparing the recipes in this book.

+ An **immersion blender** (also called a stick blender) is an inexpensive tool used to quickly blend soups to achieve a creamy texture without cream. It's easy to clean, too!
+ A **yogurt maker** is another inexpensive item that is great to have on hand if you plan to make yogurt on a regular basis.
+ A 9-cup (2.25 L) **food processor** will be essential if you want to make many of the healthy dips and some of the desserts in this book.

Nonreactive and Reactive Materials

	Nonreactive (Healthiest Option)	Reactive (Best to Avoid)
Pots and pans	✦ anodized aluminum ✦ cast iron ✦ earthenware and ceramics (test for lead in antique pieces) ✦ enamel-coated cast iron ✦ glass ✦ stainless steel (18:10 density)	✦ aluminum ✦ copper (excess exposure is considered toxic to the brain and liver) ✦ nonstick (toxic fumes are emitted at temperatures over 570°F/300°C; chemical coating is susceptible to scratches that can flake into food)
Utensils	✦ bamboo steamers ✦ spatulas and spoons made of wood or stainless steel ✦ wooden paddles	✦ aluminum ✦ plastic
Food storage	✦ BPA-free plastic (#1, #2, #4 or #5); not suitable for heating ✦ plastic wrap (low-density polyethylene or PVC-free) ✦ glass ✦ waxed or butcher paper (in lieu of plastic bags)	✦ aluminum foil ✦ plastic wrap containing PVC or BPA ✦ plastic containing BPA (#3, #6, #7)

Part 2

Ayurvedic Recipes

About the Recipes

The recipes in this book were created to be tridoshic (balancing to all doshas) unless otherwise indicated. If you gradually incorporate these dishes into your life, I trust you will get into the flow of ayurveda in no time.

Recipes that are dairy-free, gluten-free, soy-free and/or vegetarian or vegan are clearly labeled as such. If a recipe has dairy but I provide nondairy alternatives, then I have classified the recipe as "dairy-free" because it can be made without the use of dairy. Please note that a dish labeled "vegetarian" does not contain animal flesh (fish or meat) but may contain eggs or dairy (milk, yogurt, cheese or butter). The vegan recipes contain no animal flesh, eggs, dairy products or other animal-derived foods (such as honey or gelatin).

Many of the recipes include:

+ suggestions for condiments, spices or recipe modifications that can be used to target specific doshas;
+ serving suggestions to round out the energetics of a dish, especially if it is skewed toward one dosha; and/or
+ substitutions to accommodate gluten-free, dairy-free or meat-based diets.

Once you have decided on a recipe you want to prepare, read through the entire recipe first to get a feel for it. Some of the recipes have long lists of ingredients, but they generally whip up pretty quickly once the ingredients have been prepped and measured. I understand that your time is precious, so I've indicated when things can be made ahead or frozen for later use, and how you can use up leftovers.

In testing these recipes, I used a gas stove and All-Clad pans. Your cooking times and temperatures may need to be adjusted if you use a different heat source and/or pans of differing quality.

Morning Meals

If you are working with an ayurvedic practitioner, he or she will typically prescribe for you some additions to your morning routine to aid with balancing your energy. A simple routine may involve tongue scraping, oil pulling, teeth brushing, yoga, meditation or prayer, self-massage and bathing. This sequential routine helps to set the tone for your day. It's like when you hear your favorite song on the radio and instantly feel happy; the residue of the song stays with you for hours.

The morning routine is important time for you. The length of the routine is less important than the regular commitment; it should be manageable, not stressful. Record it on your calendar as a recurring appointment that has no end date.

After you have completed your morning routine, your body is ready for food. In ayurveda, the morning meal is typically a light meal designed to kindle the digestive fire for the day. Eat according to your appetite and the seasons.

In the hot summer months, our digestive fire is generally low, so you may feel satiated with a simple bowl of minted fruit (grapefruit, blueberries, apricots, strawberries, etc.) or some homemade yogurt topped with raw honey and granola. Amaranth Crêpes with Pomegranate Syrup are suitable for the summer and are gluten-free.

In the cooler fall and winter months, you may opt for a warming porridge made from amaranth, quinoa, oats or barley. Or you may want the grounding qualities of protein in the form of poached or scrambled eggs.

Lighter, drier variations of porridge (with no added milk, yogurt or sweeteners) are suitable for the wet springtime, when our bodies will be trying to remove excess water and mucus buildup from the winter. Millet Breakfast Patties are great in the spring, as they are dry and light, but they are versatile and can be eaten year-round if paired with various condiments or toppings (poached eggs, avocado or sprouts) to complement the seasonal digestive needs.

Nutty Quick Oats

Dried fruit has a different energetic than raw fruit, so while the "rule" is to eat fruit alone, the exception is when the fruit is dried. Dried fruits work well with oatmeal and porridge; bananas and juicy fruits do not. This recipe can also be made ahead in bulk (see page 103) and stored in a resealable plastic bag or jar for an instant healthy breakfast.

Makes 1 serving

Tips

To toast almonds, place them in a dry (ungreased) medium skillet over medium heat. When they begin to smell fragrant, after about 1 minute, give the pan a shake. Continue to toast, periodically shaking the pan, until the almonds are golden.

Purchase dried cranberries that have been sweetened with fruit juice (rather than refined sugar or high-fructose corn syrup).

Variations

Try adding unsalted sunflower seeds, green pumpkin seeds (pepitas) or sesame seeds.

Substitutions for the dried fruit are endless — dried apricots, blueberries, goji berries and so on.

Dairy-Free ✦ Gluten-Free ✦ Soy-Free ✦ Vegetarian

1 cup	quick-cooking rolled oats	250 mL
2 tbsp	slivered almonds, toasted (see tip, at left)	30 mL
1 tbsp	raisins	15 mL
1 tbsp	dried cranberries, chopped	15 mL
1 tbsp	unsweetened shredded coconut	15 mL
1/2 tsp	ground cinnamon	2 mL
1/4 tsp	ground cardamom	1 mL
1 1/2 cups	boiling water (approx.)	375 mL
3 tbsp	unsweetened plain yogurt (optional)	45 mL
1 tsp	raw honey	5 mL

1. In a serving bowl, combine oats, almonds, raisins, cranberries, coconut, cinnamon and cardamom. Stir in boiling water to desired consistency and let stand for 1 minute. The oats will absorb the water and become the consistency of a thick porridge. Adjust the water until you achieve the consistency you desire.

2. Top with yogurt (if using) and honey.

Dosha Modifications

✦ **Vata** can experiment with different nuts, such as walnuts, hazelnuts or pecans, in place of the almonds.

✦ If you are trying to reduce **pitta**, use cooling coconut sugar or pure maple syrup in place of the heating honey.

✦ **Kapha** may want to spice up the recipe by adding 1/8 tsp (0.5 mL) ground cloves.

Big-Batch Nutty Quick Oats

A plastic bag of this healthy mix is great for traveling when you want a quick breakfast in your hotel room without refined sugar, salt or cholesterol.

Makes 10 servings

Tip

Purchase dried cranberries that have been sweetened with fruit juice (rather than refined sugar or high-fructose corn syrup).

Gluten-Free ✦ Soy-Free ✦ Vegan

10 cups	quick-cooking rolled oats	2.5 L
1¼ cups	slivered almonds, toasted (see tip, page 102)	300 mL
⅔ cup	raisins	150 mL
⅔ cup	dried cranberries, chopped	150 mL
⅔ cup	unsweetened shredded coconut	150 mL
5 tsp	ground cinnamon	25 mL
2½ tsp	ground cardamom	12 mL

1. In a large sealable plastic bag or jar, combine oats, almonds, raisins, cranberries, coconut, cinnamon and cardamom. Seal and store in the refrigerator for up to 3 months.

2. To serve, scoop out the desired amount and prepare as directed on page 102.

Dosha Modifications

✦ **Vata** can experiment with different nuts, such as walnuts, hazelnuts or pecans, in place of the almonds.

✦ **Kapha** may want to spice up the recipe by adding ⅛ tsp (0.5 mL) ground cloves.

Warm Cashew Butter Cereal for Kids

Prepare your kids for school with this warm, grounding, moist and creamy cereal. Full of protein and brain-healthy fat, it will help them focus and give them the energy they need to power through until lunch. Active adults can eat it, too!

Makes 2 servings

Tips

As you are warming the milk mixture, be sure to stir constantly and watch as the texture changes. If it gets too thick, you can thin it out by adding more rice milk.

The amount of cashew butter you use will determine the consistency of the cereal. The more cashew butter, the thicker the cereal.

For a vegan recipe, omit the honey.

Variations

Substitute almond butter for the cashew butter.

Substitute Nut Milk (page 322) for the rice milk and omit the cashew butter.

Dairy-Free ✦ Gluten-Free ✦ Soy-Free ✦ Vegetarian

2 cups	unsweetened rice milk	500 mL
3 to 4 tbsp	organic raw cashew butter (unsalted and unsweetened)	45 to 60 mL
3 tbsp	raisins	45 mL
1/2 tsp	ground cinnamon	2 mL
1/4 tsp	ground cardamom	1 mL
2 to 3 cups	unsalted puffed rice cereal	500 to 750 mL
2 tsp	raw honey (optional)	10 mL

1. In a small pan, combine milk, cashew butter to taste, raisins, cinnamon and cardamom. Warm over medium–low heat, stirring constantly, until the cashew butter blends into the milk and thickens, about 3 minutes.

2. Divide rice puffs between two serving bowls. Pour half of the seasoned cashew milk into each bowl, stirring to combine. Sweeten with honey (if using).

Amaranth Porridge with Pear Juice, Currants and Almonds

What's old is new again! This nutty, nutritious porridge made from an ancient grain is a refreshing update of an Old World recipe. It's sure to please your palate and your waistline.

Makes 2 servings

Variation

Replace the pear juice with apple juice, pomegranate juice or additional water.

SERVING SUGGESTIONS

Top with fresh cream, yogurt, coconut milk or almond milk.

Gluten-Free ✦ Soy-Free ✦ Vegan		
½ cup	amaranth, rinsed well	125 mL
¼ cup	dried currants, raisins, cranberries or apricots, chopped as needed	60 mL
1 tsp	ground cardamom	5 mL
½ cup	unsweetened pear juice	125 mL
½ cup	water	125 mL
1 tbsp	slivered blanched almonds	15 mL

1. In a medium saucepan, combine amaranth, currants, cardamom, pear juice and water. Bring to a boil over medium heat, stirring constantly. Reduce heat and simmer, stirring occasionally, for 10 to 15 minutes or until amaranth is chewy, not crunchy. If necessary, add more water or juice until the desired consistency is reached. Transfer to serving bowls and garnish with almonds.

Dosha Modifications

✦ **Vata** can make this more "soupy" by adding more water; **kapha** may prefer a drier porridge.

✦ **Pitta** and **vata** can substitute unsweetened shredded coconut for the almonds.

✦ **Vata** and **kapha** can substitute ground cinnamon, ginger or allspice for the cardamom.

Coconut Cranberry Quinoa Porridge

Quinoa is considered tridoshic, but I find it to be drying. To add some balance for vata, stir in plain yogurt for a creamy porridge (or almond, rice or soy milk for a dairy-free creamy porridge). Garnish with fresh mint.

Makes 2 servings

Tip

Leftovers can be refrigerated overnight and reheated the next day.

Variations

Add sliced blanched almonds, green pumpkin seeds (pepitas) or unsalted sunflower seeds for a heartier breakfast.

Other dried fruits and nuts can be added as per the dosha balancing aids in the appendices (pages 328–339). Bananas and fresh fruit would not combine well with this porridge.

Replace the quinoa with amaranth, or use half amaranth and half quinoa.

Dairy-Free ✦ Gluten-Free ✦ Soy-Free ✦ Vegetarian

½ cup	quinoa, rinsed	125 mL
1 tbsp	unsweetened shredded coconut	15 mL
½ tsp	ground cinnamon or cardamom	2 mL
1½ cups	water (approx.)	375 mL
½ tsp	freshly squeezed lemon juice	2 mL
1 tbsp	dried cranberries, currants, raisins, cherries or apricots, chopped as needed	15 mL
1 tsp	raw honey	5 mL

1. In a medium saucepan, combine quinoa, coconut, cinnamon and water. Bring to a boil over medium heat. Reduce heat to low, cover and simmer, stirring occasionally, for 20 minutes or until quinoa is tender. For a thinner consistency, stir in more water. Remove from heat and stir in lemon juice.

2. Transfer to serving bowls and top with cranberries and honey.

Scrambled Egg Whites

This is a tridoshic recipe for breakfast eggs. Egg yolks are warming, so if cooking solely for vata, you can use the whole egg, but pitta should avoid yolks. Because of the cholesterol in the yolk, kapha is also generally better off with only egg whites. The cilantro is balancing to all the doshas.

Makes 1 serving

Variation

Try using ¼ cup (60 mL) chopped arugula in place of the cilantro.

SERVING SUGGESTION

Serve with Millet Breakfast Patties (page 116).

Dairy-Free ✦ Gluten-Free ✦ Soy-Free ✦ Vegetarian

2	large egg whites	2
2 tbsp	water	30 mL
1 tsp	chopped fresh cilantro	5 mL
1 tsp	sunflower oil	5 mL

1. In a bowl, whisk together egg whites, water and cilantro.
2. In a medium skillet, heat oil over medium heat. Pour in eggs and immediately reduce heat to medium-low. Using a wooden spoon, scrape around the edges of the pan, moving soft, cooked eggs toward the center. Continue scraping the bottom of the pan and redistributing the cooked eggs toward the center until eggs are cooked to desired consistency.

Dosha Modification
✦ **Kapha** could add a little hot pepper sauce or a side of Kapha Hot Onion Chutney (page 268).

Poached Eggs for Vata

Poached eggs are best for vata. Pitta can eat them on occasion if topped with cooling cilantro or sprouts. Kapha should likewise have them only on occasion and top them with sprouts.

**Makes
2 servings**

**SERVING
SUGGESTION**

Serve on top of Millet Breakfast Patties (page 116). Top with pumpkin seeds.

Dairy-Free ✦ Gluten-Free ✦ Soy-Free ✦ Vegetarian

6 cups	water	1.5 L
1 tsp	white vinegar (optional)	5 mL
2	large eggs	2

1. In a medium saucepan, heat water over medium–high heat to just below boiling. Bubbles should form on the bottom of the pan, but don't let them rise to break the surface. Adjust the heat if necessary.

2. Add white vinegar to the water to help the whites coagulate faster and help the poached eggs keep their shape.

3. Crack an egg into a small bowl. Transfer the egg to the pan by slowly sliding the egg down the side of the pan into the water. This helps keep the egg intact. Repeat with the remaining egg. Cook for 3 to 4 minutes, to desired consistency (3 minutes will be soft, longer will be a firmer yolk). Using a slotted spoon, transfer eggs to a plate lined with paper towels to drain before serving.

Minted Fingerling Potato Frittata

My Uncle Joe was famous for his frittata creations, which we devoured warm from the oven at family gatherings. "Frittata" is an Italian word meaning "fried" and refers to an egg-based dish similar to an omelet. The variations are endless.

Egg yolks have a warming energetic and are best for vata. Pitta and kapha can eat them in moderation, accompanied with a cooling salad or steamed greens.

Makes 4 servings

Tips

This frittata should be eaten the same day, as it tends to dry out overnight in the refrigerator.

Vigorous blending will incorporate air into the eggs and create a fluffier frittata; alternatively, you can use a hand whisk.

Use organic eggs from humanely treated chickens that graze on pastures.

Using fingerling potatoes with various skin colors makes for a beautiful presentation.

Variations

Substitute roasted artichoke hearts or broccoli for the asparagus.

Try basil or 1 tsp (5 mL) rosemary in place of the mint.

Gluten-Free ✦ Soy-Free ✦ Vegetarian

- Preheat broiler
- Blender
- 9-inch (23 cm) cast-iron or broiler-proof skillet

5	large eggs	5
½ tsp	grated lemon zest	2 mL
1 tbsp	chopped parsley	15 mL
1 tbsp	chopped fresh mint	15 mL
2 tbsp	ghee, butter or extra virgin olive oil	30 mL
2 cups	thinly sliced fingerling potatoes (unpeeled)	500 mL
¼ tsp	salt	1 mL
⅛ tsp	crushed black pepper	0.5 mL
½ cup	thinly sliced trimmed asparagus (sliced on the diagonal)	125 mL
3 tbsp	finely chopped green onion	45 mL

1. In blender, combine eggs and lemon zest; beat until frothy. Set aside.

2. In a small bowl, combine parsley and mint. Set aside.

3. In the cast-iron skillet, heat ghee over medium heat. Add potatoes and sprinkle with salt and pepper; cook, stirring, until edges of potatoes begin to brown. Add asparagus and green onion; cook, stirring, for 1 minute.

4. Add the egg mixture and sprinkle the herb mixture on top. As the eggs set, slide a spatula around the edge of the skillet, lifting the eggs so the uncooked liquid flows underneath.

5. When the eggs begin to firm and the bottom begins to brown but the top is still moist, about 3 minutes, transfer skillet to preheated broiler and brown the top, about 1 minute. Slice into quarters. Serve hot, cold or at room temperature.

Amaranth Crêpes with Pomegranate Syrup

Have fun making these. Smaller crêpes will be easier to flip, but will be more difficult to fold due to the inflexibility of the gluten-free batter. The first crêpe may be a disaster, but don't fret; it doesn't count. Use it to contemplate how to modify your technique so you can create future crêpes of higher quality. Note that it is difficult to have wafer-thin crêpes using gluten-free flour, so set your expectations accordingly. The coolness of the amaranth, milk and cardamom will balance the warmth of the eggs for pitta. Kapha can eat these in moderation.

Makes two 10-inch (25 cm) crêpes

Tips

The astringency of the amaranth flour and pomegranate syrup is balanced by the sweet rice flour, coconut milk and butter.

The lemon zest and cinnamon mellow the strong flavor of the amaranth flour.

Using butter or ghee will give the crêpe a caramel taste and help with browning; this will be lost if you substitute oil.

You can double the recipe so you have extra batter on hand. Leftover batter can be stored in the refrigerator for up to 3 days, but the amaranth flavor starts to overwhelm the spices with each passing day.

Gluten-Free ◆ Soy-Free ◆ Vegetarian

- 10-inch (25 cm) cast-iron skillet (or crêpe pan)

1	large egg	1
1	large egg yolk	1
1/2 cup	coconut milk (or cow's, almond or soy milk)	125 mL
2 tsp	pomegranate syrup	10 mL
2 tsp	grated lemon zest	10 mL
2 tbsp	amaranth flour, sifted	30 mL
2 tbsp	brown rice flour, sifted, or almond flour	30 mL
1 tsp	ground cinnamon (no substitutes)	5 mL
1/2 tsp	ground cardamom (no substitutes)	2 mL
1/8 tsp	Himalayan salt	0.5 mL
2 tsp	butter or ghee, melted	10 mL

1. In a medium bowl, whisk egg and egg yolk until frothy. Add coconut milk, pomegranate syrup and lemon zest, whisking until combined. Add amaranth flour, brown rice flour, cinnamon, cardamom, salt and butter, whisking until batter is thin and smooth. Cover and let set for 10 minutes in the refrigerator.

2. Meanwhile, preheat oven to 200°F (100°C).

3. Remove batter from refrigerator and whisk briefly.

Variation

Try adding ½ tsp (2 mL) almond, orange or vanilla extract.

4. Heat the skillet over medium heat. When a drop of batter placed on the pan sizzles, you are ready to cook. Lift the pan off the burner and pour in a thin layer of batter (about ¼ cup/60 mL). Gently tilt the skillet in a circular motion to spread the batter evenly across the bottom. Return the pan to the heat and patiently wait. When the bottom is done, you will see a change in color and the crêpe will easily lift from the pan. Test it by running a spatula around the edges. When the spatula easily slides under the center of the crêpe (about 2 to 3 minutes), it is time to flip. Flip the crêpe and cook for 30 seconds on the second side. Transfer crêpe to a plate and place in preheated oven while preparing the other crêpe.

Masala Dosas

These wonderful pancakes made of rice and lentils are a traditional meal served in South India. For my take on them, I've added Masala Spice Mix to the batter, and I serve the pancakes with maple syrup and a side of Vegan Vanilla Nut Yogurt (page 118). A more authentic version would be to omit the spice mix from the batter to make plain dosas, then stuff them with Masala Potatoes (page 226) and serve with Cool Coconut Chutney (page 264). For a unique variation, substitute kabocha squash for the potatoes (variation, page 226).

Makes about 10 pancakes

Tips

Poha makes the batter brown and crisp and easier to spread thin; if you omit it, the texture of the dosas will be spongier and thicker.

Chana dal makes the dosa crisper.

Fenugreek seeds add color, flavor and elasticity.

When fermenting batter, do not use an airtight container.

The batter can be made ahead through step 4 (except for preheating the oven) and stored in an airtight container in the refrigerator for up to 7 days. Bring to room temperature before cooking.

Gluten-Free ✦ Soy-Free ✦ Vegetarian

- **High-power blender**
- **10-inch (25 cm) cast-iron skillet (or crêpe pan)**

2 cups	idli rice	500 mL
½ cup	urad dal	125 mL
3 tbsp	chana dal	45 mL
1½ tsp	fenugreek seeds	7 mL
¼ cup	poha (flattened rice)	60 mL
1 tsp	salt	5 mL
1 tbsp	Masala Spice Mix (page 271)	15 mL
¼ cup	melted ghee	60 mL

1. In a large bowl, combine idli rice, urad dal, chana dal and fenugreek seeds. Add enough water to cover ingredients by 2 inches (5 cm). Soak at room temperature for 6 to 8 hours. Drain, setting aside the soaking water.

2. In blender, combine soaked rice mixture, poha and 1 to 2 cups (250 to 500 mL) of the reserved soaking water (to facilitate blending). Grind into a smooth paste (it should be thick but not grainy), adding additional soaking water if necessary.

3. Pour the mixture into a large bowl and add salt, mixing with your hands (the warmth of your hands initiates fermentation). Cover the bowl with a plate and set in a warm (80°F to 90°F/27°C to 33°C) place overnight to ferment and double in size.

4. In the morning, preheat the oven to 200°F (100°C). The batter will be frothy; beat it down with a wooden spoon for several minutes, then stir in the Masala Spice Mix. The batter will be thick but pourable; adjust with more water, if necessary.

Tips

Spreading the batter very thin will yield a crisper dosa.

Skillet temperature is key; monitor it (you can perform the water-drop dance test in step 5 between dosas to confirm the correct temperature) and adjust the heat if necessary.

5. Warm the skillet over medium heat. Do not add oil, as this may cause the batter to stick to the skillet. The pan is the correct temperature when a drop of water sprinkled on it "dances."

6. Pour $\frac{1}{3}$ cup (75 mL) batter into skillet. Using the back of a spoon, quickly stir in concentric circles, working toward the outside. Spread batter evenly and thin (it's okay if there are some holes). Drizzle some melted ghee on top of the batter. Cook until the bottom is lightly browned and lifts easily away from the pan when a spatula is slid underneath. Flip the dosa and cook the second side until lightly browned. Transfer dosa to a plate and place in warm oven while preparing the remaining dosas.

Dosha Modifications

✦ **Pitta** can sprinkle coconut flakes on their dosas.

✦ **Kapha** can add chopped chile peppers to their dosas.

Idli Rice and Poha

Idli rice (also called parboiled rice or Converted rice) has been partially boiled in the husk. Parboiling drives nutrients, especially thiamin, from the bran to the endosperm, reduces cooking time and creates a firmer, less sticky rice.

Poha (also called flattened rice) has been parboiled, rolled, flattened and dried to produce flakes. The flakes come in different thicknesses depending on the pressure used in the flattening process. They can absorb large amounts of liquid in recipes. Poha is widely used in India, with the most common preparation being a savory breakfast dish with regional ingredient variations.

Idli rice and poha can be found in Indian grocery stores.

Lime Tarragon Sweet Potato Breakfast Patties

These unique-tasting patties are great for breakfast or brunch, and are sure to please everyone. Serve with avocado slices or a poached egg (page 108).

Makes 6 patties

Tip

Flax seeds that have been ground into meal can go rancid very quickly due their high oil content. So purchase whole flax seeds and grind as needed (using a mortar and pestle or a clean spice grinder or coffee grinder) — this is also less expensive! Store whole flax seeds in a cool, dark place.

	Gluten-Free ✦ Soy-Free ✦ Vegan	
1 tbsp	flax seeds, ground	15 mL
3 tbsp	water	45 mL
3 cups	boiled cubed sweet potato (unpeeled)	750 mL
1 tbsp	arrowroot flour	15 mL
1 tbsp	chickpea (garbanzo bean) flour	15 mL
	Extra virgin olive oil	
1 cup	finely chopped onion	250 mL
1½ tsp	finely chopped gingerroot	7 mL
½ tsp	dried tarragon	2 mL
¼ tsp	dried thyme	1 mL
⅓ cup	finely chopped fresh parsley	75 mL
½ tsp	grated lime zest	2 mL
1 to 2 tbsp	freshly squeezed lime juice	15 to 30 mL
	Lime wedges (optional)	

1. In a small bowl, combine flax seeds and water. Let stand for 10 minutes.

2. In a large bowl, use a fork to coarsely mash the sweet potatoes. Set aside.

3. In a small bowl, combine flax seed mixture, arrowroot flour and chickpea flour. Set aside.

4. In a large skillet, heat 2 tbsp (30 mL) oil over medium heat. Add onions and cook, stirring, until soft. Add ginger and cook, stirring, for 30 seconds. Stir in tarragon and thyme.

Tip

The patties can be prepared ahead through step 4. Let cool, wrap individually in plastic wrap, then place in a freezer bag and store in the refrigerator for up to 2 days or the freezer for up to 2 months. Thaw for 15 minutes at room temperature, then continue with step 5.

5. Transfer onion mixture to the bowl of sweet potatoes. Stir in flax seed mixture, parsley and lime zest. Stir in lime juice 1 tbsp (15 mL) at a time, to taste. Form into 6 patties.

6. In the skillet, over medium-low heat, warm enough oil to lightly coat the bottom of the pan. Working in batches, cook patties, turning once, for 3 to 5 minutes per side or until lightly browned on both sides. Transfer to a serving plate and keep warm. Repeat with the remaining patties, adjusting heat and adding more oil between batches as necessary.

7. Serve patties garnished with lime wedges, if desired.

Dosha Modification

✦ **Kapha** can add some cayenne or chili pepper to their serving.

Millet Breakfast Patties

When vegetables are cooked together, the energetics mellow. In this recipe, the warmth of the millet is balanced by the coolness of the sweet potato. The dosha modifications given below will further smooth out the energetics.

Makes 4 patties

Tip

If you use plain cooked millet or quinoa, add some seasonings to the patty mixture — 1 tsp (5 mL) total of one or a combination of ground spices (cardamom, cinnamon, allspice, etc.).

SERVING SUGGESTIONS

Serve with avocado slices, a poached egg (page 108) or scrambled egg whites (page 107). Top with unsalted sunflower seeds, green pumpkin seeds (pepitas) or sprouts. Garnish with a lime wedge.

Dairy-Free ✦ Gluten-Free ✦ Soy-Free ✦ Vegetarian

1 cup	leftover Fluffy Cinnamon Currant Millet (page 143) or plain cooked millet or quinoa (see tip, at left)	250 mL
½ cup	mashed boiled peeled sweet potato	125 mL
3 tbsp	arrowroot flour	45 mL
⅛ tsp	Himalayan salt	0.5 mL
1	large egg, lightly beaten	1
1 tbsp	grapeseed oil or extra virgin olive oil	15 mL

1. In a medium bowl, combine millet, sweet potato, flour, salt and egg. Form into 4 patties.

2. In a large skillet, heat oil over medium heat. Add patties and cook, turning once, for 3 minutes per side or until browned on both sides.

Dosha Modifications

✦ Millet is dry and light, so **vata** will benefit from additional liquid and grounding, such as a squirt of lime juice and a slice of avocado or a poached egg.

✦ **Pitta** will benefit from adding an avocado garnish, which will both cool the dish and add healthy fat to satiate a hearty appetite.

✦ **Kapha** can garnish with sprouts to keep things light and moving — and a squirt of lime for more zest.

Creamy Yogurt

Fresh yogurt is sweet and can be served with sweet blueberries, dried fruits and/or toasted nuts. The yogurt can be spiced with cinnamon, cardamom or ginger to reduce mucus formation. Honey is a good sweetener, especially for kapha.

Makes about 3¹/₂ cups (875 mL)

Tips

Use in a Yogurt Lassi (page 323) or, for pitta, as a cooling condiment with dal dishes.

Fresh yogurt can be stored for up to 1 week in an airtight container in the refrigerator.

Gluten-Free ✦ Soy-Free ✦ Vegetarian

- **Yogurt maker**
- **Candy thermometer**

4 cups	organic whole milk	1 L
¹/₄ cup	organic plain yogurt	60 mL

1. In a large saucepan, warm milk over low heat until just below boiling (185°F to 190°F/85°C to 88°C). Cook, stirring slowly, for 20 minutes (or, for thinner yogurt, cook, stirring slowly, for 10 minutes).

2. Remove from heat and let cool for about 15 minutes or until tepid (about 110°F/43°C). If a skin forms on the top of the milk as it cools, remove and discard the skin.

3. Ladle 1 cup (250 mL) of the lukewarm milk into a small bowl and stir in the yogurt. Return to the saucepan and whisk until combined.

4. Ladle cultured milk into the jar(s) of the yogurt maker. Set to the regular cycle and leave in the yogurt maker for 8 hours to thicken (or follow the manufacturer's directions).

5. Remove jar(s) from yogurt maker and refrigerate for 2 hours before use.

Dosha Modification

✦ **Kapha** should use yogurt in moderation and add warming spices.

Vegan Vanilla Nut Yogurt

Fresh yogurt is sweet and cooling and can be made without preservatives, thickeners or a ton of added sweeteners. It is super-easy to make and is guaranteed to be fresh, with all-natural ingredients. This recipe uses a tiny amount of coconut sugar, which is necessary to feed the cultures so they will grow.

Makes 7 servings

Tips

This recipe works well with Thick-Strained Nut Milk made with almonds or cashews. It does not work with commercially prepared almond milk, cashew milk or canned coconut milk.

At the end of step 1, you can place the pan of milk in a sink filled with 1 inch (2.5 cm) of cold water or ice to accelerate the cooling. The cultures cannot survive if the temperature is too hot or too cold; they remain active between 98°F and 120°F (37°C and 49°C).

Fresh yogurt can be stored for up to 1 week in an airtight container in the refrigerator.

Gluten-Free ✦ Soy-Free ✦ Vegan

- **Yogurt maker**
- **Candy thermometer**

5¼ cups	Thick-Strained Nut Milk (page 322)	1.3 L
1 tbsp	coconut sugar or pure maple syrup	15 mL
1½	vanilla beans, split in half lengthwise (see tip, below)	1½
¼ tsp	yogurt starter culture (see tip, below)	1 mL

1. In a large saucepan, combine nut milk and coconut sugar. Using a paring knife, scrape the seeds from the vanilla beans into the pan; add the empty pods to the pan. Warm milk over low heat, stirring occasionally, for 15 minutes to infuse the milk with vanilla flavor.

2. Remove from heat and let cool for about 15 minutes or until tepid (about 110°F/43°C); it will be lukewarm to the touch. Discard vanilla bean pods.

3. Ladle 1 cup (250 mL) of the lukewarm milk into a small bowl and stir in the starter culture. Return to the saucepan and whisk until combined.

4. Ladle cultured milk into the jar(s) of the yogurt maker. Set to the regular cycle and leave in the yogurt maker for 8 hours to thicken (or follow the manufacturer's directions).

5. Remove jar(s) from yogurt maker and refrigerate for 3 hours before use.

Purchasing Tips

- Purchase soft, plump, fragrant vanilla beans with a dark brown skin; they should not feel dry or brittle.

- Purchase bottles of yogurt starter culture online or at health food stores. Alternatively, you can use ¼ cup (60 mL) unflavored commercial yogurt.

Vata Breakfast Banana

Ripe bananas are sweet, but they have a sour energetic effect, which makes them heating and mucus-forming. They are smooth and heavy, so they are ideal for vata. Pitta and kapha should avoid them, but if they want to eat bananas, they could opt for unripe (green) ones, which are soft, light, astringent and cooling.

Makes 1 serving

Tip

This is best eaten alone as a small breakfast, mid–morning snack or afternoon snack.

Variation

Substitute 1 to 2 tbsp (15 to 30 mL) light (fancy) molasses for the coconut sugar to supplement your iron intake.

Gluten-Free ✦ Soy-Free ✦ Vegetarian

2 tsp	ghee	10 mL
½ tsp	coconut sugar	2 mL
⅛ to ¼ tsp	ground cinnamon	0.5 to 1 mL
⅛ to ¼ tsp	ground cardamom	0.5 to 1 mL
⅛ to ¼ tsp	ground ginger	0.5 to 1 mL
1	ripe banana, peeled and cut into ¼-inch (0.5 cm) slices	1

1. In a medium skillet, melt ghee over low heat. Add sugar, cinnamon, cardamom and ginger, stirring to combine. Add banana slices in a single layer on top of the spice mixture and cook for 1 minute. Flip to coat the other side and cook for 1 minute. Transfer to a serving dish.

Yogurt Parfait

This breakfast or mid-morning snack is grounding for vata and cooling for pitta; kapha can eat it on occasion. It is best to avoid eating yogurt after sunset.

Makes 1 serving

Tip

To toast almonds, place them in a dry (ungreased) medium skillet over medium heat. When they begin to smell fragrant, after about 1 minute, give the pan a shake. Continue to toast, periodically shaking the pan, until the almonds are golden.

Gluten-Free ✦ Soy-Free ✦ Vegetarian

2 tbsp	green pumpkin seeds (pepitas)	30 mL
2 tbsp	unsalted sunflower seeds	30 mL
2 tbsp	slivered almonds, toasted (see tip, at left)	30 mL
2 tbsp	dried goji berries	30 mL
1 cup	Creamy Yogurt (page 117) or Vegan Vanilla Nut Yogurt (page 118)	250 mL
1 tsp	raw liquid honey	5 mL
1/4 tsp	ground cardamom	1 mL
1/4 tsp	ground cinnamon	1 mL

1. In a small bowl, combine pumpkin seeds, sunflower seeds, almonds and goji berries. Set aside.

2. Spoon half of the yogurt into an 8-oz (250 mL) cup. Sprinkle 4 tbsp (60 mL) of the seed mixture over the yogurt, making an even layer. Spoon half of the remaining yogurt on top. Add another layer of the remaining seed mixture, then add the remaining yogurt. Drizzle with honey and sprinkle with cardamom and cinnamon.

Dosha Modifications

✦ **Vata** and **pitta** could add 2 tbsp (30 mL) unsweetened shredded coconut to the seed mixture.

✦ **Vata** and **kapha** can add 2 tbsp (30 mL) chopped dried apricots to the seed mixture.

✦ **Pitta** could substitute pure maple syrup for the honey.

✦ **Kapha** should sprinkle 1/4 tsp (1 mL) ground ginger on top to balance out some of the heaviness of the yogurt.

Vegetarian Midday Meals

The recipes in this chapter are influenced by the flavors of many cuisines beyond India. Ancient grains, heirloom beans and lentils are combined thoughtfully to be satiating and easy on your digestive system. Ayurveda says a diet of light vegetarian foods promotes clarity and perception and has the ability to unfold compassion and love. You are what you eat!

The main meal should be eaten around noon (between 11:30 a.m. and 1:30 p.m.), when the digestive fire is the strongest. If you are new to beans and lentils, this is a good time to experiment – plan accordingly.

Kitchari

This light, cleansing tridoshic dish is easily digested. It can be eaten for breakfast, lunch and dinner to give the digestive system a rest for a day and restore the digestive fire.

Makes 2 servings

Tips

Use a mortar and pestle to lightly crush the coriander seeds.

If your digestion is very sensitive, reduce the mung dal to 2 tbsp (30 mL).

Variation

If you have a strong digestion and a hearty appetite, substitute long-grain brown rice for the basmati rice, increasing the amount of water to 1⅔ cups (400 mL). Start checking for doneness after 40 minutes.

SERVING SUGGESTION

Serve with steamed seasonal vegetables.

Gluten-Free ✦ Soy-Free ✦ Vegetarian

¼ cup	mung dal, sorted and rinsed	60 mL
	Water	
2 tsp	ghee	10 mL
1 tsp	cumin seeds	5 mL
¾ tsp	fennel seeds	3 mL
¾ tsp	coriander seeds, lightly crushed	3 mL
¼ cup	basmati rice	60 mL
½ tsp	ground turmeric	2 mL
½ tsp	ground cumin	2 mL
1	bay leaf	1
½ tsp	Himalayan salt	2 mL
¼ tsp	crushed black pepper	1 mL
1 tbsp	chopped fresh cilantro	15 mL

1. Place mung dal in a bowl and add enough water to cover by 2 to 3 inches (5 to 7.5 cm). Let soak at room temperature overnight. Drain.

2. In a medium saucepan, melt ghee over medium-low heat. Add cumin, fennel and coriander seeds. Cook, stirring, for about 30 seconds or until the seeds pop.

3. Stir in dal, rice, turmeric, ground cumin, bay leaf and 1½ cups (375 mL) water. Bring to a boil over high heat, stirring. Reduce heat to low, cover, leaving lid ajar, and simmer, stirring occasionally, until dal is soft and the consistency of the kitchari is to your preference (from soupy to "dry"). Check the pan after 20 minutes, then every few minutes thereafter. You may need to add water if the dal doesn't cook quickly; in that case, you may also want to add more turmeric and ground cumin. Remove from heat and stir in the salt, pepper and cilantro.

Dosha Modifications

✦ If cooking solely for **vata** and/or **kapha**, you can add ½ tsp (2 mL) black mustard seeds, ⅛ tsp (0.5 mL) ajwain seeds, ½ tsp (2 mL) chopped gingerroot or ¼ tsp (1 mL) minced garlic when cooking the spices in step 2.

✦ Sprinkle a Dosha-Specific Churna (page 272) on top.

Pitta-Cooling Summer Mung Dal

The recipe is cleansing and cooling – well suited for reducing pitta on hot summer days. The zesty lime juice adds nice flavor without adding heat.

Tips

Burdock root powder can be found in the bulk herb section of local food cooperatives or at health food stores or online herb shops. Alternatively, you can use crushed dried burdock (grind it to a powder in a clean coffee or spice grinder) or substitute 1 tsp (5 mL) finely chopped peeled fresh burdock root.

This dal is best eaten the day it is prepared; leftovers can be stored in an airtight container in the refrigerator for up to 1 day. Leftovers should be reheated as individual servings.

SERVING SUGGESTION

Serve with steamed Swiss chard for a cool, light summer meal.

Gluten-Free ✦ Soy-Free ✦ Vegan

³⁄₄ cup	mung dal, sorted and rinsed	175 mL
	Water	
1 tbsp	virgin coconut oil	15 mL
1 tsp	crushed coriander seeds	5 mL
³⁄₄ tsp	cumin seeds	3 mL
¹⁄₂ tsp	ground fennel seeds	2 mL
¹⁄₂ tsp	chopped gingerroot	2 mL
¹⁄₄ tsp	burdock root powder	1 mL
¹⁄₃ cup	chopped fresh cilantro	75 mL
¹⁄₂ tsp	Himalayan salt	2 mL
	Freshly squeezed lime juice	

1. Place mung dal in a bowl and add enough water to cover by 2 to 3 inches (5 to 7.5 cm). Let soak at room temperature overnight. Drain.

2. In a medium saucepan, melt coconut oil over medium heat. Add coriander seeds, cumin seeds, fennel seeds, ginger and burdock root powder; cook, stirring, for about 30 seconds or until fragrant.

3. Stir in dal and 1³⁄₄ cups (425 mL) water; bring to a boil over high heat. Reduce heat to low, cover and simmer, stirring occasionally, for 20 minutes. Stir and add a little more water, if necessary. Cook for 5 minutes or until dal is soft. Remove from heat and stir in cilantro, salt and lime juice to taste.

Kerala-Inspired Toor Dal

Coconut is widely used in southern Indian cooking. It is believed to have medicinal and therapeutic value, increasing vitality, nourishing the brain and nervous system, and providing antiparasitic and antibacterial properties. Coconut has a cooling energetic that offsets the spicy chiles. This dal is quite mild compared to the fiery dals I had in Kerala, but is more balancing to a Western palate (and certainly if one is aiming for a tridoshic dish).

Makes 3 servings

Tip

To peel and seed a plum (Roma) tomato, simply chop off ¼ inch (0.5 cm) from each end, then use a sharp vegetable peeler to remove the skin. Cut the tomato into quarters and scrape out the seeds using the sharp point of a knife. If you are using round tomatoes, you will need to carve out the area where the tomato was attached to the stem, then peel with a sharp vegetable peeler.

Gluten-Free ♦ Soy-Free ♦ Vegan

- Mortar and pestle
- Immersion blender or coffee or spice grinder

1 cup	toor dal, sorted and rinsed	250 mL
	Water	
1	bay leaf	1
¾ tsp	ground turmeric	3 mL
2	cloves garlic	2
1 tbsp	minced gingerroot	15 mL
⅛ tsp	Himalayan salt	0.5 mL
1 tbsp	ghee or sunflower oil	15 mL
1 tsp	cumin seeds	5 mL
8	curry leaves (fresh or dried)	8
½ cup	finely chopped seeded peeled tomato (see tip, at left)	125 mL
⅓ cup	chopped shallots or red onion	75 mL
2 tbsp	unsweetened shredded coconut (fresh or frozen)	30 mL
1 tsp	minced seeded green chile pepper (or ⅛ tsp/0.5 mL cayenne pepper)	5 mL
¼ cup	coarsely chopped fresh cilantro	60 mL

1. Place toor dal in a bowl and add enough water to cover by 2 to 3 inches (5 to 7.5 cm). Let soak at room temperature overnight. Drain.

2. In a medium saucepan, combine dal, bay leaf, turmeric and 3 cups (750 mL) water. Bring to a boil over high heat. Reduce heat and simmer, stirring occasionally, for 50 to 60 minutes or until dal is soft and has a thick porridge-like consistency. (Watch the water level and add more if the dal begins to dry out.) Discard bay leaf.

3. Meanwhile, using the mortar and pestle, pound garlic, ginger and salt to make a paste. Set aside.

4. In a large skillet, melt ghee over medium heat. Add cumin seeds and cook, stirring, for about 30 seconds or until they pop. Stir in curry leaves, tomato, shallots, coconut and chile; cook, stirring, for about 8 minutes or until the tomato is softened. Add garlic paste and sauté for 3 minutes to blend the flavors. Using an immersion blender (or transferring the mixture to a coffee or spice grinder), grind into a thick paste, adding a little water if necessary.

5. Add spice sauce to the dal and stir in cilantro.

Dosha Modifications

✦ **Pitta** should accompany this dish with Cool Coconut Chutney (page 264).

✦ **Kapha** should accompany this dish with Kapha Hot Onion Chutney (page 268).

Bangalore Toor Dal Sambhar

Toor dal is ideal for vata, as it is heavy and heating. The cool potatoes add balance for pitta, and kapha benefits from the spices.

Makes 3 servings

Tip

Be careful to not overcook the mustard seeds, as they burn easily and will make the dal taste bitter.

SERVING SUGGESTIONS

Serve with basmati rice, Cool Coconut Chutney (page 264) or Pitta-Cooling Date Chutney (page 265), cucumbers and steamed vegetables or a salad of mixed greens.

Gluten-Free ✦ Soy-Free ✦ Vegan

- **Blender**

½ cup	toor dal, sorted and rinsed	125 mL
	Water	
1	bay leaf	1
1½ cups	cubed peeled yellow-fleshed potatoes (½-inch/1 cm cubes)	375 mL
1 cup	chopped seeded peeled tomato (see tip, page 124)	250 mL
½ tsp	Himalayan salt	2 mL
¼ cup	unsweetened shredded coconut (fresh or frozen)	60 mL
1 tsp	ground cumin	5 mL
½ tsp	chopped seeded thin green chile pepper	2 mL
½ tsp	pressed or minced garlic	2 mL
¼ cup	coarsely chopped fresh cilantro	60 mL
1 tbsp	ghee or safflower oil	15 mL
1 tsp	black mustard seeds	5 mL
1 tsp	urad dal	5 mL

1. Place toor dal in a bowl and add enough water to cover by 2 to 3 inches (5 to 7.5 cm). Let soak at room temperature overnight. Drain.

2. In a large saucepan, combine dal, 1½ cups (375 mL) water and bay leaf. Bring to a boil over high heat. Reduce heat and simmer, stirring occasionally, for about 1 hour or until dal is soft and creamy. (Watch the water level and add more if the dal begins to dry out.) Drain off remaining water, discard bay leaf and return dal to the pan.

3. Stir in potatoes, tomato, salt and 2 cups (500 mL) water; bring to a boil. Reduce heat and simmer for 15 to 20 minutes or until potatoes are tender. Remove from heat.

4. In blender, combine coconut, cumin, chile, garlic and ¼ cup (60 mL) water; blend until smooth. Add to the dal mixture and stir well. Stir in cilantro.

5. In a medium skillet, melt ghee over low heat. Add mustard seeds and urad dal; cook, stirring, for about 30 seconds or until mustard seeds pop and urad dal is golden. Stir into dal.

Urad Dal with Tamarind

This mildly spiced dish is suitable for all doshas. Urad dal is heavy and warm; nevertheless, pitta can eat it on occasion, with the modifications noted below.

Makes 4 servings

Tips

Use a mortar and pestle to crush the coriander seeds to a coarse consistency or use a spice grinder for a finer texture, as desired.

Chef candles are an excellent way to remove smells from the kitchen, especially when you're using turmeric or cooking curries. Burn them while you're cooking, and the kitchen will be free of odor when the meal is served.

The curry leaves are optional, but they add a really nice flavor!

SERVING SUGGESTION

Serve with basmati rice, steamed vegetables and dosha-specific chutneys.

Gluten-Free ✦ Soy-Free ✦ Vegan

- **Immersion blender (optional)**

2 cups	urad dal, sorted and rinsed	500 mL
	Water	
1	bay leaf	1
1/4 tsp	cayenne pepper	1 mL
1 tbsp	virgin coconut oil or ghee	15 mL
1/2 tsp	pressed or minced garlic	2 mL
2 tsp	cumin seeds	10 mL
2 tsp	coriander seeds, crushed (see tip, at left)	10 mL
8	curry leaves (optional)	8
1/2 tsp	ground turmeric	2 mL
1/2 tsp	Himalayan salt	2 mL
2 tbsp	tamarind paste	30 mL
2 tbsp	chopped fresh cilantro	30 mL

1. Place urad dal in a bowl and add enough water to cover by 2 to 3 inches (5 to 7.5 cm). Let soak at room temperature overnight. Drain.

2. In a large saucepan, combine dal, bay leaf, cayenne and 4 cups (1 L) water. Bring to a boil over high heat. Reduce heat and simmer, stirring occasionally, for 60 to 90 minutes or until dal is soft and creamy. Discard bay leaf.

3. In a medium skillet, melt coconut oil over medium-low heat. Add garlic, cumin seeds, coriander seeds and curry leaves (if using); cook, stirring, for about 30 seconds or until garlic is fragrant and light golden. Reduce heat to low and stir in turmeric, salt and tamarind paste.

4. Add spice mixture to dal mixture and, if desired, lightly purée with immersion blender. Stir in cilantro.

Dosha Modifications

- ✦ For **pitta**, add more cilantro or a side of Cool Coconut Chutney (page 264).

- ✦ **Kapha** can add 1 tsp (5 mL) chopped chile pepper and/or 2 tsp (10 mL) chopped gingerroot with the garlic, or can simply add more cayenne, and can serve Kapha Hot Onion Chutney (page 268) alongside.

Gujarati Wedding Dal

This is an adaptation of a traditional sweet and sour dal recipe served at Gujarati weddings. I have modified the ingredients to be more balancing. Don't let the ingredient list put you off; the dish whips up quickly. The sweet, cooling dates make this dish ideal for vata and pitta.

Makes 4 servings

Tip

To peel and seed a plum (Roma) tomato, simply chop off ¼ inch (0.5 cm) from each end, then use a sharp vegetable peeler to remove the skin. Cut the tomato into quarters and scrape out the seeds using the sharp point of a knife. If you are using round tomatoes, you will need to carve out the area where the tomato was attached to the stem, then peel with a sharp vegetable peeler.

Variations

Substitute toor dal for the red lentils. Soak the dal overnight and increase the cooking time in step 2 to 60 minutes.

Substitute sweet potato for the yam.

Gluten-Free ✦ Soy-Free ✦ Vegan		
½ cup	chopped peeled yam	125 mL
2	Medjool dates, pitted and coarsely chopped	2
	Water	
1 cup	dried red lentils, sorted and rinsed	250 mL
7	curry leaves	7
3	whole cloves	3
1	cinnamon stick (or 1 tsp/5 mL ground cinnamon)	1
1	bay leaf	1
¼ tsp	fenugreek seeds	1 mL
1 tbsp	ghee or sunflower oil	15 mL
¼ tsp	cumin seeds	1 mL
¼ cup	finely chopped seeded peeled tomatoes (see tip, at left)	60 mL
2 tsp	minced gingerroot	10 mL
1 tsp	chopped seeded green chile pepper	5 mL
1 tsp	Himalayan salt	5 mL
½ tsp	ground turmeric	2 mL
¼ tsp	chili powder	1 mL
½ tsp	tamarind paste	2 mL
2 tbsp	chopped fresh cilantro	30 mL

1. In a small saucepan, combine yam, dates and 1½ cups (375 mL) water. Bring to a boil over high heat. Reduce heat to low, cover and simmer for about 15 minutes or until yam is parboiled.

2. Meanwhile, in a medium saucepan, combine lentils and 2 cups (500 mL) water. Bring to a boil over high heat. Reduce heat and simmer for about 10 minutes or until lentils lose their shape and are soft. Drain and return lentils to the pan. Stir in the yam mixture (including the water). Set aside.

SERVING SUGGESTIONS

Serve with basmati rice, Fluffy Cinnamon Currant Millet (page 143), Cornbread (page 294) or roti, along with steamed green vegetables and lime wedges.

3. In a small bowl, combine curry leaves, cloves, cinnamon, bay leaf and fenugreek seeds.

4. In a large skillet, melt ghee over medium heat. Add cumin seeds and cook, stirring, for about 30 seconds or until seeds pop. Add spice mixture and cook, stirring, for a few seconds.

5. Stir in tomatoes, ginger, chile, salt, turmeric, chili powder, 1 cup (250 mL) water and tamarind paste; bring to a boil over high heat. Reduce heat and simmer, stirring constantly, for 10 minutes.

6. Add tomato mixture to dal mixture and warm over low heat, stirring to combine. Discard cinnamon stick and bay leaf. Stir in cilantro.

Dosha Modifications

✦ If cooking for **vata** alone, add 2 tbsp (30 mL) toasted cashews with the yam in step 1.

✦ Kapha Hot Onion Chutney (page 268) will balance this dish for **kapha**.

Yams versus Sweet Potatoes

Yams are the edible root of the *Dioscorea* genus, largely grown in Africa and the Caribbean. They are starchy and dry, and are low in beta-carotene but high in potassium. Their skin is rough and scaly. Sweet potatoes belong to the unrelated morning glory family (*Convolvulaceae*) and are sweet and moist with high amounts of beta-carotene and sodium. Their skin is smooth and thin, and their flesh varies in color from white to orange or even purple. When the orange-fleshed variety was introduced to the United States several decades ago, they were labeled "yams" (from the African word *nyami*) to distinguish them from white sweet potatoes. Today, many sweet potatoes are incorrectly labeled as yams.

Simple Red Dal and Lime

This dish tastes great and is quick to prepare – tridoshic nourishment in 15 minutes!

Makes 3 servings

Tips

Leftovers can be stored in an airtight container in the refrigerator for up to 1 day. The dal will firm up as it sits overnight, so add a little water if reheating leftovers.

Eat the curry leaves! Ayurveda says (and research confirms) that curry leaves are antidiabetic, antioxidant, antimicrobial, anti-inflammatory, anticarcinogenic and hepatoprotective (they protect the liver from damage). They are a good source of vitamins (A, E, K, B_6 and folate) and minerals (calcium, iron, magnesium, phosphorus, potassium, zinc, copper and manganese). They have long been used in India as a home remedy for preventing graying hair and promoting hair growth.

Gluten-Free ✦ Soy-Free ✦ Vegan		
2 tbsp	ghee or virgin coconut oil	30 mL
½	onion, minced	½
3	curry leaves	3
1 tsp	ground coriander	5 mL
1 tsp	ground cumin	5 mL
1 cup	dried red lentils, sorted and rinsed	250 mL
2 cups	water	500 mL
3 tbsp	chopped fresh cilantro	45 mL
½ tsp	Himalayan salt	2 mL
¼ tsp	crushed black pepper	1 mL
¼ cup	freshly squeezed lime juice	60 mL

1. In a medium saucepan, melt ghee over medium–high heat. Add onion and cook, stirring, for 30 seconds. Add curry leaves, coriander and cumin; sauté for 1 minute.

2. Stir in lentils and water; bring to a boil. Reduce heat and simmer for about 10 minutes or until lentils lose their shape and are soft. Remove from heat and stir in cilantro, salt, pepper and lime juice.

Pitta Kapha Cannellini, Kale and Artichoke Sauté

This dish is well balanced for pitta and kapha. It is too dry for vata.

Makes 3 servings

Tip

To peel and seed a plum (Roma) tomato, simply chop off ¼ inch (0.5 cm) from each end, then use a sharp vegetable peeler to remove the skin. Cut the tomato into quarters and scrape out the seeds using the sharp point of a knife.

SERVING SUGGESTIONS

Serve with a side of couscous, quinoa, pita bread or Cornbread (page 294).

Gluten-Free ✦ Soy-Free ✦ Vegan

3 tbsp	extra virgin olive oil	45 mL
½ cup	finely chopped onion	125 mL
¼ tsp	pressed or minced garlic	1 mL
½ cup	coarsely chopped seeded peeled plum (Roma) tomatoes (see tip, at left)	125 mL
1½ cups	coarsely chopped trimmed kale leaves	375 mL
½ cup	quartered drained water-packed artichoke hearts	125 mL
1	can (14 to 19 oz/398 to 540 mL) cannellini beans, drained and rinsed	1
1¼ tsp	finely chopped fresh rosemary leaves	6 mL
½ tsp	finely chopped fresh oregano	2 mL
½ tsp	Himalayan salt	2 mL
¼ tsp	crushed black pepper	1 mL
¼ cup	water	60 mL
2 tbsp	freshly squeezed lemon juice	30 mL

1. In a large, shallow saucepan, heat oil over medium-low heat. Add onion and garlic; cook, stirring, for about 1 minute or until fragrant. Add tomatoes and cook, stirring often, for 3 minutes.

2. Remove from heat and gently stir in kale, artichokes, beans, rosemary, oregano, salt, pepper, water and lemon juice.

Puy Lentils and Artichokes in Puff Pastry

This is a wonderful dish for those transitioning to a vegetarian diet. The mushrooms add a meaty texture that will provide a feeling of fullness for pitta while being light and warm for kapha. Buttery puff pastry wouldn't be the first choice for kapha, but the filling is friendly to all three doshas (cool, light lentils, astringent and light artichoke hearts and warm, light mushrooms; cooked together with the rosemary and tarragon, the energetics mellow and become compatible). Kapha should eat this in moderation and combine it with a salad.

Makes 4 servings

Tip

Puff pastry can be purchased in the freezer section of the supermarket. Thaw it in the refrigerator overnight, then remove it from the refrigerator 10 minutes before you want to use it. Alternatively, you can thaw it at room temperature for 45 minutes. Unfold the dough onto a smooth, lightly floured surface. With a paper towel, blot any beads of moisture. If the dough has cracks because you tried to unfold it before it was completely thawed, press it back together. Flour a rolling pin. Roll from the center to the edges into the desired shape. If dough starts sticking to the work surface, lift it and scatter some flour underneath.

Soy-Free ✦ Vegetarian

- **Preheat oven to 400°F (200°C)**
- **8-inch (20 cm) glass pie plate**

1½ tbsp	ghee or extra virgin olive oil	22 mL
1	can (14 oz/398 mL) water-packed artichoke hearts, drained and thinly sliced	1
⅓ cup	chopped shallots	75 mL
2½ cups	chopped portobello mushroom (about 1 large)	625 mL
½ tsp	finely chopped fresh rosemary	2 mL
¼ tsp	dried tarragon	1 mL
1 cup	minced seeded peeled tomatoes (see tip, page 128)	250 mL
½ cup	water	125 mL
1 tbsp	tomato paste	15 mL
1 tbsp	freshly squeezed lemon juice	15 mL
1 cup	cooked Puy lentils or French green lentils (see page 62)	250 mL
¼ tsp	Himalayan salt	1 mL
¼ tsp	crushed black pepper	1 mL
18 oz	puff pastry, thawed (2 sheets)	511 g
1	medium egg, beaten	1

1. In a large, shallow saucepan, melt ghee over medium heat. Add artichokes and shallots; cook, stirring, until softened and light golden. Stir in mushroom, rosemary and tarragon; cook, stirring, until mushrooms are softened.

Variation

Replace the artichoke hearts with 1¼ cups (300 mL) peeled jicama or sliced fingerling potatoes, or 1 can (8 oz/227 g) water chestnuts, drained.

SERVING SUGGESTIONS

Serve with steamed seasonal vegetables, a leafy green salad, Puréed Parsnips with Thyme (page 215), Rosemary Roasted Root Vegetables (page 219) or Ginger Pumpkin Soup (page 189).

2. Stir in tomatoes, water, tomato paste and lemon juice; bring to a boil. Reduce heat and simmer for about 5 minutes or until sauce has thickened. Stir in lentils, salt and pepper. Remove from heat and set aside.

3. On a lightly floured work surface, roll out pastry into two ⅛-inch (3 mm) thick circles, one with a diameter of 10 inches (25 cm) and one with a diameter of 8½ inches (21 cm). Place the smaller circle in the pie plate and pour in lentil mixture. Cover with the larger circle, pressing the edges neatly together and crimping with a fork. Slice a small hole in the center and brush pastry with egg.

4. Bake in preheated oven for 20 to 25 minutes or until puffed and golden.

Rosemary-Infused Heirloom Scarlet Runners

Heirloom scarlet runners are high in protein and have a naturally nutty flavor and meaty texture. They taste great with a little rosemary, lemon juice, oil and salt – ideal for a quick weeknight dinner.

Makes 3 servings

Tips

Leftovers can be stored in an airtight container in the refrigerator for up to 3 days. Add to vegetable broth to make a quick soup.

Heirloom beans come from seeds that have been passed down through a family for several generations, preserving their unique sizes, shapes, colors and/or textures. Scarlet runners are colorful and contain healthy compounds that may reduce inflammation and prevent chronic diseases such as cancer and heart disease.

Variations

Add 1 to 3 tsp (5 to 15 mL) grated lemon zest to the dressing.

Add ¼ to ½ cup (60 to 125 mL) Roasted Kabocha Squash or its pumpkin variation (page 220) in step 3.

Gluten-Free ✦ Soy-Free ✦ Vegan		
1 cup	dried scarlet runner beans, sorted and rinsed	250 mL
	Water	
2	sprigs fresh rosemary	2
1	bay leaf	1
2 tbsp	Lemon Dressing (page 242)	30 mL
½ tsp	Himalayan salt	2 mL
¼ tsp	crushed black pepper	1 mL

1. Place beans in a bowl and add enough water to cover by 2 to 3 inches (5 to 7.5 cm). Let soak at room temperature overnight. Drain.

2. In a medium saucepan, combine beans, rosemary, bay leaf and enough water to cover by 1 inch (2.5 cm). Bring to a boil over high heat. Reduce heat to low, cover and simmer for 75 to 90 minutes or until beans are fork-tender. Drain beans and discard rosemary and bay leaf.

3. Transfer beans to a large bowl and add dressing, salt and pepper, tossing to coat. Serve warm or cold.

Dosha Modification

✦ **Kapha** can add crushed garlic or cayenne pepper to the cooking water.

Moroccan Veggie Burgers with Tangy Tamarind Sauce

These veggie burgers are easy to form into patties, and they don't fall apart during cooking. The brown rice keeps them moist, so they are well tolerated by delicate digestive systems. Served with the Tangy Tamarind Sauce, they are well balanced for all doshas.

Makes 6 burgers

Tip

The patties can be prepared through step 1, wrapped in plastic wrap and frozen in sealable freezer bags for up to 3 months. Cook from frozen, increasing the cooking time as needed (they may need an extra minute or two).

Dairy-Free ✦ Gluten-Free ✦ Soy-Free ✦ Vegetarian

- **Preheat oven to 200°F (100°C)**
- **Food processor**

1½ cups	cooked red lentils (see page 62), cooled	375 mL
1 cup	cooked long-grain brown rice (see page 72), cooled	250 mL
½ cup	minced onion	125 mL
¼ cup	green pumpkin seeds (pepitas), coarsely chopped	60 mL
3 tbsp	sunflower oil (approx.), divided	45 mL
2 tbsp	coarsely chopped fresh cilantro	30 mL
¾ tsp	Moroccan Spice Blend (page 270)	3 mL
¾ tsp	Himalayan salt	3 mL
1 tsp	tamarind paste	5 mL
6 tbsp	Tangy Tamarind Sauce (page 258)	90 mL

1. In food processor, combine lentils, rice, onion, pumpkin seeds, 2 tbsp (30 mL) oil, cilantro, spice blend, salt and tamarind paste; pulse until well combined. Form into 6 patties.

2. In a large skillet, heat the remaining oil over medium heat. Working in batches as necessary, add patties to pan and cook, turning once, for 7 to 10 minutes or until browned on both sides. Reduce heat if necessary to prevent burning. Transfer burgers to a plate and place in preheated oven. Repeat with the remaining patties, adding more oil and adjusting heat as needed between batches.

3. Serve drizzled with Tangy Tamarind Sauce.

Dosha Modifications

- **Vata** and **kapha** can add a pinch of cayenne pepper or ¼ tsp (1 mL) paprika to the patty mixture.
- **Kapha** could use mustard (or honey mustard) in place of the tamarind sauce.

Baked Falafel Balls

The brown rice and oil in this recipe balance the dryness of the chickpeas and will greatly assist vata in digestion.

**Makes
2 servings**

Tips

You should have about 1¾ cups (425 mL) drained chickpeas after soaking.

Avoid using canned chickpeas for this recipe. Canned chickpeas are precooked, and the additional baking in this recipe will create falafel balls with a soggy consistency.

Cooked falafel balls can be stored in an airtight container in the refrigerator for up to 3 days. Warm in a 200°F (100°C) oven for 15 minutes.

SERVING SUGGESTIONS

Serve 3 falafel balls in a pita pocket with Vata Sweet Onion Chutney (page 267) or Artichoke Lemon Cream Sauce (page 259) and sprinkle green pumpkin seeds (pepitas) on top. Or serve as part of a Tridoshic Mediterranean Salad Plate (page 241).

Gluten-Free ✦ Soy-Free ✦ Vegan

- **Food processor**

¾ cup	dried chickpeas	175 mL
1	4- by 1-inch (10 by 2.5 cm) strip kombu	1
½ cup	coarsely chopped onion	125 mL
¼ cup	cooked short-grain brown rice (see page 72)	60 mL
2 tbsp	coarsely chopped fresh cilantro or parsley	30 mL
2 tsp	Moroccan Spice Blend (page 270)	10 mL
½ tsp	Himalayan salt	2 mL
¼ tsp	minced garlic (optional)	1 mL
¼ cup	extra virgin olive oil	60 mL
1 tbsp	freshly squeezed lemon or lime juice	15 mL

1. Place chickpeas and kombu in a bowl and add enough water to cover by 2 to 3 inches (5 to 7.5 cm). Let soak at room temperature for 24 hours. Drain, discarding kombu.

2. Preheat oven to 350°F (180°C).

3. In food processor, combine chickpeas, onion, rice, cilantro, spice blend, salt, garlic (if using), oil and lemon juice; pulse about 30 times to a sticky, chunky paste consistency. (Do not purée until smooth.)

4. Transfer chickpea mixture to a large mixing bowl and stir to even out the spices, removing any chickpeas that did not get chopped. Form into 6 balls and place on an ungreased baking sheet.

5. Bake in preheated oven for 20 to 25 minutes or until the center of each ball is solid.

Dosha Modifications

- ✦ **Vata** and **pitta** can top with yogurt sauce (dilute plain yogurt with water to desired consistency and add a grating of lemon zest and chopped fresh cilantro).
- ✦ **Pitta** and **kapha** may opt to top with some freshly squeezed lime juice or sprouts.
- ✦ **Kapha** can add some freshly squeezed lime juice, Kapha Wasabi Dressing (page 254) or Kapha Hot Onion Chutney (page 268).

Dry-Fried Tofu

Tofu is cooling and heavy. It is suitable for pitta; vata and kapha can tolerate it with appropriate seasonings. Dry-frying prevents tofu from crumbling during cooking.

Makes 4 servings

Tips

If you plan to use the tofu in a main dish, cut it into ½-inch (1 cm) thick triangles; for use in a salad or curry, cut it into ½-inch (1 cm) cubes.

Once the tofu has been fried, you can marinate it and use in stir-fry recipes or curries.

Gluten-Free ✦ Vegan

- **Large well-seasoned cast-iron skillet**

1 lb	extra-firm tofu	500 g

1. Drain tofu and cut into desired shapes (see tip, at left). Place tofu pieces between two absorbent cotton towels and gently press to remove excess water.
2. Arrange tofu in a single layer in cast-iron skillet. Cook over medium-low heat to allow any remaining water to evaporate, pressing tofu down gently with the back of a spatula. Once the bottom is firm and golden, turn the tofu and cook the opposite side until golden.

Lime Ginger Tofu

Tofu is generally best tolerated by pitta; here, the lime ginger marinade provides some balance to vata and kapha. Serve with Asian-Style Vegetables (page 218) and purple rice with toasted pecans or Coconut Jasmine Rice (page 233).

Makes 4 servings

Variation

You can substitute shrimp or chopped boneless skinless chicken breasts for the tofu. First, boil the marinade for 5 minutes. Cook shrimp for 2 to 4 minutes or until pink, firm and opaque; cook chicken for 6 to 8 minutes or until no longer pink inside.

Gluten-Free ✦ Vegan

1 tbsp	chopped gingerroot	15 mL
¼ cup	sesame oil	60 mL
2 tbsp	freshly squeezed lime juice	30 mL
2 tbsp	tamari	30 mL
1	recipe Dry-Fried Tofu triangles (above)	1

1. In a nonmetallic bowl, whisk together ginger, oil, lime juice and tamari. Add tofu, cover and marinate in the refrigerator for 30 minutes.
2. Pour marinade into a large skillet and bring to a boil. Add tofu, reduce heat to low, cover and simmer for 2 minutes or until heated through.

Tofu Marsala

Not just for vegans, this tofu Marsala is sure to be a hit with everyone! The warmth of the mushrooms balances the cool energetic of the tofu. Kapha can be liberal with the pepper seasoning.

Makes 4 servings

Tip

Make sure to use extra-firm tofu to make the Dry-Fried Tofu. Soft or silken tofu will not hold its shape in this dish.

SERVING SUGGESTION

Serve over a bed of steamed spinach with a side of pumpkin purée for a nutritionally balanced dish with a colorful presentation.

Gluten-Free ✦ Vegan

• **Preheat oven to 200°F (100°C)**

1	recipe Dry-Fried Tofu triangles (page 137)	1
	Extra virgin olive oil or ghee	
6 oz	cremini mushrooms, thinly sliced	175 g
1/3 cup	finely chopped shallots	75 mL
1 tbsp	dried rosemary, crushed	15 mL
1/2 tsp	Himalayan salt	2 mL
1/4 tsp	crushed black pepper	1 mL
1 cup	Marsala wine	250 mL
1 tbsp	chopped fresh parsley	15 mL
1 tsp	grated lemon zest	5 mL
1/4 cup	almond milk (page 322) or soy milk	60 mL

1. Place the tofu on a plate and cover with foil. Keep warm in preheated oven.

2. Place a large skillet over medium heat and add enough oil to cover the bottom of the pan (about 1/4 cup/60 mL). Add mushrooms and cook, stirring, for about 4 minutes or until starting to brown. Add shallots, rosemary, salt and pepper; cook, stirring, for 4 minutes. Using a slotted spoon, transfer vegetables to a bowl.

3. Add Marsala to the pan and simmer, stirring constantly and scraping up any browned bits from the bottom of the pan, for about 15 minutes or until reduced by half.

4. Return the mushroom mixture to the pan and simmer, stirring, for 1 minute or until heated through. Remove from heat and stir in parsley, lemon zest and almond milk.

5. Divide tofu among four serving plates and top with mushroom Marsala sauce.

Minted Apricot Couscous

Couscous is made from durum wheat or semolina. It is sweet and cool, balancing to pitta and vata. This preparation is balanced for all doshas.

Makes
2 servings

SERVING SUGGESTIONS

Serve with Moroccan Lamb Meatballs (page 173) or Summer Vegetable Soup (page 192).

Dairy-Free ✦ Soy-Free ✦ Vegetarian

1¾ cups	water	425 mL
½ tsp	Himalayan salt	2 mL
1 cup	couscous, soaked for 10 minutes	250 mL
1 tbsp	chopped dried apricots	15 mL
1 tbsp	chopped fresh mint	15 mL

1. In a small saucepan, bring water to a boil over high heat. Stir in salt until dissolved. Stir in couscous and apricots. Remove from heat, cover and let stand for 5 minutes. Fluff couscous with a fork, stirring in mint.

Variations

For a gluten-free version, substitute white quinoa for the couscous and increase the water to 2 cups (500 mL). After adding the quinoa to the pan, reduce heat to low, cover and simmer for 10 to 12 minutes or until tender and liquid is absorbed. Remove from heat and let stand, covered, for 10 minutes before adding the mint and fluffing.

Add ½ tsp (2 mL) grated orange, lemon or lime zest with the mint.

Replace ¾ cup (175 mL) of the water with unsweetened pear or apple juice.

Replace the dried apricots (which are warming) with other dried fruit, such as cranberries, sour cherries or raisins.

Stir in ½ cup (125 mL) roasted cubed sweet potato after stirring in the mint.

Barley Sauté with Sweet Potato, Asparagus and Burdock

Barley is light, sweet, cooling and diuretic; burdock root is cool, bitter, astringent and diuretic – both are beneficial for kapha and pitta. The sweet potatoes, asparagus and tamari dressing add warmth and are grounding for vata. However, vata should eat this dish in moderation, as the energetic is not optimal, tending to be drying, bitter and cooling.

Makes 2 servings

Tips

Burdock root is bitter, cool and mildly diuretic. It promotes the flow of bile and has long been used to detoxify and purify the blood and skin. It has a slippery consistency that soothes mucous membranes. It contains a natural dietary fiber called inulin, which promotes bowel movements, lowers cholesterol and reduces the accumulation of toxins and waste in the body.

Burdock root can be found at farmers' markets, food cooperatives, Asian markets and larger grocery stores during the fall. It is a thin root, about ¾ inch (2 cm) in diameter, that is cut to about 12 inches (30 cm) long. When purchasing burdock root, look for a firm, unbroken root with taut skin.

Dairy-Free ✦ Gluten-Free ✦ Soy-Free ✦ Vegetarian

¼ cup	hulled barley	60 mL
	Water	
1 tbsp	sunflower oil	15 mL
½ cup	cubed peeled sweet potatoes (½-inch/1 cm cubes)	125 mL
2 tbsp	diced burdock root (¼-inch/0.5 cm dice)	30 mL
2 tbsp	sliced shiitake mushroom caps	30 mL
½ cup	sliced trimmed asparagus (1-inch/2.5 cm pieces)	125 mL
¼ tsp	Himalayan salt	1 mL
¼ tsp	crushed black pepper	1 mL
2 tbsp	Tridoshic Asian Tamari Dressing (page 250)	30 mL

1. Place barley in a bowl and add enough water to cover by about 1 inch (2.5 cm). Let soak at room temperature overnight. Drain.

2. In a medium saucepan, combine barley and 4 cups (1 L) water. Bring to a boil over high heat. Reduce heat to low, cover and simmer for about 1 hour or until tender. Drain, return to the pan and cover to keep warm.

Tips

To store burdock root, wrap it in a wet paper towel and seal in a plastic bag. Refrigerate in the vegetable drawer, where it may last several months. If the root becomes limp, soak it in water until firm again.

Burdock root's thin brown skin is often covered in dirt, which can be gently scrubbed off with a vegetable brush. The peel contains nutrients and shouldn't be removed. To prepare burdock root, trim the ends if they look soft and black. Cut the root into pieces of the desired size and place in cold water until ready to use, to prevent oxidation.

When cooked, burdock changes color from white to shiny gray or brown. Its earthy flavor is similar to that of artichoke hearts.

SERVING SUGGESTION

Serve with Ginger Pumpkin Soup (page 189).

3. In a large, shallow saucepan, heat oil over medium heat. Add sweet potatoes and burdock root; cook, stirring constantly with a wooden spoon, for 5 minutes. (Do not stop stirring or the vegetables will burn.) Add mushrooms and cook, stirring, for 5 minutes. Add asparagus and cook, stirring, for about 1 minute or until asparagus is just tender. Remove from heat.

4. In a medium bowl, combine barley, vegetable mixture, salt, pepper and tamari dressing, stirring gently to coat.

Dosha Modifications

✦ **Vata** can add 4 oz (125 g) grilled beef tips in step 4 for additional grounding.

✦ **Kapha** can sprinkle cayenne pepper, hot pepper flakes or minced chile peppers on their serving.

Millet Mash

Millet is warm, dry and light, but adding butter and milk brings balance to the dish.

Makes 2 servings

Tip

If you don't have an immersion blender, you can use a handheld electric mixer or a potato masher.

SERVING SUGGESTION

Serve with Bison Meatloaf with Maple Tamarind Sauce (page 174) and steamed vegetables.

Gluten-Free ✦ Soy-Free ✦ Vegetarian

- **Immersion blender (see tip, at left)**

¼ cup	millet, soaked for 10 minutes	60 mL
1¼ cups	water (approx.)	300 mL
2 tbsp	almond, rice, soy or cow's milk	30 mL
1 tbsp	unsalted butter	15 mL
¼ tsp	Himalayan salt	1 mL
¼ tsp	crushed black pepper	1 mL

1. In a medium saucepan, toast millet, stirring frequently, over low heat for 5 to 10 minutes. Add water and bring to a boil over high heat. Reduce heat to low, cover and simmer for 30 minutes or until millet is soft and has a porridge-like consistency. (You may need to add a little more water, so keep an eye on it while cooking to ensure it doesn't dry out.)

2. Remove from heat and stir in milk, butter, salt and pepper. Purée with immersion blender.

Dosha Modifications

- ✦ **Vata** can add more butter and salt to their serving.
- ✦ **Vata** and **kapha** can garnish with chopped fresh chives or parsley; add a minced clove of garlic during cooking and a squirt of lemon juice at the end; or add ¼ tsp (1 mL) ground cumin or cinnamon and/or ⅛ tsp (0.5 mL) cayenne pepper with the black pepper.

Fluffy Cinnamon Currant Millet

Millet is dry, light and heating and is ideal for kapha. Vata and pitta can enjoy it with the adjustments noted below. Omit the currants and cinnamon if you want a simpler dish.

**Makes
2 servings**

Tip

Leftovers can be added to a salad of leafy greens for pitta and kapha, or to vegetable soup for vata. Or use them to make Millet Breakfast Patties (page 116).

Variation

Make the dish sweeter by replacing ½ cup (125 mL) of the water with unsweetened apple or pear juice.

SERVING SUGGESTION

Serve with Gujarati Wedding Dal (page 128) and steamed greens.

Gluten-Free ✦ Soy-Free ✦ Vegan		
¾ cup	millet, soaked for 10 minutes	175 mL
1¾ cups	water	425 mL
1 tsp	ghee or sunflower oil	5 mL
⅛ tsp	Himalayan salt	0.5 mL
1 tbsp	dried currants or raisins	15 mL
½ tsp	ground cinnamon	2 mL

1. In a medium saucepan, bring water to a boil over high heat. Add millet, ghee and salt, reduce heat to low, cover and simmer for 20 to 25 minutes or until millet is tender and liquid is absorbed. Remove from heat and let stand, covered, for 10 minutes. Fluff millet with a fork, stirring in currants and cinnamon.

Dosha Modifications

✦ To make this dish suitable for **vata**, drizzle some melted ghee over the millet before serving or top with Basic Tahini (page 261), Tridoshic Southwest Pumpkin Seed Citrus Dressing (page 252), Vata Lemon Cashew Cream Sauce (page 262) or Vata Plum Compote (page 263).

✦ **Pitta** can add chopped fresh cilantro or Creamy Yogurt (page 117) to cool the dish.

Millet with Wild Mushroom Vegetable Ragoût

This warm, creamy dish made with cashew milk is perfect for cool, damp weather. The mint, cayenne and lemon zest lighten and balance the cashew cream sauce.

Makes 3 servings

Tips

To julienne vegetables means to cut them into long thin strips (sometimes called matchsticks).

Save the stalks from the fennel for Vegetable Broth (page 182); chop and store in an airtight container in the freezer for up to 2 months.

Try using a French press to rehydrate dried mushrooms; the plunger can be pressed down to keep the mushrooms submerged under the water.

	Gluten-Free ✦ Soy-Free ✦ Vegan	
½ oz	dried porcini mushrooms	15 g
1 cup	boiling water	250 mL
2 tbsp	ghee or extra virgin olive oil	30 mL
8 oz	cremini mushrooms, thinly sliced	250 g
½	onion, chopped	½
3 tbsp	white balsamic vinegar	45 mL
2	plum (Roma) tomatoes, peeled, seeded (see tip, page 131) and chopped	2
1	carrot, julienned (see tip, at left)	1
1	fennel bulb, julienned	1
2 tsp	dried rosemary	10 mL
1 tsp	dried oregano	5 mL
	Himalayan salt and crushed black pepper	
1	zucchini, julienned	1
¼ cup	chopped fresh parsley	60 mL
4 tsp	chopped fresh mint	20 mL
1 tsp	grated lemon zest	5 mL
¼ tsp	cayenne pepper	1 mL
⅔ cup	cashew milk (page 322) or coconut milk	150 mL
¾ cup	hot cooked millet (see page 71)	175 mL

1. In a bowl, rehydrate dried porcini mushrooms in boiling water for 30 minutes; strain, reserving the liquid. Squeeze excess liquid from mushrooms and chop mushrooms.

2. In a medium saucepan, melt ghee over medium heat. Add porcini mushrooms and cook, stirring, until golden. Add cremini mushrooms and cook, stirring, until golden. Add onion and cook, stirring, for 1 minute.

Variations

Substitute chopped string beans, asparagus or Roasted Kabocha Squash (page 220) for the zucchini.

Substitute half a 14–oz (398 mL) can of chopped artichoke hearts, drained, for the carrot.

Substitute 1 stalk of celery for the fennel.

3. Stir in vinegar, scraping up any browned bits from the bottom of the pan. Stir in tomatoes, carrot, fennel, rosemary, oregano, $\frac{1}{4}$ tsp (1 mL) salt, $\frac{1}{8}$ tsp (0.5 mL) black pepper and reserved mushroom liquid; bring to a boil. Reduce heat and simmer, stirring often, for 15 minutes.

4. Stir in zucchini, parsley, mint, lemon zest, cayenne and cashew milk. Cover and steam for about 1 minute or until zucchini is tender. If desired, season to taste with salt and pepper. Serve over millet.

Polenta with Minted Shiitake Sauce

The shiitake mushrooms (astringent, dry and heating) and polenta (sweet, dry and heating) are ideal for kapha. This preparation, however, will be tolerated by all doshas, in moderation. Vata will benefit from the moist, soupy consistency of the dish.

Makes 4 servings

Tip

Try using a French press to rehydrate dried mushrooms; the plunger can be pressed down to keep the mushrooms submerged under the water.

SERVING SUGGESTIONS

Serve with steamed bok choy or asparagus and Tridoshic Arugula, Radicchio and Cherry Salad (page 237).

Dairy-Free ✦ Gluten-Free ✦ Soy-Free ✦ Vegetarian

- **Immersion blender or handheld electric mixer**

Minted Shiitake Sauce

1/4 cup	dried shiitake mushroom caps (stems discarded)	60 mL
1/2 cup	boiling water	125 mL
2	cremini mushroom caps, stems discarded	2
2 tbsp	sunflower oil	30 mL
1/2 cup	chopped onion	125 mL
2 tsp	coconut sugar	10 mL
1/8 tsp	Himalayan salt	0.5 mL
1/8 tsp	crushed black pepper	0.5 mL
1/4 cup	water	60 mL
1/2 cup	rice milk or coconut milk	125 mL

Polenta

1	tube (18 oz/511 g) precooked polenta	1
1 1/2 cups	water	375 mL
4 tsp	chopped fresh mint	20 mL

1. *Sauce:* In a bowl, rehydrate dried shiitake mushrooms in boiling water for 30 minutes; strain, reserving the liquid. Coarsely chop shiitake and cremini mushrooms.

2. In a medium saucepan, heat oil over medium–low heat. Add shiitake and cremini mushrooms; cook, stirring, for 1 minute. Add onion and cook, stirring, for 2 minutes. Stir in coconut sugar, salt and pepper.

Tip

Substituting coconut milk for the rice milk will not impart any coconut flavor.

3. Stir in reserved mushroom liquid and ¼ cup (60 mL) water; bring to a boil, scraping up any brown bits from the bottom of the pan. Boil, whisking, for 5 minutes or until reduced by one-quarter. Remove from heat and stir in rice milk. Using an immersion blender, blend into a chunky sauce. Cover and keep warm.

4. *Polenta:* In a large, heavy saucepan, combine polenta and water. Cook over low heat, whisking, for about 5 minutes or until mixture is a thick, porridge consistency. Stir in shiitake sauce and mint until well combined. Serve immediately (the polenta will firm up as it cools).

Dosha Modifications

✦ If cooking solely for **vata**, you can replace the mushroom sauce with Vata Lemon Cashew Cream Sauce (page 262).

✦ **Pitta** and **kapha** can garnish with mung bean sprouts and/or chopped fresh cilantro.

Quinoa with Spinach Pesto "Cream" Sauce

This light dish is ideal for spring or summer. You can make the spinach pesto ahead and have it on hand for a quick weeknight meal.

Makes 3 servings

Tip

The spinach pesto can be prepared through step 1 up to 5 days in advance. Transfer to an airtight container, top with a layer of extra virgin olive oil and store in the refrigerator.

Variations

Substitute arugula for the spinach.

Replace the cayenne with 1 tsp (5 mL) minced jalapeño pepper.

Substitute almond, soy or cow's milk for the coconut milk.

SERVING SUGGESTION

Serve with Warm Beet Salad with Beet Greens (page 239).

Gluten-Free ✦ Soy-Free ✦ Vegan

- **Food processor**

5 oz	baby spinach (about 5 cups/1.25 L packed)	150 g
2½ cups	packed basil leaves, stems discarded	625 mL
1	clove garlic, pressed	1
½ tsp	grated lemon zest	2 mL
3 tbsp	extra virgin olive oil	45 mL
1 tbsp	freshly squeezed lemon juice	15 mL
⅛ tsp	Himalayan salt	0.5 mL
⅛ tsp	crushed black pepper	0.5 mL
½ cup	coconut milk	125 mL
Pinch	cayenne pepper	Pinch
1 cup	hot cooked quinoa (see page 71)	250 mL

1. In food processor, combine spinach, basil, garlic and lemon zest; pulse until finely chopped, scraping down sides of bowl as necessary. With the motor running, slowly pour the oil through the feed tube; process until smooth, stopping to scrape down sides of bowl as necessary. Add lemon juice, salt and pepper, pulsing to combine.

2. Transfer pesto to a small skillet and warm over medium heat, stirring constantly. Stir in coconut milk and cayenne. Adjust salt, pepper and milk to desired taste and consistency.

3. Divide quinoa among three serving plates. Top with pesto cream sauce.

Quinoa Tabbouleh

This quinoa variation of classic tabbouleh will especially appeal to those with a gluten allergy or sensitivity. Serve warm or cold as a salad or inside gluten-free wraps.

Makes 3 servings

Tips

Make sure the quinoa is completely cool before adding seasonings and dressing; otherwise, the dish will be soggy.

The quinoa can be cooked and the cucumbers and tomatoes prepped up to 1 day ahead; store separately in airtight containers in the refrigerator.

Leftovers can be stored in an airtight container in the refrigerator for up to 2 days.

Variations

Replace the cayenne with 1 tsp (5 mL) minced jalapeño pepper.

Add 1 tbsp (15 mL) raw liquid honey to the Lemon Dressing (if not serving this dish to vegans).

Gluten-Free ✦ Soy-Free ✦ Vegan		
3	green onions, finely chopped	3
1 1/2 cups	chopped seeded peeled plum (Roma) tomatoes (see tip, page 131)	375 mL
1 1/2 cups	chopped seeded peeled cucumbers	375 mL
1/2 cup	chopped fresh parsley	125 mL
1/2 cup	chopped fresh mint	125 mL
1 tbsp	grated lemon zest	15 mL
1/2 tsp	Himalayan salt	2 mL
1/4 tsp	crushed black pepper	1 mL
Pinch	cayenne pepper	Pinch
1 cup	cooked quinoa (see page 71), cooled	250 mL
6 to 8 tbsp	Lemon Dressing (page 242)	90 to 120 mL

1. In a large bowl, combine green onions, tomatoes, cucumbers, parsley, mint, lemon zest, salt, black pepper and cayenne. Add quinoa and gently stir to combine. Add dressing to taste and toss to coat.

Red Quinoa with Endive and Cranberries

Quinoa is a little drying and is great for kapha and pitta. Vata can enjoy this recipe with the modification noted on the facing page.

Makes 2 servings

Tips

In place of the red quinoa, you could use half red and half white, but I recommend that you do not use white quinoa alone, as it will be very bland.

Choose dried cranberries sweetened with fruit juice.

The white balsamic vinegar adds sweetness (and sourness). If you substitute another vinegar, you may want to add 1 tsp (5 mL) of a sweetener, such as raw liquid honey or coconut sugar, to the dressing.

	Gluten-Free ✦ Soy-Free ✦ Vegan	
2½ cups	cooked red quinoa (see page 71), cooled	625 mL
½ cup	coarsely chopped Belgian endive	125 mL
⅓ cup	slivered almonds, toasted (see tip, page 120)	75 mL
2 tbsp	thinly sliced green onions (sliced on the diagonal)	30 mL
2 tbsp	dried cranberries, coarsely chopped	30 mL
2 tbsp	green pumpkin seeds (pepitas) or unsalted sunflower seeds	30 mL
½ tsp	Himalayan salt	2 mL
¼ tsp	crushed black pepper	1 mL
2 tbsp	sunflower, avocado or extra virgin olive oil	30 mL
2 tbsp	white balsamic vinegar	30 mL
2 tbsp	apple cider vinegar or freshly squeezed lime juice	30 mL

1. In a large bowl, using a wooden spoon, gently combine quinoa, endive, almonds, green onions, cranberries, pumpkin seeds, salt and pepper.

2. In a small bowl, whisk together oil, balsamic vinegar and cider vinegar.

3. Pour the dressing over the salad and gently toss to coat. Let stand for 10 minutes before serving.

Dosha Modification

✦ **Vata** can use double the quantity of the vinaigrette or may substitute Vata Tamarind Honey Dressing (page 253) if their diet is not vegan.

Seasonal Variations

You can vary the ingredients by season. Here are some examples:

Summer: Substitute fennel for the endive, golden raisins for the cranberries, and chopped fresh mint for the green onions.

Fall and Winter: Substitute roasted sweet potato or pumpkin for the endive, dried sour cherries for the cranberries, and chopped fresh parsley for the green onions.

Spring: Substitute asparagus for the endive, dried apricots for the cranberries, and chopped fresh chives for the green onions.

Marco's Porcini Risotto

I learned how to make risotto from my friend Marco. He learned as a child from his dad, while living in Bolzano, Italy. Marco didn't cook from a recipe; he just tasted and adjusted seasonings as I watched and took notes. His version had about ½ cup (125 mL) Parmesan and ¼ cup (60 mL) whipping cream – it was quite delicious! This adaptation is a bit more balancing, from an ayurvedic perspective, and only slightly less tasty. The dry, warming mushrooms complement the moist, cooling rice, making the dish suitable for all doshas. *Mangia!*

Makes 4 servings

Tips

Try using a French press to rehydrate dried mushrooms; the plunger can be pressed down to keep the mushrooms submerged under the water.

When cooking risotto, keep enough liquid in the pan so that the rice doesn't stick to the bottom. Stir slowly and constantly. Observe the appearance of the rice as it absorbs the water. The exact amount of water you need will vary. Risotto-making is more art than science. If you add too much water, the rice will be soggy; too little, and the rice will be crunchy.

Gluten-Free ✦ Soy-Free ✦ Vegetarian

½ to 1 oz	dried porcini mushrooms	15 to 30 g
½ cup	boiling water	125 mL
4 to 6 cups	water (approx.)	1 to 1.5 L
1½ tbsp	extra virgin olive oil	22 mL
½ cup	finely chopped onion	125 mL
1 tsp	pressed or minced garlic	5 mL
1¼ cups	Arborio rice	300 mL
½ cup	red wine	125 mL
¼ cup	coarsely chopped parsley	60 mL
¼ cup	freshly grated Parmesan cheese	60 mL
½ tsp	Himalayan salt	2 mL
¼ tsp	crushed black pepper	1 mL

1. In a bowl, rehydrate dried mushrooms in boiling water for 30 minutes; strain, reserving the liquid. Chop mushrooms.

2. In a saucepan, bring 6 cups (1.5 L) water to a simmer; keep hot.

3. In a large, heavy saucepan, heat oil over medium heat. Add mushrooms and cook, stirring, for 5 minutes. Add onions and garlic; cook, stirring, for 2 to 4 minutes or until translucent. Stir in rice.

Variations

Add 1 tbsp (15 mL) chopped fresh rosemary with the parsley.

Add ½ cup (125 mL) chopped asparagus during the last 5 minutes of cooking.

SERVING SUGGESTION

Serve with steamed vegetables and Tridoshic Arugula, Radicchio and Cherry Salad (page 237) with Tridoshic White Balsamic Vinaigrette (page 251).

4. Add wine, stirring constantly so rice does not stick to bottom of pan. When the rice has absorbed 90% of the wine, add the reserved mushroom liquid and stir until 90% of the liquid is absorbed. Add 1 cup (250 mL) simmering water and stir until it is 90% absorbed. Continue adding water, 1 cup (250 mL) at a time, stirring until it is 90% absorbed before adding the next cup, until rice is soft and chewy.

5. Remove from heat and stir in parsley, Parmesan, salt and pepper. Serve immediately.

Citrus Spice Glass Noodle Stir-Fry

Orange, anise and a hint of heat make this dish light, lively and suitable for all doshas.

Tips

After cooking, if desired, cut the glass noodles so they are easier to eat.

Black sesame oil, sake, bunapi mushrooms, enoki mushrooms and kabocha squash are available at Asian markets and some specialty grocers and food cooperatives.

If you cannot find black sesame oil, you can use regular sesame oil.

Variations

Substitute pumpkin or any squash for the kabocha.

Replace the coconut milk and miso mixture with ½ cup (125 mL) Vegetable Broth (page 182) or Ginger Broth (page 179).

Substitute green beans for the asparagus.

Dairy-Free ✦ Gluten-Free ✦ Vegetarian		
1	package (2.4 oz/70 g) glass noodles (mung bean pasta)	1
1 tsp	grated orange zest	5 mL
¼ cup	freshly squeezed orange juice	60 mL
2 tbsp	tamari or soy sauce	30 mL
1 tbsp	black sesame oil	15 mL
1 tbsp	sake	15 mL
½ cup	coconut milk	125 mL
1 tbsp	yellow miso	15 mL
1½ tbsp	virgin coconut oil	22 mL
2 oz	bunapi or enoki mushrooms	60 g
2 tbsp	minced gingerroot	30 mL
¼ tsp	ground anise seeds	1 mL
Pinch	cayenne pepper	Pinch
1 cup	chopped trimmed asparagus	250 mL
2	green onions, chopped	2
1 cup	cubed Roasted Kabocha Squash (page 220)	250 mL
¼ cup	cashew pieces, toasted	60 mL
2 tbsp	chopped fresh cilantro	30 mL

1. Cook noodles according to package directions. Drain.

2. Meanwhile, in a small bowl, combine orange zest, orange juice, tamari, sesame oil and sake. Set aside.

3. In another small bowl, combine coconut milk and miso. Set aside.

4. In a medium skillet, melt coconut oil over medium-high heat. Add mushrooms and cook, stirring, for 30 seconds. Add ginger, anise seeds and cayenne; cook, stirring, for 30 seconds. Add asparagus and cook, stirring, for 30 seconds. Add green onions and cook, stirring, for about 15 seconds or until just wilted. Add orange juice mixture and cook, stirring, for 15 seconds. Reduce heat to medium-low and stir in coconut milk mixture. Stir in cooked noodles and squash. Remove from heat and toss in cashews and cilantro.

Kapha Mushroom and Artichoke Pesto Pizzettes

Especially suited for kapha, these gluten-free pizzettes are warm, light and easy to prepare. Pitta and vata can eat them in moderation.

Tip

The topping can be prepared through step 1 and refrigerated in an airtight container for up to 2 days.

Variations

Substitute 3 thinly sliced artichoke hearts for the mushrooms.

Substitute 1 cup (250 mL) thinly sliced fennel bulb for the mushrooms.

SERVING SUGGESTION

Serve with Tridoshic Arugula, Radicchio and Cherry Salad (page 237) with Tridoshic White Balsamic Vinaigrette (page 251).

Gluten-Free ✦ Soy-Free ✦ Vegan

- **Preheat oven to 375°F (190°C)**
- **Baking sheet, lined with foil**

1 tbsp	virgin olive oil	15 mL
½	onion, thinly sliced	½
5 oz	cremini mushrooms, thinly sliced	150 g
¼ tsp	Himalayan salt	1 mL
¼ tsp	crushed black pepper	1 mL
2 tbsp	balsamic vinegar	30 mL
4	6-inch (15 cm) organic corn tortillas	4
1 cup	Tridoshic Artichoke Pesto (page 281)	250 mL
	Hot pepper flakes	

1. In a medium skillet, heat oil over medium–high heat. Add onions and cook, stirring, for 1 minute. Add mushrooms and cook, stirring, for about 5 minutes or until mushrooms are starting to brown. Sprinkle with salt and black pepper. Add vinegar, scraping up any browned bits from the bottom of the pan. Cook, stirring, until liquid evaporates. Remove from heat.

2. Place tortillas on prepared baking sheet. Using a spoon, spread ¼ cup (60 mL) Tridoshic Artichoke Pesto in a smooth layer on each tortilla. Spread mushroom topping on top, dividing evenly. Sprinkle with hot pepper flakes.

3. Bake in preheated oven for 10 minutes.

Dosha Modifications

- ✦ **Vata** can substitute julienned beets for the mushrooms.
- ✦ **Pitta** can substitute julienned carrots for the mushrooms, and can substitute arugula for the basil in their pesto.

Zucchini Lasagna with Mary's Gravy

This is a lighter, gluten-free variation of a traditional lasagna recipe. It is most suitable for vata, but pitta and kapha can eat it on occasion with light, cooling side dishes such as Tridoshic Arugula, Radicchio and Cherry Salad (page 237).

Makes 4 servings

Tips

Broiling the zucchini slices reduces their moisture content so the lasagna isn't soggy.

The zucchini can be broiled the day before, cooled, then stored in an airtight container.

Leftover lasagna can be stored in an airtight container in the refrigerator for up to 1 day.

You can double the recipe and use a 13- by 9-inch (33 by 23 cm) metal baking pan.

If you substitute other vegetables for the zucchini, make sure they are cooked and drained; otherwise, the dish becomes soggy.

Do not add meat to this dish, as that would make it too heavy from an ayurvedic perspective.

Gluten-Free ♦ Soy-Free ♦ Vegetarian

- **Preheat broiler**
- **Broiler pan, lined with foil**
- **8-inch (20 cm) square metal baking pan**

6	8-inch (20 cm) long zucchini	6
3 tbsp	virgin olive oil, divided	45 mL
1/2	onion, thinly sliced	1/2
8 oz	cremini mushrooms, thinly sliced	250 g
2 tbsp	balsamic vinegar	30 mL
1/4 cup	chopped fresh parsley	60 mL
1/4 tsp	Himalayan salt	1 mL
1/4 tsp	crushed black pepper	1 mL
1/8 tsp	cayenne pepper	0.5 mL
1	large egg	1
1 lb	ricotta cheese, strained	500 g
1/2 cup	freshly grated Parmesan cheese	125 mL
4 to 5 cups	Mary's Gravy (page 158), divided	1 to 1.25 L
1/3 cup	freshly grated Parmesan cheese	75 mL

1. Cut zucchini lengthwise into 1/4-inch (0.5 cm) thick slices. Working in batches as necessary, arrange slices in a single layer on prepared broiler pan and brush lightly with 1 to 1 1/2 tbsp (15 to 22 mL) oil. Broil, turning once, for about 4 minutes per side or until golden. Transfer zucchini to a plate lined with paper towels.

2. Preheat oven to 350°F (180°C).

Variations

Substitute Paneer (page 160) for the ricotta cheese.

Substitute broiled artichoke hearts or summer squash for the mushrooms.

3. In a large skillet, heat the remaining oil over medium–high heat. Add onion and cook, stirring, for 4 minutes. Add mushrooms and cook, stirring, for about 4 minutes or until mushrooms are starting to brown. Add vinegar, scraping up any browned bits from the bottom of the pan. Cook, stirring, until vinegar is absorbed. Set aside.

4. In a large bowl, combine parsley, salt, black pepper, cayenne, egg, ricotta and $\frac{1}{2}$ cup (125 mL) Parmesan.

5. Spread 1 cup (250 mL) Mary's Gravy evenly in baking pan. Top with a layer of zucchini slices. Top with half the ricotta filling, spreading evenly. Sprinkle with half the onion mixture. Repeat layers of gravy, zucchini, ricotta mixture and onion mixture. Add a final layer of zucchini. Top with 1 cup (250 mL) gravy and sprinkle $\frac{1}{3}$ cup (75 mL) Parmesan cheese on top.

6. Bake for 30 minutes. Let cool for 10 minutes, then cut into 4 pieces and transfer to individual plates. Spoon the remaining gravy on top, as desired.

Mary's Gravy

This tomato sauce is adapted from my Italian grandmother's recipe. She never added sugar because she used only naturally sweet San Marzano tomatoes, an heirloom variety with less citric acid than other tomatoes. Mary always added fennel seeds – and a lot of love – to her sauce. Fennel cools and balances the tomatoes.

Makes about 5 cups (1.25 L)

Tip

Once the sauce has cooled, you can divide it into 1- to 2-cup (250 to 500 mL) portions and store it in airtight containers in the refrigerator for up to 3 days or in the freezer for up to 1 month.

Variation

Substitute ¼ cup (60 mL) balsamic vinegar for the red wine.

Dairy-Free ♦ Gluten-Free ♦ Soy-Free ♦ Vegetarian

• Blender

2	cans (each 28 oz/796 mL) whole peeled San Marzano tomatoes, with juice	2
1 tbsp	dried basil	15 mL
2 tsp	dried oregano	10 mL
2 tsp	dried rosemary	10 mL
2 tsp	fennel seeds	10 mL
1 tsp	dried savory	5 mL
1 tsp	dried thyme	5 mL
1 tsp	Himalayan salt	5 mL
½ tsp	crushed black pepper	2 mL
4 tbsp	virgin olive oil	60 mL
½	onion, finely chopped	½
2	cloves garlic, pressed or minced	2
1	bay leaf	1
½ cup	dry red wine (such as Chianti)	125 mL
¼ cup	chopped fresh basil	60 mL
¼ cup	chopped fresh parsley	60 mL

1. In blender, purée tomatoes and their juice until smooth. Set aside.

2. In a small bowl, combine dried basil, oregano, rosemary, fennel seeds, savory, thyme, salt and pepper. Set aside.

3. In a large pan, heat oil over medium-high heat. Add onion and garlic; cook, stirring, for 30 seconds. Stir in herb mixture.

4. Stir in puréed tomatoes and bay leaf; bring to a boil. Stir in wine, reduce heat and simmer, stirring occasionally, for 1 hour. The sauce will thicken and reduce. Discard bay leaf. Stir in fresh basil and parsley. If desired, adjust seasoning with salt and pepper.

Dairy, Fish and Meat Midday Meals

The recipes in this chapter are a mix of light meals derived from animal protein. Small portions of organic meat from animals that were treated humanely can be balancing, grounding and rejuvenating, especially for vata. It is best to consume these dishes as your main meal around noon (between 11:30 a.m. and 1:30 p.m.), when the digestive fire is the strongest – plan accordingly.

Ayurveda is rooted in Hindu culture and the philosophy of yoga, which are premised on compassion and nonviolence. Animal flesh in general is not consumed, because taking the life of another breaches these traditions and results in bad karma. In addition, both yoga and ayurveda teach that animal flesh is heating and heavy and creates feelings of dullness, depression and sleepiness.

However, ayurveda recognizes that animal flesh (and bones) can be beneficial when the body is depleted. In these cases, it prescribes specific meats for specific conditions (for example, rabbit for menstrual issues or mutton for anemia). Meat was traditionally prepared in soups or stews that were cooked for many hours (sometimes days) with specific herbs for optimal assimilation. In addition to the healthy meat recipes in this chapter, look for some restorative soups – Slow Cooker Bone Broth (page 180), Chicken, Lemongrass and Quinoa Soup (page 202) and Iron-Boosting Pomegranate Lamb Soup (page 204) – in the Anytime Soups and Stews chapter. All three soups are based on traditional ayurvedic recipes.

Paneer

Freshly made paneer is considered tridoshic; it is sweet, light and cooling. You may be thinking back to the Food Combining table (page 42) and wondering why I am combining lime with milk here. Well, that table refers to foods that are raw. If you drank a glass of milk and then had lime juice, it would curdle in your stomach and might create digestive issues. But when you cook the milk and lime together, the curdling occurs during the cooking process, so when you ingest the cooked product, it does not create as much of a digestive burden.

Makes 8 oz (250 g)

Tips

Avoid skim or nonfat milk, which generally don't have enough milk fat to separate into curds and whey.

Do not use ultra-high pasteurized milk (UHT); this pasteurization method changes the protein structure in a way that prevents separation.

Do not use a colored cloth; the colors may bleed onto the cheese.

The cheese can be stored, tightly wrapped in plastic wrap, in the refrigerator for up to 1 week. As the cheese ages, its properties change to sour, heating and heavy, so discard any unused portions after a week.

SERVING SUGGESTIONS

Cut paneer into cubes and add it to curries, or crumble it and add it to main-dish salads.

Gluten-Free ♦ Soy-Free ♦ Vegetarian

- **Medium or large sieve or colander**
- **Cheesecloth or thin cotton cloth (undyed)**

8 cups	whole milk (see tips, at left)	2 L
6 tbsp	plain yogurt	90 mL
1 to 4 tbsp	freshly squeezed lime or lemon juice	15 to 60 mL

1. In a large pot, bring milk to a boil over medium heat. Gently stir in yogurt and return to a boil. Stir in 1 tbsp (15 mL) lime juice. The milk should immediately split (the curd solids will separate from the whey liquid). If it doesn't, keep adding lime juice 1 tbsp (15 mL) at a time until the milk splits. Immediately remove from heat and let rest for 2 minutes.

2. Line the sieve with cheesecloth and set over a bowl. Strain curdled mixture through lined sieve. Lift the cloth (with the cheese) from the sieve and fold the cloth around the cheese, squeezing out more liquid as you fold; set the cloth containing the cheese on a plate.

3. Place a heavy pan or dish on top of the cheese and transfer to the refrigerator. The weight will press the moisture out of the cheese. Refrigerate until most of the liquid has drained and the cheese has firmed, about 30 minutes.

Amaranth Crêpes with Pomegranate Syrup (page 110)

Millet Breakfast Patties (page 116)

Yogurt Parfait (page 120)

Gujarati Wedding Dal (page 128)
with Kapha Hot Onion Chutney (page 268)

Baked Falafel Balls (page 136)

Barley Sauté with Sweet Potato, Asparagus and Burdock (page 140)

Red Quinoa with Endive and Cranberries (page 150)

Ginger Salmon Hand Rolls (page 164)

Broiled Lime Ginger
Shrimp (page 162)

Fennel-Crusted Paneer with Balsamic Reduction

This dish is well balanced, especially with the recommended serving suggestions. Fresh paneer is tridoshic.

Makes 3 servings

Variations

Try Tangy Tamarind Sauce (page 258) or Tridoshic Pomegranate Orange Reduction Sauce (page 257) in place of the balsamic reduction.

Substitute extra-firm tofu, cut into 2-inch (5 cm) triangles, for the paneer.

Replace the paneer with 3 halibut fillets (each 8 oz/250 g). In step 3, cook until fish is opaque and flakes easily when tested with a fork.

SERVING SUGGESTIONS

Serve with Kapha Hot Onion Chutney (page 268), steamed vegetables or Brussels Sprout and Sweet Potato Sauté (page 223) and saffron basmati rice.

Gluten-Free ✦ Soy-Free ✦ Vegetarian

Balsamic Reduction Sauce

1	small clove garlic, cut in half	1
1 cup	balsamic vinegar	250 mL

Fennel-Crusted Paneer

3 tbsp	ghee or sunflower oil (approx.)	45 mL
1 tbsp	fennel seeds	15 mL
2 tsp	cumin seeds	10 mL
1½ tsp	ground coriander	7 mL
¼ tsp	pressed or minced garlic	1 mL
¼ tsp	crushed black pepper	1 mL
¼ tsp	ground turmeric	1 mL
1½ lbs	paneer, cut into 2-inch (5 cm) triangles or squares	750 g
	Chopped fresh cilantro	
	Grated lemon zest	

1. *Sauce:* In a small saucepan, combine garlic and vinegar. Bring to a boil over medium–high heat, stirring. Reduce heat and simmer for about 15 minutes or until vinegar is reduced by half (or more if a thicker consistency is desired). Remove from heat and discard garlic. Let cool to room temperature.

2. *Paneer:* In a large, shallow saucepan, melt ghee over medium heat. Add fennel seeds and cumin seeds; cook, stirring, for about 30 seconds or until the seeds pop. Immediately reduce heat to low and add coriander, garlic, pepper and turmeric; cook, stirring, for 1 minute.

3. Add more ghee, if needed, then add paneer in a single layer on top of spices. Cook, gently turning once, until browned on both sides. The seeds will stick to the paneer and make a crunchy coating.

4. Place paneer on a serving plate and drizzle with some of the sauce. Garnish with cilantro and lemon zest. Serve the remaining sauce on the side.

Broiled Lime Ginger Shrimp

These are a perfect blend of zest and zip – there won't be any leftovers!

Variation

Replace the shrimp with boneless skinless chicken breasts, cut into 1-inch (2.5 cm) cubes. Thread chicken onto metal skewers and arrange in a single layer on prepared broiler pan. Broil for 4 minutes per side or until no longer pink inside.

SERVING SUGGESTIONS

Serve with Coconut Purple Rice (page 232) and Asian-Style Vegetables (page 218) or Cinnamon Lotus Edamame Sauté (page 228).

Dairy-Free ◆ Gluten-Free

- **Broiler pan, lined with foil**

1 tbsp	chopped gingerroot	15 mL
1 tsp	coconut sugar	5 mL
1/4 cup	sesame oil	60 mL
2 tbsp	freshly squeezed lime juice	30 mL
2 tbsp	tamari	30 mL
8 oz	large shrimp, peeled and deveined	250 g

1. In a large nonmetallic bowl, whisk together ginger, sugar, oil, lime juice and tamari. Stir in shrimp, cover and marinate in the refrigerator for 1 hour.
2. Meanwhile, preheat broiler.
3. Remove shrimp from marinade, discarding marinade, and place on prepared broiler pan. Broil, turning once, for 1 to 2 minutes per side or until shrimp are pink, firm and opaque.

Dosha Modification

◆ If cooking for **kapha** only, you can add minced chile pepper and garlic to the marinade.

Broiled Salmon in Maple Lime Marinade

Wild salmon is lean and heating – ideal for vata. Pitta and kapha will benefit from eating this lean protein in moderation (note the serving size of this recipe) and served with green vegetables.

Makes 2 servings

SERVING SUGGESTIONS

Serve with purple rice and steamed vegetables (such as asparagus, green beans, carrots, kale or bok choy) or a salad of mixed greens.

Dairy-Free ✦ Gluten-Free

- Broiler pan, lined with foil

6 tbsp	sunflower oil	90 mL
3 tbsp	freshly squeezed lime juice	45 mL
2 tbsp	pure maple syrup	30 mL
1 tbsp	tamari	15 mL
8 oz	skin-on wild salmon fillet, rinsed	250 g

1. In a small bowl, whisk together oil, lime juice, maple syrup and tamari.
2. Place salmon, skin side down, in a shallow nonmetallic dish and pour marinade on top. Turn fish so it is skin side up, cover with plastic wrap and marinate in the refrigerator for 20 minutes.
3. Meanwhile, preheat broiler.
4. Remove salmon from marinade, discarding marinade, and transfer salmon, skin side down, to prepared broiler pan. Broil for 3 to 4 minutes per 1-inch (2.5 cm) thickness. Turn fish over and cook for 2 minutes or until fish is opaque and firm to the touch, the center is a little rare (it will continue cooking while resting) and the meat separates easily from the skin. If it is flaky, it is overdone and will be dry. Let rest for a few minutes before serving.

Dosha Modifications

- ✦ **Vata** can replace 1 tbsp (15 mL) of the sunflower oil with sesame oil.
- ✦ If cooking solely for **vata** or **kapha**, you can add 1 tsp (5 mL) grated orange zest and $\frac{1}{2}$ tsp (2 mL) ground cinnamon to the marinade.
- ✦ If cooking solely for **kapha**, you can skip the marinade and broil the salmon with a little sesame oil, then top with Kapha Wasabi Dressing (page 254).

Ginger Salmon Hand Rolls

Hand rolls are an easy entry into the world of sushi. They are healthy and light, with endless variations to keep meals fun!

Makes 2 servings

Variations

Vary the fillings as per the dosha balancing aids (pages 328–339), but keep them simple — only one or two per roll. Traditional fillings include baby bok choy, watercress, cucumber, avocado, sprouts, lettuce, pickled daikon, green onions, cooked shrimp and cilantro.

Dairy-Free ✦ Gluten-Free

- **Steamer basket**
- **Small food processor**

5 cups	water (approx.)	1.25 L
4 oz	skinless wild salmon fillet (about 1 inch/2.5 cm thick)	125 g
8	asparagus stalks	8
1½ tsp	minced gingerroot	7 mL
1 tbsp	tamari	15 mL
1 tbsp	sesame oil	15 mL
2 tsp	apple cider vinegar	10 mL
2 tbsp	coarsely chopped fresh cilantro	30 mL
2	toasted nori sheets	2
1 cup	cooked short-grain brown rice (see page 72), cooled	250 mL
	Sesame seeds	

1. Pour water into a large, shallow saucepan (the pan should be about half filled with water; adjust accordingly). Bring the water to a boil and then reduce heat until water is slightly simmering. Add the salmon and cook, turning once, for 4 to 5 minutes per side, or until fish is opaque and flakes easily when tested with a fork. Using a slotted spoon, transfer the salmon to a plate lined with a paper towel. Let cool completely.

2. Meanwhile, in a steamer basket set over a pot of boiling water, steam asparagus for about 5 minutes or until just tender-crisp. Let cool slightly, then trim stalks to 5½ inches (14 cm) long. Set aside.

3. In food processor, combine salmon, ginger, tamari, oil and vinegar; pulse until ground into a sticky mixture. Transfer to a small bowl and stir in cilantro.

SERVING SUGGESTIONS

Serve with Dashi Clear Broth (page 178) or miso soup in the winter, or with Wakame Daikon Salad (page 240) in the summer.

4. Cut nori sheets in half, so you have four $7\frac{1}{2}$- by $4\frac{1}{2}$-inch (19 by 11 cm) sheets. With dry hands, place one of the half sheets, shiny side down, on a clean, dry work surface, positioning it so the longer edges of the rectangle are parallel to you. Spread $\frac{1}{4}$ cup (60 mL) rice along the left edge of the nori sheet. Moisten your fingers with water and gently press the rice, spreading it toward the right until it covers one-third of the sheet.

5. Position 2 asparagus stems diagonally across the rice, with the tips overhanging the top left corner. Place one-quarter of the salmon mixture diagonally on top of the asparagus. Sprinkle some sesame seeds on top.

6. Bring the bottom left corner to meet the upper right corner where the rice ends, making a cone shape. Press tightly, then roll in the shape of an ice cream cone to the right edge of the nori sheet. Seal the edge with a few drops of water or a few grains of rice. Let dry for 5 minutes before serving. Repeat with the remaining nori sheets to make 4 hand rolls.

Dosha Modifications
+ **Vata** and **kapha** can add Kapha Wasabi Dressing (page 254) to their rolls.
+ **Pitta** can add tamari and/or lime juice to their rolls.

Chicken Tikka Masala

This dish is inspired by Chef Jasmer Singh's fish tikka masala, which I enjoyed at the Metropolis Hotel in Old Delhi, India. He was very kind to share the ingredients, and I created a nondairy version using chicken. Serve over steamed rice or quinoa.

Makes 4 servings

Tips

To peel and seed a plum (Roma) tomato, simply chop off ¼ inch (0.5 cm) from each end, then use a sharp vegetable peeler to remove the skin. Cut the tomato into quarters and scrape out the seeds using the sharp point of a knife.

To julienne ginger, use a paring knife to peel off the skin. Trim one side to create a flat surface and rest the ginger on that side. Cut the ginger lengthwise into long, thin slices. Stack the slices and cut thin slices through them to make even slivers, or "matchsticks."

Dairy-Free ✦ Gluten-Free ✦ Soy-Free

- **High-speed blender**

3	cloves garlic, pressed or minced, divided	3
2 tsp	minced gingerroot	10 mL
½ tsp	ground cumin	2 mL
½ tsp	ground cardamom	2 mL
½ tsp	Himalayan salt	2 mL
¼ tsp	crushed black pepper	1 mL
¼ tsp	ground turmeric	1 mL
¼ tsp	paprika	1 mL
⅛ tsp	ground anise seeds	0.5 mL
¼ cup	sunflower oil	60 mL
2 tbsp	freshly squeezed lemon juice	30 mL
1 lb	organic boneless skinless chicken breasts and/or thighs, cut into ½-inch (1 cm) cubes	500 kg
2 tbsp	unsalted cashews	30 mL
3	plum (Roma) tomatoes, peeled, seeded (see tip, at left) and coarsely chopped	3
½	onion, cut into quarters	½
1	½-inch (1 cm) piece gingerroot, coarsely chopped	1
1 tbsp	Masala Spice Mix (page 271)	15 mL
¼ cup	chopped fresh cilantro	60 mL
¼ cup	cashew milk (page 322; optional)	60 mL
1 tbsp	julienned gingerroot (optional)	15 mL

1. In a large nonmetallic bowl, combine two-thirds of the garlic, minced ginger, cumin, cardamom, salt, pepper, turmeric, paprika, anise seeds, oil and lemon juice. Add chicken, stirring to coat. Cover and refrigerate for 1 hour.

2. Meanwhile, in a small saucepan of boiling water, boil cashews for 10 minutes. Drain.

3. In blender, combine cashews, the remaining garlic, tomatoes, onion and coarsely chopped ginger; purée until smooth.

4. Transfer purée to a medium saucepan and stir in Masala Spice Mix. Cook, stirring, over medium heat for 2 minutes. Add chicken and marinade; bring to a boil. Reduce heat to low, cover and simmer for 20 minutes or until chicken is no longer pink inside. Stir in cilantro and cashew milk (if using).

5. Divide chicken mixture among four bowls and, if desired, top with julienned ginger.

Spanish Chicken

Hints of cinnamon, orange and sweet paprika lend an international flair to this dish. It is mildly flavored and suitable for all doshas, in moderation.

Makes 4 servings

Tip

If you substitute additional oil for the butter, the chicken will not brown.

Variation

Substitute shrimp for the chicken. Use 1 lb (500 g) large shrimp, peeled and deveined, tails removed. Simmer the sauce for 5 minutes, then add the shrimp and squash; cook for 3 to 5 minutes or until shrimp are pink, firm and opaque and squash is tender.

SERVING SUGGESTION

Serve with Spanish Saffron Rice (page 231), made with the optional steamed peas.

Dairy-Free ◆ Gluten-Free ◆ Soy-Free		
3 tbsp	sunflower oil	45 mL
1 tbsp	butter	15 mL
4	organic bone-in skinless chicken thighs	4
½ cup	finely chopped onion	125 mL
1 tsp	pressed or minced garlic	5 mL
1	bay leaf	1
1 tsp	ground cinnamon	5 mL
1 tsp	ground cumin	5 mL
1 tsp	paprika	5 mL
1 tsp	coconut sugar	5 mL
½ tsp	chili powder	2 mL
½ tsp	Himalayan salt	2 mL
¼ tsp	crushed black pepper	1 mL
2 tbsp	tomato paste	30 mL
2 tsp	grated orange zest	10 mL
1½ cups	water	375 mL
½ cup	freshly squeezed orange juice	125 mL
1 tsp	apple cider vinegar	5 mL
2 tsp	arrowroot flour	10 mL
2 tsp	water	10 mL
¾ cup	chopped yellow summer squash	175 mL

1. In a large, shallow saucepan, heat oil and butter over medium heat. Add chicken and cook, turning, until browned on all sides. Transfer chicken to a plate.

2. Add onion and garlic to the pan and cook, stirring, for 2 minutes. Add bay leaf, cinnamon, cumin, paprika, sugar, chili powder, salt, pepper, tomato paste and orange zest; cook, stirring, for 1 minute. Stir in 1½ cups (375 mL) water, orange juice and vinegar; bring to a boil.

3. Return chicken and any accumulated juices to the pan. Reduce heat to low, cover and simmer for about 10 minutes or until chicken is no longer pink inside.

4. In a small bowl, combine arrowroot flour and water. Stir into chicken mixture. Remove from heat and stir in squash. Cover and simmer for 5 minutes or until squash is tender and sauce is thickened.

Lemon Rosemary Turkey Sausages

These go well with Puréed Parsnips with Thyme (page 215) or Millet with Wild Mushroom Vegetable Ragoût (page 144).

Makes 6 sausages

Tips

If cooking solely for kapha and pitta, use white turkey meat; for vata only, use dark. Otherwise, mix half dark, half white.

The sausages can be prepared through step 1 and stored in a sealable freezer bag in the refrigerator for up to 1 day or in the freezer for up to 2 months. When ready to cook, place frozen sausages on prepared broiler pan and place in unheated oven. Turn on broiler and cook for 5 to 8 minutes or until sausages are browned on top. (As the broiler warms up, it will defrost the sausages.) Turn sausages over and cook until browned on top and a meat thermometer inserted in the center of a sausage registers 165°F (74°C).

Variation

Substitute organic ground chicken for the turkey.

Dairy-Free ✦ Gluten-Free ✦ Soy-Free

- Preheat broiler
- Broiler pan, lined with foil
- Meat thermometer

1	large egg	1
1	clove garlic, pressed or minced	1
2 tbsp	grated onion	30 mL
1 tbsp	chopped fresh rosemary	15 mL
1½ tsp	grated lemon zest	7 mL
¾ tsp	Himalayan salt	3 mL
½ tsp	crushed black pepper	2 mL
1 lb	organic ground turkey (see tip, at left)	500 kg

1. In a large bowl, whisk together egg, garlic, onion, rosemary, lemon zest, salt and pepper. Add turkey, using your hands to combine it with the seasonings. Divide into 6 portions and roll into 6- by ½-inch (15 by 1 cm) sausage links.

2. Place sausages on the prepared broiler pan. Broil for 3 to 5 minutes or until well browned on top; turn sausages over and cook until browned on top and a meat thermometer inserted in the center of a sausage registers 165°F (74°C).

Roasted Turkey Breast with Tarragon Cream Sauce

The cream sauce in this recipe is very light, but moderation and balance are still key. For an even lighter version, use rice milk instead of whipping cream.

Makes 4 servings

Tip

After meat is removed from the oven, it continues to cook and its internal temperature continues to rise. This is called carryover cooking. The larger and denser the piece of meat, the greater the amount of carryover cooking. In a turkey breast this size, the temperature may increase by as much as 5°F (3°C), so you may want to remove it from the oven when the internal temperature is 160°F (71°C). Always let meat rest after removing it from the oven, to allow heat to distribute from the outside to the cool inner core.

Gluten-Free ◆ Soy-Free

- **Preheat oven to 400°F (200°C)**
- **Large ovenproof skillet**
- **Meat thermometer**

2 tbsp	ghee or sunflower oil	30 mL
1½ lb	organic boneless skin-on turkey breast	750 g
½ cup	coarsely chopped shallots	125 mL
1 cup	water	250 mL
1	bay leaf	1
1 tsp	dried tarragon	5 mL
½ tsp	Himalayan salt	2 mL
¼ tsp	crushed black pepper	1 mL

Tarragon Cream Sauce

½ tsp	grated lemon zest	2 mL
3 tbsp	freshly squeezed lemon juice	45 mL
1 tsp	chopped fresh tarragon	5 mL
3 tbsp	heavy or whipping (35%) cream or rice milk	45 mL

1. In ovenproof skillet, melt ghee over medium heat. Add turkey breast and brown both sides. Transfer turkey to a plate.

2. Add shallots to the pan and sauté for 1 minute. Add water, scraping up any browned bits from the bottom of the pan. Return turkey and any accumulated juices to the pan. Add bay leaf and sprinkle with dried tarragon, salt and pepper.

SERVING SUGGESTIONS

Serve with Cranberry Relish (page 269), white or red quinoa and steamed escarole, kale, spinach, green beans or broccoli. Leftover turkey, quinoa and vegetables can be added to Ginger Broth (page 179) or Miso Soup (page 183) and simmered on low heat for 1 minute.

3. Transfer pan to preheated oven and roast (uncovered) for 30 minutes. Baste turkey with pan juices. If the skin is getting too crispy, tent turkey with foil to inhibit additional browning. Roast for 10 to 20 minutes or until a meat thermometer inserted in the thickest part of the breast registers 165°F (74°C). Transfer turkey to a serving platter, cover with foil and let rest for 15 minutes. Discard bay leaf.

4. *Sauce:* Meanwhile, place pan with drippings over medium heat on the stovetop. Add lemon zest and juice; whisk, scraping up any brown bits from the bottom of the pan. Remove from heat and whisk in fresh tarragon and cream.

5. Slice turkey across the grain and serve with sauce.

Dosha Modification

✦ **Kapha** should use a minimal amount of the cream sauce or omit it.

Turkey Cilantro Meatballs

These tiny meatballs are great to add to soups. They cook quickly and can be made ahead of time and frozen for later use.

Makes 18 mini meatballs

Tips

You can make your own gluten-free bread crumbs by toasting a few slices of gluten-free bread and then chopping them in a food processor to coarse crumbs. Store in an airtight container in the freezer to prevent mold growth for up to 2 months.

The meatballs can be prepared through step 1 and frozen in sealable freezer bags for up to 2 months. You do not need to defrost them before adding to soup. Simmer frozen meatballs, covered, in liquid for 10 minutes or until cooked through.

SERVING SUGGESTIONS

Add these to Dashi Clear Broth (page 178) or serve with Escarole with Pomegranate and Sweet Balsamic Dressing (page 212), Cinnamon Lotus Edamame Sauté (page 228) or Ginger-Braised Fennel and Sweet Potato (page 224).

Dairy-Free ✦ Gluten-Free

- **Preheat oven to 350°F (180°C)**
- **Rimmed baking sheet, lined with foil**

4 oz	organic ground turkey (dark meat)	125 g
4 tsp	finely chopped fresh cilantro	20 mL
1½ tsp	dry bread crumbs (gluten-free or regular)	7 mL
1 tsp	grated lemon zest (optional)	5 mL
⅛ tsp	crushed black pepper	0.5 mL
⅛ tsp	Himalayan salt	0.5 mL

1. In a bowl, combine turkey, cilantro, bread crumbs, lemon zest (if using), pepper and salt. Shape into 18 mini meatballs, each about ¾ inch (2 cm) in diameter. Place on prepared baking sheet.

2. Bake in preheated oven for 15 to 20 minutes or until no longer pink inside.

Moroccan Lamb Meatballs

You may be inspired to bring out the candles and linens when the aroma of Moroccan spices starts wafting from the oven! Simple to prepare, yet sophisticated in taste, these meatballs will add a spark to your weeknight meal. I've used quinoa instead of bread crumbs to lighten and cool the heavy, heating lamb – and keep it gluten-free.

Makes 2 servings

Tip

The meatballs can be prepared through step 1 and stored in a sealable freezer bag in the freezer for up to 2 months. Bake from frozen, placing the meatballs in a cold oven, then setting it to 350°F (180°C). As the oven warms up, it will defrost the meatballs. The total cooking time will increase by about 10 minutes.

Variation

Substitute organic ground chicken (half white/half dark meat) for the lamb and omit the garlic.

SERVING SUGGESTIONS

Serve with Minted Apricot Couscous (page 139), steamed green vegetables and Pitta-Cooling Date Chutney (page 265) or, for kapha, Kapha Hot Onion Chutney (page 268).

Gluten-Free ✦ Soy-Free

- **Preheat oven to 350°F (180°C)**
- **Meat thermometer**

8 oz	organic ground lamb	250 g
1	large egg, beaten	1
1/4 cup	minced onion	60 mL
1/2 tsp	pressed or minced garlic	2 mL
2 tsp	cooked white quinoa (see page 71), cooled	10 mL
2 tsp	finely chopped fresh mint	10 mL
1 tsp	Moroccan Spice Blend (page 270)	5 mL
1/4 tsp	Himalayan salt	1 mL

1. In a large bowl, combine lamb, egg, onion, garlic, quinoa, mint, spice blend and salt. Form into 6 balls.

2. Place on a baking sheet so they are not touching. Bake in preheated oven for 20 minutes or until a meat thermometer inserted in the center of a meatball registers 160°F (71°C).

Bison Meatloaf with Maple Tamarind Sauce

Bison is a lean red meat that is heavy, heating and strengthening. The tarragon and quinoa lend coolness and lightness, bringing balance. All doshas can eat this meatloaf in moderation. Kapha and pitta can add a side of sprouts.

Makes 5 servings

Tips

Do not use honey in place of the maple syrup in the sauce; ayurveda states that honey should never be cooked.

Sweet in taste and cooling in action, kuzu root starch is used to aid digestion, clear toxins, rejuvenate the skin, improve longevity, strengthen vitality and rejuvenate the male reproductive system. It is a versatile thickener that dissolves quickly in cold liquid and has no perceptible taste. It is very low in calories and contains no fat. Kuzu binds more strongly than arrowroot but is generally more expensive.

Make extra sauce and serve the leftovers on a corn tortilla with steamed Swiss chard for a gluten-free lunch the next day.

Dairy-Free ♦ Gluten-Free

- Preheat oven to 350°F (180°C)
- Food processor
- 8- by 4-inch (20 by 10 cm) nonstick metal loaf pan
- Meat thermometer

Maple Tamarind Sauce

1/4 cup	tomato paste	60 mL
1 tbsp	tamari	15 mL
1 1/2 tsp	apple cider vinegar	7 mL
1 tsp	pure maple syrup, light (fancy) molasses or coconut sugar	5 mL
1/2 tsp	tamarind paste	2 mL

Bison Meatloaf

1 lb	ground bison	500 g
1 3/4 cups	cooked white quinoa (see page 71), cooled	425 mL
3/4 cup	shredded onion	175 mL
2 tbsp	coarsely chopped fresh parsley	30 mL
1 tsp	dried oregano	5 mL
1 tsp	dried tarragon	5 mL
1 tsp	dried summer savory	5 mL
1/2 tsp	Himalayan salt	2 mL
1/2 tsp	crushed black pepper	2 mL

Gravy (Optional)

2 tsp	crushed kuzu root starch (see tip, at left)	10 mL
2 tsp	water	10 mL

1. *Sauce:* In a small bowl, whisk together tomato paste, tamari, vinegar, maple syrup and tamarind paste.

2. *Meatloaf:* In food processor, combine bison, quinoa, onion, parsley, oregano, tarragon, savory, salt, pepper and 2 tbsp (30 mL) of the sauce; pulse to combine.

SERVING
SUGGESTIONS

Serve with basmati
rice or Millet Mash
(page 142) with
gravy and steamed
asparagus, or with
Puréed Parsnips with
Thyme (page 215)
and steamed
summer squash.

3. Transfer meat mixture to loaf pan and pat down into the pan with the back of a spoon. Top with the remaining sauce, spreading evenly.

4. Bake in preheated oven for 1 hour or until a meat thermometer inserted in the center of the meatloaf registers 160°F (71°C). Transfer meatloaf to a platter and let stand for 10 minutes.

5. *Gravy:* Meanwhile, if desired, place a fine-mesh sieve over a small saucepan and strain the juices from the meatloaf pan into the saucepan. In a small bowl, combine kuzu root starch and water; stir into the juices. Bring to a boil over high heat. Reduce heat and simmer, whisking constantly, until reduced to desired thickness. Serve gravy with meatloaf.

Dosha Modification

✦ **Kapha** and **pitta** can replace half of the bison with ground turkey or chicken.

Rabbit Coconut Fenugreek Stew

This stew is relatively balanced for all doshas. Rabbit is cool and dry, but the coconut sauce balances it. The fenugreek is heating; it reduces vata and kapha and kindles the digestive fire. The black sesame oil gives the dish a rich, distinct flavor. Rabbit cooked in this manner is nourishing, toning and rejuvenative for women's menstrual cycles.

Makes 4 servings

Tips

You can purchase black sesame oil at Asian markets and international stores.

Use a mortar and pestle to coarsely crush the fenugreek seeds.

Cumin seeds (called *jeera* in Indian markets) are generally added whole in Indian cooking. If you find the flavor too strong, experiment with reducing the quantity.

Variation

You can substitute organic chicken parts for the rabbit.

SERVING SUGGESTIONS

Serve with Cornbread (page 294) or wheat chapati.

Dairy-Free ✦ Gluten-Free ✦ Soy-Free

1 lb	bone-in rabbit, cut into parts	500 g
1 cup	chopped onion	250 mL
2 tsp	minced gingerroot	10 mL
1 tsp	fenugreek seeds, coarsely crushed	5 mL
1/2 tsp	coriander seeds, crushed	2 mL
1/2 tsp	cumin seeds	2 mL
1/2 tsp	Himalayan salt	2 mL
1/4 tsp	crushed black pepper	1 mL
5	curry leaves	5
1	can (14 oz/398 mL) coconut milk	1
1 cup	water	250 mL
1 to 2 tbsp	black sesame oil	15 to 30 mL
1 1/2 cups	cubed peeled sweet potatoes (1/2-inch/1 cm cubes)	375 mL
1 cup	green peas	250 mL
2 tbsp	chopped fresh cilantro	30 mL

1. In a large pot, combine rabbit, onion, ginger, fenugreek, coriander, cumin, salt, pepper, curry leaves, coconut milk, water and oil to taste. Bring to a boil over high heat. Reduce heat and simmer, stirring occasionally, for 1 hour or until meat begins to fall off the bones.

2. Stir in sweet potatoes and simmer for 20 minutes. Remove from heat and stir in peas and cilantro; cover and let stand for 5 minutes to steam the peas.

Dosha Modification

✦ **Kapha** can add some minced chile peppers or hot pepper flakes to their serving.

Anytime Soups and Stews

Soups and stews are a great meal any time of day. They are the easiest way to make a tridoshic meal, because when foods are cooked together, the qualities tend to mellow and balance each other. I like to purée soups to give them a creamy texture without the added unhealthy fat or calories of cream, so you'll see a lot of puréed soups in this chapter (an immersion blender will come in very handy). It's a healthy way to prepare a rich-tasting soup.

Commercial broths, stocks and bouillon cubes are generally high in sodium. As a healthier and lower-cost option, the recipes here use water or homemade broth as their base. The flavor comes from the herbs, vegetables and other ingredients in the soup, rather than salt.

Dashi Clear Broth

This recipe makes a concentrated broth that can be used in small quantities as a flavor boost for soups, stews and sauces, or in larger amounts to make Miso Soup (page 183), Dashi Puy Lentil Soup (page 193) or Dashi Noodle Soup (page 200). When used to make soup, it is diluted with an equal amount of water.

Makes about 4 cups (1 L)

Tips

Traditionally, kombu is not boiled, as that is said to make it bitter.

Tororo-kombu is pickled, softened kombu that is layered, pressed and thinly shaved into threads. The light gray strands are then folded and packaged. The texture resembles old, deteriorated gauze fabric. It is generally only found at Japanese stores.

The concentrated broth can be cooled and stored in the freezer for up to 2 months. Use 2-cup (500 mL) airtight freezer containers if you plan to use it to make soup. For use as a flavoring, pour it into ice cube trays; once the cubes are frozen, transfer them to a sealable freezer bag. Each cube is equal to about 2 tbsp (30 mL) broth. Thaw overnight in the refrigerator before use.

Gluten-Free ✦ Vegan

- Sieve lined with paper towels or a thin cotton cloth

1	5-inch (12.5 cm) stick kombu	1
2	dried shiitake mushrooms	2
4 cups	water	1 L
½ oz	tororo-kombu (optional)	15 g
2½ tbsp	tamari	37 mL
2 tbsp	sake	30 mL
2 tsp	mirin or coconut sugar	10 mL

1. Gently wipe kombu with a clean cloth. In a medium saucepan, combine kombu, mushrooms and water. Place a small plate on the mushrooms to keep them submerged. Let stand for 4 hours. Remove the plate.

2. Bring mushroom mixture to just below a boil over medium heat. Using a slotted spoon, remove kombu and mushrooms. Discard kombu. If necessary, cut off shiitake stems and discard. Thinly slice shiitake caps and return caps to the water.

3. Add tororo-kombu (if using), reduce heat and simmer for 5 minutes. Stir in tamari, sake and mirin; simmer for 2 minutes.

4. Strain broth through lined sieve into a spouted 4-cup (1 L) measuring cup and discard solids.

Dashi Clear Broth Soup with Meatballs

To transform this broth into a hearty soup, combine 3 cups (750 mL) each Dashi Clear Broth and water in a medium saucepan. Bring to a boil over medium heat. Add 12 Turkey Cilantro Meatballs (page 172), reduce heat and simmer for 5 minutes. (If using frozen meatballs, simmer for 10 minutes.)

Ginger Broth

Ginger is pungent and warming, and is especially balancing when the weather is cool and damp. Ginger broth can be substituted for water in any recipe that will benefit from a subtle infusion of ginger flavor, such as Red Lentil Winter Stew with Turmeric Root and Kale (page 206), Puréed Orange Ginger Yams (page 222) or Ginger-Braised Fennel and Sweet Potato (page 224).

Makes about 1 cup (250 mL)

Tip

The broth can be cooled and stored in an airtight glass container in the refrigerator for up to 3 days.

Gluten-Free ✦ Soy-Free ✦ Vegan

1 tbsp	chopped gingerroot	15 mL
1½ cups	water	375 mL

1. In a small pan, combine ginger and water. Bring to a boil over high heat. Reduce heat and simmer for 15 minutes or until reduced by one-third. Strain through a fine-mesh sieve and discard ginger.

Slow Cooker Bone Broth

The nutrients in bone broths are easily assimilated and are a great way to restore vitamins and minerals supportive to overall health. Research has shown that trace minerals and gelatin support bone, cartilage and tendon repair. Drink this concentrated broth undiluted. Double the recipe (and use a 4-quart slow cooker) to have homemade broth on hand for cold and flu season.

Makes about 4 cups (1 L)

Tips

Look for pippali at Indian grocery stores. If you can only find whole pippali seed, use 1 seed in place of the ground pippali.

The broth can be cooled and stored in an airtight container in the refrigerator for up to 3 days. Or divide it into 1- to 2-cup (250 to 500 mL) portions and store in airtight containers in the freezer for up to 1 month. Alternatively, pour it into ice cube trays, then, once the cubes are frozen, transfer them to a sealable freezer bag. Use the cubes, which are equal to about 2 tbsp (30 mL), in recipes calling for smaller amounts of broth. Either way, thaw overnight in the refrigerator before use.

Dairy-Free ✦ Gluten-Free ✦ Soy-Free

- **Small (2-quart) slow cooker**

1 lb	organic beef shank	500 g
1	stalk celery, chopped	1
1	clove garlic, pressed or minced	1
½	red onion, chopped	½
2 tsp	chopped gingerroot	10 mL
1 tsp	fenugreek seeds	5 mL
1 tsp	crushed coriander seeds	5 mL
1 tsp	fennel seeds	5 mL
½ tsp	dried oregano	2 mL
¼ tsp	Himalayan salt	1 mL
¼ tsp	ground pippali (Indian long pepper)	1 mL
1	bay leaf	1
2 tsp	apple cider vinegar	10 mL
	Water	

1. In slow cooker, combine beef shank, celery, garlic, onion, ginger, fenugreek seeds, coriander seeds, fennel seeds, oregano, salt, pippali, bay leaf and vinegar. Add enough water to cover the bone, but only fill the cooker three-quarters full (about 6 cups/1.5 L).

2. Cover and cook on High for 2 hours, then cook on Low for 24 to 48 hours. The broth will reduce by about one-quarter.

Tip

If you don't have a slow cooker, the broth can be made on the stovetop. In a large pot, over medium heat, melt enough virgin coconut oil to cover the bottom. Add garlic, onion and ginger; cook, stirring, for 1 minute. Add beef shank, celery, fenugreek, coriander, fennel, oregano, salt, pippali, bay leaf, vinegar and enough water to cover the bones by 1 inch (2.5 cm). Bring to a boil, then reduce heat to low, cover loosely and simmer, stirring occasionally and monitoring the liquid level, for 10 hours. The liquid will reduce by about one-quarter; however, add water if at any point the bones are not completely submerged.

Variation

Any organic bone can be used in place of the beef shank in this recipe.

3. Using a slotted spoon, scoop out the bone and any large pieces of meat. (The meat can be added to the broth or to another recipe.) Strain broth through a fine-mesh sieve and discard solids.

Ayurvedic Wisdom

Ayurveda says, "For all living beings, meat soup is nourishing. This is regarded as nectar for those suffering from consumption [tuberculosis], during convalescence, for the emaciated, and for those desirous of strength and luster. Meat soup prepared accordingly alleviates many diseases. It promotes voice, youth, intelligence, power of sense organs and longevity."

— *Charaka Samhita I, XXVII, 312–315*

Vegetable Broth

When vegetables are cooked together, their flavors meld and their energetics are balanced. This mildly spiced vegetable combination is a great tridoshic broth to drink on its own or use as a base for other soups.

Makes about 4 cups (1 L)

Tips

The broth can be cooled and stored in an airtight container in the refrigerator for up to 3 days. Or divide it into 1- to 2-cup (250 to 500 mL) portions and store in airtight containers in the freezer for up to 1 month. Alternatively, pour it into ice cube trays, then, once the cubes are frozen, transfer them to a sealable freezer bag. Use the cubes, which are equal to about 2 tbsp (30 mL), in recipes calling for smaller amounts of broth. Either way, thaw overnight in the refrigerator before use.

Save the trimmed ends of asparagus or fennel stalks from other recipes to add to the broth. Chop them and store in an airtight container in the freezer for up to 2 months.

Gluten-Free ♦ Soy-Free ♦ Vegan		
2 tbsp	extra virgin olive oil	30 mL
1 cup	coarsely chopped leek	250 mL
2	shiitake mushrooms (with stems)	2
1	clove garlic, pressed or minced	1
2	stalks celery with leaves, coarsely chopped	2
2	carrots, coarsely chopped	2
1/3 cup	chopped daikon radish	75 mL
1	bay leaf	1
8 cups	water	2 L
1	3-inch (7.5 cm) strip wakame	1
1 tbsp	chopped peeled turmeric root	15 mL
1 tbsp	dried parsley	15 mL
1/2 tsp	Himalayan salt	2 mL

1. In a medium saucepan, heat oil over medium heat. Add leek and cook, stirring, for 45 seconds. Add mushrooms and garlic; cook, stirring, for 45 seconds.

2. Stir in celery, carrots, radish, bay leaf and water; bring to a boil. Stir in wakame, turmeric, parsley and salt; reduce heat and simmer, stirring occasionally, for about 1½ hours or until broth is reduced by half. Strain through a fine-mesh sieve and discard solids.

Variations

Substitute 1 cup (250 mL) chopped parsnip or turnip for the carrots.

Substitute onion or shallots for the leek.

Substitute 5 sprigs of fresh parsley, tied together, for the dried parsley.

Substitute button or cremini mushrooms for the shiitake mushrooms.

Miso Soup

In Far Eastern cultures, miso is associated with health and longevity. It has been used to aid digestion, reduce acidity, fight intestinal infections and improve libido. Some studies have shown that it provides protection against cancer and exposure to radiation and heavy metals. The energetics of the sweeter varieties (white and yellow) are more balancing for all constitutions.

Makes 2 servings

Tips

If you cannot find ready-to-use wakame, use a 3-inch (7.5 cm) long strip. Rehydrate as directed in step 1, then drain, chop and measure ½ cup (125 mL) for use in this recipe.

To retain its health benefits, miso should not be boiled. When adding it to a dish, dissolve the required amount in a little water and add it after cooking is complete.

Gluten-Free ✦ Vegan

1 tbsp	ready-to-use wakame	15 mL
	Water	
1 tbsp	non-GMO, gluten-free white miso	15 mL
2 cups	Dashi Clear Broth (page 178)	500 mL
1 tbsp	chopped green onions	15 mL
1 tbsp	chopped fresh cilantro	15 mL

1. Place wakame in a small bowl and add enough water to cover by about 1 inch (2.5 cm); soak for 15 minutes. Drain and set aside.

2. In a small bowl, dissolve miso in 1 tsp (5 mL) water.

3. In a medium saucepan, combine dashi broth and 2 cups (500 mL) water. Warm over medium heat until heated through. Remove from heat and stir in wakame, miso mixture, green onions and cilantro.

Dosha Modification

✦ **Pitta** or **kapha** can add 2 tbsp (30 mL) cooked barley.

Chilled Avocado Soup

This main-dish soup is cooling for pitta and grounding for vata. Kapha should add a lot more spice (see the modification below), follow the serving suggestions and eat only on occasion.

Makes 3 servings

Tip

Store leftovers in an airtight container in the refrigerator for up to 2 days.

SERVING SUGGESTIONS

Serve as a light summertime meal with sides of Tridoshic Arugula, Radicchio and Cherry Salad (page 237) and Cornbread (page 294), or as an accompaniment to Kapha Mushroom and Artichoke Pesto Pizzettes (page 155). Kapha can garnish with thin radish slices.

Gluten-Free ✦ Soy-Free ✦ Vegan

- Blender

5	avocados, peeled and pitted	5
1/4 cup	chopped fresh cilantro	60 mL
1/2 tsp	Himalayan salt	2 mL
1/4 tsp	paprika	1 mL
5 cups	Vegetable Broth (page 182)	1.25 L
1/4 cup	freshly squeezed lime juice	60 mL
	Additional chopped fresh cilantro (optional)	
	Julienned radish (optional)	

1. In blender, combine avocados, cilantro, salt, paprika, broth and lime juice; purée until smooth. Refrigerate for 1 hour, until chilled.

2. Ladle soup into bowls. If desired, garnish with cilantro and radish.

Dosha Modification

✦ **Kapha** can warm this up by adding 1/4 tsp (1 mL) cayenne pepper or wasabi paste to their serving.

Creamy Beet Leek Soup

Beets are sweet with a warming energy, making them suitable for vata and kapha. When cooked, the flavor of beets mellows. Some of my pitta friends feel that peeling beets reduces their pungency. I have found that beets vary significantly depending on where they were grown. So experiment for yourselves and follow your intuition.

Makes 4 servings

Tips

If you don't have an immersion blender, you can purée the soup in batches in a regular blender.

Before puréeing the soup, transfer a few beet pieces to a cutting board and cut into ½-inch (1 cm) cubes to use as a garnish.

Variation

Beet Sweet Potato Soup: Substitute 2½ cups (625 mL) chopped peeled sweet potato for the carrots and reduce the beets to 2 cups (500 mL) to create a cooler energetic with a beautiful magenta color!

SERVING SUGGESTIONS

Serve with Moroccan Veggie Burgers with Tangy Tamarind Sauce (page 135), Baked Falafel Balls (page 136), Lime Ginger Tofu (page 137) or Marco's Porcini Risotto (page 152).

Gluten-Free ✦ Soy-Free ✦ Vegan

- **Immersion blender (see tip, at left)**

1 tbsp	ghee or sunflower oil	15 mL
1 cup	chopped leeks (white and light green parts only)	250 mL
3 cups	chopped peeled beets	750 mL
1½ cups	chopped carrots	375 mL
1 tsp	ground coriander	5 mL
1 tsp	Himalayan salt	5 mL
½ tsp	crushed black pepper	2 mL
2 tsp	grated orange zest	10 mL
4 cups	water	1 L

1. In a large saucepan, melt ghee over medium–low heat. Add leeks and cook, stirring, until translucent, about 3 minutes.

2. Stir in beets, carrots, coriander, salt, pepper, orange zest and water; bring to a boil. Reduce heat to low, cover and simmer, stirring occasionally, for about 25 minutes or until vegetables are tender. Purée soup with immersion blender.

Dosha Modification

✦ **Vata** and **pitta** can top their serving with 1 tbsp (15 mL) minted yogurt. To make minted yogurt, whisk together 1 cup (250 mL) plain yogurt (regular or dairy-free), 2 tsp (10 mL) chopped fresh mint and 1 tsp (5 mL) rice syrup, coconut sugar or pure maple syrup. Leftovers can be stored in an airtight container in the refrigerator for up to 5 days.

Chilled Carrot Soup with Avocado

This tridoshic main-dish soup can be served hot when the weather is cool or chilled in the summer.

**Makes
3 servings**

Tips

You can also use an immersion blender in this recipe, but a regular or high-powered blender will produce a velvety smooth texture.

If chilling the soup, wait to chop the avocados until just prior to serving.

Store leftovers in an airtight container in the refrigerator for up to 2 days.

Change up the garnish: try julienned gingerroot (for kapha or vata), toasted sliced almonds, steamed heirloom carrot slices, pea sprouts or Cranberry Relish (page 269).

Variation

Add 1 cup (250 mL) chopped fennel bulb with the shallots.

**SERVING
SUGGESTIONS**

Pair with Mizuna Mixed Greens Salad (page 236) and Lime Ginger Tofu (page 137) or Moroccan Lamb Meatballs (page 173).

Gluten-Free ✦ Soy-Free ✦ Vegan

- Blender

2 tbsp	extra virgin olive oil	30 mL
½ cup	chopped shallots	125 mL
1 tsp	finely chopped gingerroot	5 mL
½ tsp	Himalayan salt	2 mL
½ tsp	ground cinnamon	2 mL
¼ tsp	ground nutmeg	1 mL
4	carrots, chopped	4
3 cups	Vegetable Broth (page 182)	750 mL
1 cup	water	250 mL
½ cup	chopped fresh cilantro	125 mL
Pinch	cayenne pepper (optional)	Pinch
½ cup	coconut milk	125 mL
1 tsp	grated lime zest	5 mL
2 tbsp	freshly squeezed lime juice	30 mL
6 tbsp	cubed avocados	90 mL
	Additional chopped fresh cilantro (optional)	

1. In a medium saucepan, heat oil over medium heat. Add shallots and ginger; cook, stirring, until fragrant. Sprinkle in salt, cinnamon and nutmeg; cook, stirring, for 30 seconds.

2. Stir in carrots, broth and water; bring to a boil. Reduce heat to medium-low, cover, leaving lid ajar, and simmer, stirring occasionally, for about 30 minutes or until carrots are tender.

3. Working in batches, transfer soup to a blender and add cilantro, cayenne (if using), coconut milk, lime zest and lime juice; purée until smooth. Serve hot or cover and refrigerate for 1 hour, until chilled.

4. Divide avocados among three bowls and ladle soup on top. Garnish with cilantro, if desired.

Creamy Corn Soup

This soup is well balanced for pitta and kapha. Vata can enjoy it with the modifications noted below.

Makes 2 servings

Tips

If you don't have an immersion blender, you can purée the soup in batches in a regular blender.

Do not substitute a nondairy alternative for the butter or ghee, as butter is the main flavoring in this soup.

A quick way to steam frozen corn is to add it to a skillet, cover and steam over low heat for 1 or 2 minutes or just until warm to the touch. There is normally some ice on the corn from being frozen that will serve to steam it; if not, add about ¼ cup (60 mL) water to the pan.

SERVING SUGGESTIONS

Serve with Moroccan Veggie Burgers with Tangy Tamarind Sauce (page 135), Bison Meatloaf with Maple Tamarind Sauce (page 174) or Warm Beet Salad with Beet Greens (page 239).

Gluten-Free ✦ Soy-Free ✦ Vegetarian

- **Immersion blender (see tip, at left)**

2 tsp	unsalted butter or ghee	10 mL
1 cup	chopped onion	250 mL
1 cup	chopped peeled yellow-fleshed potato (such as Yukon Gold)	250 mL
½ tsp	Himalayan salt	2 mL
4 cups	water	1 L
10 oz	frozen organic corn, steamed (see tip, at left)	300 g

1. In a medium saucepan, melt butter over medium-low heat. Add onion and cook, stirring, for 3 minutes.

2. Stir in potato, salt and water; bring to a boil. Reduce heat and simmer, stirring occasionally, for about 15 minutes or until potato is tender.

3. Remove from heat and stir in half the corn. Purée with immersion blender. Stir in half of the remaining corn.

4. Ladle soup into bowls and garnish with the remaining corn.

Dosha Modification

✦ **Vata** should add extra salt and ghee or butter to their serving.

Mushroom Tarragon Purée

The coconut milk and tarragon help cool the energetics of the warm mushrooms. The small amount of coconut milk does not impart any coconut taste.

Makes 2 servings

Tips

Try using a French press to rehydrate dried mushrooms; the plunger can be pressed down to keep the mushrooms submerged under the water.

Coconut milk is readily available in the international food aisle of most grocery stores. It comes in 13.5- or 14-oz (400 mL) cans and has a long shelf life. The milk and cream tend to separate inside the can, so shake the can vigorously before opening it. Once opened, transfer unused coconut milk to an airtight container and store in the refrigerator for up to 1 week.

SERVING SUGGESTIONS

Serve with a salad of mixed greens and Red Quinoa with Endive and Cranberries (page 150) or Autumn Wild Rice Salad (page 246).

Gluten-Free ✦ Soy-Free ✦ Vegan

- **Immersion blender (see tip, page 187)**

¼ cup	dried shiitake mushroom caps (stems discarded)	60 mL
1 cup	boiling water	250 mL
2 tbsp	sunflower oil	30 mL
1½ tsp	minced shallots	7 mL
½ cup	sliced button mushroom caps	125 mL
½ cup	sliced portobello or cremini mushroom caps	125 mL
¾ cup	chopped peeled red-skinned potato	175 mL
¼ tsp	Himalayan salt	1 mL
⅛ tsp	crushed black pepper	0.5 mL
⅛ tsp	dried tarragon	0.5 mL
1¼ cups	water	300 mL
¼ cup	coconut milk	60 mL
1 tbsp	freshly squeezed lemon juice	15 mL

1. In a bowl, rehydrate shiitake mushrooms in boiling water for 30 minutes; strain, reserving the liquid. Slice mushrooms.

2. In a medium saucepan, heat oil over medium–low heat. Add shallots and cook, stirring gently, for 2 minutes. Add shiitake, button and portobello mushroom caps; cook, stirring constantly, for 2 minutes.

3. Stir in potato, salt, pepper, tarragon, water and reserved mushroom liquid; bring to a boil. Reduce heat and simmer, stirring occasionally, for 15 to 20 minutes or until potato is tender.

4. Remove from heat and stir in coconut milk and lemon juice. Purée with immersion blender.

Dosha Modification

✦ If cooking solely for **pitta**, increase the potato to 1 cup (250 mL) and reduce the lemon juice to 1 tsp (5 mL).

Ginger Pumpkin Soup

Fresh ginger and a touch of cinnamon puréed into a creamy soup – tridoshic heaven for fall, winter or spring!

Tips

For a thinner consistency, increase the water to 4 cups (1 L) in step 3.

Grated orange zest makes an appealing garnish for this soup.

Variations

Substitute acorn or butternut squash for the pumpkin.

Add a star anise pod or a pinch of ground mace with the water. (Discard star anise at the end of cooking.)

For a heartier dish, add ½ cup (125 mL) cooked quinoa (see page 71) with the pumpkin.

SERVING SUGGESTIONS

Serve with Puy Lentils and Artichokes in Puff Pastry (page 132), French Lentil Salad (page 242), Fennel-Crusted Paneer with Balsamic Reduction (page 161) or Moroccan Lamb Meatballs (page 173).

Gluten-Free ✦ Soy-Free ✦ Vegan

- Immersion blender (see tip, page 187)

1 tsp	coconut sugar or pure maple syrup	5 mL
½ tsp	Himalayan salt	2 mL
½ tsp	ground coriander	2 mL
½ tsp	ground cinnamon	2 mL
⅛ tsp	paprika	0.5 mL
1 tbsp	unsalted butter or sunflower oil	15 mL
½ cup	chopped onion	125 mL
1 tsp	chopped gingerroot	5 mL
2 cups	chopped seeded peeled pumpkin	500 mL
1 cup	chopped peeled sweet potato	250 mL
3 cups	water	750 mL
2 tbsp	green pumpkin seeds (pepitas)	30 mL

1. In a small bowl, combine sugar, salt, coriander, cinnamon and paprika.

2. In a medium saucepan, melt butter over medium heat. Add onion and ginger; cook, stirring, for 2 minutes. Stir in spice mixture.

3. Stir in pumpkin, potato and water; bring to a boil. Reduce heat and simmer, stirring occasionally, for 15 to 20 minutes or until vegetables are tender. Purée with immersion blender. Serve garnished with pumpkin seeds.

Puréed Potato-Leek Soup with Asparagus and Lemon

This tridoshic main-dish soup can be served warm or chilled (see tip) to balance seasonal energies. It pairs well with Tridoshic Arugula, Radicchio and Cherry Salad (page 237). For a heartier meal, serve with Lemon Rosemary Turkey Sausages (page 169), Broiled Lime Ginger Shrimp (page 162) or Autumn Wild Rice Salad (page 246).

Makes 3 servings

Tips

To prepare leeks, remove the tough outer stalks. Slice about ¼ inch (0.5 cm) from the bottom (white) end and discard. Slice the dark green tops off and discard. Cut the leek in half lengthwise and rinse under cold water, spreading apart the layers to remove dirt.

To serve chilled, prepare through step 6, then transfer the soup and the garnish ingredients to separate airtight containers and refrigerate for 1 hour.

Dairy-Free ✦ Gluten-Free ✦ Soy-Free ✦ Vegetarian

• **Blender or immersion blender**

10	stalks asparagus, trimmed	10
1 tbsp	ghee or extra virgin olive oil	15 mL
2 cups	chopped leeks (white and light green parts only)	500 mL
1 cup	chopped fennel bulb, fronds reserved	250 mL
3 cups	chopped peeled yellow-fleshed potatoes (such as Yukon gold)	750 mL
3	sprigs fresh thyme, tied together	3
1	bay leaf	1
¾ tsp	Himalayan salt	3 mL
½ tsp	crushed black pepper	2 mL
	Water	
1 tsp	grated lemon zest	5 mL
¼ cup	freshly squeezed lemon juice	60 mL
	Lemon wedges (optional)	

1. Cut off the top 2 inches (5 cm) of the asparagus tips, holding the knife on the diagonal; set aside. Chop the remaining asparagus stalks.

2. In a medium saucepan, melt ghee over medium heat. Add leeks and cook, stirring, for about 2 minutes or until wilted. Add fennel bulb and cook, stirring, for about 3 minutes or until softened.

3. Stir in chopped asparagus stalks, potatoes, thyme, bay leaf, salt, pepper and 4 cups (1 L) water; bring to a boil. Reduce heat and simmer, stirring occasionally, for about 15 minutes or until potatoes are tender. Discard thyme and bay leaf.

4. Meanwhile, in a small saucepan, add enough water to cover the bottom of the pan by $\frac{1}{4}$ inch (0.5 cm). Bring to a boil over medium heat. Add asparagus tips and boil until bright green and tender. Set aside.

5. Cut the reserved fennel fronds into 1-inch (2.5 cm) lengths. Set aside.

6. Working in batches, transfer soup to blender and purée (or purée in the pan with an immersion blender). Be careful not to over-blend, or the soup will get gluey. Stir in lemon zest and lemon juice.

7. Ladle soup into bowls and garnish with asparagus tips and fennel fronds. Serve warm, with a wedge of lemon, if desired.

Summer Vegetable Soup

Fresh seasonal vegetables are the star of this simple, light, healthy midweek meal. Cooking vegetables together in a soup balances out the energetics, so have some fun and experiment with your favorite veggies.

Makes 3 servings

Tips

Leeks have a sweet, mild oniony taste. If you can't find them, substitute an onion.

If you use fresh tarragon and savory, chop ¾ tsp (3 mL) each and add them during the last few minutes of cooking.

Variations

Add ½ cup (125 mL) cooked cannellini beans or chickpeas for a heartier soup.

Substitute 1 tbsp (15 mL) lemon juice for the apple cider vinegar.

SERVING SUGGESTIONS

Serve with a salad of mixed greens, Minted Apricot Couscous (page 139) or Bhutanese red rice.

Gluten-Free ✦ Soy-Free ✦ Vegan		
1½ tbsp	sunflower oil	22 mL
½ cup	chopped leeks (white and light green parts only)	125 mL
½ tsp	Himalayan salt	2 mL
¼ tsp	crushed black pepper	1 mL
¼ tsp	dried tarragon	1 mL
¼ tsp	dried savory	1 mL
1 cup	chopped red-skinned potato (¾-inch/2 cm pieces)	250 mL
½ cup	coarsely chopped carrots	125 mL
¼ cup	coarsely chopped seeded peeled tomatoes (see tip, page 128)	60 mL
3 cups	water	750 mL
½ cup	chopped green beans	125 mL
¼ cup	coarsely chopped yellow summer squash	60 mL
¼ tsp	apple cider vinegar	1 mL

1. In a medium saucepan, heat oil over low heat. Add leeks and cook, stirring, until fragrant. Stir in salt, pepper, tarragon and savory.

2. Stir in potato, carrots, tomatoes and water; bring to a boil. Reduce heat to low, cover and simmer, stirring occasionally, for about 10 minutes or until potato and carrots are almost tender. Add beans, squash and vinegar; simmer for about 5 minutes or until vegetables are tender.

Winter Chestnut Soup

This creamy soup is balancing for vata; pitta and kapha can eat it on occasion.

Makes 3 servings

Tip

If you don't have an immersion blender, you can purée the soup in batches in a regular blender.

Variation

To make this recipe vegan, substitute almond milk or a cashew cream sauce for the cream.

SERVING SUGGESTION

Serve with Ginger Almond Squash Pie (page 221).

Gluten-Free ◆ Soy-Free ◆ Vegetarian

- **Immersion blender (see tip, at left)**

3 tbsp	sunflower oil	45 mL
1	bay leaf	1
1 cup	finely chopped onion	250 mL
1	jar (15 oz/425 mL) peeled roasted chestnuts, drained	1
1/2 tsp	Himalayan salt	2 mL
1/2 tsp	crushed black pepper	2 mL
1/2 tsp	dried sage	2 mL
4 cups	water	1 L
1/4 cup	cream (any type)	60 mL

1. In a medium saucepan, heat oil over medium heat. Add bay leaf and onion; cook, stirring, for about 3 minutes or until onion is light golden. Add chestnuts, salt, pepper and sage; cook, stirring, for 2 minutes.

2. Add the water and bring to a boil. Reduce heat and simmer, stirring occasionally, for about 10 minutes or until chestnuts are tender. Remove from heat and stir in cream. Purée with immersion blender.

Dashi Puy Lentil Soup

Grounding and light, this is my favorite meal when I've had a stressful day and don't have much energy or time to cook.

Makes 2 servings

Gluten-Free ◆ Vegan

1/2 cup	Puy lentils	125 mL
1/2 cup	thinly sliced carrots	125 mL
2 cups	Dashi Clear Broth (page 178)	500 mL
2 cups	water	500 mL

1. In a medium saucepan, combine lentils, carrots, broth and water. Bring to a boil over high heat. Reduce heat and simmer, stirring occasionally, for about 20 minutes or until carrots and lentils are tender.

Borscht Lentil Soup

This soup made of vegetables and lentils is easy for all digestive systems and provides a hearty, balanced meal. The warm, pungent beets are cooled by the bitter beet greens. Mild napa cabbage is the easiest cabbage for vata to tolerate, especially in a soup.

Makes 3 servings

SERVING SUGGESTIONS

Serve with Paneer (page 160) or Fennel-Crusted Paneer with Balsamic Reduction (page 161).

Gluten-Free ✦ Soy-Free ✦ Vegan

4	beets, with greens	4
1 tbsp	sunflower oil	15 mL
1/2 cup	chopped onion	125 mL
1 cup	shredded napa cabbage	250 mL
1/2 cup	diced carrots	125 mL
1/2 cup	Puy lentils	125 mL
5 cups	water	1.25 L
1/2 tsp	dried dillweed	2 mL
1/2 tsp	Himalayan salt	2 mL
1/4 tsp	crushed black pepper	1 mL
2 tbsp	freshly squeezed lemon juice	30 mL
1 tbsp	white balsamic vinegar	15 mL

1. Remove beet greens from beets, trim off tough stems and chop leaves into 1-inch (2.5 cm) pieces; set aside. Peel beets and cut into 1/2-inch (1 cm) cubes.

2. In a medium saucepan, heat oil over medium heat. Add onion and cook, stirring, for 3 minutes.

3. Stir in beets, cabbage, carrots, lentils and water; bring to a boil. Reduce heat and simmer, stirring occasionally, for about 20 minutes or until beets and lentils are tender.

4. Remove from heat and stir in beet greens, dill, salt, pepper, lemon juice and vinegar. Cover and let stand for about 5 minutes or until beet greens are wilted.

Dosha Modification

✦ **Vata** and **pitta** can garnish their serving with a large dollop of plain yogurt.

Mung Dal Cilantro Soup

This is my re-creation of a dish I would eat at the Tandoori Grill in Boulder, Colorado. When I worked late and was too tired to cook, I would pair this soup with naan smothered in ghee and call it dinner. It is my Indian comfort food. The lentils are well soaked, making them more balancing to vata. The mild spices are suitable for pitta; kapha can sprinkle some hot pepper flakes on their serving.

**Makes
3 servings**

Tips

If you don't have an immersion blender, you can purée the soup in batches in a regular blender.

For a vegan soup, replace the ghee with sunflower oil.

Be careful not to burn the mustard seeds or they will impart a bitter taste to your dish.

SERVING SUGGESTIONS

Serve with steamed green vegetables and roti or corn tortillas. For a midday meal, add a serving of brown rice and steamed vegetables.

Gluten-Free ✦ Soy-Free ✦ Vegetarian

• **Immersion blender (see tip, at left)**

1 cup	mung dal, sorted and rinsed	250 mL
	Water	
1	bay leaf	1
1/4 tsp	ground turmeric	1 mL
1 tbsp	grapeseed oil	15 mL
2 tsp	ghee	10 mL
1 tsp	cumin seeds	5 mL
1/2 tsp	coriander seeds, crushed	2 mL
1/2 tsp	black mustard seeds	2 mL
4	curry leaves	4
1 tsp	pressed or minced garlic	5 mL
1/2 tsp	Himalayan salt	2 mL
1/8 tsp	crushed black pepper	0.5 mL
3 tbsp	coarsely chopped fresh cilantro	45 mL

1. Place mung dal in a bowl and add enough water to cover by 2 to 3 inches (5 to 7.5 cm). Let soak at room temperature overnight. Drain.

2. In a medium saucepan, combine dal, bay leaf, turmeric, 2½ cups (625 mL) water and grapeseed oil; bring to a boil. Reduce heat and simmer for about 20 minutes or until dal is soft. Discard bay leaf. Purée soup with immersion blender, cover and keep warm.

3. In a medium skillet, melt ghee over medium–low heat. Add cumin seeds, coriander seeds and black mustard seeds; cook, stirring, for about 30 seconds or until the mustard seeds pop. Stir in curry leaves and garlic.

4. Add spice mixture to dal and season with salt and pepper. Stir in cilantro.

Puréed Lemon Chickpea Soup

If you like hummus and other Middle Eastern dishes, you'll love this – and it's a great intro to vegetarian cooking! The oregano and bay leaf add warmth to the cool energetics of the chickpeas, aiding digestibility.

Makes 3 servings

Tip

If you don't have an immersion blender, you can purée the soup in batches in a regular blender.

SERVING SUGGESTIONS

Serve with blue corn chips or pita bread, or with Moroccan Veggie Burgers with Tangy Tamarind Sauce (page 135) or Autumn Wild Rice Salad (page 246).

Gluten-Free ✦ Soy-Free ✦ Vegan

- Immersion blender (see tip, at left)

1 tbsp	avocado or sunflower oil	15 mL
½ cup	chopped onion	125 mL
1	can (14 to 19 oz/398 to 540 mL) chickpeas, drained and rinsed	1
1	bay leaf	1
1 tsp	dried oregano	5 mL
½ tsp	Himalayan salt	2 mL
¼ tsp	crushed black pepper	1 mL
4 cups	water	1 L
2 tbsp	freshly squeezed lemon juice	30 mL

1. In a large saucepan, heat oil over medium-low heat. Add onion and cook, stirring, until translucent.

2. Stir in chickpeas, bay leaf, oregano, salt, pepper and water; increase heat and bring to a boil. Reduce heat and simmer, stirring occasionally, for 30 minutes. Discard bay leaf. Add lemon juice. Purée with immersion blender.

Dosha Modifications

✦ **Vata** and **pitta** can serve with Vata Pitta Avocado Cucumber Salad (page 238); vata can add a tahini dressing.

✦ **Vata** and **kapha** can add ½ tsp (2 mL) pressed garlic or cayenne pepper with the onion.

✦ **Pitta** and **kapha** can serve with a chicory and mixed greens salad with lime juice.

Kapha Pitta Barley Kale Soup

This hearty one-dish meal is balancing for pitta and kapha. Vata can enjoy it with the modifications noted below.

Makes 2 servings

Tip

Hulled barley is a whole grain with only the inedible outer hull removed. It is brown in color and contains gluten. For optimal digestion, soak the barley overnight. If I know I'm going to make a barley recipe during the week, I will soak it on Sunday night, then on Monday morning, drain, transfer to an airtight container and store it in the refrigerator until I'm ready to use it later in the week.

Soy-Free ◆ Vegan

6 tbsp	hulled barley	90 mL
	Water	
1½ tsp	sunflower oil	7 mL
1 tsp	cumin seeds, coarsely ground	5 mL
½ tsp	dried savory	2 mL
½ cup	chopped onion	125 mL
½ tsp	pressed or minced garlic	2 mL
¼ cup	water chestnuts, cut in half	60 mL
⅛ tsp	cayenne powder	0.5 mL
½ tsp	Himalayan salt	2 mL
¼ tsp	crushed black pepper	1 mL
4 cups	water	1 L
½ cup	sliced carrot (¼-inch/0.5 cm slices)	125 mL
½ cup	chopped red-skinned potato (½-inch/1 cm cubes)	125 mL
1 cup	chopped trimmed kale leaves (1-inch/2.5 cm pieces)	250 mL
1 tsp	freshly squeezed lemon juice	5 mL

1. Place barley in a bowl and add enough water to cover by about 1 inch (2.5 cm). Let soak at room temperature overnight. Drain.

2. In a medium saucepan, heat oil over medium heat. Add cumin seeds and savory; cook, stirring, for about 30 seconds or until fragrant. Add onion and garlic; cook, stirring, for 1 minute.

3. Stir in barley, water chestnuts, cayenne, salt, black pepper and water; bring to a boil. Reduce heat to low, cover and simmer for 40 minutes. Add carrot and potato; cover and simmer for about 20 minutes or until barley and vegetables are tender.

4. Remove from heat and stir in kale and lemon juice. Cover and let stand for about 5 minutes or until kale is wilted.

Dosha Modification

◆ For **vata**, substitute sweet potato for the red potato and replace the kale with asparagus.

Thai Lemongrass Vermicelli Soup

This warm, moist, sweet and sour soup is perfect for vata while still offering reasonable balance for the other doshas. Vary it for taste and dosha by adding more cooling, grounding coconut milk for pitta and vata or by omitting the coconut milk if cooking only for kapha (or if you are trying to lose weight).

<table>
<tr><td colspan="3" align="center">Gluten-Free ✦ Vegan</td></tr>
<tr><td>2 oz</td><td>rice vermicelli noodles</td><td>60 g</td></tr>
<tr><td>1</td><td>lemongrass stalk, tough outer layers removed</td><td>1</td></tr>
<tr><td>2</td><td>large (or 4 small) lime leaves (fresh or frozen)</td><td>2</td></tr>
<tr><td>1/4 cup</td><td>thinly sliced shiitake mushroom caps (stems discarded)</td><td>60 mL</td></tr>
<tr><td>3 cups</td><td>water</td><td>750 mL</td></tr>
<tr><td>1/4 cup</td><td>minced shallots or red onion</td><td>60 mL</td></tr>
<tr><td>2 tbsp</td><td>finely chopped gingerroot</td><td>30 mL</td></tr>
<tr><td>1 tsp</td><td>pressed or minced garlic</td><td>5 mL</td></tr>
<tr><td>1/2 tsp</td><td>minced thin green chile pepper (or cayenne pepper)</td><td>2 mL</td></tr>
<tr><td>1/2 cup</td><td>chopped napa cabbage</td><td>125 mL</td></tr>
<tr><td>1 tsp</td><td>coconut sugar</td><td>5 mL</td></tr>
<tr><td>1/4 cup</td><td>coconut milk</td><td>60 mL</td></tr>
<tr><td>1 to 3 tsp</td><td>fish sauce (optional)</td><td>5 to 15 mL</td></tr>
<tr><td>2 tbsp</td><td>chopped fresh cilantro</td><td>30 mL</td></tr>
<tr><td>2 tbsp</td><td>chopped fresh basil</td><td>30 mL</td></tr>
<tr><td>1 tbsp</td><td>tamari</td><td>15 mL</td></tr>
<tr><td>1 tbsp</td><td>freshly squeezed lime juice</td><td>15 mL</td></tr>
</table>

Makes 2 servings

Tip

Select firm lemongrass stalks that are pale yellow at the lower end and green at the upper end. They can be purchased at larger grocery stores or Asian markets in the produce section. Wrap them tightly in plastic or place them in an airtight container and store in the refrigerator for up to 1 week or in the freezer for up to 2 months. Frozen lemongrass will thaw in 5 minutes at room temperature.

SERVING SUGGESTIONS

Serve with Cornbread (page 294) or corn tortillas.

1. In a medium saucepan of boiling water, cook vermicelli for 2 to 3 minutes or until tender. Drain and rinse under cold water; drain again. Set aside.

2. Place lemongrass on a cutting board and trim 1 inch (2.5 cm) from each end. Using the back of a knife blade, bruise the lemongrass (or pound it with a mallet).

3. In a large pot, combine lemongrass, lime leaves, mushrooms and water (the lemongrass will stick out of the pan). Bring to a boil over high heat. Stir in shallots, ginger, garlic and chile.

Variations

Substitute glass noodles for the rice vermicelli noodles.

Substitute chopped summer squash, diced carrots or chopped bok choy for the cabbage, adjusting the cooking time as needed.

At the end of step 3, add 8 oz (250 g) boneless skinless chicken thighs, diced. Cook for 10 minutes before proceeding with step 4. At the end of step 4, make sure the chicken is no longer pink inside before proceeding with step 5.

Add cooked Turkey Cilantro Meatballs (page 172) with the cabbage and cook until heated through.

Add 8 oz (250 g) shrimp, peeled and deveined, with the cabbage and cook until firm, pink and opaque.

Add 8 oz (250 g) extra-firm tofu, cubed, with the cabbage and cook until heated through.

4. Reduce heat to low and stir in cabbage, coconut sugar, coconut milk and fish sauce (if using); simmer for about 3 minutes or until cabbage is tender-crisp.

5. Remove from heat and discard lemongrass and lime leaves. Stir in vermicelli, cilantro, basil, tamari and lime juice.

Dosha Modifications

+ **Vata** can add a splash of sesame oil and/or additional coconut milk in step 5 for more grounding.
+ **Pitta** can add additional coconut milk and cilantro to cool things down.
+ **Kapha** can omit the coconut milk entirely and increase the amount of chile pepper, if desired.

Dashi Noodle Soup

Traditional noodle soups use vermicelli or udon noodles. I prefer glass noodles because their light, cooling energetic complements the heavy, warming broth. Experiment and decide for yourself! Prep the broth the night before and you can whip this soup up in 15 minutes when you get home from work, then enjoy a relaxing evening at home.

Makes 2 servings

Tips

Canned sliced water chestnuts are widely available at supermarkets, health food stores, food cooperatives and Asian markets.

To retain the benefits of the micronutrients from the kombu, do not boil the Dashi Clear Broth.

Variations

Substitute fine rice vermicelli noodles or udon noodles for the glass noodles.

Add cooked or frozen Turkey Cilantro Meatballs (page 172) with the water chestnuts.

Gluten-Free ♦ Vegan

8 oz	glass noodles	250 g
4	water chestnut slices, drained	4
1 cup	broccoli crowns, sliced like thin trees	250 mL
½ cup	thinly sliced carrots	125 mL
2 cups	Dashi Clear Broth (page 178)	500 mL
2 cups	water	500 mL
	Chopped fresh cilantro	
	Lime wedges	

1. In a pot of boiling water, cook vermicelli for 2 minutes. Drain and rinse under cold water; drain again. Set aside.

2. In a medium saucepan, combine water chestnuts, broccoli, carrots, broth and water; cook over medium heat for 10 to 15 minutes or until vegetables are tender (see tip, at left).

3. Remove from heat and stir in vermicelli. Serve garnished with cilantro and lime.

Puy Lentil Soup with Pork Sausage

If you are new to lentils or are serving them to people unaccustomed to eating lentils, this dish is a nice introduction. Puy lentils are relatively easy on the digestive system and the well-seasoned broth makes them even more so. The small amount of sausage in the dish provides some heaviness and grounding, which carnivores generally seek in their meals.

**Makes
3 servings**

Variations

For a vegan version, omit the pork and use sunflower oil.

Try adding ¼ tsp (1 mL) organic dried lavender with the thyme.

**SERVING
SUGGESTIONS**

Serve with Tridoshic Arugula, Radicchio and Cherry Salad (page 237) and crusty French bread or Cornbread (page 294).

Dairy-Free ✦ Gluten-Free ✦ Soy-Free

1 tbsp	unsalted butter or sunflower oil	15 mL
8 oz	pork sausage, cut into 1-inch (2.5 cm) slices	250 g
½ cup	chopped onion	125 mL
1	bay leaf	1
½ tsp	finely chopped fresh rosemary	2 mL
¼ tsp	crushed black pepper	1 mL
⅛ tsp	dried tarragon	0.5 mL
⅛ tsp	dried thyme	0.5 mL
1 cup	Puy lentils	250 mL
¾ cup	thinly sliced carrots	175 mL
2	whole cloves	2
¼ tsp	Himalayan salt	1 mL
4 cups	water	1 L

1. In a large saucepan, melt butter over medium heat. Add sausage and cook, stirring, until browned on both sides. Add onion, bay leaf, rosemary, pepper, tarragon and thyme; cook, stirring, for 1 minute.

2. Stir in lentils, carrots, cloves, salt and water; bring to a boil. Reduce heat and simmer, stirring occasionally, for about 20 minutes or until lentils are soft.

Chicken, Lemongrass and Quinoa Soup

This light, nourishing soup with lemongrass and ginger is designed to move stagnant energy and open the channels for well-being. It is perfect for cold and flu season or any time you need to restore and energize. If you're congested, try adding a pinch of cayenne pepper to your serving.

Makes 6 servings

Tips

Pippali, also called Indian long pepper, is warm and nourishing. It is tridoshic in moderation, but in excess it can aggravate pitta. It is considered a rejuvenating tonic for kapha and the lungs. It is said to scrape ama from cell walls, arteries and tissues to promote weight loss. It kindles the digestive fire to aid nutrient absorption. It is generally available only at Indian grocery stores.

To remove the chicken from the pot, slide a long (14 inch/35 cm) metal slotted spoon into the cavity of the chicken and slowly lift it out of the pot, allowing the broth to drain back in.

Gluten-Free ✦ Soy-Free

2 tsp	fenugreek seeds	10 mL
1 tsp	fennel seeds	5 mL
1 tsp	dried thyme	5 mL
½ tsp	Himalayan salt	2 mL
¼ tsp	ground pippali (Indian long pepper)	1 mL
1 tbsp	ghee	15 mL
½	onion, chopped	½
2 tsp	minced gingerroot	10 mL
1	organic chicken (about 4 lbs/2 kg)	1
	Water	
2	stalks celery, chopped	2
1 tbsp	ume plum vinegar	15 mL
2	carrots, diced	2
½ cup	quinoa, rinsed and soaked (see page 71)	125 mL
2 cups	chopped green beans	500 mL
4	curry leaves	4
1 tsp	minced peeled turmeric root	5 mL
½ tsp	crushed black pepper	2 mL
6	lemongrass stalks, cut in half and bruised	6
½ cup	chopped fresh parsley	125 mL
	Lemon wedges (optional)	

1. In a small bowl, combine fenugreek seeds, fennel seeds, thyme, salt and pippali.

2. In a large pot, melt ghee over medium heat. Add onion and ginger; cook, stirring, until fragrant. Add spice mixture and cook, stirring, for 30 seconds.

Tips

Store the soup in an airtight container in the refrigerator for up to 2 days. The gelatin (from the bones) will congeal, creating a thick mass, but this will dissolve once the soup is reheated.

Follow steps 1 to 4 to make a broth that can be frozen for up to 2 months for later use. Divide it into 1- to 2-cup (250 to 500 mL) portions and store in airtight containers. Or pour it into ice cube trays, then, once the cubes are frozen, transfer them to a sealable freezer bag. Use the cubes, which are equal to about 2 tbsp (30 mL), in recipes calling for smaller amounts of broth. Either way, thaw overnight in the refrigerator before use.

3. Add chicken and cover with water (about 11 cups/2.75 L). Increase heat to high and bring to a boil. Add celery and vinegar. Reduce heat to medium-low, cover, leaving lid ajar, and simmer, stirring occasionally, for 2 hours. Transfer chicken to a cutting board to cool (see tip, at left).

4. Strain broth through a fine-mesh sieve into a large spouted measuring cup. Pour the strained broth back into the pot.

5. Using a paring knife, remove the meat from the chicken bones, discarding skin and bones. Chop meat into small pieces.

6. Add meat to the pot and stir in carrots and quinoa. Bring to a boil, then reduce heat to low. Add green beans, curry leaves, turmeric and pepper. Cover, leaving lid ajar, and simmer for 20 minutes. Add lemongrass and simmer for 10 minutes. Discard lemongrass. Remove from heat and stir in parsley. If desired, serve garnished with lemon wedges.

Compatible Substitutions

The ingredients in this recipe were selected for specific nutritional and medicinal qualities, and for their compatibility. However, if you have trouble locating certain ingredients, the following substitutions will not alter the energetics:

- Substitute virgin coconut oil for the ghee.
- Substitute apple cider vinegar for the ume plum vinegar.
- Omit the quinoa and serve the soup over bowls of cooked glass noodles.
- Substitute broccoli for the green beans.
- Substitute $\frac{1}{2}$ tsp (2 mL) ground turmeric for the turmeric root.

Iron-Boosting Pomegranate Lamb Soup

This soup is adapted from an ancient recipe used to treat iron-deficiency anemia that was prepared for me when I was in Kerala, India. Ayurveda says meat prepared in broth is easiest to digest, promoting maximum assimilation of protein, iron and nutrients. Iron absorption is optimized when vitamin C is eaten at the same time. Pomegranates are loaded with vitamin C, and research has linked them with red (and white) blood cell production, along with a wide variety of other health benefits.

**Makes
6 servings**

Tip

To prepare the pomegranates for this recipe, use a sharp paring knife to slice $\frac{1}{4}$-inch (0.5 cm) off each end. Discard the ends. Make $\frac{1}{8}$-inch (3 mm) deep slices along the six natural indentations in the skin, from blossom end to stem end. Pry open the six sections (like you would open an orange) to expose the seeds. Use your fingers to separate the seeds from the membrane. Discard the membrane, reserving the seeds and the peel.

Dairy-Free ♦ Gluten-Free ♦ Soy-Free

- Mortar and pestle

1 tbsp	virgin coconut oil	15 mL
6	curry leaves	6
2 tsp	cumin seeds	10 mL
2 lbs	lamb shoulder chops	1 kg
2	pomegranates, seeded, peels reserved (see tips, at left and opposite)	2
1 tsp	dried rosemary, ground with a mortar and pestle	5 mL
$\frac{1}{2}$ tsp	Himalayan salt (approx.)	2 mL
$\frac{1}{2}$ tsp	ground pippali (Indian long pepper)	2 mL
$\frac{1}{2}$ tsp	crushed black pepper	2 mL
$\frac{1}{2}$ tsp	ground ginger	2 mL
Pinch	ground asafoetida (hing)	Pinch
9 cups	water (approx.)	2.25 L
1 tsp	grated lemon zest	5 mL

1. In a large pot, melt coconut oil over low heat. Add curry leaves and cumin seeds; cook, stirring, for about 30 seconds or until cumin seeds start to pop.

2. Add lamb, pomegranate seeds and peels, rosemary, salt, pippali, black pepper, ginger and asafoetida. Add enough water to cover meat by about 1 inch (2.5 cm). Increase heat to high and bring to a boil.

Tips

Pomegranate juice can stain and sometimes splatters when you open the fruit, so lay a cloth under your cutting board and wear an apron. To remove stains from your hands, scrub with lemon juice and salt.

Curry leaves, pippali and asafoetida (hing) are traditional Indian spices that are readily available at Indian grocery stores. In addition to adding a subtle but distinct flavor, they provide added nutrients and aid in digestion, absorption and assimilation.

3. Reduce heat to medium–low, cover, leaving lid ajar, and simmer, stirring occasionally, for about 2 hours or until the meat is falling off the bone and broth has reduced by about half.

4. Using a slotted spoon, transfer lamb and pomegranate seeds and peels to a large bowl, discarding bones. Using a mortar and pestle and working in batches, crush the meat and pomegranate seeds and peels, making sure to thoroughly crush the seeds. Return the crushed mixture to the pot. Stir in lemon zest. Adjust salt to taste, if desired.

Red Lentil Winter Stew with Turmeric Root and Kale

Warm and grounding, this stew is ideal for a cold winter or damp spring day. It is made with fresh turmeric root, which fortifies the immune system. Studies have shown that the efficacy of turmeric is increased when it is combined with pepper (black pepper, cayenne, etc.), so enjoy a little spice – it's good for your immune system!

Makes 2 servings

Tips

For a vegan stew, substitute sunflower oil for the ghee.

If you cannot find fresh turmeric root, you can substitute ½ tsp (2 mL) ground turmeric.

This soup is best eaten the day it is prepared, but leftovers can be stored in an airtight container in the refrigerator for up to 1 day. Reheat leftovers as individual servings.

Variation

Substitute ½ tsp (2 mL) apple cider vinegar for the lime juice.

Gluten-Free ✦ Soy-Free ✦ Vegetarian

1 tbsp	ghee	15 mL
¼ cup	finely chopped shallots	60 mL
½ tsp	pressed or minced garlic	2 mL
1 tsp	cumin seeds	5 mL
½ tsp	fennel seeds	2 mL
½ tsp	crushed coriander seeds	2 mL
2 to 4 tsp	minced gingerroot	10 to 20 mL
1 tsp	finely chopped peeled turmeric root	5 mL
½ cup	short-grain brown rice	125 mL
½ cup	dried red lentils, sorted and rinsed	125 mL
½ tsp	Himalayan salt	2 mL
¼ tsp	crushed black pepper	1 mL
3 cups	Ginger Broth (page 179) or water	750 mL
1 cup	chopped trimmed kale leaves (stems removed)	250 mL
1 tsp	freshly squeezed lime juice	5 mL

1. In a medium saucepan, melt ghee over medium heat. Add shallots and garlic; cook, stirring, for 2 minutes. Add cumin seeds, fennel seeds and coriander seeds; cook, stirring, for 1 minute. Add ginger and turmeric; cook, stirring, until fragrant.

2. Stir in rice, lentils, salt, pepper and broth; bring to a boil. Reduce heat to medium–low, cover, leaving lid ajar, and simmer, stirring occasionally, for about 40 minutes, or until rice is tender. Remove from heat and stir in kale and lime juice. Cover and let stand for 5 minutes or until kale is wilted.

Moroccan-Spiced Chickpea Stew

This stew is big on flavor without a lot of fuss. It's mildly spiced, so all doshas can enjoy it. Kapha can add a pinch of cayenne pepper to their serving, if desired.

Makes 3 servings

Tips

Dried chickpeas can be purchased in bulk and are often less expensive than canned chickpeas. To substitute dried chickpeas, use ½ cup (125 mL) and follow the soaking and cooking instructions on page 64. They can be cooked up to 3 days in advance, drained and stored in an airtight container in the refrigerator.

The kabocha squash can be prepped up to 24 hours in advance. Using a serrated knife, use a sawing motion to cut a circle ½ inch (1 cm) around the stem; remove the stem. Cut the squash in half, then into quarters. Using a spoon, scrape the seeds off the inside and discard. The skin is edible, so there is no need to peel it; simply remove any blemishes and chop squash to desired size. Store in an airtight container in the refrigerator.

Gluten-Free ✦ Soy-Free ✦ Vegan

2 tbsp	extra virgin olive oil	30 mL
⅓ cup	chopped shallots	75 mL
2 tsp	chopped gingerroot	10 mL
1 tbsp	Moroccan Spice Blend (page 270)	15 mL
1 cup	chopped seeded peeled tomato (see tip, page 230)	250 mL
1	can (14 to 19 oz/398 to 540 mL) chickpeas, drained and rinsed	1
1 cup	chopped organic kabocha squash (see tip, at left)	250 mL
½ tsp	Himalayan salt	2 mL
¼ tsp	crushed black pepper	1 mL
2 cups	Vegetable Broth (page 182)	500 mL
2 cups	water	500 mL
1 cup	chopped green beans	250 mL
¼ cup	chopped fresh cilantro	60 mL
1 tbsp	grated orange zest	15 mL

1. In a medium saucepan, heat oil over medium heat. Add shallots and ginger; cook, stirring, for about 30 seconds or until fragrant. Sprinkle with spice blend and cook, stirring, for 30 seconds. Add tomato and cook, stirring, for 1 minute.

2. Add chickpeas, squash, salt, pepper, broth and water; bring to a boil. Reduce heat and simmer, stirring occasionally, for 30 minutes or until squash is tender. Stir in beans and simmer for about 3 minutes or until tender.

3. Remove from heat and stir in cilantro and orange zest.

Variations

Add 1 tsp (5 mL) ground cinnamon and ½ tsp (2 mL) chili powder with the spice blend.

Substitute peeled pumpkin or other squash varieties for the kabocha.

Substitute Roasted Kabocha Squash (page 220) for the raw kabocha; add in step 3.

Lemon Farro Cannellini Stew

This stew of farro and cannellini cooked in a lemony broth is perfect for fall, winter and spring. It is ideal for pitta and kapha. It is a little rough for vata, who should eat it in moderation.

Makes 4 servings

Tips

Dried cannellini beans can be purchased in bulk and are often less expensive than canned cannellini beans. To substitute dried cannellini beans, use ½ cup (125 mL) and follow the soaking and cooking instructions on page 64. They can be cooked up to 3 days in advance, drained and stored in an airtight container in the refrigerator.

For a vegan stew, substitute extra virgin olive oil for the ghee.

Variations

Substitute delicata squash or pumpkin for the kabocha squash.

Substitute 1 oz (30 g) dried porcini mushrooms, rehydrated, for the cremini mushrooms.

Substitute trimmed kale or Swiss chard for the escarole.

Soy-Free ◆ Vegetarian		
½ cup	farro	125 mL
2 tbsp	ghee	30 mL
¼ cup	minced shallots	60 mL
2 oz	cremini mushrooms	60 g
½ tsp	dried thyme	2 mL
½ tsp	Himalayan salt	2 mL
¼ tsp	crushed black pepper	1 mL
1	can (14 to 19 oz/398 to 540 mL) cannellini beans, drained and rinsed	1
4 cups	Vegetable Broth (page 182)	1 L
1 tbsp	tomato paste	15 mL
2 cups	chopped escarole	500 mL
1 cup	chopped Roasted Kabocha Squash (page 220)	250 mL
1 tsp	grated lemon zest	5 mL
¼ cup	freshly squeezed lemon juice	60 mL

1. Place farro in a bowl and add enough water to cover by about 1 inch (2.5 cm). Let soak at room temperature overnight. Drain.

2. In a medium saucepan, melt ghee over medium heat. Add shallots and cook, stirring, for about 30 seconds or until fragrant. Add mushrooms and cook, stirring, until just browned. Stir in the thyme, salt and pepper.

3. Stir in farro, beans, broth and tomato paste; bring to a boil. Reduce heat to medium–low, cover, leaving lid ajar, and simmer, stirring occasionally, for 30 minutes or until farro is soft and chewy.

4. Remove from heat and stir in escarole and squash. Continue stirring until escarole is wilted. Stir in lemon zest and lemon juice.

Caribbean Adzuki Bean Stew

Astringent adzuki beans are ideal for pitta and kapha. They are cool and light, so I've warmed them up and grounded the energetics a bit with allspice, cinnamon, ginger and sweet potato for vata. These beans are still a little rough for a sensitive constitution, so vata should eat this stew in moderation.

Makes 3 servings

SERVING SUGGESTIONS

Serve with a green leaf or spinach salad and Coconut Jasmine Rice (page 233), Cornbread (page 294) or corn tortillas.

Gluten-Free ✦ Soy-Free ✦ Vegan

1/4 tsp	ground allspice	1 mL
1/4 tsp	ground cinnamon	1 mL
1/4 tsp	ground cumin	1 mL
1/4 tsp	dried thyme	1 mL
1/8 tsp	ground nutmeg	0.5 mL
1/8 tsp	cayenne pepper	0.5 mL
3 tbsp	sunflower oil	45 mL
1/2 cup	minced onion	125 mL
2 tbsp	minced gingerroot	30 mL
1 cup	cubed peeled sweet potato, squash or pumpkin (1/2-inch/1 cm cubes)	250 mL
1/4 tsp	Himalayan salt	1 mL
1/4 tsp	crushed black pepper	1 mL
1 1/2 cups	water	375 mL
2 tbsp	light (fancy) molasses or coconut sugar	30 mL
1	can (14 to 19 oz/398 to 540 mL) adzuki beans, drained and rinsed	1
3/4 cup	frozen corn kernels	175 mL
2 tbsp	chopped fresh cilantro	30 mL
2 tbsp	freshly squeezed lime juice	30 mL

1. In a small bowl, combine allspice, cinnamon, cumin, thyme, nutmeg and cayenne.

2. In a medium saucepan, heat oil over medium heat. Add onion and ginger; cook, stirring, for 3 to 5 minutes or until onion is soft and translucent. Add spice mixture and cook, stirring, for 1 minute.

3. Stir in yam, salt, black pepper, water and molasses; bring to a boil. Reduce heat and simmer, stirring occasionally, for about 15 minutes or until yams are tender and sauce is thickened. Stir in beans and simmer for 1 minute.

4. Remove from heat and stir in corn. Cover and let stand for 5 minutes or until corn is tender. Stir in cilantro and lime juice.

Brazilian Black Bean Stew

Beans in general are best for pitta and kapha, due to their cold, dry qualities and astringent taste. Vata can eat this stew on occasion.

Variation

Add 4 oz (125 g) fresh chorizo or linguiça sausage, broiled and cut into ¼-inch (0.5 cm) slices, with the cilantro. (Chorizo and linguiça are spicy sausages; purchase a brand that is uncured and nitrate-free or substitute any uncured nitrate-free spicy sausage.)

SERVING SUGGESTIONS

Serve with basmati rice or Coconut Jasmine Rice (page 233) and a salad of mixed greens with Tridoshic White Balsamic Vinaigrette (page 251).

Gluten-Free ✦ Soy-Free ✦ Vegan

2 tbsp	sunflower oil	30 mL
½ cup	chopped onion	125 mL
½ tsp	minced gingerroot	2 mL
1	can (14 to 19 oz/398 to 540 mL) black beans, drained and rinsed	1
1 cup	minced seeded peeled tomatoes (see tip, page 230)	250 mL
1 cup	cubed peeled sweet potatoes (½-inch/1 cm cubes)	250 mL
½ tsp	Himalayan salt	2 mL
½ tsp	crushed black pepper	2 mL
¾ cup	water	175 mL
2 tsp	pure maple syrup	10 mL
¾ cup	frozen corn kernels	175 mL
½ cup	chopped frozen green beans	125 mL
2 tbsp	chopped fresh cilantro	30 mL
2 tbsp	freshly squeezed lime juice	30 mL

1. In a medium saucepan, heat oil over medium heat. Add onion and ginger; cook, stirring, for 2 minutes.

2. Stir in black beans, tomatoes, sweet potatoes, salt, pepper, water and maple syrup; bring to a boil. Reduce heat to low, cover and simmer for about 15 minutes or until sweet potatoes are tender.

3. Stir in corn and green beans; simmer, uncovered, for 3 minutes. Remove from heat and stir in cilantro and lime juice.

Vegetable Side Dishes

When you use fresh, seasonal, local vegetables, preparation can be simple: for pitta and kapha, gently steam some greens; for vata, purée cooked root vegetables with almond or cashew milk. Garnish with lemon or lime wedges, top with toasted nuts and voila – you've composed a side dish!

If you're feeling a little more adventurous, check out the recipes in this chapter. Most of the veggies can be prepped (cut and stored in an airtight container in the refrigerator) the night before so you're not rushed when you get home from work. If you follow the serving suggestions, you will delight your senses with layers of complementary flavors, textures and colors while filling your belly with nourishment. Are you ready to eat your veggies?

Escarole with Pomegranate and Sweet Balsamic Dressing

This escarole side dish is suitable for all doshas year-round. Fresh pomegranate seeds are readily available in the fall; dried cranberries are a good substitution at other times of the year.

Makes 3 servings

Tips

To toast almonds, place them in a dry (ungreased) medium skillet over medium heat. When they begin to smell fragrant, after about 1 minute, give the pan a shake. Continue to toast, periodically shaking the pan, until the almonds are golden.

Leftovers can be stored in an airtight container in the refrigerator for up to 1 day.

Variations

Substitute kale for the escarole.

Substitute pine nuts for the almonds.

Turn this into a main dish by adding 4 oz (125 g) crumbled goat cheese or Paneer (page 160) in step 2.

	Gluten-Free ♦ Soy-Free ♦ Vegan	
2 tbsp	extra virgin olive oil	30 mL
1/4 cup	minced leeks (white and light green parts only)	60 mL
1/4 tsp	Himalayan salt	1 mL
5 cups	chopped escarole	1.25 L
1/4 cup	pomegranate seeds	60 mL
1/4 cup	slivered almonds, toasted (see tip, at left)	60 mL
Pinch	cayenne pepper	Pinch
2 tbsp	Sweet Balsamic Dressing (page 246)	30 mL

1. In a large skillet, heat oil over medium heat. Add leeks and cook, stirring, until lightly browned. Sprinkle salt over leeks. Add escarole and cook, stirring, for about 15 seconds or until just wilted.

2. Transfer leek mixture to a medium nonmetallic bowl. Add pomegranate seeds, almonds and cayenne. Add dressing and toss to coat.

Shaved Fennel in Orange Sauce

Fresh fennel is sweet, cooling and tridoshic. Its mild licorice aroma and flavor mellow significantly when it is cooked. Citrus juice adds a delightful splash of harmonizing flavor.

Makes 2 servings

SERVING SUGGESTIONS

Serve with Moroccan Veggie Burgers with Tangy Tamarind Sauce (page 135), Red Quinoa with Endive and Cranberries (page 150), Polenta with Minted Shiitake Sauce (page 146), Minted Apricot Couscous (page 139), Marco's Porcini Risotto (page 152) or Mushroom Tarragon Purée (page 188).

Gluten-Free ♦ Soy-Free ♦ Vegan

1	large bulb fennel	1
½ tsp	grated orange zest	2 mL
½ cup	freshly squeezed orange juice	125 mL
2 tbsp	sunflower oil	30 mL
1 tbsp	white balsamic vinegar	15 mL

1. Trim the base of the fennel. Remove the top stalks (with the fronds); chop and reserve 1 tsp (5 mL) fronds for garnish. Holding the fennel in your hand, run a vegetable peeler lengthwise down one side. Repeat several more times on this side. Flip and shave the opposite side. Repeat until all four sides have been shaved and all that remains is the inner core. Place shaved fennel in a medium bowl and set aside. Discard inner core.

2. In a small bowl, whisk together orange zest, orange juice, sunflower oil and vinegar. Pour over shaved fennel and gently toss to coat.

3. Transfer fennel mixture to a large skillet and cook over medium–low heat, stirring constantly, for 1 to 2 minutes or until fennel is tender but has a slight crunch in the middle. Serve sprinkled with reserved fennel fronds.

Okra with Ginger Lemongrass Sauce

This recipe for broiled okra is light and flavorful, without the slimy texture often associated with okra dishes. Serve over couscous, brown rice or coconut rice. Okra (also called lady's finger) is high in fiber and is loaded with antioxidants, vitamins (A, B$_6$, C and K) and minerals (zinc, copper, calcium, manganese and magnesium). It has a low glycemic load. In ayurveda, it has long been used as a remedy for constipation, ulcers, eye health, heart health, sexual dysfunction, lung inflammation and diabetes.

Makes 3 servings

Tips

The sauce can be prepared up to 1 day ahead and stored in an airtight container in the refrigerator.

Leftovers can be stored in an airtight container in the refrigerator for up to 2 days.

To minimize secretion of okra's slimy mucilage, quick-cook okra whole (not cut) using dry heat (baking, broiling or grilling). When stewed or cooked with liquid, okra often becomes slimy.

Variation

Instead of broiling, place okra on a baking pan, drizzle with oil and sprinkle with salt. Roast at 450°F (230°C), turning once, for 5 minutes per side. Proceed with step 3.

Gluten-Free ✦ Soy-Free ✦ Vegan

- **Preheat broiler**
- **Rimmed baking sheet, lined with foil**

Ginger Lemongrass Sauce

1 tbsp	sunflower oil	15 mL
¼ cup	chopped shallots	60 mL
Pinch	Himalayan salt	Pinch
1	clove garlic, crushed	1
1 tbsp	minced gingerroot	15 mL
2 tsp	minced lemongrass (white inner stalk only)	10 mL
1 to 2 tsp	minced seeded serrano or jalapeño pepper	5 to 10 mL
1 tbsp	sake	15 mL
2 tbsp	freshly squeezed lime juice	30 mL

Okra

12	whole okra	12
1 tbsp	sunflower oil	15 mL

1. *Sauce:* In a small skillet, heat oil over medium heat. Add shallots and salt; cook, stirring, for about 5 minutes or until shallots begin to brown. Add garlic, ginger, lemongrass and serrano pepper; cook, stirring, for 30 seconds. Stir in sake, scraping up any browned bits from the bottom of the pan. Remove from heat and stir in lime juice. Set aside.

2. *Okra:* Place okra on prepared baking sheet and drizzle with oil. Broil, turning once, for about 5 minutes per side or until fork-tender.

3. Transfer okra to medium bowl. Add sauce and toss to coat. Serve immediately.

Puréed Parsnips with Thyme

Parsnips and carrots are in the same family and share similar energetics: sweet, cooling and mildly astringent. They are most balancing for vata and pitta. The garlic and thyme balance this dish for kapha.

Makes 2 servings

Tips

If garlic turns brown when you're sautéing it, it will taste bitter; discard and start fresh.

If you don't have an immersion blender, you can purée the parsnip mixture in a regular blender or a food processor.

Variation

Add 1 tbsp (15 mL) minced shallots, chives or green onions with the garlic.

SERVING SUGGESTIONS

Serve as a side dish with fish, poultry, Bison Meatloaf with Maple Tamarind Sauce (page 174), Autumn Wild Rice Salad (page 246) or French Lentil Salad with Lemon Dressing (page 242).

Gluten-Free ✦ Soy-Free ✦ Vegan

- **Immersion blender (see tip, at left)**

1 cup	chopped parsnips	250 mL
2 cups	water	500 mL
1 tbsp	sunflower oil or unsalted butter	15 mL
¼ tsp	pressed or minced garlic	1 mL
¼ tsp	chopped fresh thyme	1 mL
¼ cup	Vata Lemon Cashew Cream Sauce (page 262), heavy cream or whipping (35%) cream	60 mL
½ tsp	Himalayan salt	2 mL
¼ tsp	crushed black pepper	1 mL

1. In a medium saucepan, combine parsnips and water. Bring to a boil over high heat. Reduce heat and simmer for about 15 minutes or until parsnips are tender. Drain, reserving ¼ cup (60 mL) of the cooking water, then return parsnips to the pan and set aside.

2. In a medium skillet, heat oil over low heat. Add garlic and cook, stirring, until fragrant. Whisk in thyme and cashew cream sauce; simmer gently for 2 minutes to combine the flavors.

3. Add sauce to parsnips, along with the reserved cooking water, salt and pepper; purée with immersion blender.

Dosha Modification

✦ If serving only **kapha** or **pitta**, you can substitute potatoes for the parsnips.

Steamed Rainbow Chard with Lemon Juice

Rainbow chard has a softer texture and milder flavor than other bitter greens and tends to be tolerated by all doshas.

Makes 3 servings

Variation

Substitute escarole for the rainbow chard.

SERVING SUGGESTIONS

Serve with Marco's Porcini Risotto (page 152) or Kapha Broiled Polenta Slices (page 227).

Gluten-Free ✦ Soy-Free ✦ Vegan		
1	bunch rainbow chard (about 7 leaves)	1
	Water	
½ tsp	Himalayan salt	2 mL
3 tbsp	freshly squeezed lemon juice	45 mL

1. Using a chef's knife, remove the main stem from the chard, leaving two halves. Chop the stem and set aside. Stack 4 half leaves on top of each other (larger leaves on the bottom and smaller leaves on top). Tightly roll up lengthwise. Slice into ¼-inch (0.5 cm) ribbons. Keep the stems and leaves separate.

2. Add ¼ inch (0.5 cm) water to a large, shallow saucepan and bring to a gentle boil over medium heat. Add chard stems and cook, stirring, over medium–high heat until just tender. Add more water if necessary to prevent burning. Add chard ribbons and sprinkle with salt; cook, stirring, until wilted.

3. Drain chard and transfer to a serving bowl. Add lemon juice and toss to coat.

Summer Squash Pasta

This dish is balancing to all three doshas. The dry-frying removes some of the moisture to make the vegetables suitable for kapha.

Tip

Instead of the box grater, you can also use a mandoline or food processor with a julienne blade, a spiral vegetable slicer or a knife to create long strands of zucchini and summer squash.

SERVING SUGGESTIONS

Serve with Artichoke Lemon Cream Sauce (page 259) and broiled chicken, shrimp or tofu marinated in Tridoshic Lime Cumin Vinaigrette (page 251) or the lime ginger marinade on page 137. Start the meal with Borscht Lentil Soup (page 194).

Gluten-Free ✦ Soy-Free ✦ Vegan

8 oz	zucchini (about 2 small)	250 g
8 oz	yellow summer squash (about 2 small)	250 g

1. Cut ends off zucchini and summer squash. Place a box grater on its side, with the largest holes on top, over a clean work surface. Hold a zucchini lengthwise and slide it across the grater, making long, thin strands. When you reach the seeds at the core, flip the zucchini over and grate the opposite side. Continue working your way around the zucchini. Discard the seeds and core. Repeat with the other zucchini and both summer squash.

2. In a large nonstick skillet, cook vegetables over low heat, stirring constantly, for about 3 minutes or until slightly wilted. Transfer to a plate lined with paper towels to drain excess moisture.

Dosha Modification

✦ If serving to **vata** only, sauté the zucchini and summer squash in 1 tbsp (15 mL) sunflower oil instead of dry-frying.

Asian-Style Vegetables

Colorful fresh veggies tossed with a zesty vinaigrette are sure to add a spark to your week. Prep the veggies and vinaigrette the night before and this tridoshic goodness whips up in minutes when you get home from work.

Makes 2 servings

Tip

To julienne vegetables means to cut them into long thin strips (sometimes called matchsticks).

SERVING SUGGESTIONS

Serve with Broiled Lime Ginger Shrimp (page 162) or its chicken variation.

Dairy-Free ✦ Gluten-Free ✦ Vegetarian

2 cups	water, divided	500 mL
1/2 cup	thinly shredded red cabbage	125 mL
1	carrot, julienned (see tip, at left)	1
1	zucchini, julienned	1
1/4 cup	Tridoshic Asian Lime Vinaigrette (page 249)	60 mL

1. In a large skillet, bring 1 cup (250 mL) water to a boil. Add cabbage and boil for about 5 minutes or until wilted. Drain and transfer to a plate lined with paper towels to cool (the color will bleed onto everything it touches, so handle with care).

2. Add the remaining water to the skillet and bring to a boil. Add carrots and boil until tender-crisp (begin checking after 30 seconds). Using a slotted spoon, transfer carrots to a plate lined with paper towels to cool.

3. Add zucchini to the boiling water and boil until tender-crisp (begin checking after 30 seconds). Drain and transfer to a plate lined with paper towels to cool.

4. Transfer vegetables to a bowl, add vinaigrette and toss gently to coat.

Rosemary Roasted Root Vegetables

Turnips are in the same family as radishes and are balancing to kapha. Parsnips are related to carrots and, when cooked, are balancing to vata and pitta. Brussels sprouts are part of the cabbage family, so they are best tolerated by pitta and kapha.

Makes 4 servings

Tips

For the most even cooking, cut all of the root vegetables into 1-inch (2.5 cm) cubes.

Leftovers can be added to soup, couscous salad or rice salad the next day.

Variations

Substitute 1½ tsp (7 mL) dried oregano for the rosemary.

Toss the vegetables with 2 tbsp (30 mL) coarsely chopped fresh parsley after roasting.

Gluten-Free ✦ Soy-Free ✦ Vegan

- Preheat oven to 400°F (200°C)
- 13- by 9-inch (33 by 23 cm) metal baking pan, oiled

4	Brussels sprouts, cut into quarters	4
1 cup	cubed red-skinned potatoes (see tip, at left)	250 mL
1 cup	cubed sweet potato or yam	250 mL
1 cup	cubed red or yellow beets	250 mL
½ cup	cubed turnips	125 mL
½ cup	cubed parsnips	125 mL
1 tbsp	dried rosemary	15 mL
½ tsp	Himalayan salt	2 mL
¼ tsp	crushed black pepper	1 mL
2 tbsp	sunflower oil	30 mL
1 tbsp	freshly squeezed lemon juice	15 mL

1. In a large bowl, combine Brussels sprouts, potatoes, sweet potato, beets, turnips and parsnips. Add rosemary, salt, pepper, oil and lemon juice; toss with your hands until vegetables are evenly coated. Spread vegetables out in a single layer on prepared pan.

2. Roast in preheated oven for about 1 hour, turning halfway through, until vegetables are tender.

Roasted Kabocha Squash

Kabocha squash (also called Japanese pumpkin) is a good source of beta-carotene (which the body converts to vitamin A), vitamin C and B vitamins. It is antioxidant, anti-inflammatory and antidiabetic, with insulin-regulating properties. Plus, it is considered an aphrodisiac. The culinary possibilities for roasted kabocha are endless: add it to quinoa or adzuki bean salad; add it to stews or soups; or purée it with spices to make a soup or pie and custard fillings. Make ahead on Sunday and you'll have delicious squash ready for your weekday meals.

Makes about 6 cups (1.5 L)

Variation

Substitute pumpkin or any other squash (such as acorn, butternut or delicata) for the kabocha, adjusting the roasting time depending on the size of the squash.

Gluten-Free ✦ Soy-Free ✦ Vegan

- **Preheat oven to 375°F (190°C)**

| 1 | organic kabocha squash (about 4 lbs/2 kg) | 1 |
| 2 tbsp | virgin coconut oil | 30 mL |

1. Cut kabocha in half (see tip, below). Using a metal spoon, scrape out seeds and stringy fiber. Using your fingers, rub coconut oil into the flesh. Place kabocha, cut side down, on a baking sheet.

2. Roast in preheated oven for about 30 minutes or until fork–tender. Let cool.

3. Using your fingers or a paring knife, remove the skin, if desired. Coarsely chop kabocha and serve warm.

Tips for Success

- Kabocha is widely available in the late summer and early fall. Select squash that is blemish- and bruise-free and feels heavy for its size. It can be stored for 1 month or more in cool, dry conditions.

- To cut a kabocha in half, use a serrated knife to pierce it about $1/2$ inch (1 cm) from the stem. Using a sawing motion, cut a circle around the stem. Pull out and discard the stem. Slice the kabocha in half from top to bottom, using a sawing motion. (Alternatively, you can use a cleaver to slice it in half.)

- The skins of kabocha squash are edible. Make sure the squash you purchase is organic or at least pesticide-free.

- Roasted kabocha can be stored in an airtight container in the refrigerator for up to 3 days.

- If desired, reserve the seeds to make Roasted Ginger Kabocha Seeds (page 279).

Ginger Almond Squash Pie

This light-textured pie is grounded with a gluten-free crust of nuts and dates. The naturally sweet filling is tempered with warm ginger and cinnamon, resulting in multiple layers of flavor and nutrition for all doshas.

Makes 6 servings

Tip

If you don't have an immersion blender, you can use a handheld electric mixer or transfer the vegetable mixture in batches to a regular blender.

Variations

Add 2 drops of rose water and 1/2 tsp (2 mL) ground cardamom with the orange zest.

Substitute coconut milk for the almond milk.

Substitute a 9-inch (23 cm) ready-made organic pie crust.

SERVING SUGGESTIONS

For a midday meal, serve with Tridoshic Arugula, Radicchio and Cherry Salad (page 237) and Puy Lentil Soup with Pork Sausage (page 201) or its vegan variation. Or serve with Autumn Wild Rice Salad (page 246) topped with Dry-Fried Tofu (page 137).

Gluten-Free ✦ Soy-Free ✦ Vegetarian

- **Preheat oven to 300°F (150°C)**
- **Immersion blender (see tip, at left)**

2 cups	cubed peeled acorn squash	500 mL
2 cups	chopped peeled sweet potato	500 mL
1 cup	chopped peeled yellow-fleshed potato (such as Yukon Gold)	250 mL
4 cups	water	1 L
1 tbsp	minced gingerroot	15 mL
1 tsp	coconut sugar	5 mL
1/2 tsp	ground cinnamon	2 mL
1/2 tsp	Himalayan salt	2 mL
1/4 tsp	crushed black pepper	1 mL
1 tbsp	ghee or sunflower oil	15 mL
1	large egg, beaten	1
1/4 cup	almond milk	60 mL
1/2 tsp	grated orange zest	2 mL
1/4 tsp	almond extract	1 mL
1	The Nutty Date Pie Crust (page 300)	1

1. In a large saucepan, combine squash, sweet potato, potato and water. Bring to a boil over high heat. Boil for about 10 minutes or until vegetables are starting to soften. Drain and transfer to a large bowl. Set aside.

2. In a small bowl, combine ginger, sugar, cinnamon, salt and pepper.

3. In a skillet, melt ghee over low heat. Add ginger mixture and cook, stirring, for 1 minute.

4. Pour ginger mixture over vegetables. Add egg, almond milk, orange zest and almond extract. Purée with immersion blender until just combined. Pour into pie crust, smoothing top.

5. Bake in preheated oven for 45 to 60 minutes or until top of pie is firm to the touch.

Puréed Orange Ginger Yams

Here's a tridoshic alternative to mashed white potatoes that is easy on the digestive system.

Tips

If you don't have an immersion blender, you can use a handheld electric mixer.

Leftovers can be added to a soup broth (in lieu of tomatoes) for a sweet, cooling energetic, or can be used to make Millet Breakfast Patties (page 116).

**SERVING
SUGGESTIONS**

Serve with Bison Meatloaf with Maple Tamarind Sauce (page 174) or broiled fish or chicken.

Gluten-Free ✦ Soy-Free ✦ Vegan

• **Immersion blender (see tip at left)**

2 cups	diced peeled yams or sweet potatoes	500 mL
4 cups	water	1 L
2 tbsp	ghee or sunflower oil	30 mL
1 tbsp	grated gingerroot	15 mL
1 tsp	grated orange zest	5 mL
1/4 tsp	ground nutmeg	1 mL
1/4 tsp	ground mace	1 mL
1/4 tsp	ground cinnamon	1 mL
1/2 to 1 cup	plain yogurt or almond milk	125 to 250 mL
1 tbsp	raw liquid honey (optional)	15 mL
3 tbsp	toasted sliced almonds (optional)	45 mL

1. In a large saucepan, combine yams and water. Bring to a boil over medium heat. Boil for about 20 minutes or until tender. Drain and transfer yams to a bowl; set aside.

2. Add ghee to the pan and melt over medium heat. Add ginger and cook, stirring, for about 30 seconds or until fragrant. Add orange zest, nutmeg, mace and cinnamon; cook, stirring, for 1 minute. Remove from heat and return yams to the pan, stirring to coat.

3. Add 1/2 cup (125 mL) yogurt and purée with immersion blender to desired consistency, adding more yogurt as necessary. If desired, stir in honey and garnish with almonds.

Brussels Sprout and Sweet Potato Sauté

Brussels sprouts are astringent, mildly heating and diuretic – ideal for pitta and kapha. Here, they are combined with sweet potatoes to bring some balance and grounding for vata without upsetting pitta.

Makes 2 servings

Tip

Use a mortar and pestle to lightly crush the cumin and fennel seeds.

SERVING SUGGESTIONS

Serve with Mushroom Tarragon Purée (page 188) and brown rice; with Creamy Beet Leek Soup (page 185) and brown rice or Minted Apricot Couscous (page 139); or with Fennel-Crusted Paneer with Balsamic Reduction (page 160). For omnivores, this goes well with broiled white fish, such as fennel-crusted halibut.

Gluten-Free ✦ Soy-Free ✦ Vegan

1 cup	Brussels sprouts	250 mL
1 tbsp	sunflower oil or melted butter (approx.)	15 mL
1/2 tsp	cumin seeds, lightly crushed (see tip, at left)	2 mL
1/4 tsp	fennel seeds, lightly crushed	1 mL
1 1/2 cups	chopped peeled sweet potato (1/2-inch/1 cm cubes)	375 mL
1/4 tsp	Himalayan salt	1 mL
1/2 tsp	grated lemon zest	2 mL
2 tbsp	freshly squeezed lemon juice	30 mL

1. Trim bottoms of Brussels sprouts and remove any wilted outer leaves. Cut lengthwise into wedges. Set aside.

2. Add just enough oil to a medium skillet to make a thin layer on the bottom. Heat oil over medium heat. Add cumin seeds and fennel seeds; cook, stirring, for 30 seconds. Add sweet potato and cook, stirring constantly, for 5 minutes, adding more oil if the pan is drying out.

3. Add Brussels sprouts and cook, stirring, for 2 to 3 minutes or until tender. (Be careful not to overcook the Brussels sprouts or they will taste bitter.) Remove from heat and stir in salt, lemon zest and lemon juice.

Dosha Modifications

✦ Brussels sprouts are very drying, so **vata** may want to add butter to their serving (or a nut butter sauce, a seed butter sauce or a vinaigrette).

✦ If serving for **vata** or **kapha** only, toss in some chopped cooked beets at the end of step 3.

Ginger-Braised Fennel and Sweet Potato

This light and nutritious side dish is easy to make and tastes great! Ayurveda says fennel is soothing for the digestive system, with a sweet post-digestive effect. The sweet potatoes and ginger broth add some grounding to the dish, making it suitable for fall and not too heavy for summer. It is ideal for pitta and vata; kapha can eat it in moderation with the addition of some cayenne pepper or fresh ginger slices.

Makes 2 servings

Tips

To julienne vegetables or herbs means to cut them into long thin strips (sometimes called matchsticks).

Fresh fennel has a strong licorice aroma that mellows considerably after cooking.

The vegetables can be julienned the night before and stored in an airtight container in the refrigerator.

Variation

Substitute miso broth (¾ cup/175 mL water mixed with 1 tbsp/15 mL yellow miso) for the Ginger Broth.

SERVING SUGGESTIONS

Serve with couscous, quinoa or fish.

Gluten-Free ✦ Soy-Free ✦ Vegan

2 tsp	ghee, butter or extra virgin olive oil	10 mL
1 cup	julienned fennel bulb (see tip, at left)	250 mL
1 cup	julienned peeled sweet potato	250 mL
¼ tsp	Himalayan salt	1 mL
¾ cup	Ginger Broth (page 179)	175 mL
1 tbsp	freshly squeezed lemon juice	15 mL
1 tbsp	julienned fresh mint	15 mL

1. In a large skillet, melt ghee over medium heat. Arrange fennel and sweet potato in a single layer on bottom of pan and sprinkle with salt. Cook for about 4 minutes or until lightly browned. Using tongs, flip vegetables and lightly brown the other side. Add broth and immediately cover the pan. Reduce heat to low and simmer for about 3 minutes or until liquid is reduced by half.

2. Remove from heat and stir in lemon juice, scraping up any browned bits from the bottom of the pan.

3. Transfer fennel and sweet potato to a serving platter or individual bowls. Drizzle with broth from the pan and garnish with mint.

Dosha Modification

✦ **Kapha** can substitute daikon radish for the fennel and/or potatoes for the sweet potatoes.

Sweet Potato Fries

Broiled, not fried, these healthier fries are ideal for vata and pitta. Kapha can eat them on occasion, with the modification noted below.

Makes 2 servings

SERVING SUGGESTION

Serve with Moroccan Veggie Burgers with Tangy Tamarind Sauce (page 135).

Gluten-Free ✦ Soy-Free ✦ Vegan

- Preheat broiler
- Rimmed baking sheet, lined with foil

2	large sweet potatoes, scrubbed	2
3 tbsp	sunflower oil	45 mL
$\frac{1}{4}$ tsp	Himalayan salt	1 mL
$\frac{1}{4}$ tsp	crushed black pepper	1 mL

1. Cut sweet potatoes in half lengthwise. Slice lengthwise into wedges about $\frac{3}{4}$ inch (2 cm) thick.
2. In a large bowl, combine oil, salt and pepper. Add sweet potatoes and toss to lightly coat. Transfer to prepared baking sheet.
3. Broil for about 3 minutes or until top is just starting to turn golden. Turn the wedges and cook for about 2 minutes or until just starting to brown.

Dosha Modification

✦ **Kapha** should add crushed garlic or cayenne pepper with the oil.

Masala Potatoes

"Masala" is a Hindi word meaning "mixture of spices." This recipe sautés the potatoes in a special blend of spices to create an authentic South Indian flavor (but with much less heat, as I've used far fewer chile peppers). Serve as a side dish or stuff inside Masala Dosas (page 112).

**Makes
4 servings**

Tip

Eat the curry leaves — they are good for you! Ayurveda says, and research confirms, that curry leaves are antidiabetic, antioxidant, antimicrobial, anti–inflammatory, anticarcinogenic and hepatoprotective (they protect the liver from damage). They are a good source of vitamins (A, E, K, B_6 and folate) and minerals (calcium, iron, magnesium, phosphorus, potassium, zinc, copper and manganese).

Variation

Substitute 2 cups (500 mL) chopped Roasted Kabocha Squash (page 220) or leftover potatoes for the fingerling potatoes. Omit step 1 and add the cooked squash or potatoes and the salt with the spice mix (do not cook for 5 minutes after adding them; just cook until heated through).

Gluten-Free ✦ Soy-Free ✦ Vegan		
2 cups	chopped fingerling potatoes (unpeeled)	500 mL
	Water	
2 tbsp	ghee or extra virgin olive oil (approx.)	30 mL
¼	onion, chopped	¼
½ tsp	Himalayan salt	2 mL
1 tbsp	Masala Spice Mix (page 271)	15 mL
⅛ tsp	ground asafoetida (hing) (optional)	0.5 mL
5	curry leaves	5
2 tbsp	unsweetened shredded coconut	30 mL

1. Place potatoes in a medium saucepan and add enough water to cover by ½ inch (1 cm). Bring to a boil over high heat. Reduce heat and simmer for 10 minutes or until potatoes are soft but still holding their shape. Drain well.

2. In a large skillet, melt ghee over medium heat. Add onion and cook, stirring, for 30 seconds. Add potatoes and salt; cook, stirring, for 5 minutes. Sprinkle with spice mix and asafoetida (if using); cook, stirring, until potatoes are tender, adding more ghee if necessary to prevent sticking. Add curry leaves and coconut; cook, stirring, until curry leaves are wilted.

Kapha Broiled Polenta Slices

These polenta slices can be prepared in minutes and make a light, satisfying dish for kapha. Vata can eat on occasion, with extra gravy. Pitta can eat them on occasion, but should omit the cayenne.

Makes 3 servings

Tip

The polenta slices can be stored in an airtight container in the refrigerator for up to 3 days. Store the gravy in a separate container so the polenta stays firm.

Variations

Add 1 tsp (5 mL) chopped fresh oregano or 1 tbsp (15 mL) chopped fresh parsley in addition to or in place of the basil.

Avoid adding cheese to this recipe. Cheese is heavy, cold and kapha-provoking.

SERVING SUGGESTIONS

Serve with Steamed Rainbow Chard with Lemon Juice (page 216), Pitta Kapha Cannellini, Kale and Artichoke Sauté (page 131) or Puréed Lemon Chickpea Soup (page 196).

Gluten-Free ✦ Soy-Free ✦ Vegan

- **Preheat broiler**
- **Rimmed baking sheet, lined with foil**

¼ cup	chopped fresh basil	60 mL
½ tsp	paprika	2 mL
Pinch	cayenne pepper	Pinch
¼ cup	virgin olive oil	60 mL
1	tube (18 oz/511 g) precooked polenta	1
1 cup	Mary's Gravy (page 158)	250 mL

1. In a shallow dish, combine basil, paprika, cayenne and oil.

2. Cut polenta into ½-inch (1 cm) slices. Dip one slice in the basil mixture, coating both sides. Place on prepared baking sheet. Repeat with the remaining polenta slices, arranging them in a single layer.

3. Broil, turning once, for about 5 minutes or until golden on both sides. Transfer to serving dishes and top with gravy.

Cinnamon Lotus Edamame Sauté

Lotus root is said to be a symbol of longevity and love. It is a mild diuretic and was traditionally used to cleanse the lymphatic system, pushing waste from the blood. Cinnamon is pungent and is used in ayurveda to facilitate purification of the blood and lymph via removal of phlegm.

Makes 3 servings

Tips

Sliced peeled lotus root can be found frozen at Indian markets or fresh, packed in a saltwater solution, at Asian markets. Fresh lotus root should be peeled, sliced thin and placed in a bowl of vinegar until ready to use (otherwise, it discolors); rinse just before use.

If you cannot find black sesame oil, you can substitute regular sesame oil.

	Gluten-Free ✦ Vegan	
½ tsp	ground cinnamon	2 mL
¼ tsp	ground anise seeds	1 mL
Pinch	cayenne pepper	Pinch
1 tbsp	coconut sugar	15 mL
2 tbsp	tamari	30 mL
1 tbsp	unseasoned rice vinegar	15 mL
1 tbsp	sake	15 mL
1 tsp	black sesame oil	5 mL
½ cup	water	125 mL
1 tsp	yellow miso	5 mL
3 tbsp	sunflower oil	45 mL
1	small clove garlic, pressed or minced	1
1 tbsp	minced gingerroot	15 mL
1	package (5 oz/150 g) lotus root slices, rinsed and drained	1
3	shiitake mushroom caps, thinly sliced	3
2	green onions, chopped	2
½ cup	shelled edamame (thawed if frozen)	125 mL

1. In a small bowl, combine cinnamon, anise seeds and cayenne. Set aside.

2. In another small bowl, combine sugar, tamari, vinegar, sake and sesame oil. Set aside.

Variations

Substitute ¼ cup (60 mL) chopped enoki mushrooms for the shiitakes.

Substitute black soybeans for the edamame.

SERVING SUGGESTIONS

Serve with Miso Soup (page 183) and Mizuna Mixed Greens Salad (page 236) or Roasted Kabocha Squash (page 220).

3. In a third small bowl, combine water and miso. Set aside.

4. In a large skillet, heat sunflower oil over medium–high heat. Add garlic and ginger; cook, stirring, for about 30 seconds or until fragrant. Add lotus root slices in a single layer. Cook on one side for 2 minutes, then flip and cook for 2 minutes. Add mushrooms and cook, stirring, for 1 minute. Add green onions, edamame and cinnamon mixture; cook, stirring, for 1 minute. Stir in tamari mixture, scraping up any brown bits on the bottom of the pan. Remove from heat and stir in miso mixture.

Mexican Rice

This version of Mexican rice uses much less oil than traditional recipes. Serve with black beans or grilled chicken and an arugula salad. It is best for vata and kapha; pitta can eat it on occasion.

**Makes
3 servings**

Tips

To peel and seed a plum (Roma) tomato, simply chop off $\frac{1}{4}$ inch (0.5 cm) from each end, then use a sharp vegetable peeler to remove the skin. Cut the tomato into quarters and scrape out the seeds using the sharp point of a knife. If you are using round tomatoes, you will need to carve out the area where the tomato was attached to the stem, then peel with a sharp vegetable peeler.

At the end of the simmering time, remove the rice from the heat and check for doneness. If it is still crunchy after all of the liquid is absorbed, add 2 to 3 tbsp (30 to 45 mL) more water and simmer for a few minutes or until the rice is the desired consistency.

Gluten-Free ✦ Soy-Free ✦ Vegan		
1 cup	long-grain white rice	250 mL
$\frac{1}{2}$ cup	chopped seeded peeled tomatoes (see tip, at left)	125 mL
$\frac{1}{2}$ cup	chopped onion	125 mL
1 tsp	minced seeded jalapeño pepper	4 mL
$\frac{1}{2}$ tsp	Himalayan salt	2 mL
$1\frac{1}{2}$ cups	water	375 mL
$\frac{1}{2}$ tsp	sunflower oil	2 mL
$\frac{1}{4}$ cup	chopped fresh cilantro	60 mL

1. In a saucepan, combine rice, tomatoes, onion, jalapeño, salt, water and oil. Bring to a boil over high heat. Reduce heat to low, cover with a tight-fitting lid and simmer for 20 to 25 minutes or until liquid is absorbed and rice is tender. Remove from heat, cover and let rest for 5 minutes. Fluff rice and stir in cilantro.

Variation

You can substitute long-grain brown rice, but increase the water to $2\frac{1}{4}$ cups (550 mL) and the simmering time to 35 to 40 minutes.

Spanish Saffron Rice

The strands of saffron give this rice a beautiful yellow color and an exotic flavor. Pair it with Spanish Chicken (page 168) to replicate the local flavors of the Iberian Peninsula. This preparation is balancing to vata and pitta; kapha can eat it on occasion.

Tip

At the end of the simmering time, remove the rice from the heat and check for doneness. If it is still crunchy after all of the liquid is absorbed, add 2 to 3 tbsp (30 to 45 mL) more water and simmer for a few minutes or until the rice is the desired consistency.

Gluten-Free ✦ Soy-Free ✦ Vegan

1 cup	long-grain white rice	250 mL
1/2 cup	chopped onion	125 mL
1/2 tsp	paprika	2 mL
1/2 tsp	Himalayan salt	2 mL
5 to 8	saffron threads	5 to 8
1 1/2 cups	water	375 mL
1 tsp	virgin olive oil	5 mL
1/2 cup	peas (optional)	125 mL

1. In a saucepan, combine rice, onion, paprika, salt, saffron to taste, water and oil. Bring to a boil over high heat. Reduce heat to low, cover with a tight-fitting lid and simmer for 20 to 25 minutes or until liquid is absorbed and rice is tender. Remove from heat, stir in peas (if using), cover and let rest for 5 minutes. Fluff rice.

Coconut Purple Rice

According to legend, purple rice was once eaten exclusively by the emperors of China, as it was believed to enrich health and ensure longevity. Thus, it was nicknamed "forbidden rice." In traditional Chinese medicine, it is considered a blood tonifier. It has a nutty taste, soft texture and beautiful deep purple color. Iron-rich, it is balancing to vata and pitta. Kapha should avoid it or eat it only in very small amounts.

**Makes
3 servings**

Tip

At the end of the simmering time, remove the rice from the heat and check for doneness. If it is still crunchy after all of the liquid is absorbed, add 2 to 3 tbsp (30 to 45 mL) more water and simmer for a few minutes or until the rice is the desired consistency.

Gluten-Free ✦ Soy-Free ✦ Vegan

1 cup	purple rice	250 mL
3 tbsp	unsweetened shredded coconut	45 mL
1⅔ cups	water	400 mL

1. In a saucepan, combine rice, coconut and water. Bring to a boil over high heat. Reduce heat to low, cover with a tight-fitting lid and simmer for 30 minutes or until liquid is absorbed and rice is tender. Remove from heat, cover and let rest for 5 minutes. Fluff rice.

Dosha Modifications

✦ **Vata** can stir in toasted nuts (pecans, almonds, walnuts) while fluffing the rice.

✦ **Pitta** and **vata** can add chopped fresh cilantro while fluffing the rice or serve with Pitta-Cooling Date Chutney (page 265).

Coconut Jasmine Rice

Jasmine rice was first cultivated for the royalty of the kingdom of Siam. It was named after the sweet-smelling jasmine flower because of the scent it releases while cooking. Sweet, light, cool and astringent, it is perfect for pitta. Pairing it with coconut and coconut milk makes it balancing for vata, but rather heavy and cool for kapha. Kapha should avoid this dish or eat it only in very small amounts.

**Makes
3 servings**

**SERVING
SUGGESTION**

Serve with Miso Soup
(page 183).

Gluten-Free ◆ Soy-Free ◆ Vegan

- **Rice cooker**

1 cup	jasmine rice	250 mL
6 tbsp	minced onion	90 mL
2 tbsp	unsweetened shredded coconut	30 mL
1/4 tsp	Himalayan salt	1 mL
1 1/2 cups	water (approx.)	375 mL
3/4 cup	coconut milk	175 mL
1/2 tsp	sunflower oil	2 mL

1. In rice cooker, combine rice, onion, coconut, salt, water, coconut milk and oil. Cover and turn the cooker on. When the cooker switches to the Warm setting, check for doneness. If the rice is still crunchy, stir in 1 to 2 tbsp (15 to 30 mL) more water; cover and steam on the Warm setting for 10 minutes or until rice is the desired consistency. Fluff rice.

Kelp Noodles with Almond Sauce

This dish is balancing for pitta and kapha; vata should use the almond sauce liberally to balance out the dryness of the kelp noodles. The suitability of the suggested toppings for the doshas is indicated by the abbreviations in parentheses.

Makes 3 servings

Tip

Although soy sauce contains wheat, tamari is wheat-free; however, if you are allergic or sensitive to gluten, always read labels to make sure the manufacturer did not add wheat. Also check to make sure traditional brewing methods were used, as this ensures the highest quality.

Gluten-Free ✦ Vegan

½ tsp	minced seeded jalapeño pepper	2 mL
⅛ tsp	chili powder	0.5 mL
½ cup	water	125 mL
3 tbsp	almond butter	45 mL
1 tbsp	pure maple syrup or coconut sugar	15 mL
2 tsp	tamari	10 mL
1 tsp	apple cider vinegar	5 mL
12 oz	kelp noodles, rinsed	375 g

Suggested Toppings

Chopped fresh cilantro (VPK)
Finely chopped raw fennel (VPK)
Steamed finely chopped cabbage (PK)
Steamed julienned carrots (VPK)
Finely chopped green onions (VK)
Sesame seeds (V)
Green pumpkin seeds (VPK)

1. In a large skillet, combine jalapeño, chili powder, water, almond butter, maple syrup, tamari and vinegar. Cook, stirring, over low heat for 5 to 10 minutes or until thickened. (Do not let boil.)

2. Stir in kelp noodles and cook, stirring, for about 2 minutes or until noodles are softened and infused with flavors.

3. Serve with any of the suggested toppings, as desired.

Kelp Noodles

Kelp noodles are low in fat and are a good source of iron, calcium, iodine and other trace minerals. They are gluten-free, low in calories and low in carbohydrates, with a neutral taste. The drying process and removal of the outer skin make them suitable for kapha and pitta, even though they are salty. While they can be eaten raw (they are dry and crunchy), I recommend lightly sautéing them to moisten them and aid digestion. For vata, kelp noodles must be cooked and served with a moist, heavy, grounding sauce or in a soup, and should be eaten in moderation.

Salads and Dressings

Ayurveda recommends that foods be cooked before they are eaten, to make them easier to digest. While it is true that raw foods have more enzymes than their cooked counterparts, one must have a very strong digestive fire to unlock the energy of the enzymes and receive their benefits. Understanding this logic, we should try to minimize raw foods. To the extent that you partake in uncooked foods, you can assist their digestion, absorption and assimilation by adding warming herbs, sauces and dressings; consuming them at midday, when the digestive fire is strongest; and letting moderation and balance be your guide.

Vata can eat softer salads with a base of baby arugula, escarole or baby spinach, but should avoid rough vegetables (cabbage, cauliflower, kale, corn, radish). They should apply liberal amounts of oils and lemon or top with a warming dressing, such as tahini or umeboshi vinaigrette.

Fiery pitta can benefit from cool salads, in moderation, adding lime juice to aid digestion or tamari for flavoring.

A spicy dressing, such as Kapha Wasabi Dressing, will balance a salad for kapha. Dressings prepared with a small amount of high-quality corn oil or sesame oil are also beneficial for balancing kapha.

Mizuna Mixed Greens Salad

Mizuna is mildly heating, with a peppery taste. It is well tolerated by all three doshas.

Tip

Mizuna can be purchased at Asian markets and larger grocery stores. If you cannot find it, arugula is a good substitute.

Dairy-Free ✦ Gluten-Free ✦ Vegetarian

2 cups	chopped mizuna	500 mL
1 cup	chopped chicory (frisée)	250 mL
1 cup	chopped red leaf lettuce	250 mL
2 tbsp	Tridoshic Asian Tamari Dressing (page 250)	30 mL

1. In a bowl, combine mizuna, chicory and lettuce. Add dressing and toss to coat.

Dosha Modification

✦ **Vata** can add extra dressing, if desired.

Tridoshic Arugula, Radicchio and Cherry Salad

Cooling and colorful radicchio balances this salad visually and energetically. Ancient Romans considered radicchio a blood purifier and natural sedative. Modern studies show it is high in antioxidants and is nutrient-rich — good for you and tastes good too!

Makes 3 servings

SERVING SUGGESTIONS

Serve as a side with Summer Vegetable Soup (page 192), Marco's Porcini Risotto (page 152) or Ginger Almond Squash Pie (page 221). For a main-dish salad that serves two, top with Paneer (page 160) or Fennel-Crusted Paneer with Balsamic Reduction (page 161).

Dairy-Free ✦ Gluten-Free ✦ Soy-Free ✦ Vegetarian

2 cups	baby arugula	500 mL
1 cup	chopped curly green leaf lettuce	250 mL
1 cup	chopped radicchio	250 mL
2 tbsp	unsweetened dried cherries, chopped	30 mL
2 tbsp	Tridoshic White Balsamic Vinaigrette (page 251)	30 mL

1. In a bowl, combine arugula, lettuce, radicchio and cherries. Add dressing and toss to coat.

Dosha Modification

✦ **Vata** can add extra dressing, if desired, and can serve with a side of Vata Plum Compote (page 263) or Vata Sweet Onion Chutney (page 267).

Vata Pitta
Avocado Cucumber Salad

Avocados are astringent, cooling and sweet, making them ideal for pitta. They are also heavy, oily and soft, which is balancing to vata. Cucumbers are sweet and cooling – ideal for pitta – and are soft and liquid, which balances vata. Kapha should avoid both avocados and cucumbers, so this salad is not a good choice for them.

**Makes
2 servings**

Variation

Use Tridoshic White Balsamic Vinaigrette (page 251) to dress the salad.

Dairy-Free ✦ Gluten-Free ✦ Vegetarian		
2 cups	mizuna or baby spinach	500 mL
1 cup	chopped seeded peeled cucumber ($^3/_4$-inch/2 cm pieces)	250 mL
1	avocado, cut into $^1/_2$-inch (1 cm) pieces	1
2 tbsp	green pumpkin seeds (pepitas)	30 mL
1$^1/_2$ tbsp	Tridoshic Asian Tamari Dressing (page 250)	22 mL

1. Arrange mizuna on a serving plate and top with cucumber and avocado. Sprinkle with pumpkin seeds. Drizzle with dressing.

Dosha Modification
✦ **Vata** can add extra dressing, if desired.

Warm Beet Salad with Beet Greens

The cool beet greens balance the warm beets in this tridoshic salad.

Tips

For the beets, use a mixture of colors: gold, red, etc. Boil the beets separately; otherwise, the darker colors will bleed onto the lighter colors.

To remove beet stains from a wooden cutting board, scrub with lemon juice, then sprinkle with baking soda; let set for 5 minutes, then rinse.

SERVING SUGGESTIONS

This is a great salad to bring to work for lunch; add a wrap made from Lemony Cannellini Bean Spread (page 285), hummus (pages 282–284) or Baked Falafel Balls (page 136). Alternatively, serve as a salad plate with Lemony Cannellini Bean Spread, artichoke hearts and chickpeas or broiled chicken marinated in Tridoshic Lime Cumin Vinaigrette (page 251).

Dairy-Free ✦ Gluten-Free ✦ Soy-Free ✦ Vegetarian

2 cups	chopped peeled beets (1-inch/2.5 cm chunks)	500 mL
	Beet greens, trimmed and chopped into $\frac{1}{2}$-inch (1 cm) pieces	
2 tbsp	chopped fresh mint leaves	30 mL
1 tbsp	finely chopped fresh chives	15 mL
1 tsp	chopped fresh thyme leaves	5 mL
1 tbsp	freshly squeezed lemon juice	15 mL

1. In a saucepan of boiling water, cook beets for about 20 minutes or until tender. Using a slotted spoon, transfer beets to a plate lined with paper towels and let cool.

2. Add beet greens to boiling water and cook for about 30 seconds or until wilted. Drain, transfer to another plate lined with paper towels and let cool.

3. In a bowl, combine beets, beet greens, mint, chives, thyme and lemon juice, tossing to coat.

Variation

Substitute 2 tsp (10 mL) white balsamic vinegar for the lemon juice.

Wakame Daikon Salad

Wakame is cleansing, cooling and decongesting. It promotes smooth downward motion in the colon, which benefits vata; it has a light, decongesting effect that benefits kapha; and it offers a cooling energetic that benefits pitta. With warming daikon radish and carrots to aid digestion, the salad is tolerated by all doshas.

**Makes
2 servings**

Tips

Canned sliced water chestnuts are widely available at supermarkets, health food stores, food cooperatives and Asian markets.

Purchase seaweed (such as wakame) from trusted suppliers that test for heavy metals and pesticides. Avoid seaweed that has been harvested around nuclear power plants or near an industrial zone.

SERVING SUGGESTION

Serve with Dashi Noodle Soup (page 200).

Dairy-Free ✦ Gluten-Free ✦ Vegetarian

⅓ cup	ready-to-use wakame	75 mL
	Warm water	
2 tsp	Tridoshic Asian Tamari Dressing (page 250)	10 mL
½ cup	shredded daikon radish	125 mL
¼ cup	shredded carrots	60 mL
12	water chestnut slices	12
2 tsp	sesame seeds	10 mL

1. Place wakame in a bowl with enough warm water to cover; soak for 15 minutes. Drain and return to bowl. Add dressing and stir to coat evenly.

2. Divide water chestnuts between two serving plates, arranging them in a single layer. Layer wakame mixture on top, then daikon, then carrots, dividing evenly. Sprinkle with sesame seeds.

Dosha Modifications

✦ **Vata** or **pitta** can add chopped cucumber and/or avocado slices.

✦ **Kapha** can add some sprouts.

Tridoshic Mediterranean Salad Plate

This versatile salad comes together quickly and is great for vegetarian potlucks and picnics. For a heartier dish, add stuffed grape leaves, tabbouleh, hummus, chickpeas, Tridoshic Zucchini Hummus (page 283) or white couscous with lemon juice.

Makes 2 servings

Tip

To peel and seed a plum (Roma) tomato, simply chop off ¼ inch (0.5 cm) from each end, then use a sharp vegetable peeler to remove the skin. Cut the tomato into quarters and scrape out the seeds using the sharp point of a knife. If you are using round tomatoes, you will need to carve out the area where the tomato was attached to the stem, then peel with a sharp vegetable peeler.

Variation

Replace the tomatoes with Marinela's Stuffed Grape Leaves (page 276).

SERVING SUGGESTIONS

Serve with Cornbread (page 294) or pita bread.

Dairy-Free ✦ Gluten-Free ✦ Soy-Free ✦ Vegetarian

¾ cup	cubed peeled beets (½-inch/1 cm cubes)	175 mL
1¼ cups	torn red leaf lettuce	300 mL
1¼ cups	spinach leaves	300 mL
6	Baked Falafel Balls (page 136)	6
6	kalamata olives	6
¾ cup	chopped seeded peeled cucumber	175 mL
¾ cup	chopped seeded peeled tomatoes (see tip, at left)	175 mL
¾ cup	quartered drained canned or thawed frozen artichoke hearts	175 mL
3 tbsp	Oregano Vinaigrette (page 249)	45 mL
	Lemon wedges	

1. In a saucepan of boiling water, cook beets for about 15 minutes or until tender. Using a slotted spoon, transfer beets to a plate lined with paper towels and let cool.

2. Arrange lettuce and spinach on a serving plate. Place beets, falafel balls, olives, cucumber, tomatoes and artichoke hearts in small clusters on top. Drizzle with vinaigrette and garnish with lemon wedges.

Dosha Modifications

✦ **Vata** can dress the salad with Basic Tahini (page 261) or Vata Lemon Cashew Cream Sauce (page 262) in place of the vinaigrette.

✦ **Pitta** and **kapha** can try Pitta Kapha Pomegranate Vinaigrette (page 253).

French Lentil Salad with Lemon Dressing

This salad is a very balanced dish that is easy to digest. It can be prepared ahead, making it ideal for lunches and parties.

Makes 2 servings

Tips

If you overcook these lentils, they will lose their shape and become soggy, but they will still be edible.

If preparing this salad ahead, store it in an airtight container in the refrigerator for up to 2 days.

Variations

Add ½ cup (125 mL) diced fennel bulb, celery or carrot in step 2.

Add a few sprigs of chopped fresh tarragon and mint with the parsley.

SERVING SUGGESTIONS

Serve as a main dish with a side of mixed greens, Puréed Parsnips with Thyme (page 215) or Creamy Corn Soup (page 187). Or serve as a side dish alongside poached fish.

Gluten-Free ◆ Soy-Free ◆ Vegan		
1 cup	dried French or Puy lentils, sorted and rinsed	250 mL
1	bay leaf	1
2 cups	water	500 mL
1 tbsp	grated lemon zest	15 mL
1 tbsp	chopped fresh chives or green onions	15 mL
1 tbsp	coarsely chopped fresh parsley	15 mL
¾ tsp	coarsely ground black pepper	3 mL
½ tsp	Himalayan salt	2 mL
Lemon Dressing		
1 tbsp	freshly squeezed lemon juice	15 mL
1 tbsp	sunflower oil	15 mL

1. In a medium saucepan, combine lentils, bay leaf and water. Bring to a boil over high heat. Reduce heat and simmer, skimming off any foam that accumulates on the surface of the water, for 20 minutes or until lentils are tender. Drain, discarding bay leaf, and let cool to room temperature.

2. In a large bowl, combine cooked lentils, lemon zest, chives, parsley, pepper and salt.

3. *Dressing:* In a bowl, whisk together lemon juice and oil.

4. Drizzle dressing over salad and toss gently to coat.

Dosha Modifications

◆ **Vata** can add more oil and salt to their serving.

◆ **Kapha** may omit the oil in step 3 and instead whisk together fresh lemon juice and 1 clove of pressed or minced garlic.

Black Bean Avocado Salad

This dish is best for pitta. The avocados are a little heavy for kapha, but the lightness of the beans and heat of the spices make the dish fine in moderation. Vata can eat it on occasion, with liberal amounts of the dressing.

Makes 4 servings

Tips

Avocado is astringent, cooling, oily and heavy, so it provides balance to pitta and vata.

Black beans are astringent (dry) and cooling, providing balance to pitta and kapha.

SERVING SUGGESTION

Serve with Creamy Corn Soup (page 187).

Dairy-Free ✦ Gluten-Free ✦ Soy-Free ✦ Vegetarian

2 tsp	sunflower oil	10 mL
½ tsp	finely chopped seeded green chile pepper	2 mL
½ tsp	pressed or minced garlic	2 mL
1	can (14 to 19 oz/398 to 540 mL) black beans, drained and rinsed	1
8 oz	frozen corn kernels, thawed	250 g
½ tsp	chili powder	2 mL
4 to 6 tbsp	Tridoshic Lime Cumin Vinaigrette (page 251)	60 to 90 mL
¼ cup	chopped green onions	60 mL
2 tbsp	chopped fresh cilantro	30 mL
1	avocado, chopped	1
	Lime wedges	

1. In a medium saucepan, heat oil over medium–low heat. Add chile pepper and garlic; cook, stirring, for 30 seconds. Add beans, corn and chili powder; cook, stirring gently, for 3 minutes to warm all the ingredients.

2. Transfer bean mixture to a large bowl. Add vinaigrette and toss well to evenly coat the beans. Add green onions, cilantro and avocado, tossing to combine. Garnish with lime wedges.

Summer Israeli Couscous Salad

This light salad is satisfying on a hot summer day. If you soak and cook the chickpeas earlier in the week (or use canned chickpeas), the rest of the dish whips up in minutes. Easy!

**Makes
2 servings**

Variation

Vary the vegetables according to the seasons or your dosha, using the dosha balancing aids (pages 328–339).

SERVING SUGGESTIONS

As a main dish, serve with a side of Vata Sweet Onion Chutney (page 267) and grilled polenta. As a side dish, serve with Broiled Lime Ginger Shrimp (page 162).

Dairy-Free ✦ Soy-Free ✦ Vegetarian

¾ cup	Israeli couscous	175 mL
2 cups	water, divided	500 mL
½ tsp	Himalayan salt, divided	2 mL
½ cup	chopped trimmed kale leaves	125 mL
¼ cup	diced carrot (¼-inch/0.5 cm dice)	60 mL
¼ cup	cooked chickpeas (see page 64), cooled	60 mL
¼ cup	chopped fresh mint	60 mL
2 tbsp	sultana raisins, raisins or chopped dried apricots	30 mL
2 tbsp	chopped fresh chives	30 mL
2 tbsp	Tridoshic Southwest Pumpkin Seed Citrus Dressing (page 252)	30 mL

1. In a small saucepan, bring 1½ cups (375 mL) water to a boil over high heat. Add couscous and ¼ tsp (1 mL) salt; reduce heat to low, cover and simmer, stirring occasionally, for about 10 minutes or until water is absorbed and couscous is tender. Remove from heat and fluff with a fork. Let rest, covered, while you complete step 2.

2. In a medium saucepan, bring the remaining water to a boil. Add kale and carrot; boil for 1 to 2 minutes or until tender. Drain, transfer to a plate lined with paper towels and pat dry.

3. In a bowl, combine couscous, kale mixture, chickpeas, mint, raisins, chives and the remaining salt.

4. Divide salad among two serving plates and drizzle dressing over top.

Dosha Modifications

✦ **Vata** can add extra dressing, if desired.

✦ Couscous is a little heavy for **kapha**, so they should add some cayenne pepper to their serving. Kapha may also substitute an equal amount of freshly squeezed lime juice for the citrus dressing.

Soba Noodle Salad

Fresh mint and basil add a lightness to this dish and complement the sweet and tangy dressing, creating a great summertime meal for all doshas.

Makes 3 servings

Tips

Soba noodles are traditionally made with buckwheat flour, which is gluten-free, but if you are allergic or sensitive to gluten, always check the label to make sure wheat flour was not added.

You can cook the noodles and toss them with the dressing the day before; cover and refrigerate overnight.

SERVING SUGGESTIONS

Serve with Lime Ginger Tofu (page 137) or its shrimp variation and Miso Soup (page 183).

Dairy-Free ◆ Gluten-Free ◆ Vegetarian

- Steamer basket

12 oz	gluten-free soba noodles	375 g
1/2 cup	frozen peas, thawed	125 mL
3 tbsp	Tridoshic Asian Lime Vinaigrette (page 249)	45 mL
1 cup	diced seeded peeled cucumber	250 mL
1/4 cup	chopped fresh basil	60 mL
1/4 cup	chopped fresh mint	60 mL
1/2 cup	black sesame seeds	125 mL
1 tbsp	green pumpkin seeds (pepitas)	15 mL
	Lime wedges	

1. In a large saucepan of boiling salted water, cook noodles, stirring occasionally, for 3 to 6 minutes or until tender. Drain well. Rinse under cold water and drain again. Transfer noodles to a plate lined with paper towels to drain.

2. Meanwhile, in a steamer basket set over boiling water, steam peas for about 2 minutes or until tender.

3. Transfer noodles to a medium bowl. Add dressing and toss to coat. Add peas, cucumber, basil and mint, tossing gently.

4. Arrange salad on a platter. Sprinkle with sesame seeds and pumpkin seeds. Garnish with lime wedges.

Dosha Modifications

- ◆ **Vata** can add roasted cashews with the seeds.
- ◆ **Kapha** can add 1/4 to 1/2 tsp (1 to 2 mL) minced chile pepper to their serving.

Autumn Wild Rice Salad

This salad is light and warming. The earthy flavor of the wild rice is balanced by the sweet (and sour) balsamic dressing.

Tip

Do not overcook the Brussels sprouts or they will taste bitter.

Variations

Substitute pumpkin or sweet potato for the acorn squash.

Substitute chopped asparagus or string beans for the Brussels sprouts.

Replace the cranberries with other cooling dried fruits, such as dates or currants.

Use red rice or short-grain white rice in place of the brown rice.

SERVING SUGGESTIONS

For a main dish, top the salad with ¾ cup (175 mL) crumbled Paneer (page 160) or cubes of Dry-Fried Tofu (page 137); serve with Beet Sweet Potato Soup (variation, page 185) or Chilled Avocado Soup (page 184).

Dairy-Free ✦ Gluten-Free ✦ Soy-Free ✦ Vegetarian

1 tbsp	sunflower oil (approx.)	15 mL
1 cup	cubed peeled acorn squash	250 mL
1 cup	quartered trimmed Brussels sprouts	250 mL
½ cup	cooked wild rice (see page 72), cooled	125 mL
¼ cup	cooked short-grain brown rice (see page 72), cooled	60 mL
¼ cup	dried cranberries, chopped	60 mL
2 tbsp	finely chopped fresh chives	30 mL
2 tbsp	chopped fresh mint	30 mL
¼ tsp	Himalayan salt	1 mL
¼ tsp	crushed black pepper	1 mL

Sweet Balsamic Dressing

1½ tbsp	sunflower oil	22 mL
2½ tsp	white balsamic vinegar	12 mL
½ tsp	raw liquid honey	2 mL

1. Warm a medium skillet over medium heat. Add enough oil to coat the bottom of the pan in a very thin layer. Add squash and cook, stirring, for 5 minutes or until outer edges are browned and center is tender. Using a slotted spoon, transfer squash to a plate.

2. Add more oil to skillet, if necessary. Add Brussels sprouts and cook, stirring, for 2 to 3 minutes or until tender. Add to plate with squash and cool to room temperature.

3. *Dressing:* In a bowl, whisk together oil, vinegar and honey until blended.

4. In a large bowl, combine wild rice, brown rice, cranberries, chives, mint, salt and pepper. Add dressing and stir to coat. Stir in squash and Brussels sprouts.

Dosha Modifications

✦ **Vata** can top with toasted nuts and/or replace the dressing with Vata Tamarind Honey Dressing (page 253).

✦ **Pitta** and **kapha** can add ½ cup (125 mL) cooked chickpeas or steamed cauliflower.

Build Your Own Salad

This book includes recipes for some great tridoshic salads and dressings. If you want to experiment with a dosha-specific salad, or need help at the salad bar, use this chart to help you build your own.

	Vata	Pitta	Kapha
Greens	baby arugula baby spinach chicory (endive/frisée) mizuna mustard greens	chicory (endive/frisée) dandelion greens green lettuce kale mizuna radicchio spinach	arugula chicory (endive/frisée) dandelion greens kale mizuna mustard greens radicchio
Vegetables	asparagus (cooked) beets (cooked) cilantro cucumber fennel	artichokes (cooked) celery cilantro cucumber fennel jicama	artichokes (cooked) beets (cooked) celery chile peppers cilantro corn (cooked) fennel mushrooms onions
Protein (cooked)	French lentils	adzuki beans black beans cannellini beans chickpeas French lentils	adzuki beans black beans cannellini beans chickpeas French lentils
Fruits	avocado black olives dried apricots	avocado dried dates dried figs raisins	dried apricots dried cranberries
Toppings	paneer umeboshi plums	paneer sprouts	chives daikon radish green onions paneer radish sprouts wasabi
Dressing	Basic Tahini (page 261) lemon juice Vata Tamarind Honey Dressing (page 253)	lime juice Pitta Kapha Pomegranate Vinaigrette (page 253)	lime juice Pitta Kapha Pomegranate Vinaigrette (page 253) Kapha Wasabi Dressing (page 254)

Create Your Own Vinaigrette

The salad recipes in this book have been paired with complementary vinaigrettes, but for those who want to venture on their own, the chart below will help you create your signature dressing.

A basic vinaigrette can be made by blending together 3 tbsp (45 mL) oil, 1 tbsp (15 mL) vinegar and a pinch of salt and black pepper. Decide which oil and vinegar you would like to use from among the options that are suitable for your dosha. From there, you can add as many optional ingredients to your dressing as you like, choosing dosha-appropriate additions from the chart. Combine all of the ingredients in a clean, dry 8-oz (250 mL) glass jar; close the lid tightly and shake vigorously until well combined. Store in the refrigerator for up to 1 week (exception: if you use raw garlic, use up the dressing within 3 days).

	Vata	Pitta	Kapha	Tridoshic
Oil (3 tbsp/45 mL)	almond avocado olive sesame sunflower	avocado olive soy sunflower	corn mustard sunflower	sunflower
Vinegar (1 tbsp/15 mL)	apple cider balsamic rice white	apple cider balsamic rice white	apple cider	apple cider
Citrus juice (1 tsp/5 mL)	grapefruit lemon lime orange	lime orange	lime	lime
Flavoring (¼ tsp/1 mL)	tamarind paste umeboshi paste			
Sweetener (½ tsp/2 mL)	coconut sugar raw liquid honey rice syrup	coconut sugar pure maple syrup pomegranate syrup rice syrup	apple or pear juice concentrate raw liquid honey pomegranate syrup	coconut sugar
Dried herbs and spices (¼ tsp/1 mL unless otherwise noted)	cayenne pepper (a pinch) cumin (ground) dillweed fennel seeds oregano parsley tarragon	cumin (ground) dillweed fennel seeds tarragon	cayenne pepper (a pinch) cumin (ground) dillweed dry mustard fennel seeds oregano	cumin (ground) dillweed fennel seeds
Fresh herbs and spices (¾ tsp/3 mL minced)	chives garlic green onions mint parsley	cilantro dill mint tarragon	chives garlic green onions mint parsley rosemary	mint

Oregano Vinaigrette

Oregano is a warming spice that aids digestion. It is great combined with cool foods such as salad greens, beans and lentils. It especially works well paired with Mediterranean and Mexican dishes.

Makes ¹/₂ cup (125 mL)

Tip

Store in the refrigerator for up to 1 week.

Dairy-Free ♦ Gluten-Free ♦ Soy-Free ♦ Vegetarian

¹/₂ tsp	dried oregano	2 mL
¹/₂ tsp	Himalayan salt	2 mL
¹/₄ tsp	crushed black pepper	1 mL
6 tbsp	avocado oil or extra virgin olive oil	90 mL
2 tbsp	freshly squeezed lemon juice	30 mL
1 tsp	apple cider vinegar	5 mL
¹/₂ tsp	raw liquid honey	2 mL

1. In a glass jar, combine oregano, salt, pepper, oil, lemon juice, vinegar and honey; cover tightly and shake vigorously until well combined.

Tridoshic Asian Lime Vinaigrette

This dressing is sweet and tangy, with a balanced energetic. To make it vegan, you can substitute an equal amount of coconut sugar for the honey, but the energetic will be a little more cooling, and less tridoshic, so kapha should use the dressing in moderation.

Makes ¹/₄ cup (60 mL)

Tip

Store in the refrigerator for up to 1 week.

SERVING SUGGESTIONS

Serve over Asian-Style Vegetables (page 218) or Mizuna Mixed Greens Salad (page 236).

Dairy-Free ♦ Gluten-Free ♦ Vegetarian

¹/₈ tsp	cayenne pepper	0.5 mL
1 tbsp	freshly squeezed lime juice	15 mL
1 tbsp	sunflower oil	15 mL
1 tbsp	sesame oil	15 mL
1 tbsp	raw liquid honey	15 mL
2¹/₄ tsp	tamari	11 mL
1¹/₂ tsp	apple cider vinegar	7 mL

1. In a glass jar, combine cayenne, lime juice, sunflower oil, sesame oil, honey, tamari and vinegar; cover tightly and shake vigorously until well combined. Let stand for 15 minutes to allow the flavors to blend before using.

Tridoshic Asian Tamari Dressing

This lightly sweetened dressing has a balanced energetic and tastes clean on the palate.

Makes ¹/₄ cup (60 mL)

Tips

Store in the refrigerator for up to 1 week.

Although soy sauce contains wheat, tamari is wheat-free; however, if you are allergic or sensitive to gluten, always read labels to make sure the manufacturer did not add wheat. Also check to make sure traditional brewing methods were used, as this ensures the highest quality.

SERVING SUGGESTIONS

Serve over Wakame Daikon Salad (page 240) or Barley Sauté with Sweet Potato, Asparagus and Burdock (page 140).

Dairy-Free ✦ Gluten-Free ✦ Vegetarian

¹/₄ tsp	cayenne pepper	1 mL
2 tbsp	sunflower oil	30 mL
4 tsp	tamari	20 mL
1 tbsp	unseasoned rice vinegar	15 mL
2 tsp	sesame oil	10 mL
2 tsp	raw liquid honey	10 mL

1. In a glass jar, combine cayenne, sunflower oil, tamari, vinegar, sesame oil and honey; cover tightly and shake vigorously until well combined. Let stand for 15 minutes to allow the flavors to blend before using.

Tridoshic Lime Cumin Vinaigrette

Cumin is a digestive aid, making this a great vinaigrette for lentils and beans.

Makes ¹/₂ cup (125 mL)

Tip
Store in the refrigerator for up to 1 week.

Variation
To use as a marinade, substitute coconut sugar for the honey.

SERVING SUGGESTIONS

Serve with Black Bean Avocado Salad (page 243) or over a salad of mixed greens. Or use as a tridoshic marinade for fish.

Dairy-Free ◆ Gluten-Free ◆ Soy-Free ◆ Vegetarian

¹/₂ tsp	cumin seeds, lightly crushed	2 mL
¹/₂ tsp	ground cumin	2 mL
¹/₂ tsp	ground coriander	2 mL
¹/₂ tsp	Himalayan salt	2 mL
¹/₂ tsp	crushed black pepper	2 mL
6 tbsp	sunflower oil	90 mL
2 tbsp	freshly squeezed lime juice	30 mL
1 tbsp	raw liquid honey	15 mL

1. In a glass jar, combine cumin seeds, ground cumin, coriander, salt, pepper, oil, lime juice and honey; cover tightly and shake vigorously until well combined. Let stand for 15 minutes to allow the flavors to blend before using.

Tridoshic White Balsamic Vinaigrette

White balsamic vinegar is made from white Trebbiano grapes. It is milder (less sour) and less heating than regular balsamic vinegar.

Makes ¹/₂ cup (125 mL)

Tip
Store in the refrigerator for up to 1 week.

Dairy-Free ◆ Gluten-Free ◆ Soy-Free ◆ Vegetarian

¹/₈ tsp	Himalayan salt	0.5 mL
¹/₈ tsp	crushed black pepper	0.5 mL
6 tbsp	sunflower oil	90 mL
2 tbsp	white balsamic vinegar	30 mL
1 tsp	raw liquid honey	5 mL

1. In a glass jar, combine salt, pepper, oil, vinegar and honey; cover tightly and shake vigorously until well combined.

Tridoshic Southwest Pumpkin Seed Citrus Dressing

This dressing captures the essential seasonings of the American Southwest: cinnamon, cumin, orange and chiles. I've kept the heat to a minimum so all doshas can enjoy!

Makes ¹/₂ cup (125 mL)

Tip

Store in the refrigerator for up to 1 week.

Variation

Add 1 tbsp (15 mL) chopped fresh mint and/or cilantro.

SERVING SUGGESTIONS

Serve with Summer Israeli Couscous Salad (page 244) or Black Bean Avocado Salad (page 243).

Dairy-Free ◆ Gluten-Free ◆ Soy-Free ◆ Vegetarian

- Small food processor or mini chopper

¹/₃ cup	green pumpkin seeds (pepitas)	75 mL
¹/₂ tsp	chili powder	2 mL
¹/₂ tsp	ground coriander	2 mL
¹/₂ tsp	ground cumin	2 mL
¹/₂ tsp	ground cinnamon	2 mL
¹/₈ tsp	Himalayan salt	0.5 mL
Pinch	cayenne pepper	Pinch
1 tsp	grated orange zest	5 mL
¹/₄ cup	freshly squeezed orange juice	60 mL
1 tbsp	freshly squeezed lime juice	15 mL
1 tbsp	sunflower oil	15 mL
³/₄ tsp	raw liquid honey	3 mL
2 to 3 tbsp	water	30 to 45 mL

1. In food processor, combine pumpkin seeds, chili powder, coriander, cumin, cinnamon, salt, cayenne, orange zest, orange juice, lime juice, oil and honey; pulse until pumpkin seeds are coarsely chopped.

2. Transfer to a glass jar and add 2 tbsp (30 mL) water; cover tightly and shake vigorously until well combined. For a thinner dressing, add another 1 tbsp (15 mL) water and shake to combine. Let stand for 20 minutes to allow the flavors to blend before using.

Vata Tamarind Honey Dressing

Tamarind paste is ideal for vata, as the sour taste adds moisture and warmth, which are beneficial to digestion. Pitta and kapha can use it in moderation.

Makes ¹/₂ cup (125 mL)

Tip

Store in the refrigerator for up to 1 week.

Variation

To use as a marinade, replace the honey with coconut sugar.

Dairy-Free ✦ Gluten-Free ✦ Soy-Free ✦ Vegetarian

¹/₈ tsp	Himalayan salt	0.5 mL
¹/₄ cup	water	60 mL
¹/₄ cup	sunflower oil	60 mL
1 tbsp	raw liquid honey	15 mL
2 tsp	freshly squeezed lime juice	10 mL
2¹/₂ tsp	tamarind paste	12 mL

1. In a glass jar, combine salt, water, oil, honey, lime juice and tamarind paste; cover tightly and shake vigorously until well combined.

Pitta Kapha Pomegranate Vinaigrette

Cool and astringent, this dressing is ideal for pitta and kapha. Serve over salads or use as a marinade for seafood or chicken.

Makes ²/₃ cup (150 mL)

Tips

Store in the refrigerator for up to 1 week.

Pomegranate syrup (also known as pomegranate molasses) can be purchased at international grocery stores or in the international aisle of major grocery stores.

Gluten-Free ✦ Soy-Free ✦ Vegan

6 tbsp	sunflower oil	90 mL
2 tbsp	pomegranate syrup	30 mL
¹/₄ tsp	grated lime, orange or lemon zest	1 mL
1 tbsp	freshly squeezed lime juice	15 mL
1 tbsp	apple cider vinegar	15 mL

1. In a glass jar, combine oil, pomegranate syrup, lime zest, lime juice and vinegar; cover tightly and shake vigorously until well combined.

Kapha Wasabi Dressing

Hot and pungent, this dressing has a kick that will get kapha moving! Serve over salads, rice or broiled fish.

Makes ½ cup (125 mL)

Tips

Store in an airtight container in the refrigerator for up to 1 week.

Ayurvedic practitioners believe raw honey has many benefits, including scraping fat and cholesterol from the body's tissues, making it the go-to sweetener for kapha or anyone trying to reduce kapha in their body.

SERVING SUGGESTION

Serve with Ginger Salmon Hand Rolls (page 164).

Dairy-Free ✦ Gluten-Free ✦ Vegetarian

4 tsp	wasabi powder	20 mL
2 tsp	water	10 mL
2 tsp	grated gingerroot	10 mL
Pinch	cayenne pepper (optional)	Pinch
¼ cup	sesame oil	60 mL
4 tsp	unseasoned rice vinegar	20 mL
2 tsp	raw liquid honey	10 mL
2 tsp	tamari	10 mL
2 tsp	freshly squeezed lemon juice	10 mL

1. In a small bowl, mix wasabi powder and water to form a thick paste. Whisk in ginger, cayenne (if using), oil, vinegar, honey, tamari and lemon juice. Let stand for 20 minutes to allow the flavors to blend before using.

Sauces, Chutneys and Spice Blends

Unlike the other chapters, the majority of recipes in this chapter are dosha-specific, designed to produce an energy that will help to balance vata, pitta or kapha. Use the sauces, chutneys and spice blends to accompany meals where the energetic needs to be modified and toned down to suit your constitution. The recipes here allow you to cheat a little and eat the foods you love without the heartache (or heartburn or bloating) of food choices that are less than ideal.

This is my favorite chapter. When I'm feeling creative, I'll often design a meal around one of these recipes, having fun with the interplay of the foods' energetics. If you love cooking, this chapter will be a playground from which you can conduct your own experiments. If that sounds too ambitious, don't worry: all of the recipes feature serving suggestions that will help you pair them with other recipes in this book. The recipes are not labor-intensive and do not require special culinary skills. All can be made in advance to help you flow through your weekday meal routines with ease.

I have included some churnas – dosha-specific spice combinations – at the end of the chapter. In ayurveda, these are typically sprinkled on meals or taken at the end of a meal to regulate digestion. If making churnas feels like too much of an effort, you can chew a few fennel seeds or ajwain seeds at the end of a meal instead.

Ghee

Ayurveda advocates the consumption of dairy products because, in Hindu culture, the cow is sacred and is the giver of life. Ingesting dairy products is akin to receiving love and nutrients from your mother. Ghee was traditionally made from cream that was fermented into yogurt, churned into butter, then simmered slowly until it transformed into a golden liquid. Ghee is special because it can both detoxify and rejuvenate at the same time when specific protocols are followed. It is still widely used today because it has a higher smoking point than butter and adds a delicious flavor to your cooking.

Makes about 14 oz (400 g)

Tips

Ghee is the most refined end product of milk. Anything present in milk — including antibiotics, hormones (where legally permitted), chemical pesticides, etc. — is concentrated in ghee, so it is best to use organic butter to make it.

Try using cultured butter to approximate the traditional Indian preparation.

Moisture permits bacteria to grow and will spoil the ghee. Be sure to use clean, dry utensils when scooping out ghee. If you store ghee in the refrigerator, condensation may form as you move the jar in and out; this condensation can spoil the ghee.

Gluten-Free ✦ Soy-Free ✦ Vegetarian

- **Fine-mesh sieve, lined with cheesecloth**
- **Clean, dry 1-pint (500 mL) glass jar or container with lid**

| 1 lb | organic unsalted butter | 454 g |

1. In a medium, heavy-bottomed saucepan, melt butter over medium heat. Bring to a boil. Immediately reduce heat to low and simmer gently. The water content will evaporate and milk solids (small white curds) will form, fall to the bottom of the pan and begin to turn brown. Using a dry spoon, skim the froth from the top and discard. The ghee is done in 25 to 30 minutes when the sputtering ceases, the ghee is clear, the color is golden and it smells like popcorn.

2. Immediately remove ghee from heat and let cool for 15 minutes. Place the lined sieve over the glass jar. Slowly pour ghee into the sieve, straining out the curds. Let cool to room temperature. Cover and store in a cool, dark place for up to 3 months.

Ghee and the Doshas

Ghee is considered tridoshic, but it is especially good for vata, who can benefit immensely from its lubricating qualities. Ghee's cooling energetics make it suitable for pitta; kapha can tolerate it in moderation. People with high ama, high cholesterol, obesity or fever should not use ghee.

Spanish Chicken (page 168) over Spanish Saffron Rice (page 231)

Dashi Noodle Soup (page 200)

Caribbean Adzuki Bean Stew (page 209)
over Coconut Jasmine Rice (page 233), with Cornbread (page 294)

Kelp Noodles with Almond Sauce (page 234)

Tridoshic Mediterranean Salad Plate (page 241)
made with Marinela's Stuffed Grape Leaves (page 276)

Endive
with Honeyed
Goat Cheese
(page 274)

Lemony Cannellini Bean Spread (page 285), Traditional Mexican
Salsa (page 290) and Mexican Black Bean Spread (page 286)

Pomegranate Orange Chip Cookies
(variation, page 306)

Lavender Essence
Tea Bread (page 293)

Truffles (page 309)

Tridoshic Pomegranate Orange Reduction Sauce

Pomegranate is astringent and is best for balancing pitta and kapha. The sourness of the vinegar and the sweetness of the orange juice round out the flavors and provide balance for vata.

**Makes about
3/4 cup (175 mL)**

Tip

Pomegranate syrup (also known as pomegranate molasses) can be purchased at international grocery stores or in the international aisle of major grocery stores.

Variation

Add ¼ tsp (1 mL) chopped fresh herbs, such as mint, tarragon, basil or rosemary — whatever complements your dish — after the sauce is reduced.

SERVING SUGGESTIONS

Serve drizzled over Fennel-Crusted Paneer (page 161), grilled halibut, scallops, chicken breasts or venison.

Gluten-Free ✦ Soy-Free ✦ Vegan		
¾ cup	water	175 mL
¼ tsp	grated orange zest	1 mL
6 tbsp	freshly squeezed orange juice	90 mL
3 tbsp	pomegranate syrup	45 mL
2 tbsp	white balsamic vinegar	30 mL
1 tbsp	freshly squeezed lemon juice	15 mL

1. In a small saucepan, whisk together water, orange zest, orange juice, pomegranate syrup, vinegar and lemon juice. Bring to a boil over high heat. Reduce heat and simmer, whisking often, for 15 to 20 minutes or until sauce is thickened and reduced by half.

Tangy Tamarind Sauce

The moist, warm, heavy, sweet and sour qualities of this dressing are ideal for vata. It can be used on any dish that needs grounding. Pitta and kapha can use it in moderation on a cold, light dish.

Makes about ³/₄ cup (175 mL)

Tip

Store in an airtight nonmetallic container in the refrigerator for up to 2 weeks.

SERVING SUGGESTIONS

Drizzle over Moroccan Veggie Burgers (page 135) or Fennel-Crusted Paneer (page 161).

Dairy-Free ♦ Gluten-Free ♦ Soy-Free ♦ Vegetarian

¹/₂ cup	water	125 mL
6 tbsp	raw liquid honey	90 mL
2 tbsp	tamarind paste	30 mL

1. In a small bowl, whisk together water, honey and tamarind paste.

Artichoke Lemon Cream Sauce

Artichokes are astringent, light and warm, and cashews are sweet, heavy and warm, so this sauce is ideal for vata. It's a little warm for pitta and a little heavy for kapha, but okay in moderation. It will balance dry, light dishes.

Makes about
³/₄ cup (175 mL)

Tips

Omit the salt if the canned artichokes were packed with salt.

Store in an airtight nonmetallic container in the refrigerator for up to 1 week.

Variation

Substitute chopped baby arugula or chopped zucchini for the artichoke hearts.

SERVING SUGGESTIONS

Serve over Summer Squash Pasta (page 217), wheat pasta or steamed vegetables, or as a dipping sauce for Baked Falafel Balls (page 136).

Gluten-Free ✦ Soy-Free ✦ Vegan		

• **Food processor**

½ cup	drained canned unsalted water-packed artichoke hearts	125 mL
½ cup	water	125 mL
¼ cup	raw cashew butter (page 280)	60 mL
1 tbsp	freshly squeezed lemon juice	15 mL
¼ tsp	Himalayan salt (see tip, at left)	1 mL
⅛ tsp	crushed black pepper	0.5 mL

1. In food processor, combine artichoke hearts, water, cashew butter, lemon juice, salt and pepper; pulse until smooth.

Tzatziki

This cucumber dill sauce is best for vata and pitta; kapha can eat in moderation if the yogurt is fresh (not more than 3 days old).

Makes about 1 cup (250 mL)

Tip

Store in an airtight nonmetallic container in the refrigerator for up to 1 week.

Variation

Substitute 2 small mint leaves, finely chopped, for the dill.

SERVING SUGGESTIONS

Serve with Marinela's Stuffed Grape Leaves (page 276) or mung dal.

Gluten-Free ✦ Soy-Free ✦ Vegetarian

- **Food processor**

1 cup	plain full-fat yogurt	250 mL
1/2 cup	coarsely chopped seeded peeled cucumber	125 mL
1/4 to 1/2 tsp	fresh dill	1 to 2 mL
1/4 tsp	pressed or minced garlic	1 mL
1/8 tsp	Himalayan salt	0.5 mL
1/2 tsp	grated lemon zest	2 mL
1/2 tsp	freshly squeezed lemon juice	2 mL

1. Place yogurt in a fine-mesh sieve and let drain for about 30 minutes.
2. In food processor, combine yogurt, cucumber, dill to taste, garlic, salt, lemon zest and lemon juice; purée until smooth. Cover and refrigerate for 1 hour before serving.

Basic Tahini

Sesame seeds are heating, oily and heavy, so tahini is ideal for vata. Pitta can use it in moderation or with cooling herbs such as cilantro or mint. Kapha should avoid tahini unless it is thinned in a sauce and accompanied by a dish that is very drying, such as millet.

Makes about ¹/₂ cup (125 mL)

• **Food processor**

1 cup	unhulled raw sesame seeds	250 mL
¹/₄ cup	sunflower oil	60 mL

1. In a large dry skillet, toast sesame seeds over medium heat for 5 minutes, tossing frequently with a wooden spatula until fragrant and lightly browned. Let cool for 20 minutes.

2. Transfer sesame seeds to food processor and add oil. Process for 2 minutes to the consistency of nut butter.

Tips

Unhulled brown or black sesame seeds are high in calcium and are a good dairy-free solution to supplement your calcium intake. When the raw unhulled seeds are crushed, as in tahini, their nutrients are more easily digested.

Store in a glass jar in the refrigerator for up to 2 months.

To make a sauce for salads or vegetables, add ¹/₂ tsp (2 mL) freshly squeezed lemon juice to 1 tbsp (15 mL) tahini, then thin with water to desired consistency.

SERVING SUGGESTIONS

Use to replace peanut butter in sandwiches; to replace butter in baking recipes (be aware that it will impart a sesame flavor); or as a base for salad dressings and sauces for vegetables.

Vata Lemon Cashew Cream Sauce

This sauce is sweet, a little sour, heavy and warming – ideal for grounding vata.

Variations

Add one or two of
the following: 1 tsp
(5 mL) tamari, a pinch
of cayenne pepper,
¹/₈ tsp (0.5 mL) ground
cinnamon, a pinch of
ground allspice, 1 tsp
(5 mL) chopped fresh
mint, ¹/₂ tsp (2 mL) fresh
thyme leaves, ¹/₂ tsp
(2 mL) fresh savory
leaves or ¹/₂ tsp (2 mL)
grated orange zest.

SERVING
SUGGESTIONS

Season with ¹/₈ tsp
(0.5 mL) ground
cinnamon and serve
over millet, couscous
or polenta.

Gluten-Free ✦ Soy-Free ✦ Vegan

- **Small food processor or mini chopper**

1 tbsp	coarsely chopped fresh parsley	15 mL
¹/₂ tsp	Himalayan salt	2 mL
¹/₄ cup	raw cashew butter (page 280)	60 mL
¹/₄ cup	water (approx.)	60 mL
¹/₂ tsp	grated lemon zest	2 mL
1 tbsp	freshly squeezed lemon juice	15 mL

1. In food processor, combine parsley, salt, cashew butter, water, lemon zest and lemon juice; process until smooth and creamy. If you desire a thinner consistency, add more water.

Vata Plum Compote

I love the sweet juicy goodness of ripe in-season plums. This delicately spiced compote is easy to make and will fill your kitchen with the smell of the harvest and the memory of all things sweet.

**Makes about
$\frac{1}{2}$ cup (125 mL)**

Tips

Purchase plums that are plump, richly colored and sweet–smelling and that yield to gentle pressure from your finger. Avoid plums with shriveled skin, brown discolorations or mushy spots.

Store in an airtight glass container in the refrigerator for up to 1 week. Serve cold or gently warm the amount you want to use in a small saucepan over low heat.

SERVING SUGGESTIONS

Serve alongside Fluffy Cinnamon Currant Millet (page 143), couscous, quinoa or rice.

	Gluten-Free ✦ Soy-Free ✦ Vegan	
1½ cups	quartered organic plums	375 mL
1 tbsp	coconut sugar or pure maple syrup	15 mL
½ tsp	Himalayan salt	2 mL
¼ tsp	ground cloves	1 mL
¼ cup	water	60 mL
1 tsp	grated orange zest	5 mL
2 tsp	freshly squeezed lemon juice	10 mL

1. In a small saucepan, combine plums, sugar, salt, cloves, water, orange zest and lemon juice. Bring to a boil over high heat. Reduce heat and simmer, stirring occasionally, for 20 minutes or until plums become a chunky sauce.

Cool Coconut Chutney

The chile pepper gives this chutney a mildly spicy flavor, but the coconut provides an overall cooling energetic. You can reduce or omit the chile pepper if you prefer a sweeter chutney.

Makes about ²/₃ cup (150 mL)

Tips

Do not use dried coconut in place of the fresh or frozen.

For a vegan chutney, substitute sunflower oil for the ghee.

Store in an airtight container in the refrigerator for up to 1 week.

SERVING SUGGESTIONS

Serve with Bangalore Toor Dal Sambhar (page 126), Kerala-Inspired Toor Dal (page 124) or Urad Dal with Tamarind (page 127).

Gluten-Free ✦ Soy-Free ✦ Vegetarian

• **Small food processor or mini chopper**

1½ tsp	ghee	7 mL
1½ tsp	urad dal, sorted	7 mL
¼ cup	coarsely chopped onion	60 mL
2 tsp	finely chopped gingerroot	10 mL
4	curry leaves	4
½ tsp	tamarind paste	2 mL
½ cup	unsweetened fresh or frozen shredded coconut	125 mL
¼ tsp	sliced seeded thin green chile pepper	1 mL
¼ tsp	Himalayan salt	1 mL
6 tbsp	water (approx.)	90 mL
1½ tsp	freshly squeezed lime juice	7 mL
2 tsp	chopped fresh cilantro leaves	10 mL

1. In a small saucepan, melt ghee over medium heat. When ghee is hot, but not smoking, add urad dal; cook, stirring, until starting to brown. Stir in onion, ginger, curry leaves and tamarind paste until well combined; cook, stirring, for 3 minutes. Add coconut, chile and salt; cook, stirring, for 3 minutes to blend the flavors.

2. Transfer coconut mixture to food processor and add water and lime juice. Pulse to a thick, smooth paste, adding more water as needed to achieve the desired consistency. Garnish with cilantro.

Pitta-Cooling Date Chutney

This chutney is sweet, heavy and cool – balancing for pitta. Vata can eat it in moderation; kapha should avoid it, as it is too sweet.

Makes about 1 cup (250 mL)

Tip

Store in an airtight nonmetallic container in the refrigerator for up to 2 weeks.

SERVING SUGGESTION

Serve alongside dishes with a warming energetic, such as Polenta with Minted Shiitake Sauce (page 146) or a spicy dal.

Gluten-Free ✦ Soy-Free ✦ Vegan

⅔ cup	coarsely chopped Medjool dates	150 mL
½ cup	coarsely chopped peeled Bartlett pear or red apple	125 mL
¼ cup	finely chopped onion	60 mL
⅛ tsp	ground cardamom	0.5 mL
1 cup	water	250 mL
¼ tsp	balsamic vinegar	1 mL

1. In a small saucepan, combine dates, pear, onion, cardamom, water and vinegar. Bring to a boil over high heat. Reduce heat and simmer, stirring occasionally, for about 15 minutes or until liquid is reduced and chutney is chunky.

2. Remove from heat and mash pears a bit with the back of a fork.

Kapha Spicy Pear Chutney

Lightly sweet, with a kick of heat, this chutney will help kapha balance cooler and heavier dishes.

Makes about 1½ cups (375 mL)

Tip

Store in an airtight nonmetallic container in the refrigerator for up to 2 weeks.

SERVING SUGGESTIONS

Serve warm as an accompaniment to rice dishes, meat dishes (such as Bison Meatloaf with Maple Tamarind Sauce, page 174) or Baked Falafel Balls (page 136).

Gluten-Free ✦ Soy-Free ✦ Vegan		
2 cups	chopped peeled Bartlett pears or red apple	500 mL
1 tsp	coconut sugar, pure maple syrup or pomegranate syrup	5 mL
1 tsp	grated orange zest	5 mL
¼ tsp	ground cloves	1 mL
¼ tsp	Himalayan salt	1 mL
⅛ to ¼ tsp	cayenne pepper	0.5 to 1 mL
½ cup	water	125 mL
½ tsp	apple cider vinegar	2 mL

1. In a small saucepan, combine pears, coconut sugar, orange zest, cloves, salt, cayenne, water and vinegar. Bring to a boil over high heat. Reduce heat to low; cover and simmer for 20 minutes or until the pears are soft.

2. Remove from heat and mash pears with a fork to create a chunky chutney.

Vata Sweet Onion Chutney

This sweet and sour chutney with a mildly warming energetic will soothe and ground vata while also stimulating the digestive fire to help vata digest cooler dishes.

**Makes about
1 cup (250 mL)**

Tip

The cooled chutney can be stored in a glass jar in the refrigerator for up to 1 week.

SERVING SUGGESTION

Serve with Moroccan Veggie Burgers (page 135).

Gluten-Free ◆ Soy-Free ◆ Vegan

• **Small food processor or mini chopper**

2½ tbsp	sunflower oil, divided	37 mL
1 cup	chopped onion	250 mL
½ tsp	pressed or minced garlic	2 mL
½ tsp	finely chopped seeded thin green chile pepper	2 mL
5	curry leaves	5
¼ tsp	tamarind paste	1 mL
¼ cup	water (approx.)	60 mL
1 tsp	urad dal, sorted	5 mL
1 tsp	mustard seeds	5 mL
½ tsp	Himalayan salt	2 mL
1 tsp	tomato paste	5 mL

1. In a large skillet, heat 1½ tsp (7 mL) oil over medium heat. Add onion, garlic and chile; cook, stirring, for 1 minute or until fragrant and golden. Reduce heat to low and stir in curry leaves and tamarind paste; cook, stirring for 1 minute.

2. Transfer onion mixture to food processor and add water; pulse to a thick consistency.

3. In the same skillet, heat the remaining oil over medium heat. Add urad dal and cook, stirring, until fragrant and golden. Add mustard seeds and cook, stirring, for about 30 seconds or until the seeds pop. Stir in onion mixture, salt and tomato paste. If the mixture is sticking to the pan, add a few teaspoons (10 to 15 mL) water. Cook, stirring, for about 20 minutes or until chutney is thickened. Let cool completely.

Kapha Hot Onion Chutney

This chutney is balancing for kapha. A little goes a long way – 1 or 2 tbsp (15 or 30 mL) is all you need.

Makes about 1/2 cup (125 mL)

Tip

Store in an airtight nonmetallic container in the refrigerator for up to 2 weeks.

SERVING SUGGESTIONS

Serve with rice dishes, heavy dals (such as Urad Dal with Tamarind, page 127) and meat dishes (such as Bison Meatloaf with Maple Tamarind Sauce, page 174).

Dairy-Free ♦ Gluten-Free ♦ Soy-Free ♦ Vegetarian

1 tsp	tomato paste	5 mL
1 tsp	water	5 mL
1/2 tsp	pressed or minced garlic	2 mL
1/4 to 1/2 tsp	cayenne pepper	1 to 2 mL
1 tsp	apple cider vinegar	5 mL
1/4 tsp	raw liquid honey	1 mL
1/2 cup	minced onion	125 mL
1 tsp	coarsely chopped fresh cilantro or parsley	5 mL

1. In a bowl, whisk together tomato paste and water to make a thick sauce. Whisk in garlic, cayenne, vinegar and honey. Add onions and cilantro, stirring to evenly coat onions with seasonings. Let stand for 15 minutes to blend the flavors.

Cranberry Relish

A healthier twist on cranberry relish from a can, this recipe is easy to make and can be served warm or chilled. Cranberries are astringent, sour and heating, making them well suited for kapha. But cooking them with maple syrup cools things down, and the orange zest rounds out the flavors.

Makes about 1 cup (250 mL)

Tip

Store in an airtight container in the refrigerator for up to 4 days.

Variations

Substitute lemon zest for the orange zest.

Add a star anise pod or 3 whole cloves with the maple syrup; discard after removing from the heat.

SERVING SUGGESTIONS

Serve with Roasted Turkey Breast with Tarragon Cream Sauce (page 170), Lemon Rosemary Turkey Sausages (page 169) or Roasted Kabocha Squash (page 220).

Gluten-Free ✦ Soy-Free ✦ Vegan

1½ cups	cranberries	375 mL
¼ cup	water	60 mL
¼ cup	pure maple syrup	60 mL
¾ tsp	grated orange zest (optional)	3 mL

1. In a small saucepan, combine cranberries, water and maple syrup. Bring to a boil over high heat. Reduce heat and boil gently, stirring constantly, until reduced by half. Stir in orange zest (if using). Remove from heat and let cool for 20 minutes. Serve warm or cover and refrigerate for 1 hour, until chilled.

Moroccan Spice Blend

This is a mildly warming spice blend, well tolerated by vata and kapha. Pitta can use it in moderation. Use as a rub on fish or meat, or sprinkled in lentil or chickpea stew, to experience the flavors of Morocco.

Makes about 8 tsp (40 mL)

Tip

Store spices and spice blends in a cool, dark place. Try to use them up within 6 months; after that, the spices will start to lose their zing.

SERVING SUGGESTIONS

Serve with Moroccan Veggie Burgers (page 135), Baked Falafel Balls (page 136) or Moroccan Lamb Meatballs (page 173).

Gluten-Free ◆ Soy-Free ◆ Vegan

2 tsp	ground coriander	10 mL
2 tsp	ground cumin	10 mL
1½ tsp	ground cinnamon	7 mL
1 tsp	ground ginger	5 mL
½ tsp	paprika	2 mL
½ tsp	Himalayan salt	2 mL
¼ tsp	ground nutmeg	1 mL
¼ tsp	ground turmeric	1 mL
¼ tsp	ground allspice	1 mL
¼ tsp	dried oregano	1 mL

1. In a glass jar or other airtight container, combine coriander, cumin, cinnamon, ginger, paprika, salt, nutmeg, turmeric, allspice and oregano.

Masala Spice Mix

This versatile blend of spices has a very mild amount of heat with a great depth of flavor – suitable for all doshas.

Makes about 1/2 cup (125 mL)

Tips

Toasting the spices releases the essential oils and flavors.

Grind the spices to a fine powder if you plan to use the mix to make desserts or you prefer a silkier finish.

Store in an airtight glass container at room temperature for up to 3 months.

This recipe can be doubled if you find yourself using it a lot.

SERVING SUGGESTIONS

Use in Masala Dosas (page 112), Chicken Tikka Masala (page 166) or Masala Potatoes (page 226). Or sprinkle on porridge, Creamy Yogurt (page 117), Kabocha Caramel Custard (page 310) or any food to lend a touch of exotic taste.

Gluten-Free ✦ Soy-Free ✦ Vegan

- Mortar and pestle
- Coffee or spice grinder

4	2½-inch (6 cm) cinnamon sticks	4
3 tbsp	green cardamom pods	45 mL
6	star anise pods	6
2	bay leaves	2
2 tbsp	coriander seeds	30 mL
2 tsp	cumin seeds	10 mL
½ tsp	whole black peppercorns	2 mL
1 tsp	ground turmeric	5 mL
½ tsp	ground nutmeg	2 mL
½ tsp	cayenne pepper	2 mL

1. Using a mortar and pestle, lightly crush cinnamon sticks and cardamom pods.

2. In a small skillet, over medium heat, toast cinnamon, cardamom, star anise, bay leaves, coriander seeds, cumin seeds and peppercorns, stirring constantly, for 30 seconds. Let cool.

3. Transfer spice mixture to coffee grinder and grind to a coarse powder. Stir in turmeric, nutmeg and cayenne. Let cool completely.

Variations

Add 4 whole cloves in step 1 for a more intense flavor and more heat (pitta should use this version with caution).

Add 1 dried chile pepper in step 1 for more heat (not advisable for pitta).

Dosha-Specific Churnas

Churna means "powder" in Sanskrit. Churnas are often used medicinally in ayurveda to balance the energies of doshas, aid digestion, calm stressed nervous systems and move stagnant energy. These churnas were designed to regulate and maintain balance for specific constitutions. They contain all the tastes, except sour. Sprinkle ¼ to ½ tsp (1 to 2 mL) over your food to assist with digestion, or sip with warm water at the end of a meal. Keep some at work or in your briefcase or laptop bag so you always have it handy.

Makes about 5 tsp (25 mL)

Tips

For Pitta: If you have high blood pressure, substitute fennel powder for the licorice.

These churnas can be stored in their airtight containers at room temperature for up to 2 months.

The recipes yield a small amount. If you find them to be of benefit, you can double or triple them so you have enough to last for a month at a time.

Gluten-Free ✦ Soy-Free ✦ Vegan

Vata

2 tsp	ground cumin	10 mL
2 tsp	ground ginger	10 mL
1 tsp	ground cardamom	5 mL
½ tsp	Himalayan salt	2 mL
¼ tsp	ground turmeric	1 mL

1. In an airtight container, combine cumin, ginger, cardamom, salt and turmeric.

Pitta

2 tsp	ground coriander	10 mL
2 tsp	ground cumin	10 mL
1 tsp	licorice powder (see tip, at left)	5 mL
1 tsp	unsweetened finely shredded dried coconut	5 mL
¼ tsp	ground turmeric	1 mL
⅛ tsp	Himalayan salt	0.5 mL

1. In an airtight container, combine coriander, cumin, licorice, coconut, turmeric and salt.

Kapha

1 tsp	ground ginger	5 mL
1 tsp	ground cumin	5 mL
1 tsp	ground black pepper	5 mL
1 tsp	ground fennel seeds	5 mL
¼ tsp	ground turmeric	1 mL
⅛ tsp	Himalayan salt	0.5 mL

1. In an airtight container, combine ginger, cumin, pepper, fennel seeds, turmeric and salt.

Snacks, Dips and Spreads

Ayurveda does not recommend snacks. The theory is that we should be giving our digestive systems adequate time in between meals to process and assimilate nutrients from the last meal. If we eat well-balanced meals at regular intervals, there should be no need (or desire) for snacking.

But for most people these days, meals tend to be haphazard in their timing and are not generally balanced as per an ayurvedic definition. As such, I feel there is a need for some healthy snacks that can be eaten on the go (in the car, on the train, at your office). You may be thinking that eating on the go violates one of the top 10 rules: eating mindfully. True. But if the alternative is consuming fast food laden with sodium, sugar and/or fat, then I feel that eating a healthy snack is preferable.

This chapter includes many dips and spreads, which are quick to prepare, can be made ahead and will keep in the refrigerator for several days. Add to an insulated lunch box for kids or adults. They can be used as spreads for wraps and sandwiches, used as base toppings for bruschetta, served with a salad, eaten with organic corn chips and much more. Dips and spreads are best stored in tightly sealed glass jars in the refrigerator. Use a clean, dry utensil when scooping out the contents, to avoid contamination and potential bacteria growth.

I have included a basic recipe for nut or seed butter. Nut and seed butters can be purchased at most grocery stores, but they are often quite expensive and contain unnecessary salt and preservatives. Making your own is a low-cost, healthy, dairy-free way to tailor recipes to your individual needs.

Aside from the recipes in this chapter, consider making a snack of minted fruit (grapefruit, blueberries, watermelon, apricots, papaya or peaches) for a refreshing burst of energy, especially in the heat of summer. Minted fruit can be prepared ahead and stored in an airtight container in the refrigerator for up to 1 day.

Endive with Honeyed Goat Cheese

Pairing cold, heavy cheese with light endive and warming honey and cayenne makes for a compatible food combination. Made with goat cheese, this snack is best for vata and pitta; made with fresh paneer, it is tridoshic.

**Makes
2 servings**

Tips

Belgian endive is also called French endive, witloof or chicory. Its leaves are slightly bitter and are moist and crunchy. Heads with green tips are more bitter than those with yellow tips.

If you cannot find endive, radicchio is a good substitute, but tends to be more bitter (more cooling).

Variation

Replace the cayenne with ½ tsp (2 mL) grated lemon or orange zest.

Gluten-Free ✦ Soy-Free ✦ Vegetarian

¼ cup	soft goat cheese or crumbled Paneer (page 160)	60 mL
1 tsp	raw liquid honey	5 mL
⅛ tsp	cayenne pepper	0.5 mL
8	Belgian endive or radicchio leaves	8
	Toasted walnuts or almonds (optional)	

1. In a small bowl, using a fork, combine cheese, honey and cayenne, mixing thoroughly.
2. Divide cheese mixture into eight portions and place one portion in each endive leaf. Serve garnished with nuts, if desired.

Jicama Lime Sticks

Jicama is a cool, sweet, crunchy and moist tuberous root with a neutral flavor. It is ideal for pitta, but is also tolerated (with appropriate heating spices) by vata and kapha in the summer. Add jicama sticks to a crudités platter, or to salads for a crunchy surprise.

Makes 4 servings

Tips

Jicama is a dietary staple in Latin America. Other names for it include Mexican potato, Mexican yam bean, ahipa, saa got, Chinese turnip, lo bok and Chinese potato. You can find it in the produce section of most supermarkets. Jicama looks like a giant round potato. Its skin is thin and can be gray, tan or brown; the inner flesh is white. When purchasing jicama, select tubers that are firm and dry. Jicama is high in vitamin C and fiber, is low in sodium and has no fat.

Jicama sticks can be stored in an airtight container in the refrigerator for up to 4 days.

Gluten-Free ✦ Soy-Free ✦ Vegan

$\frac{1}{2}$	small jicama (about 2 lbs/1 kg)	$\frac{1}{2}$
2 tbsp	chopped cilantro	30 mL
$\frac{1}{2}$ tsp	crushed black pepper	2 mL
$\frac{1}{4}$ tsp	Himalayan salt	1 mL
$\frac{1}{4}$ tsp	chili powder	1 mL
$\frac{1}{8}$ to $\frac{1}{4}$ tsp	cayenne pepper (optional)	0.5 to 1 mL
3 tbsp	freshly squeezed lime juice	45 mL

1. Peel jicama and cut into 3-inch (7.5 cm) sticks, about $\frac{1}{4}$ inch (0.5 cm) thick.

2. In a bowl, combine jicama sticks, cilantro, black pepper, salt, chili powder, cayenne (if using) and lime juice, tossing to coat.

Dosha Modifications

✦ **Kapha** and **vata** must add the cayenne to warm the jicama up.

✦ **Vata** and **pitta** can serve with a side of guacamole.

✦ **Kapha** can serve with Traditional Mexican Salsa (page 290).

Marinela's Stuffed Grape Leaves

This recipe comes from my neighbor Marinela and was handed down from her mom in Greece, where these snacks are called dolmathakia. Grape leaves are cool and astringent; combined with rice and spices, they are tridoshic. Serve with Tzatziki (page 260) or Basic Tahini (page 261).

Makes 20 rolls

Tips

To make tomato pulp, cut a tomato in half, then grate the fleshy side with the coarse side of a box grater. Discard skins.

These rolls will keep, wrapped tightly in plastic wrap, in the refrigerator for 2 to 3 days.

Gluten-Free ♦ Soy-Free ♦ Vegan

1 cup	Arborio rice	250 mL
	Water	
1 tsp	grated lemon zest	5 mL
6 tbsp	freshly squeezed lemon juice, divided	90 mL
¼ cup	olive oil, divided	60 mL
1 cup	finely chopped onion	250 mL
1 cup	finely chopped green onions	250 mL
⅓ cup	tomato pulp (see tip, at left)	75 mL
¾ cup	finely chopped fresh parsley	175 mL
¼ cup	finely chopped fresh dill	60 mL
¼ cup	chopped fresh mint	60 mL
3 tbsp	chopped fresh basil	45 mL
¾ tsp	Himalayan salt	3 mL
¼ tsp	crushed black pepper	1 mL
30	grape leaves (packed in water), rinsed, drained and patted dry, stems removed	30

1. Place rice in a large bowl and add enough water to cover; let soak for 1 hour. Drain, rinse with cold water and drain again. Return to the bowl and stir in 2 tbsp (30 mL) lemon juice. Set aside.

2. In a large, shallow saucepan, heat 2 tbsp (30 mL) oil over medium–high heat. Add onion and green onions; cook, stirring, for 3 to 4 minutes or until onion is translucent.

3. Stir in rice mixture, 1 cup (250 mL) water and tomato pulp; bring to a boil. Reduce heat and simmer for 7 to 10 minutes or until water is absorbed (the rice will not be fully cooked).

4. Meanwhile, in a small bowl, combine parsley, dill, mint, basil, salt and pepper.

Variation

Add ½ cup (125 mL) cooked ground beef or lamb to the rice mixture.

SERVING SUGGESTION

Add to a Tridoshic Mediterranean Salad Plate (page 241).

5. Remove pan from heat and stir in herb mixture, lemon zest and 2 tbsp (30 mL) lemon juice. Let cool for 10 minutes.

6. Sort through grape leaves, selecting 20 medium leaves that are well shaped, without any holes. Use the remaining leaves to line the bottom of a large, heavy pot, making a bed of several layers.

7. Lay out the 20 leaves shiny side down, with their stem ends facing you. Place 1 tbsp (15 mL) rice mixture at the center of the stem end of a leaf. Fold the bottom of the leaf up to cover the filling, then fold in the sides and roll the packet up to the top of the leaf (like rolling a burrito or spring roll). Do not roll too tightly or the leaves will burst open as the rice expands during cooking. Repeat until all the rice mixture and leaves are used.

8. Place rolls, seam side down, on top of the bed of grape leaves, arranging them in a circular pattern and packing them in snugly (this helps keep the leaves intact as they cook). Add layers on top until all the stuffed leaves are in the pan. Pour the remaining oil and lemon juice over the rolls. Add enough water to cover by ½ inch (1 cm). Place a heatproof plate on top of the rolls to keep them submerged during cooking.

9. Heat over medium–high heat until water just begins to bubble. Reduce heat to low, cover and simmer for 30 to 40 minutes or until leaves are fork-tender and rice is tender but chewy.

Trail Mix

This make-ahead snack is quick to prepare and travels well — it's great for children to bring to school.

Makes 2 cups (500 mL)

Tips

To toast almonds, place them in a dry (ungreased) medium skillet over medium heat. When they begin to smell fragrant, after about 1 minute, give the pan a shake. Continue to toast, periodically shaking the pan, until the almonds are golden.

Trail mix will keep for several months in an airtight container at room temperature. Portion it out as needed into plastic baggies to take with you when traveling or any time you need a healthy burst of energy.

SERVING SUGGESTIONS

Sprinkle on your breakfast porridge or layer into Yogurt Parfait (page 120).

Gluten-Free ✦ Soy-Free ✦ Vegan

½ cup	green pumpkin seeds (pepitas)	125 mL
½ cup	unsalted raw sunflower seeds	125 mL
½ cup	toasted slivered almonds (see tip, at left)	125 mL
½ cup	dried goji berries or raisins	125 mL

1. In an airtight container, combine pumpkin seeds, sunflower seeds, almonds and goji berries.

Roasted Ginger Kabocha Seeds

These crunchy treats are full of protein, magnesium, potassium, iron and fiber. Store in airtight containers or plastic bags at work, in your car, in your children's lunch boxes or when traveling, for healthy snacks on the go.

Makes ¹/₂ cup (125 mL)

Tips

One kabocha squash will yield about ¹/₂ cup (125 mL) seeds.

Store in an airtight container at room temperature for up to 2 weeks.

Variation

Substitute pumpkin seeds or other squash seeds.

Gluten-Free ♦ Soy-Free ♦ Vegan

¹/₂ cup	kabocha squash seeds (see tip, at left)	125 mL
	Water	
¹/₂ tsp	grated gingerroot	2 mL
¹/₄ tsp	Himalayan salt	1 mL
Pinch	cayenne pepper	Pinch
2 tbsp	freshly squeezed lemon juice	30 mL
1 tbsp	virgin olive oil	15 mL

1. In a fine-mesh sieve, rinse seeds under cold water, using your fingers to remove the stringy fibers from the seeds.

2. Place seeds in a medium saucepan and add enough water to cover by 1 inch (2.5 cm). Bring to a boil over high heat. Reduce heat and simmer for 75 minutes or until outer skins are softened. Drain and pat dry with a paper towel.

3. Meanwhile, preheat oven to 375°F (190°C).

4. In a small bowl, combine seeds, ginger, salt, cayenne, lemon juice and oil. Spread seeds in an even layer on a baking sheet.

5. Bake for 5 minutes. Using a spatula, turn the seeds over. Bake for 5 to 7 minutes or until golden. Serve warm or at room temperature.

Dosha Modifications

♦ **Vata** can try this lemony variation: Soak the boiled seeds overnight in a mixture of ¹/₂ tsp (2 mL) salt, ¹/₂ tsp (2 mL) grated lemon zest, ¹/₂ cup (125 mL) freshly squeezed lemon juice and 2 tbsp (30 mL) extra virgin olive oil. Bake as directed.

♦ **Kapha** can add 1 tsp (5 mL) minced lemongrass and additional cayenne in step 4.

Basic Nut or Seed Butter

You can use any nuts or seeds, or combination of nuts and seeds, in this recipe, though you'll get the most use out of mild-flavored cashew butter or almond butter, which can be substituted in many baking recipes calling for butter. Almonds, when peeled and blanched, are considered tridoshic. Other nuts are generally heavy and oily and are thus most suited for vata, but on occasion, in moderation and properly spiced, nut butters can be enjoyed by all.

Makes about ¹/₂ cup (125 mL)

Variation

Sweeten with 1 tsp (5 mL) raw liquid honey or add a pinch of salt.

SERVING SUGGESTIONS

Use to replace peanut butter in sandwiches or to replace butter in baking recipes. Or combine with lemon juice and/or water and spices to make a sauce for salads or vegetables.

Dairy-Free ✦ Gluten-Free ✦ Soy-Free ✦ Vegan

- **Food processor**

| 1 cup | unsalted raw nuts (peeled, if necessary) or unsalted raw seeds | 250 mL |
| 1 to 2 tbsp | sunflower oil | 15 to 30 mL |

1. In a large dry skillet, toast nuts over medium heat for 5 minutes, tossing frequently with a wooden spatula, until light golden. Let cool for 20 minutes.
2. Transfer nuts to food processor and add 1 tbsp (15 mL) oil. Process to the consistency of nut butter, scraping the sides of the bowl and adding more oil as needed.

Nut Butter Tips

- Refer to the dosha balancing aids (pages 328–339) for dosha-specific nut and seed recommendations.
- Nut butters should be stored in a glass container with an airtight lid in the refrigerator. Be sure to use clean, dry utensils when scooping out the butter to avoid contamination and potential bacterial growth. A butter made solely of nuts and oil (no herbs, garlic, lemon juice, etc.) will keep for a few months.
- You can make creamy sauces by whisking together ¹/₄ cup (60 mL) nut butter and 1 cup (250 mL) water. Season to taste with tamari, cayenne pepper, ground cinnamon, ground allspice, chopped fresh mint, thyme or savory, or grated orange or lemon zest.

Tridoshic Artichoke Pesto

Here's a nice tridoshic alternative to traditional pesto. Artichokes are astringent, heating and sweet – most suitable for pitta and kapha – but the sweet basil and warm oil bring balance to the spread for vata.

**Makes about
$1/_2$ cup (125 mL)**

Tip

The pesto will keep for up to 5 days in the refrigerator if you are diligent about keeping it covered with oil and not contaminating the jar with water or other food.

Variations

Add $1/_3$ cup (75 mL) arugula with the basil for an earthier flavor.

To make pesto sauce, add an equal amount of water, plus enough heavy or whipping (35%) cream to achieve the desired consistency; purée with an immersion blender or in a regular blender or food processor. Warm over low heat and serve over pasta or vegetables.

SERVING SUGGESTIONS

Spread over toast or crackers; serve as a dip with raw vegetables; or use as a base for a veggie sandwich or wrap, adding lettuce, tomatoes, sprouts and cucumbers.

Gluten-Free ✦ Soy-Free ✦ Vegan

- **Food processor**

1$1/_3$ cups	basil leaves, stems discarded	325 mL
$2/_3$ cup	rinsed drained water-packed canned artichoke hearts	150 mL
$1/_4$ cup	blanched almonds	60 mL
$1/_4$ tsp	pressed or minced garlic	1 mL
$1/_8$ tsp	Himalayan salt	0.5 mL
$1/_8$ tsp	crushed black pepper	0.5 mL
1$1/_2$ tsp	freshly squeezed lemon juice	7 mL
4 tsp	avocado oil	20 mL
	Additional avocado oil	

1. In food processor, combine basil, artichokes, almonds, garlic, salt, pepper and lemon juice. With the motor running, through the feed tube, slowly pour in oil. (The more slowly you pour, the smoother the texture will be and the less likely the sauce will separate later.) Process until pesto has the consistency of a light paste.

2. Scoop into a glass jar and pour a layer of oil on top to act as a preservative.

Dosha Modification
✦ **Vata** can use 2 tbsp (30 mL) avocado oil instead of 4 tsp (20 mL).

Lemony Hummus

This healthy, low-calorie snack has lots of versatility for those who find themselves eating on the go. Vata-approved, it has been carefully seasoned to be suitable for all constitutions. Although beans have a cold, light and dry energy, which can be aggravating to vata, the tahini, lemon juice, garlic and oil help to balance the energetics of the beans. My friend's nine-year-old daughter loves this hummus as an after-school snack.

Makes about 1½ cups (375 mL)

Tips

Store in an airtight container in the refrigerator for up to 5 days.

Pack in an insulated lunch box with some carrots or rice crackers for a protein-packed tasty treat!

Canned food may contain additives and potentially harmful chemicals that leach from the cans, so I prefer using dried chickpeas when time permits. I soak them overnight, then cook them in the morning. If this doesn't fit your schedule, replace the cooked chickpeas with a 14- to 19-oz (398 to 540 mL) can.

SERVING SUGGESTIONS

Serve with fresh fennel slices or use as a spread for a veggie wrap.

Gluten-Free ✦ Soy-Free ✦ Vegan

• **Food processor**

1½ cups	cooked chickpeas (see page 64), cooled	375 mL
¼ tsp	pressed or minced garlic	1 mL
½ tsp	Himalayan salt	2 mL
Pinch	cayenne pepper	Pinch
¾ tsp	grated lemon zest	3 mL
2 tbsp	freshly squeezed lemon juice	30 mL
2 tbsp	tahini (store-bought or see recipe, page 261)	30 mL
2 tbsp	extra virgin olive oil	30 mL
2 tbsp	water (approx.)	30 mL

1. In food processor, combine chickpeas, garlic, salt, cayenne, lemon zest, lemon juice, tahini, oil and water; process, adding more water as needed to achieve the desired consistency.

Dosha Modifications

✦ To further warm and ground the dish for **vata**, add ½ cup (125 mL) cooked diced golden beets.

✦ If serving for **pitta** or **kapha**, you can experiment with other beans. For example, try replacing ¼ cup (60 mL) of the chickpeas with fava or cannellini beans.

Tridoshic Zucchini Hummus

This bean-free hummus is much easier on the digestive system than traditional hummus. It's easy to prepare, stores well and is a great way to meet your daily vegetable requirements.

Makes about 2 cups (500 mL)

Tip

Store in an airtight nonmetallic container in the refrigerator for up to 4 days.

SERVING SUGGESTIONS

Serve as a dip with carrots, radishes or celery; spoon onto Belgian endive leaves; wrap in radicchio leaves; or serve with minted grilled vegetables, Coconut Purple Rice (page 232) or a bulgur salad with cucumber, green onions and lemon vinaigrette.

Gluten-Free ✦ Soy-Free ✦ Vegan

• **Food processor**

3 cups	chopped zucchini	750 mL
$\frac{1}{2}$ tsp	paprika	2 mL
$\frac{1}{2}$ tsp	Himalayan salt	2 mL
$\frac{1}{8}$ tsp	cayenne pepper	0.5 mL
$\frac{1}{8}$ tsp	crushed black pepper	0.5 mL
$\frac{1}{2}$ tsp	grated lemon zest	2 mL
2 tbsp	freshly squeezed lemon juice	30 mL
2 tbsp	tahini (store-bought or see recipe, page 261)	30 mL

1. In food processor, combine zucchini, paprika, salt, cayenne, black pepper, lemon zest, lemon juice and tahini; process until smooth.

Tridoshic Red Lentil Hummus

This version of hummus is perfect for more sensitive digestive systems. Light, cooling red lentils are balanced with warm mushrooms and spices targeted to aid digestion and delight your palate.

Makes about 2 cups (500 mL)

Tips

Remove dirt from mushroom caps by gently dusting them with a paper towel.

Leftover hummus can be stored in an airtight container in the refrigerator for 2 days; however, it will thicken as it chills.

Variation

Add ¼ cup (60 mL) crumbled Paneer (page 160) in step 4 for a richer-tasting spread.

Gluten-Free ✦ Soy-Free ✦ Vegetarian

- Food processor

½ cup	dried red lentils, sorted and rinsed	125 mL
1½ cups	water	375 mL
1 tsp	Himalayan salt, divided	5 mL
½ tsp	crushed black pepper, divided	2 mL
½ tsp	chili powder	2 mL
¼ tsp	ground coriander	1 mL
¼ tsp	ground cumin	1 mL
⅛ tsp	cayenne pepper	0.5 mL
⅛ tsp	ground turmeric	0.5 mL
1 tbsp	sunflower oil	15 mL
1 tsp	unsalted butter	5 mL
2 cups	chopped cremini mushroom caps	500 mL
1 cup	chopped onion	250 mL
½ tsp	pressed or minced garlic	2 mL
1 tsp	grated orange zest	5 mL
¼ cup	freshly squeezed orange juice	60 mL
2 tbsp	raw liquid honey	30 mL

1. In a medium saucepan, combine lentils and water. Bring to a boil over high heat. Reduce heat and simmer for about 10 minutes or until lentils lose their shape and are soft. Strain through a fine-mesh sieve, gently pressing lentils with the back of a spoon to remove excess water. Set aside.

2. In a small bowl, combine ½ tsp (2 mL) salt, ¼ tsp (1 mL) pepper, chili powder, coriander, cumin, cayenne and turmeric.

3. In a medium saucepan, heat oil and butter over medium heat. Add mushrooms, onion and garlic; cook, stirring, for 5 minutes. Add spice mixture and cook for about 1 minute or until fragrant. Stir in orange zest and orange juice, scraping up any brown bits from the bottom of the pan. Add lentils and cook, stirring, until liquid has evaporated. Remove from heat and let cool to room temperature.

4. In food processor, combine lentil mixture, honey and the remaining salt and pepper; purée until smooth.

Lemony Cannellini Bean Spread

Seasoned with lemon zest, oregano, basil and rosemary, this cannellini bean spread will take you on a trip to Tuscany any night of the week. It's suitable for all doshas, in moderation.

Makes about 1¹/₂ cups (375 mL)

Tips

To substitute dried beans, use ¹/₂ cup (125 mL) and follow the soaking and cooking instructions on page 64.

The fresh herbs can be replaced with dried herbs. Use ¹/₂ tsp (2 mL) dried oregano and ¹/₄ tsp (1 mL) each dried basil and rosemary.

This spread can be stored in an airtight nonmetallic container in the refrigerator for up to 3 days; however, it will dry out as the beans continue to absorb moisture.

SERVING SUGGESTIONS

Use as the base layer on bruschetta, topped with chopped tomatoes tossed in olive oil and oregano. Or spread on a sandwich or wrap and add cucumbers, lettuce, tomatoes and shredded fennel.

Gluten-Free ✦ Soy-Free ✦ Vegan

- **Food processor**

2¹/₂ tbsp	olive oil (approx.), divided	37 mL
¹/₂ tsp	pressed or minced garlic	2 mL
1	can (14 to 19 oz/398 to 540 mL) cannellini beans, drained and rinsed	1
1 tsp	chopped fresh oregano	5 mL
³/₄ tsp	chopped fresh basil	3 mL
³/₄ tsp	chopped fresh rosemary	3 mL
¹/₂ tsp	Himalayan salt	2 mL
¹/₄ tsp	crushed black pepper	1 mL
1 tsp	grated lemon zest	5 mL
2 tbsp	freshly squeezed lemon juice	30 mL

1. In a small skillet, heat 1 tbsp (15 mL) oil over medium heat. Add garlic and cook, stirring, for about 2 minutes or until softened and fragrant.

2. In food processor, combine garlic, beans, oregano, basil, rosemary, salt, pepper, lemon zest, lemon juice and the remaining oil; pulse until smooth and creamy.

Dosha Modifications

✦ **Vata** can eat this spread in moderation, but may need to increase the oil by 1 to 2 tbsp (15 to 30 mL) and/or double the lemon juice.

✦ **Pitta** can omit the garlic.

✦ **Kapha** can add a bit of cayenne pepper or skip step 1 and use raw garlic.

Mexican Black Bean Spread

This spread is well balanced for pitta and kapha. The oregano and cumin are digestive aids, which will allow vata to eat it in moderation on occasion.

Tips

To substitute dried black beans, use $\frac{1}{2}$ cup (125 mL) and follow the soaking and cooking instructions on page 64. They can be cooked up to 3 days in advance, drained and stored in an airtight container in the refrigerator.

This spread can be stored in an airtight nonmetallic container in the refrigerator for up to 3 days; however, it will dry out as the beans continue to absorb moisture.

SERVING SUGGESTIONS

Use as the base layer on bruschetta, topped with Traditional Mexican Salsa (page 290) and oregano. Or spread on a sandwich or wrap and add avocado and lettuce or endive.

Gluten-Free ✦ Soy-Free ✦ Vegan

- **Food processor**

1	can (14 to 19 oz/398 to 540 mL) black beans, drained and rinsed	1
$\frac{1}{2}$ tsp	chili powder	2 mL
$\frac{1}{2}$ tsp	ground cumin	2 mL
$\frac{1}{2}$ tsp	Himalayan salt	2 mL
$\frac{1}{4}$ tsp	crushed black pepper	1 mL
$\frac{1}{8}$ tsp	cayenne pepper	0.5 mL
$\frac{1}{8}$ tsp	dried oregano	0.5 mL
2 tbsp	avocado oil or sunflower oil	30 mL
5 tsp	freshly squeezed lime juice	25 mL
2 tbsp	chopped fresh cilantro	30 mL

1. In food processor, combine beans, chili powder, cumin, salt, black pepper, cayenne, oregano, oil and lime juice; pulse until smooth and creamy. Add cilantro and pulse until combined.

Tridoshic Carrot (with a Kick) Spread

This versatile, tasty spread is tridoshic and simple to make. Add it to your kids' insulated lunch boxes with some crackers to make sure they get their daily vitamin A.

Makes about 1¹/₂ cups (375 mL)

Tip

Store in an airtight nonmetallic container in the refrigerator for up to 3 days.

SERVING SUGGESTIONS

Serve as a dip with crudités or on roasted garlic spelt chips, wheat crackers or toasted baguette slices. Or spread on pita bread and add sprouts, lettuce, tomato, avocado and green pumpkin seeds (pepitas).

Gluten-Free ♦ Soy-Free ♦ Vegan

• **Food processor**

1	clove garlic	1
1¹/₂ cups	chopped carrots	375 mL
¹/₂ cup	chopped peeled yellow-fleshed potato (such as Yukon Gold)	125 mL
4 cups	water	1 L
1 tbsp	ground coriander	15 mL
1¹/₂ tsp	ground cumin	7 mL
¹/₄ tsp	cayenne pepper	1 mL
¹/₄ tsp	Himalayan salt	1 mL
¹/₈ tsp	crushed black pepper	0.5 mL
1 tbsp	sunflower oil	15 mL
1 tbsp	freshly squeezed lemon juice	15 mL

1. In a medium saucepan, combine garlic, carrots, potatoes and water. Bring to a boil over high heat. Reduce heat and boil gently for about 20 minutes or until carrots and potato are tender. Drain and let cool. Discard garlic clove.

2. In food processor, combine carrot mixture, coriander, cumin, cayenne, salt, black pepper, oil and lemon juice; process until smooth.

Mushroom Almond Pâté

This spread is relatively balanced for all three doshas. The heavy, oily qualities of the nuts are balanced by the light, dry qualities of the lentils and shiitakes. Serve with crackers or crudités, or as part of a salad plate.

Makes about 1¹/₂ cups (375 mL)

Tips

Try using a French press to rehydrate dried mushrooms; the plunger can be pressed down to keep the mushrooms submerged under the water.

In excess, mushrooms may increase ama (toxins) in the body and blood; ayurveda says they should be avoided when there is fever or infection.

Leftovers can be stored in an airtight container in the refrigerator for up to 2 days; however, the pâté will thicken as it chills.

Gluten-Free ✦ Soy-Free ✦ Vegan

- **Food processor**
- **2-cup (500 mL) pâté mold or serving dish**

¹/₃ cup	dried French lentils, sorted and rinsed	75 mL
1 cup	water	250 mL
4 oz	dried shiitake mushrooms	125 g
1 cup	boiling water	250 mL
³/₄ tsp	thyme	3 mL
¹/₂ tsp	paprika	2 mL
¹/₂ tsp	crushed black pepper	2 mL
¹/₄ tsp	Himalayan salt	1 mL
¹/₈ tsp	ground allspice	0.5 mL
1 tbsp	butter or sunflower oil	15 mL
¹/₂ cup	coarsely chopped onion	125 mL
¹/₄ cup	toasted almonds	60 mL
¹/₂ tsp	grated lemon zest	2 mL
3 tbsp	freshly squeezed lemon juice	45 mL
2 tbsp	coarsely chopped fresh parsley	30 mL

1. In a medium saucepan, combine lentils and water. Bring to a boil over high heat. Reduce heat and simmer for about 20 minutes or until lentils are very soft. Strain through a fine-mesh sieve, gently pressing lentils with the back of a spoon to remove excess water. Set aside.

2. In a bowl, rehydrate dried mushrooms in boiling water for 30 minutes; strain, reserving the liquid. Remove and discard shiitake stems. Coarsely chop mushroom caps. Set aside.

3. In a small bowl, combine thyme, paprika, pepper, salt and allspice.

Variation

Add ½ tsp (2 mL) chopped fresh mint with the parsley to lighten the dish.

4. In a large, shallow saucepan, melt butter over medium heat. Gently stir in spice mixture. Add mushrooms and onion; cook, stirring, for 5 to 10 minutes or until mushrooms are golden brown and onion is soft. Remove from heat and let cool.

5. In food processor, combine lentils, mushroom mixture, almonds, lemon zest and lemon juice; process until smooth. Add parsley and pulse briefly to combine.

6. Transfer pâté to mold or serving dish, cover and refrigerate for 1 hour to blend the flavors.

Dosha Modification

✦ If preparing for **vata** only, replace the almonds with cashews.

Traditional Mexican Salsa

A friend in Los Angeles taught me how to make this simple salsa, which he has loved since his childhood in Guanajuato, Mexico. I've modified the recipe (less salt and less jalapeño) to make it more balancing for pitta. It is balancing for kapha, and vata can eat it in moderation. Pitta can eat it in moderation, with cilantro and lime.

Makes about 1 cup (250 mL)

Tips

To peel and seed a plum (Roma) tomato, simply chop off ¼ inch (0.5 cm) from each end, then use a sharp vegetable peeler to remove the skin. Cut the tomato into quarters and scrape out the seeds using the sharp point of a knife. If you are using round tomatoes, you will need to carve out the area where the tomato was attached to the stem, then peel with a sharp vegetable peeler.

Store in an airtight nonmetallic container in the refrigerator for up to 3 days.

SERVING SUGGESTIONS

Serve with broiled chicken, red snapper or halibut marinated in Tridoshic Lime Cumin Vinaigrette (page 251), with Mexican Rice (page 230) and Mexican Black Bean Spread (page 286).

Gluten-Free ✦ Soy-Free ✦ Vegan

1 cup	chopped seeded peeled ripe red tomatoes (see tip, at left)	250 mL
2 tbsp	thinly sliced green onion	30 mL
1 tbsp	coarsely chopped fresh cilantro	15 mL
½ tsp	finely chopped seeded jalapeño pepper	2 mL
¼ tsp	Himalayan salt	1 mL
¼ tsp	crushed black pepper	1 mL
1 tbsp	freshly squeezed lime juice	15 mL
1 tsp	extra virgin olive oil	5 mL

1. In a bowl, combine tomatoes, green onion, cilantro, jalapeño, salt, pepper, lime juice and oil, mixing gently with a wooden spoon. Cover and refrigerate for 30 minutes before serving.

Breads and Treats

This chapter perhaps stretches the limits of what should be included in an ayurvedic wellness cookbook. However, I have a sweet tooth, and if the alternative is purchasing a candy bar containing refined sugar, chemical preservatives and additives, a homemade sweet is a better choice.

My preferred sweetener is coconut sugar. It has a low glycemic index (releasing glucose slowly and steadily into the blood), is minimally refined and is high in minerals and vitamins. It is cooling, sweet and heavy, making it ideal for vata and pitta. I find it to be sweeter than cane sugar, and I generally use about 25% less than I normally would in recipes, which makes it less unbalancing to kapha. It costs more than refined cane sugar, but since you use less, the true cost is comparable.

To accommodate a variety of tastes, some of the recipes have a range for the sugar amount. In such cases, prepare the recipe with the lower amount of sugar the first time you make it. If it's not sweet enough for your taste, you can use the larger amount of sugar the next time.

For best results, do not reduce the sugar any further, especially in the gluten-free recipes. Sugar provides moisture and texture, as does gluten.

Honey is the best sweetener for kapha, because of its heating energetic and scraping properties. I have included a recipe for Turkish Halva made from toasted sesame seeds and raw honey – suitable for kapha, in moderation.

Italian Flatbread

This amazing gluten-free flatbread with a soft, chewy texture is an ideal accompaniment to soups and salads.

Makes 12 flatbreads

Tips

A well-seasoned cast-iron skillet will give the best results, as will a very flexible silicone spatula.

Avoid leftovers, as the chickpea flour will become stronger with each passing day, imparting a bitter taste to the bread. However, you can prepare the flour mixture up to 3 months in advance and store it in an airtight container; when ready to use, scoop out the desired quantity and add water — for one flatbread, use 2 tbsp (30 mL) flour mixture and about 2½ tbsp (37 mL) water; continue with step 2.

Variation

If serving with Indian curries, omit the oregano and rosemary and add 1 tsp (5 mL) ground cumin, ¼ tsp (1 mL) ground turmeric and a pinch of ajwain (optional, to aid digestion).

Gluten-Free ✦ Soy-Free ✦ Vegan

- 9-inch (23 cm) cast-iron skillet or crêpe pan

¾ cup	chickpea flour	175 mL
¼ cup	brown rice flour	60 mL
2 tbsp	arrowroot flour	30 mL
1 tsp	gluten-free baking powder	5 mL
1 tsp	dried oregano	5 mL
1 tsp	dried rosemary	5 mL
¾ tsp	Himalayan salt	3 mL
1 cup	water (approx.)	250 mL
	Extra virgin olive oil	

1. In a large bowl, combine chickpea flour, rice flour, arrowroot flour, baking powder, oregano, rosemary and salt. Whisk in water until lumps are dissolved. The batter should be pourable but not runny; adjust water if necessary.

2. Preheat the cast-iron skillet over medium-low heat. You'll know the temperature of the pan is correct when a drop of water placed on the surface "dances." If the water evaporates, the pan is too hot.

3. Lift the pan away from the heat and pour about 3 tbsp (45 mL) batter onto the pan, tilting the pan in a circular motion to spread batter out into a very thin circle (the thinner the better). Place the pan back on the burner and cook for about 1 minute or until tiny bubbles appear in the batter. Drizzle a few drops of oil on top. Using a flexible spatula, gently flip flatbread over. (If the edges don't lift easily from the pan, the bread isn't ready to flip.) Drizzle a few drops of oil on the other side and cook for about 2 minutes or until lightly browned, with a soft and flexible texture. Repeat with the remaining batter.

Lavender Essence Tea Bread

This reduced-sugar tea bread can be eaten in moderation by all doshas. Lavender is calming, and this bread will be soothing to pitta and vata – in moderation. The addition of flax seeds is helpful for kapha.

Makes 9 servings

Tips

Prepare the recipe with the lower amount of coconut sugar the first time you make it. If it's not sweet enough for your taste, you can use the larger amount of sugar the next time.

Use a mortar and pestle to lightly crush the lavender leaves.

Make sure all ingredients are at room temperature before starting step 1.

Store the cooled bread (without confectioners' sugar or lemon zest), wrapped in plastic wrap, in a large sealable freezer bag in the freezer for up to 1 month. Unwrap and thaw at room temperature for 2 hours before serving.

Soy-Free ◆ Vegetarian

- Preheat oven to 350°F (180°C)
- 8- by 4-inch (20 by 10 cm) loaf pan, greased and bottom lined with parchment paper

1¼ cups	pastry flour	300 mL
½ cup	almond flour (see box, page 303)	125 mL
1 tbsp	flax seeds	15 mL
1 tsp	baking powder	5 mL
¼ tsp	baking soda	1 mL
¼ tsp	Himalayan salt	1 mL
¾ to 1 cup	coconut sugar (see tip, at left)	175 to 250 mL
⅓ cup	unsalted butter, at room temperature	75 mL
1½ tsp	organic lavender leaves, lightly crushed	7 mL
1 tsp	vanilla extract	5 mL
2	large eggs, at room temperature	2
1 cup	plain yogurt, at room temperature	250 mL
2 tbsp	confectioners' (icing) sugar	30 mL
½ tsp	grated lemon zest	2 mL

1. In a medium bowl, whisk together pastry flour, almond flour, flax seeds, baking powder, baking soda and salt.

2. In a large bowl, using an electric mixer, cream coconut sugar and butter until fluffy. Stir in lavender and vanilla. Beat in eggs until well combined. Gently fold in flour mixture alternately with yogurt, making three additions of flour and two of yogurt. Spoon batter into prepared pan.

3. Bake in preheated oven for 40 to 45 minutes or until the bread starts to separate from the edges of the pan and a tester inserted in the middle comes out clean. Let cool in pan on a wire rack for 20 minutes, then turn out onto the rack to cool completely. Dust with confectioners' sugar and garnish with lemon zest.

Cornbread

Corn is heating and dry – ideal for kapha. The coconut milk and maple syrup cool and moisten the bread. This cornbread is best paired with lentils, beans and salads. Pitta can eat it in moderation. Vata should apply liberal amounts of butter or ghee.

Makes 9 servings

Tips

The coconut milk does not impart a coconut flavor to this bread.

Be sure to use full-fat coconut milk, as the added protein and fat enhance the structure, texture and moisture in the bread.

Glutinous rice flour (also known as sweet rice flour) is ground from short-grain glutinous rice (also known as sticky rice), which is used in making sushi. It has a much higher starch content than other types of rice, but it does not contain gluten. It can be purchased at Asian grocery stores.

Store the cooled bread in an airtight container for up to 2 days.

SERVING SUGGESTIONS

Serve with Caribbean Adzuki Bean Stew (page 209), Lime Ginger Tofu (page 137) or Puy Lentil Soup with Pork Sausage (page 201) and a salad.

Gluten-Free ✦ Soy-Free ✦ Vegetarian

- Preheat oven to 425°F (220°C)
- 8-inch (20 cm) square metal baking pan, greased

1 cup	full-fat coconut milk	250 mL
1 tbsp	freshly squeezed lime juice	15 mL
2 cups	yellow cornmeal	500 mL
1/4 cup	glutinous rice flour	60 mL
2 tbsp	arrowroot flour	30 mL
1 tsp	gluten-free baking powder	5 mL
1/2 tsp	Himalayan salt	2 mL
1/4 tsp	baking soda	1 mL
1	large egg	1
3 tbsp	unsalted butter, melted	45 mL
2 tbsp	pure maple syrup	30 mL

1. In a small bowl, combine coconut milk and lime juice; let stand for 10 minutes.

2. Meanwhile, in a large bowl, whisk together cornmeal, rice flour, arrowroot flour, baking powder, salt and baking soda. Set aside.

3. In a medium bowl, whisk egg. Whisk in coconut milk mixture, butter and maple syrup until well combined.

4. Gradually add the egg mixture to the cornmeal mixture, swiftly combining with a wooden spoon. Do not overmix. Pour into prepared baking pan.

5. Bake in preheated oven for 15 to 18 minutes or until the bread starts to separate from the edges of the pan and a tester inserted in the middle comes out clean. Let cool in pan on a wire rack for 10 minutes, then turn out onto the rack to cool completely.

Zucchini Trail Bread

This hearty quick bread can be eaten for breakfast or packed as a snack for travel, a long day at the office or any other time you may be missing meals.

Makes 9 servings

Tips

Arrowroot flour is cooling, demulcent, mildly laxative and nutritive. I often add it to gluten-free baking recipes, as it is a "healthy" starch. It relieves acidity, indigestion and colic.

Do not reduce the amount of coconut sugar in this recipe; if you do, the texture will be very dry and the taste bland.

Wrap the cooled bread in waxed paper, then foil, to keep it fresh for up to 2 days. Or place the wrapped bread in a large sealable freezer bag and store in the freezer for up to 1 month.

Variations

Substitute dark chocolate chips for the cherries.

Substitute 1 tbsp (15 mL) orange zest for the orange extract.

Dairy-Free ✦ Gluten-Free ✦ Soy-Free ✦ Vegetarian

- Preheat oven to 350°F (180°C)
- 8- by 4-inch (20 by 10 cm) loaf pan, greased and bottom lined with parchment paper

1¾ cups + 1 tbsp	almond flour (see box, page 303)	440 mL
¼ cup	amaranth flour	60 mL
5 tsp	arrowroot flour	25 mL
1½ tsp	baking powder	7 mL
½ tsp	baking soda	2 mL
½ tsp	ground ginger	2 mL
½ tsp	Himalayan salt	2 mL
7 tsp	green pumpkin seeds (pepitas)	35 mL
7 tsp	dried cherries, halved	35 mL
1	large egg	1
2 tbsp	avocado oil	30 mL
3½ tbsp	thick-strained cashew milk (page 322)	52 mL
1 tsp	freshly squeezed lemon juice	5 mL
½ cup	coconut sugar	125 mL
¾ tsp	orange extract	3 mL
1 cup	shredded zucchini	250 mL

1. In a large bowl, combine almond flour, amaranth flour, arrowroot flour, baking powder, baking soda, ginger and salt. Stir in pumpkin seeds and cherries. Set aside.

2. In a medium bowl, whisk together egg and oil. Whisk in cashew milk and lemon juice. Whisk in sugar and orange extract. Stir in zucchini.

3. Add the egg mixture to the flour mixture, stirring until blended. Immediately spoon into prepared loaf pan.

4. Bake in preheated oven for about 40 minutes or until a tester inserted in the center comes out with a few crumbs attached. Let cool completely in pan on a wire rack.

Kabocha Cranberry Bread

Kabocha, or Japanese pumpkin, is abundant in the fall and early winter. It has a mild, sweet flavor – sweeter than a pumpkin, not quite as sweet as a sweet potato. It is reputed to be an aphrodisiac and is loaded with vitamins A and C.

**Makes
9 servings**

Tips

If using frozen cranberries, there's no need to thaw them; they can easily be cut in half while frozen.

Coconut milk is readily available in the international food aisle of most grocery stores. It comes in 13.5- or 14-oz (400 mL) cans and has a long shelf life. The milk and cream tend to separate inside the can, so shake the can vigorously before opening it. Once opened, transfer unused coconut milk to an airtight container and store in the refrigerator for up to 1 week.

Wrap the cooled bread in waxed paper, then foil, to keep it fresh for up to 2 days. Or place the wrapped bread in a large sealable freezer bag and store in the freezer for up to 1 month.

Variation

Add ½ cup (125 mL) toasted walnuts with the cranberries.

Dairy-Free ✦ Gluten-Free ✦ Soy-Free ✦ Vegetarian

- **Preheat oven to 350°F (180°C)**
- **8- by 4-inch (20 by 10 cm) loaf pan, greased and bottom lined with parchment paper**
- **Blender**

Cinnamon Topping

1 tsp	coconut sugar	5 mL
½ tsp	ground cinnamon	2 mL

Bread

1 cup	almond flour (see box, page 303)	250 mL
1 cup	brown rice flour	250 mL
1½ tbsp	ground cinnamon	22 mL
1 tbsp	arrowroot flour	15 mL
2¼ tsp	gluten-free baking powder	11 mL
½ tsp	Himalayan salt	2 mL
½ tsp	ground nutmeg	2 mL
¼ tsp	ground anise seeds	1 mL
¼ tsp	baking soda	1 mL
1 cup	fresh or frozen cranberries, cut in half	250 mL
⅓ cup	coconut sugar	75 mL
2	large eggs	2
½ cup	peeled Roasted Kabocha Squash (page 220)	125 mL
⅓ cup	full-fat coconut milk	75 mL
½ tsp	almond extract	2 mL

1. *Cinnamon Topping:* In a small bowl, combine coconut sugar and cinnamon. Set aside.

2. *Bread:* In a large bowl, combine almond flour, rice flour, cinnamon, arrowroot flour, baking powder, salt, nutmeg, anise and baking soda. Add cranberries, tossing to coat. Set aside.

3. In blender, combine sugar, eggs, squash, coconut milk and almond extract.

4. Add the egg mixture to the flour mixture, stirring with a wooden spoon until combined. Immediately spoon batter into prepared loaf pan. Sprinkle with topping.

5. Bake in preheated oven for 50 minutes or until a tester inserted into the middle comes out clean. Let cool completely in pan on a wire rack.

Maple Orange Scones

All three doshas can eat these scones in moderation. They're great for breakfast on the run or with afternoon tea.

Makes 5 scones

Tips

The higher fat content in full-fat yogurt helps to tenderize the scones and achieve a soft texture.

To toast pecans, place them in a dry (ungreased) skillet over medium heat. When they begin to smell fragrant, after about 1 minute, give the pan a shake. Continue to toast, periodically shaking the pan, until they begin to turn a darker color. Remove from heat immediately, as they can burn quickly.

Store in an airtight container at room temperature for up to 2 days.

Soy-Free ✦ Vegetarian

- **Preheat oven to 400°F (200°C)**
- **Baking sheet, greased**

1½ cups	whole wheat pastry flour (approx.)	375 mL
¼ cup	wheat germ	60 mL
2 tsp	baking powder	10 mL
½ tsp	Himalayan salt	2 mL
½ cup	quick-cooking rolled oats	125 mL
1 tbsp	flax seeds	15 mL
6 tbsp	ghee	90 mL
2 tbsp	grated orange zest	30 mL
2 tbsp	pure maple syrup	30 mL
2 tbsp	full-fat plain yogurt	30 mL
½ cup	coarsely chopped pecans, toasted (see tip, at left)	125 mL
1	large egg, beaten	1

1. In a large bowl, sift together flour, wheat germ, baking powder and salt. Stir in oats and flax seeds. Add ghee, stirring with a fork until mixture is crumbly but starting to cling together. Set aside.

2. In a small bowl, combine orange zest, maple syrup and yogurt.

3. Add the orange zest mixture to the flour mixture and stir with a fork to combine. Add pecans. Using your hands, work the dough until it becomes soft and firm. It should not be sticky; add more flour if necessary.

4. Divide dough into 5 equal pieces, transfer to a lightly floured surface and pat out to 1¼ inch (3 cm) thick. Form each scone into the desired shape (triangles, circles, etc.) and place on prepared baking sheet. Brush top and sides of scones with egg.

5. Bake in preheated oven for 18 to 22 minutes or until tops are lightly golden and scones feel slightly firm when pressed with a finger. Let cool on pan on a wire rack for 10 minutes. Serve warm.

Chocolate Almond Rose Cake with Ganache and Minted Whipped Cream

This decadent gluten-free cake is guaranteed to satisfy your chocolate cravings. All doshas should eat it in moderation, on special occasions.

Makes 8 servings

Tip

It is important to use good-quality chocolate. I prefer Green & Black's, which is organic, fair-trade and gluten-free, and has a smooth, creamy texture.

Gluten-Free ◆ Soy-Free ◆ Vegetarian

- **Preheat oven to 350°F (180°C)**
- **Double boiler**
- **8-inch (20 cm) springform pan, greased and bottom lined with parchment paper**

Cake

1 cup + 2 tbsp	chopped gluten-free dark chocolate (70% cacao)	280 mL
²/₃ to 1 cup	coconut sugar (see tip, opposite)	150 to 250 mL
¹/₂ cup	unsalted butter	125 mL
4	large egg yolks	4
¹/₂ tsp	rose water	2 mL
1¹/₂ cups	almond flour (see box, page 303)	375 mL
¹/₄ tsp	Himalayan salt	1 mL
4	large egg whites, at room temperature	4
1 tsp	coconut sugar	5 mL

Ganache

²/₃ cup	organic heavy or whipping (35%) cream	150 mL
1 cup	chopped gluten-free dark chocolate (¹/₂-inch/1 cm pieces), at room temperature	250 mL

Minted Whipped Cream

1¹/₄ cups	organic heavy or whipping (35%) cream	300 mL
¹/₄ tsp	rose water	1 mL
1 tbsp	coconut sugar	15 mL
1 tbsp	minced fresh mint leaves	15 mL

Tips

Prepare the recipe with the lower amount of sugar the first time you make it. If it's not sweet enough for your taste, you can use the larger amount of sugar the next time.

Store the cake in an airtight container in a cool, dark place for up to 4 days.

1. *Cake:* In the top of a double boiler, over simmering water, melt chocolate, stirring often. Remove from heat and let cool.

2. In a large bowl, cream ⅔ to 1 cup (150 to 250 mL) sugar and butter. Beat in melted chocolate, egg yolks and rose water until well combined. Fold in the almond flour and salt.

3. In another large bowl, using an electric mixer, beat egg whites on medium–high speed until frothy. Add 1 tsp (5 mL) sugar and beat until soft peaks form.

4. Gently fold half of the egg whites into the chocolate mixture. Fold in the remaining egg whites. Pour batter into prepared pan.

5. Bake in preheated oven for 25 to 35 minutes or until a tester inserted in the center comes out clean with just a few crumbs attached and the center of the cake bounces back after it is lightly touched (but no fingerprints should remain on the surface). Let cool in pan on a wire rack for 10 minutes, then invert the cake onto the rack and lift off the pan.

6. *Ganache:* In a medium saucepan, bring cream to a boil over medium heat. Immediately remove from heat and whisk in chocolate until melted and smooth. Let cool for 10 minutes. Spread ganache in a smooth layer over the top and sides of the cake.

7. *Whipped Cream:* In a medium bowl, using an electric mixer, beat cream and rose water on medium–high speed until frothy. Add sugar and mint; beat until soft peaks form. Spoon whipped cream onto cake.

The Nutty Date Pie Crust

This crust is moist and grounding for vata, while also being cooling for pitta. The heavy, oily nuts are least beneficial for kapha, so kapha should eat pies made with this crust only on special occasions.

Makes one 9-inch (23 cm) pie crust

Tip

To toast pecan halves and macadamia nuts, place them in a single layer in a dry (ungreased) skillet over medium heat. (You will likely need to toast them in batches.) When they begin to smell fragrant, after about 1 minute, give the pan a shake. Continue to toast, periodically shaking the pan, until they begin to turn a darker color. Remove from heat immediately, as they can burn quickly.

SERVING SUGGESTIONS

Use to make Ginger Almond Squash Pie (page 221) or fill with Puréed Parsnips with Thyme (page 215), chocolate pudding, coconut cream filling, key lime filling or pomegranate lemon mascarpone.

Gluten-Free ✦ Soy-Free ✦ Vegan

- Food processor
- 9-inch (23 cm) pie pan

6 tbsp	unsweetened shredded coconut	90 mL
2 tsp	virgin coconut oil	10 mL
1/2 cup	Medjool dates, pitted	125 mL
1 1/2 cups	macadamia nuts, toasted (see tip, at left)	375 mL
1 cup	pecan halves, toasted	250 mL
1/2 tsp	Himalayan salt	2 mL

1. In food processor, combine coconut and coconut oil; process for about 5 minutes, to the consistency of a nut butter. Add dates and pulse until finely chopped. Add macadamia nuts and pulse until finely chopped. Add pecans and salt; pulse for about 1 minute, to the consistency of a thick paste.

2. Press batter into the bottom and up the sides of pie pan, pressing it to about 1/4 inch (0.5 cm) thick. (If you spread the batter too thin, it will break apart when you slice the pie.) Use immediately or cover with plastic wrap and refrigerate for up to 1 day.

Making a Pie

To make a pie with this crust, add the desired filling and bake in a 325°F (160°C) oven for 25 minutes. The crust must be cooked on low heat or the exposed edges will burn.

Variation

Add 1 tsp (5 mL) grated orange or lemon zest with the dates.

Adzuki Bean Squares

Adzuki beans have a sweet taste and are often used in Japanese desserts, cooked down with sugar to make a paste. Cool and light, they are balancing to pitta and kapha. In this recipe, the wheat will help balance things for vata. But all three doshas should eat these squares in moderation.

Makes 16 squares

Tips

Dried beans take a little more preparation time, but are less costly than canned and have no added salt, sugar or preservatives. To save time, you may use 1½ cups (375 mL) canned adzuki beans, drained and rinsed, in place of the cooked dried beans.

Carefully remove individual squares from the pan; the dough topping tends to crumble (because the rice flour is dry).

Store the cooled squares, wrapped in waxed paper, then foil, at room temperature for up to 3 days.

Soy-Free ✦ Vegetarian

- **Preheat oven to 350°F (180°C)**
- **Immersion blender or handheld mixer (optional)**
- **Food processor, preferably fitted with the dough blade**
- **8-inch (20 cm) square metal baking pan, greased and lined with parchment paper**

Filling

¾ cup	coconut sugar	175 mL
½ cup	cooked adzuki beans (see page 64)	125 mL
½ tsp	ground cardamom	2 mL
¼ tsp	Himalayan salt	1 mL

Dough

1½ cups	almond flour (see box, page 303)	375 mL
1 cup	all-purpose flour	250 mL
1 cup	white rice flour	250 mL
½ cup	coconut sugar	125 mL
1 cup	cold unsalted butter, cut into ½-inch (1 cm) cubes	250 mL
1 tsp	almond extract	5 mL

1. *Filling:* In a medium saucepan, over medium–low heat, combine sugar, beans, cardamom and salt. Reduce heat to low and cook, stirring occasionally, for 10 minutes or until mixture resembles a chunky paste. If a smoother consistency is desired, purée with an immersion blender. Remove from heat and let cool.

2. *Dough:* In food processor, combine almond flour, all-purpose flour, rice flour, sugar, butter and almond extract; pulse until the mixture resembles moist crumbs.

3. Press half the dough mixture into the bottom of the prepared pan, pressing with the back of a metal spoon to level the surface. Spread filling on top. Sprinkle the remaining dough crumbs on top.

4. Bake in preheated oven for 20 to 30 minutes or until the dough topping is golden, but not brown. Let cool in pan on a wire rack for 10 minutes. Cut into squares, then let cool completely in pan on rack.

Gluten-Free Adzuki Bean Squares

I created this gluten-free version of Adzuki Bean Squares for my ayurveda classmate Laura. It is suitable for all doshas, in moderation.

Makes 16 squares

Tips

Dried beans take a little more preparation time, but are less costly than canned and have no added salt, sugar or preservatives. To save time, you may use 1½ cups (375 mL) canned adzuki beans, drained and rinsed, in place of the cooked dried beans.

Butter with a higher fat content (such as European-style 85% fat) works well with gluten-free recipes to help with structure and moisture.

Gluten-Free ✦ Soy-Free ✦ Vegetarian

- Preheat oven to 350°F (180°C)
- Immersion blender or handheld mixer (optional)
- Food processor, preferably fitted with the dough blade
- 8-inch (20 cm) square metal baking pan, greased and bottom lined with parchment paper

Filling

¾ cup	coconut sugar	175 mL
½ cup	cooked adzuki beans (see page 64)	125 mL
½ tsp	ground cardamom	2 mL
¼ tsp	Himalayan salt	1 mL

Dough

2 cups	almond flour (see box, opposite)	500 mL
¾ cup	brown rice flour	175 mL
½ cup	chickpea flour	125 mL
¼ cup	arrowroot flour	60 mL
⅔ cup	coconut sugar	150 mL
¼ tsp	Himalayan salt	1 mL
¾ cup + 2 tbsp	cold unsalted butter (see tip, at left), cut into ½-inch (1 cm) cubes	205 mL
1	large egg, beaten	1
1½ tsp	almond extract	7 mL

1. *Filling:* In a medium saucepan, over medium–low heat, combine sugar, beans, cardamom and salt. Reduce heat to low and cook, stirring occasionally, for 10 minutes or until mixture resembles a chunky paste. If a smoother consistency is desired, purée with an immersion blender. Remove from heat and let cool.

Tips

Allow the squares to cool completely. They will firm up as they cool, making removal from the pan easier.

Store the cooled squares, wrapped in waxed paper, then foil, at room temperature for up to 3 days.

2. *Dough:* In food processor, combine almond flour, rice flour, chickpea flour, arrowroot flour, sugar, salt and butter; process until combined. Add egg and almond extract; process until dough is consistently moist and holds together.

3. Press half the dough mixture into the bottom of the prepared pan, pressing with the back of a metal spoon to level the surface. Bake in preheated oven for 10 minutes.

4. Remove pan from oven, leaving oven on, and spread filling evenly on top of dough. Use your fingers to spread and lightly press the remaining dough on top. Using a fork, prick the top to make even columns of tiny holes.

5. Bake for about 20 minutes or until top is light golden, but not brown. Let cool in pan on a wire rack for 10 minutes. Cut into squares, then let cool completely in pan on rack.

Almond Flour

If you make your own almond milk (page 322), you should definitely make your own almond flour! This simple recipe makes good use of the leftover strained nut meat and is really easy to make: Spread almond nut meat evenly on a rimmed baking sheet lined with parchment paper. Bake in a 170°F (80°C) oven for about 3 hours or until completely dried out. Let cool to room temperature, then transfer to a food processor and pulse to a fine consistency. Store in an airtight container in the refrigerator for up to 3 months.

Turkish Halva

Fresh halva is soft, moist and easy to prepare. It has a warm energetic and is oily, making it best for vata; pitta can substitute cooling maple syrup for the honey; kapha can try the coffee flavoring (see variations). This lightly sweetened version is suitable for all doshas, in moderation.

**Makes
16 squares**

Tips

Ayurvedic practitioners believe raw honey has many benefits, including scraping fat and cholesterol from the body's tissues, making it the go-to sweetener for kapha or anyone trying to reduce kapha in their body.

Store squares in an airtight container in the refrigerator for up to 1 month.

Variations

Replace the cardamom with any of the following: 1 tsp (5 mL) vanilla extract; $\frac{1}{2}$ tsp (2 mL) instant coffee dissolved in $\frac{1}{2}$ tsp (2 mL) boiling water; $\frac{1}{2}$ tsp (2 mL) orange extract; 1 tsp (5 mL) unsweetened cocoa powder; $1\frac{1}{2}$ tbsp (22 mL) chopped pistachios; $1\frac{1}{2}$ tbsp (22 mL) chopped blanched almonds.

Dairy-Free ✦ Gluten-Free ✦ Soy-Free ✦ Vegetarian

- Food processor
- 8-inch (20 cm) square glass baking dish

$\frac{3}{4}$ cup	unhulled raw sesame seeds	175 mL
$\frac{1}{4}$ tsp	ground cardamom	1 mL
1 cup	Basic Tahini (page 261)	250 mL
2 tbsp	raw liquid honey	30 mL
1 tsp	rose water	5 mL

1. In food processor, grind sesame seeds to a coarse consistency (about 2 minutes). Add cardamom, tahini, honey and rose water; pulse until combined.

2. Transfer to baking dish, smoothing the top with the back of a metal spoon. Cover and refrigerate for 1 hour. Cut into squares.

Dark Chocolate Cherry Nut Slices

These bars can be made in a flash and are always a hit at parties. Moist and cool, they are perfect for vata and pitta, but a bit heavy for kapha. All doshas should eat them in moderation.

Makes 24 bars

Tips

It is important to use good-quality chocolate. I prefer Green & Black's, which is organic, fair-trade and gluten-free, and has a smooth, creamy texture.

Melt the chocolate in a small, heavy-bottomed pan over low heat, stirring constantly so it doesn't burn.

The bars can be stored in sealable freezer bags in the freezer for up to 1 month. Thaw for 10 minutes before serving.

Variations

Substitute orange sauce (variation, page 311) for the Cherry Sauce.

Add ¼ cup (60 mL) toasted shredded coconut to the chocolate while melting it.

Gluten-Free ✦ Soy-Free ✦ Vegetarian

- Food processor
- 8-inch (20 cm) square metal baking pan, greased, bottom lined with parchment (or waxed) paper

Base

¾ cup	unsweetened shredded coconut	175 mL
¼ cup	Cherry Sauce (page 311)	60 mL
1 tbsp	virgin coconut oil	15 mL
1 tbsp	almond butter	15 mL
6	Medjool dates	6
1 cup	macadamia nuts, lightly toasted (see tip, page 300)	250 mL
1 cup	pecan halves, lightly toasted	250 mL

Toppings

¼ cup	Cherry Sauce (page 311)	60 mL
½ cup	chopped dark (85%) chocolate, melted (see tip, at left)	125 mL

1. *Base:* In food processor, combine coconut, Cherry Sauce, coconut oil and almond butter; pulse for 3 to 5 minutes, to the consistency of a paste. Add dates, macadamia nuts and pecans. Pulse until batter is well incorporated and sticks together (it will be very thick).

2. Spread batter evenly across the bottom of the prepared pan.

3. *Toppings:* Spread Cherry Sauce in an even layer over batter. Pour melted chocolate on top, spreading until evenly coated. Refrigerate for 20 minutes, then cut into bars.

Pomegranate Orange Chip Bars

The merger of chocolaty, chewy goodness with heart-healthy oats and pomegranate created this divine bar – a taste of bliss in every bite. All doshas should eat it in moderation.

Makes 16 bars

Tips

Store the squares in an airtight container at room temperature for up to 3 days.

The batter can be stored in an airtight container in the refrigerator for up to 1 week.

Variations

Substitute white chocolate chunks in place of the dark chocolate.

Substitute lemon zest in place of the orange zest.

You can also use this batter to make 1 dozen cookies. At the end of step 1, form batter into 12 equal balls. Gently press onto a baking sheet lined with parchment paper, placing them ½ inch (1 cm) apart. Bake for 7 to 8 minutes or until the edges are starting to brown. The cookies will be soft coming out of the oven but will firm up as they cool on a wire rack.

Gluten-Free ✦ Soy-Free ✦ Vegetarian

- **Preheat oven to 350°F (180°C)**
- **8-inch (20 cm) square metal baking pan, lined with parchment paper**

½ cup	coconut sugar	125 mL
½ tsp	ground cinnamon	2 mL
1 tsp	grated orange zest	5 mL
¼ tsp	Himalayan salt	1 mL
¾ cup	almond butter	175 mL
¼ cup	unsalted butter	60 mL
1 tbsp	pomegranate syrup (see tip, page 316)	15 mL
1	large egg, beaten	1
¾ tsp	baking soda	3 mL
1½ cups	quick-cooking rolled oats	375 mL
¼ cup	gluten-free dark chocolate chunks (70% to 85% cacao)	60 mL

1. In a large bowl, combine sugar, cinnamon, orange zest, salt, almond butter, butter and pomegranate syrup. Stir in egg. The batter will be very thick and oily. Stir in baking soda. Stir in oats and chocolate chunks until well incorporated. Spoon into prepared baking pan.

2. Bake in preheated oven for 20 to 22 minutes or until the edges just start to brown. (If the entire top is brown, the bars are overcooked and will be very dry. The dough should be soft coming out of the oven.) Let cool in pan on a wire rack for 10 minutes, then cut into bars and transfer bars to the rack to cool completely.

Chewy Choco-Orange Macaroons

Lightly sweetened, infused with ginger and topped with dark chocolate, these macaroons are delightful. Coconut is cooling, sweet and heavy – balancing for pitta and vata. The ginger adds a little warmth for kapha, but in general, kapha should eat these in moderation.

Makes 2 dozen cookies

Tips

Full-fat coconut milk will yield a moist, chewy macaroon.

Do not reduce the sugar in this recipe. If you desire sweeter macaroons, however, you can increase the sugar by 2 to 4 tbsp (30 to 60 mL).

For the best texture, use 2½ cups (625 mL) finely shredded coconut and 1 cup (250 mL) long-thread coconut.

When forming the macaroons, dip your fingers in cold water to minimize dough sticking to your fingers.

If desired, you can omit the chocolate drizzle, for a lighter treat.

Variations

Substitute lime or lemon zest for the orange zest.

Substitute rose water for the vanilla.

Gluten-Free ✦ Soy-Free ✦ Vegetarian

- **Preheat oven to 325°F (160°C)**
- **Baking sheet, lined with parchment paper**

1	can (14 oz/400 mL) full-fat coconut milk	1
½ cup	coconut sugar	125 mL
1½ tsp	grated orange zest	7 mL
¼ tsp	grated gingerroot	1 mL
Pinch	Himalayan salt	Pinch
½ tsp	vanilla extract	2 mL
3½ cups	unsweetened shredded coconut	875 mL
2	large egg whites, at room temperature	2
⅓ cup	chopped gluten-free dark chocolate (85% cacao), melted	75 mL

1. In a small saucepan, over medium-low heat, cook coconut milk and sugar, stirring occasionally, for about 25 minutes or until reduced by three-quarters. Stir in orange zest, ginger, salt and vanilla.

2. Transfer coconut milk mixture to a large bowl. Stir in coconut. Let cool.

3. In a medium bowl, using an electric mixer, beat egg whites on medium-high speed until soft peaks form. Gently fold into coconut mixture.

4. Using about 2 tbsp (30 mL) dough for each ball, roll dough into 24 balls. Place ½ inch (1 cm) apart on prepared baking sheet.

5. Bake in preheated oven for 28 minutes or until golden. Transfer cookies to a wire rack and let cool completely.

6. Drizzle melted chocolate over macaroons.

Cardamom Almond Balls

While attending ayurveda school in Albuquerque, New Mexico, I would frequent Anupurna's World Vegetarian Café for healthy ayurvedic meals, a cup of chai and their amazing sweets. This recipe was inspired by their cardamom cookies.

Makes about 30 cookies

Tips

Use a clean coffee grinder or a mini food processor to grind the almonds and flax seeds, using a few pulses to get a coarse grind.

Place a piece of parchment paper under the cooling rack to catch any sugar that falls through the rack. Then you can roll the paper into a cone shape and funnel the sugar back into its container — easy cleanup and no waste!

Cooled cookies can be stored in an airtight container at room temperature for up to 3 days.

Soy-Free ✦ Vegetarian

- **Preheat oven to 350°F (180°C)**
- **Baking sheet, greased**

½ cup	whole wheat pastry flour	125 mL
½ cup	unbleached all-purpose flour	125 mL
¾ tsp	gluten-free baking powder	3 mL
½ tsp	Himalayan salt	2 mL
¼ tsp	baking soda	1 mL
⅓ cup	coconut sugar	75 mL
½ cup	unsalted butter, softened	125 mL
1	large egg, beaten	1
2 tsp	grated lemon zest	10 mL
1 tsp	vanilla extract	5 mL
1½ cups	blanched slivered almonds, coarsely ground (see tip, at left)	375 mL
3 tbsp	flax seeds, coarsely ground	45 mL
1 tbsp	ground cardamom	15 mL
3 tbsp	confectioners' (icing) sugar	45 mL

1. In a small bowl, sift together pastry flour, all-purpose flour, baking powder, salt and baking soda.

2. In a large bowl, cream sugar and butter until fluffy. Beat in egg, lemon zest and vanilla until light and fluffy. Stir in almonds, flax seeds and cardamom until well combined. Stir in flour mixture until thoroughly combined. (The dough will be oily from the almonds.)

3. Using about 1½ tsp (7 mL) dough for each ball, roll dough into 30 balls. Place 1 inch (2.5 cm) apart on prepared baking sheet.

4. Bake in preheated oven for 8 minutes or until cookies are just beginning to brown slightly on the bottom. (Be careful, as they will quickly burn and dry out if baked for too long.) Transfer cookies to a wire rack (see tip, at left) and let cool for 5 minutes.

5. Place confectioners' sugar in a sieve. Hold the sieve above the cookies and gently tap it to allow a fine powder to sprinkle onto the cookies.

Truffles

These decadent truffles are a crowd-pleaser and great for parties. But keep in mind that chocolate is bitter, astringent, acidic and contains caffeine. Minimize these treats, especially in the evening. Eat them in moderation and share with friends. The suitability of the suggested toppings for the doshas is indicated by the abbreviations in parentheses.

Makes 30 truffles

Tips

It is important to use good-quality chocolate. I prefer Green & Black's, which is organic, fair-trade and gluten-free, and has a smooth, creamy texture.

If the ganache gets too warm, it will start to melt and stick to your hands. You can put it in the freezer for 5 or 10 minutes to firm it up, then continue making balls. Rinsing your hands with cold water will also help.

Store the truffles in the refrigerator for up to 1 week or in the freezer for up to 1 month.

Variation

Replace some of the dark chocolate with a flavored dark chocolate (such as Green & Black's Maya Gold).

Gluten-Free ✦ Soy-Free ✦ Vegetarian

½ cup	organic heavy or whipping (35%) cream	125 mL
5 tsp	unsalted butter	25 mL
1 cup	chopped gluten-free dark chocolate (85% cacao)	250 mL
1 tbsp	raw liquid honey	15 mL

Suggested Toppings

Sifted unsweetened cocoa powder (PK)

Unsweetened shredded coconut (VP)

Ground toasted almonds, hazelnuts, cashews or pecans (V)

1. In a small saucepan, heat cream and butter over medium-low heat, stirring constantly. When the mixture reaches just below boiling (you will see tiny bubbles beginning to form), remove from heat and add chocolate, stirring with a flexible spatula until melted and smooth. Let cool completely, then stir in honey.

2. Transfer to a small bowl, cover with plastic wrap and refrigerate for 1 to 2 hours or until ganache is firm enough to roll into balls.

3. Place desired toppings on plates. Scoop out 1 tsp (5 mL) ganache and mold into a small ball using the palm of your hand. Roll ball in topping. Continue making balls, placing them in a single layer in an airtight container.

Kabocha Caramel Custard

This custard is light and delicately flavored with ginger and a hint of saffron.

Tips

Prepare the custard with
¼ cup (60 mL) sugar
and taste it at the end of
step 4; if it doesn't seem
sweet enough, add the
additional sugar.

Custards are thickened
primarily by egg
proteins, which "set"
below 212°F (100°C).
If placed directly in a
300°F (150°C) oven,
they are likely to
overcook and tighten or
shrink, which will cause
the custard to crack or
separate into curdled egg
and liquid. Using a water
bath protects the proteins
from the high heat of the
oven and ensures slow,
even cooking. The dish
for the bath should be
just large enough to hold
the ramekins.

Dairy-Free ✦ Gluten-Free ✦ Soy-Free ✦ Vegetarian

- **Preheat oven to 300°F (150°C)**
- **Blender**
- **Four ¾-cup (175 mL) ramekins**
- **Glass baking dish large enough to hold ramekins snugly**

Caramel

2 tbsp	water	30 mL
¼ cup	coconut sugar	60 mL
¼ cup	pure maple syrup	60 mL

Custard

4	saffron threads	4
1 cup	thick-strained cashew milk (page 322), divided	250 mL
2 cups	peeled Roasted Kabocha Squash (page 220)	500 mL
1 tsp	minced gingerroot	5 mL
¼ to ⅓ cup	coconut sugar (see tip, at left)	60 to 75 mL
2	large eggs	2
	Hot (not boiling) water	

1. *Caramel:* In a small saucepan, warm water over low heat. Add sugar and maple syrup; simmer, stirring constantly to prevent scorching, until caramel has thickened. Divide evenly among ramekins and set aside to let the caramel harden.

2. *Custard:* In a small bowl, soak saffron in 1 tsp (5 mL) cashew milk for 5 minutes.

3. In blender, combine squash, ginger, saffron-infused milk and the remaining cashew milk; purée until smooth.

4. Transfer squash mixture to a medium saucepan and warm over medium–low heat until small bubbles begin breaking the surface. (Do not let boil.) Whisk in sugar, then remove from heat.

5. In a medium bowl, whisk eggs. Gradually whisk eggs into custard. Pour custard into ramekins, dividing evenly. Place ramekins in baking dish.

Tip

You may use an 8-inch (20 cm) glass pie plate in place of the 4 ramekins. The custard will take a little longer to cook, so begin checking for doneness after 25 minutes.

6. Place baking dish in preheated oven. Slowly add hot water to the baking dish, creating a bath for the custard. The water should come up to the level of the custard inside the ramekins. Be careful not to spill water into the custard.

7. Bake in preheated oven for 20 to 30 minutes or until the outer edges are firm but the center is still jiggly. Be careful when removing the pan from the oven, so as not to slosh any water into the ramekins. Let cool to room temperature. Wrap with plastic wrap and refrigerate for about 30 minutes or until firm.

Cherry Sauce

This sweet cherry sauce can be used any time you need natural cherry flavoring. Mix it with chocolate, pour it over desserts or pancakes, or combine it with mineral water for a refreshing summer spritzer.

Makes about ¹/₂ cup (125 mL)

Tip

Store in a nonreactive airtight container in the refrigerator for up to 7 days or in the freezer for up to 2 months.

Variation

Substitute 1 cup (250 mL) chopped apricots, pears or oranges for the cherries.

Gluten-Free ✦ Soy-Free ✦ Vegan

● **Blender**

8 oz	fresh or thawed frozen sweet cherries, pitted	250 g
2 tsp	coconut sugar	10 mL
2 tsp	freshly squeezed lemon juice	10 mL

1. In blender, combine cherries, sugar and lemon juice; purée until smooth.

2. Transfer cherry mixture to a small saucepan and bring to a boil over medium heat. Reduce heat and simmer, stirring often, until reduced by half.

Rice Pudding

This low-sugar version of rice pudding is the ultimate comfort food when you're recovering from an illness. It is building and nurturing.

**Makes
4 servings**

Tips

This recipe is the consistency of a moist risotto; if you desire a thinner consistency, increase the amount of cashew milk.

Store in an airtight container in the refrigerator for up to 3 days. Bring to room temperature or warm in a saucepan over low heat before eating.

Variations

Garnish with toasted pistachios, pine nuts or sliced almonds.

Add 2 tbsp (30 mL) sultanas with the maple syrup.

Add 1 tsp (5 mL) grated lemon or orange zest with the maple syrup.

Gluten-Free ✦ Soy-Free ✦ Vegetarian

Pinch	saffron threads	Pinch
2 cups	thick-strained cashew milk (page 322), divided	500 mL
1 tbsp	ghee	15 mL
½ cup	Arborio rice	125 mL
1	vanilla bean, split lengthwise	1
¼ tsp	ground cardamom	1 mL
⅛ tsp	Himalayan salt	0.5 mL
2 to 3 tbsp	pure maple syrup	15 to 30 mL
	Julienned fresh mint (optional)	

1. In a small bowl, soak saffron in 1 tbsp (15 mL) cashew milk for 5 minutes.

2. In a medium saucepan, melt ghee over medium heat. Add rice and cook, stirring, for about 5 minutes or until golden.

3. Stir in saffron-infused milk, the remaining cashew milk, vanilla bean, cardamom, salt and maple syrup to taste; bring to a boil. Reduce heat and boil gently, stirring often, for about 15 minutes or until rice is tender. Discard vanilla bean.

4. Divide pudding among four serving dishes and serve warm, garnished with mint, if desired.

Beverages

Ayurveda considers clean, pure water served warm or at room temperature to be the ideal drink. The recommended daily intake is determined by several factors, including your constitution (kapha needs the least); your lifestyle (if you sweat a lot, you need to drink more); your diet (if you eat a lot of salty or dry foods, you need to drink more); and the climate (you will need to drink more in a dry or hot climate). Ayurveda recommends avoiding iced drinks.

Alcohol is occasionally recommended in small amounts – for example, $1/4$ cup (60 mL) wine diluted with an equal amount of water – to stimulate digestion before a meal, but in general, alcohol causes imbalance and is best avoided.

Likewise, coffee is best avoided, as caffeine stresses the adrenal glands. An ayurvedic antidote to minimize the impact on the adrenals is to add a pinch of cardamom or cinnamon to your coffee. If you are interested in reducing your caffeine intake, try substituting an herbal coffee, such as Teeccino. Teeccino is astringent and bitter, making it well balanced for kapha or pitta; vata will need to add some steamed milk (or nondairy alternative) and honey to balance it out.

Dosha-Specific Drinks and Juices

Drinks

In ayurveda, clean, warm water is the drink of choice. But herbal teas and milks are often used to balance doshas. The following table outlines some drinks that are used to ground vata, cool down pitta and get kapha moving. In addition to the teas and milks, I have concocted some fun and tasty recipes to provide you with alternatives to sugary sodas, caffeinated drinks and alcohol. Our culture revolves around gatherings where we consume beverages; these drinks will allow you to fit in, and will provide you with unique conversation starters so you stand out!

Vata	Pitta	Kapha
◆ Vata Blood Orange Mojito Mocktail (page 315) ◆ Vata Pitta Vitality Drink (page 320) ◆ Go-to-Sleep Nutmeg Milk (page 321) ◆ Vata Pitta Coconut Chai Shake (page 324) ◆ Vata Pitta Ginger Tea (page 326) ◆ masala chai	◆ Pitta Pomegranate Lime Mocktail (page 316) ◆ Pitta-Soothing Mint Rose Water Drink (page 317) ◆ Pitta-Refreshing Aloe Lime Drink (page 318) ◆ Vata Pitta Vitality Drink (page 320) ◆ Pitta-Cooling Coriander Milk (page 320) ◆ Go-to-Sleep Nutmeg Milk (page 321) ◆ Vata Pitta Coconut Chai Shake (page 324) ◆ Vata Pitta Ginger Tea (page 326)	◆ Kapha Lime Ginger Mint Mocktail (page 317) ◆ Kapha Ginger Tea (page 325)

Juices

The following table presents some dosha-specific juice combinations. Kapha should dilute their fruit juices 50% with water so as to minimize their sugar intake. Some ayurvedic doctors advise that the juice of fruits not be combined with the juice of vegetables. I have followed that advice in preparing this table. It is not necessary to add sweeteners to these juices.

Vata	Pitta	Kapha
◆ carrot-ginger-beet ◆ orange-lime ◆ *Optional herbs and spices:* gingerroot, mint	◆ apple-cranberry ◆ apple-lime ◆ carrot-kale ◆ coconut water ◆ watermelon ◆ *Optional herbs and spices:* cilantro, mint	◆ apple-lemon ◆ kale-carrot-parsley ◆ pomegranate-lime-ginger-apple ◆ *Optional herbs and spices:* fresh gingerroot, cayenne pepper, mint

Vata Blood Orange Mojito Mocktail

This is a refreshing drink for vata on a summer day. Blood oranges are less acidic than navel oranges and, depending on the variety, may be sweet or slightly sour. This blend of orange, mint and lime is a revitalizing combination of vitamins and minerals.

Makes 1 serving

Tips

When muddling the mint leaves, you want to bruise the leaves to release the flavor; do not grind them to the point that they tear.

Vata doesn't need bubbles (movement) so it's best to not use sparkling (carbonated) water.

This recipe can be multiplied and stored in an airtight container in the refrigerator for up to 4 days. Bring to room temperature before drinking.

Gluten-Free ✦ Soy-Free ✦ Vegan

- **Wooden pestle or wooden spoon**

10	fresh mint leaves	10
1/2 tsp	coconut sugar	2 mL
3/4 cup	non-carbonated mineral water	175 mL
1/4 cup	freshly squeezed blood orange juice	60 mL
1 tsp	freshly squeezed lime juice	5 mL

1. In a tall glass, combine mint and sugar. Using a wooden pestle or spoon, gently muddle mint for about 10 seconds. Stir in mineral water, blood orange juice and lime juice. Serve immediately.

Pitta Pomegranate Lime Mocktail

This drink is sweet and cooling, perfect for when pitta is running high!

Makes 1 serving

Tips

Pomegranate syrup (also known as pomegranate molasses) can be purchased at international grocery stores or in the international aisle of major grocery stores.

This recipe can be multiplied and stored in an airtight container in the refrigerator for up to 4 days. If you're trying to reduce pitta, you can drink it chilled. Otherwise, bring to room temperature before drinking.

Variations

Substitute Cherry Sauce (page 311) for the pomegranate syrup.

Add 3 fresh mint leaves.

Substitute coconut water for the mineral water.

Gluten-Free ✦ Soy-Free ✦ Vegan

1 cup	non-carbonated mineral water	250 mL
1½ tsp	pomegranate syrup	7 mL
1 tsp	freshly squeezed lime juice	5 mL
	Lime wedge (optional)	

1. In a tall glass, combine mineral water, pomegranate syrup and lime juice. If desired, garnish with a lime wedge.

Kapha Lime Ginger Mint Mocktail

This light and pungent drink is invigorating for kapha.

Makes 1 serving

Tip

This recipe can be multiplied and stored in an airtight container in the refrigerator for up to 4 days. Bring to room temperature before drinking.

Variation

Add a pinch of cayenne pepper or dash of hot pepper sauce.

	Gluten-Free ◆ Soy-Free ◆ Vegan	
• **Glass jar with lid**		
10	fresh mint leaves	10
2 tbsp	chopped gingerroot	30 mL
1 cup	sparkling mineral water	250 mL
2 tsp	freshly squeezed lime juice	10 mL

1. In jar, combine mint, ginger, mineral water and lime juice. Cover tightly and shake vigorously for 30 seconds. Let stand for 10 minutes to allow the flavors to infuse the water.

2. Strain into a glass and serve at room temperature.

Pitta-Soothing Mint Rose Water Drink

Mint calms pitta. Combined with cooling rose water and sweet maple syrup, it makes a deliciously soothing drink.

Makes 1 serving

	Dairy-Free ◆ Gluten-Free ◆ Soy-Free ◆ Vegetarian	
• **Glass jar with lid**		
1 tsp	chopped fresh mint	5 mL
1 cup	water	250 mL
$\frac{1}{2}$ tsp	pure maple syrup	2 mL
$\frac{1}{4}$ tsp	rose water	1 mL

1. In jar, combine mint, water, maple syrup and rose water. Cover tightly and shake to blend. Transfer to a glass and serve.

Pitta-Refreshing Aloe Lime Drink

Coconut sugar is cooling, and the wisdom of the ancients says aloe vera juice is good for the liver. Cilantro is also cooling and helps to pacify feelings of anger.

Makes 1 serving

Tip

Aloe vera juice can be purchased at health food stores, food cooperatives and large grocery stores. Choose high-quality aloe vera that is preservative-free, has the official IASC (International Aloe Science Council) seal on the package or container and lists aloe vera gel as the first ingredient (if water is the first ingredient, the contents are likely reconstituted powder). Choose the "inner fillet," which is nutrient-rich, cooling and gently cleansing. The "whole-leaf" option has a strong laxative effect.

Gluten-Free ✦ Soy-Free ✦ Vegan

1 tsp	coconut sugar	5 mL
1/2 cup	water	125 mL
1 tsp	chopped fresh cilantro	5 mL
1/4 cup	aloe vera juice (see tip, at left)	60 mL
1 tsp	freshly squeezed lime juice	5 mL

1. In a small saucepan, heat coconut sugar and water over medium heat, stirring gently until sugar is dissolved. Let cool to room temperature.
2. Pour into a glass and stir in cilantro, aloe vera juice and lime juice.

Pitta Green Tonic

This is a cooling and gently cleansing drink for pitta. Ideal in the summer, it is best to avoid in cooler weather.

**Makes
3 servings**

Tips

Store in a glass jar in the refrigerator for up to 2 days; shake before serving.

Ayurveda recommends that drinks be consumed at room temperature or warm (not with ice). Using a high-power blender may result in a lukewarm drink, as it will slightly "cook" the kale. If you prefer something cooler, place the freshly rinsed kale in the freezer for 30 minutes (or overnight) before blending.

Gluten-Free ✦ Soy-Free ✦ Vegan

- **High-power blender**

4 cups	trimmed coarsely chopped kale leaves	1 L
⅛ to ¼	lemon, with peel	⅛ to ¼
1 tbsp	dulse	15 mL
1	½-inch (1 cm) piece gingerroot	1
1 cup	aloe vera juice (see tip, page 318)	250 mL
1 cup	water	250 mL

1. In blender, combine kale, lemon to taste, dulse, ginger, aloe vera juice and water; blend until smooth.

Vata Pitta Vitality Drink

This drink is grounding and replenishing to vata, cooling and restorative to pitta. Drink in a calm, peaceful environment before sunrise.

Makes 1 serving

Tip

The dates and almonds will end up falling to the bottom of the cup. I typically eat them with a spoon.

Gluten-Free ♦ Soy-Free ♦ Vegan

- **Mortar and pestle**

3	fresh dates	3
	Water	
8	blanched almonds	8
2	saffron threads	2
⅛ tsp	ground cardamom	0.5 mL
1 cup	organic milk or unsweetened almond milk	250 mL

1. Place dates in a bowl and add enough water to cover. Let soak overnight at room temperature. Drain, pit and chop.
2. Using a mortar and pestle, crush almonds into small pieces.
3. In a small saucepan, combine dates, almonds, saffron, cardamom and milk. Bring to a boil over medium heat. Reduce heat and simmer for 3 minutes. Remove from heat and let cool for 5 minutes before serving.

Pitta-Cooling Coriander Milk

I concocted this spiced milk when I was experiencing hot flashes. One cup, 30 minutes before bed, produced a cool, restful sleep.

Makes 1 serving

Tips

Use a mortar and pestle to coarsely crush the coriander seeds.

If desired, strain the milk before serving.

Gluten-Free ♦ Soy-Free ♦ Vegan

1 cup	organic milk or nondairy alternative (unsweetened soy or almond)	250 mL
1 tsp	coriander seeds, coarsely crushed	5 mL

1. In a small saucepan, heat milk and coriander seeds over medium heat until just beginning to boil. Remove from heat and let cool for 5 minutes before serving.

Go-to-Sleep Nutmeg Milk

This sleepy-time milk is ideal for vata or pitta. Mellow kapha probably doesn't need it. Prepare this a half-hour before you head to bed.

Makes 1 serving

Gluten-Free ✦ Soy-Free ✦ Vegan		
1 cup	organic milk or unsweetened almond milk	250 mL
Pinch	ground nutmeg	Pinch

1. In a small saucepan, bring milk to a boil over medium heat. Add nutmeg, reduce heat and simmer for 5 minutes. Transfer to your favorite mug and drink slowly.

Turmeric Milk

Warm milk makes you sleepy and the benefits of turmeric in ayurveda are seemingly endless. It's generally good for the immune system, and turmeric milk is recommended daily before bed as a preventive health measure. This recipe is tridoshic if made with cow's milk or almond milk. Prepare it a half-hour before you head to bed.

Makes 1 serving

Variation
Add a pinch of saffron with the turmeric.

Gluten-Free ✦ Soy-Free ✦ Vegan		
1 cup	organic milk or unsweetened almond milk	250 mL
¼ tsp	ground turmeric	1 mL

1. In a small saucepan, bring milk to a boil over medium heat. Add turmeric, reduce heat and simmer for 5 minutes. Transfer to your favorite mug and drink slowly.

Nut Milk

This great-tasting nut milk contains no preservatives or thickeners. The natural goodness is ready in seconds using a high-power blender.

Tips

Store for up to 4 days in an airtight glass container in the refrigerator. If prepared through step 1, the nut meat will separate from the milk, so you will need to shake it before serving. If prepared through step 3, the milk will not separate and will be thick. If you want to make yogurt using nut milk, you *must* prepare through step 3.

Leftover nut meat can be stored in an airtight glass container in the refrigerator for up to 4 days. Add it to soups to impart a nutty essence and added nutrients. Add ¼ cup (60 mL) to Tridoshic Artichoke Pesto (page 281) or Mushroom Almond Pâté (page 288). Leftover almond nutmeat can be used to make Almond Flour (see box, page 303).

Gluten-Free ✦ Soy-Free ✦ Vegan

- **High-power blender**
- **Fine-mesh strainer (optional)**

1 cup	blanched nuts (almonds or cashews)	250 mL
3 cups	water	750 mL

1. In blender, combine nuts and water; purée until smooth. Serve as is or continue with step 2.

Thick–Strained Nut Milk

2. For a smoother and thicker consistency, place a strainer over a medium pan. Pour the puréed nut milk through the strainer into the pan. Using a spoon, scoop out the nut meat to facilitate the flow of milk.

3. Warm the strained milk over medium heat. Bring to a gentle boil, then reduce heat and simmer, stirring constantly, to desired thickness. Serve warm or chill in the refrigerator.

Variations

Add ¼ tsp (1 mL) ground cinnamon, ground cardamom or vanilla extract in step 1, before puréeing.

Add 1 split vanilla bean pod (and its seeds) to the milk in step 3. Simmer for at least 15 minutes, stirring constantly, for a delicious vanilla infusion. Strain out vanilla pod and seeds.

Yogurt Lassi

A lassi is a traditional Indian drink often taken with meals as a digestive aid. It is made by diluting yogurt with room-temperature water and adding sweet, savory or spicy flavorings. The following are some delish dosha-specific lassis.

Makes 1 serving

Tips

Use fresh yogurt, as it is light, it is easy to digest, and it improves assimilation of nutrients.

Vata can drink the Savory Lassi with lunch to aid digestion, but should not drink it at dinner.

Pita can drink the Sweet Rose Lassi at lunch or dinner, when pitta is high.

Kapha can drink the Spicy Lassi with lunch to stimulate digestion, but should not drink it at dinner.

Gluten-Free ♦ Soy-Free ♦ Vegetarian

$\frac{1}{2}$ cup	Creamy Yogurt (page 117)	125 mL
$\frac{1}{2}$ cup	water	125 mL

Savory Lassi (for Vata)

$\frac{1}{4}$ tsp	ground cumin	1 mL
1 tsp	chopped fresh cilantro	5 mL
Pinch	Himalayan salt	Pinch

Sweet Rose Lassi (for Pitta)

2	drops rose water	2
$\frac{1}{2}$ tsp	pure maple syrup	2 mL
Pinch	ground cardamom (optional)	Pinch

Spicy Lassi (for Kapha)

$\frac{1}{2}$ tsp	ground ginger	2 mL
$\frac{1}{8}$ tsp	ground cinnamon	0.5 mL
$\frac{1}{8}$ tsp	ground cardamom	0.5 mL

1. In a tall glass, whisk together yogurt, water and desired seasonings until well combined (or shake together in a tightly covered jar, then pour into a glass).

Vata Pitta Coconut Chai Shake

This shake is best for vata and pitta, but kapha can enjoy it with the modifications noted below.

Makes 1 serving

Tips

Coconut milk is readily available in the international food aisle of most grocery stores. It comes in 13.5- or 14-oz (400 mL) cans and has a long shelf life. The milk and cream tend to separate inside the can, so shake the can vigorously before opening it. Once opened, transfer unused coconut milk to an airtight container and store in the refrigerator for up to 1 week.

Leftover coconut milk can be used to make Thai Lemongrass Vermicelli Soup (page 198).

Variations

Sprinkle chopped mint over top before serving.

Sweeten with 1 tbsp (15 mL) minced Medjool dates.

Gluten-Free ✦ Soy-Free ✦ Vegan

* **Glass jar with lid**

1	bay leaf	1
1	star anise	1
1 tsp	coconut sugar	5 mL
¼ tsp	ground cinnamon	1 mL
¼ tsp	ground cardamom	1 mL
¼ tsp	ground ginger	1 mL
Pinch	ground cloves	Pinch
1 cup	coconut milk (full-fat or light)	250 mL

1. In a small saucepan, combine bay leaf, star anise, coconut sugar, cinnamon, cardamom, ginger, cloves and coconut milk. Bring to a simmer over low heat. Simmer for 5 minutes to infuse the milk with flavor. Let cool.

2. Strain into a glass jar and refrigerate for 1 hour. Shake, pour into a glass and serve.

Dosha Modification

✦ **Kapha** should dilute with ¼ cup (60 mL) water and omit the coconut sugar.

Cardamom Tea

Fragrant cardamom tea is soothing to the senses and a time-honored aid to digestion. Ayurveda recognizes cardamom as having the qualities of an expectorant (removing mucus from the stomach and lungs), a heart tonic and a carminative (alleviating stomach pain, indigestion and gas). It is a delicious treat after dinner or any time of day.

Makes 1 serving

Variation
Add ¼ cup (60 mL) unsweetened almond milk or cashew milk.

Gluten-Free ✦ Soy-Free ✦ Vegan

- **Mortar and pestle**

5	green cardamom pods	5
1 cup	water	250 mL
	Raw liquid honey (optional)	

1. Using a mortar and pestle, lightly crush cardamom pods.
2. In a small saucepan, combine crushed cardamom and water. Bring to a boil over high heat. Reduce heat and simmer for 5 minutes.
3. Strain tea into a mug and (if adding honey) let cool to lukewarm. If desired, sweeten with honey.

Kapha Ginger Tea

Ginger is warm and stimulates digestion. This is a great tea for when kapha is feeling a little sluggish.

Makes 1 serving

Gluten-Free ✦ Soy-Free ✦ Vegan

1 cup	water	250 mL
½ tsp	ground ginger	2 mL
	Raw liquid honey (optional)	

1. In a small saucepan, combine water and ginger. Bring to a boil over high heat. Reduce heat and simmer for 3 minutes.
2. Pour tea into a mug and (if adding honey) let cool to lukewarm. If desired, sweeten with honey.

Vata Pitta Ginger Tea

This is a nice alternative to a caffeinated tea any time you want a little nurturing in between meals. Fresh ginger is mildly heating and is said to cleanse the blood.

Makes 1 serving

Gluten-Free ✦ Soy-Free ✦ Vegan

1 cup	water	250 mL
½ tsp	chopped gingerroot	2 mL
	Raw liquid honey or pure maple syrup (optional)	

1. In a small saucepan, combine water and ginger. Bring to a boil over high heat. Reduce heat and simmer for 3 minutes.
2. Pour tea into a mug and (if adding honey) let cool to lukewarm. Sweeten if desired, using honey for vata and maple syrup for pitta.

Tridoshic Mint Tea

The smell of mint is soothing and has a cooling effect on the emotions. When the leaves are steeped into a tea, that calming energetic gets transferred. Some mint can have a bit of a pungent (heating) aftereffect, which would not be ideal if one were trying to reduce pitta.

Makes 1 serving

Gluten-Free ✦ Soy-Free ✦ Vegan

2 tbsp	fresh mint leaves	30 mL
1 cup	boiling water	250 mL

1. In a mug, steep mint leaves in boiling water for 3 minutes. Strain into a glass and serve.

Ginger Lemongrass Tea

Sip this tea during flu season or on cold, damp days to bring a sense of overall well-being. The combination of lemongrass and ginger has a warm and stimulating energetic, ideal for clearing kapha congestion. Lemongrass tea is an ancient remedy for curing chest congestion, colds and coughs. Ginger is traditionally used to improve cardiovascular health and to treat and prevent nausea, joint pain, inflammation, colds and bacterial and viral infections.

Makes 4 servings

Tips

Lemongrass has several tightly wrapped layers surrounding a tender white core. Select firm lemongrass stalks that are pale yellow at the lower end and green at the upper end. Remove the tough outer layers before use.

Store leftover tea in a glass jar in the refrigerator for up to 5 days. Reheat individual servings as desired.

You can sweeten the tea with honey or coconut sugar. If using honey, let the tea cool to lukewarm first.

Gluten-Free ✦ Soy-Free ✦ Vegan

2	stalks lemongrass	2
1	2-inch (5 cm) piece gingerroot	1
8 cups	water	2 L

1. Using a mallet or the dull side of a knife blade, bruise lemongrass stalks. Cut each stalk into 3 pieces.
2. In a medium saucepan, combine lemongrass, ginger and water. Bring to a boil over medium–high heat. Reduce heat and simmer for 15 minutes. Strain into a glass and serve.

Appendix A
Vata Balancing Aids

Signs and Symptoms of Imbalance

+ anxiety
+ asthma
+ black circles under eyes
+ bloating
+ breathlessness
+ constipation
+ cracked heels
+ difficulty with speech
  (such as stuttering)
+ dry skin
+ emaciation
+ fatigue
+ fearfulness
+ forgetfulness
+ gas

+ heart palpitations
+ hiccups
+ inability to concentrate/racing thoughts
+ insecurity
+ insomnia
+ loneliness
+ nervousness
+ neuromuscular disorders (tremors, spasms, numbness, tingling)
+ nightmares
+ osteoporosis
+ popping joints
+ sciatic pain
+ vague abdominal pain and distention
+ wheezing

Causes of Imbalance

+ astringent food
+ bitter food
+ excess cold (food, drink, environment)
+ excess dry (food, environment)
+ excess talking
+ jumping
+ leftover foods

+ pungent foods
+ running
+ staying up late
+ suppressing natural urges (burping, defecation, urination, flatulence, etc.)
+ travel
+ windy days

Balancing and Unbalancing Choices

	Balancing	Unbalancing
Tastes	salty, sour, sweet	astringent, bitter, pungent
Qualities	cloudy, gross, heavy, oily, smooth, stable, warm	astringent, clear, cold, dry, light, mobile, rough, subtle
Fruits	apricots, avocados, bananas, blueberries, cantaloupe, cherries, coconut, dates, figs, grapefruit, grapes, kiwifruit, lemons, limes, mangos, olives (black), oranges, papayas, peaches, pineapple, plums, prunes (soaked), raisins (soaked), rhubarb, umeboshi plums	apples, bitter melon, cranberries, pears, persimmons, pomegranates, raisins (unsoaked), strawberries, watermelon
Vegetables	asparagus, beets, carrots (cooked), chicory (endive, frisée), chile peppers, cucumbers, fennel, green beans, leeks (cooked), mizuna, mustard greens, okra, onions (cooked), parsnips, sweet potatoes, rutabaga, spinach, zucchini	artichokes, beet greens, bell peppers, broccoli, Brussels sprouts, burdock root, cabbage, carrots (raw), cauliflower, celery, corn, dandelion greens, eggplant, kale, kohlrabi, lettuce, mushrooms, onions (raw), peas, potatoes, radishes, sprouts, tomatoes, turnips, winter squash
Grains	amaranth, Durham flour, oats (cooked), quinoa, rice (basmati, brown, white), seitan, wheat	barley, buckwheat, corn, millet, oat bran, pasta (wheat), rice cakes, rye, sago, soy flour and powder, spelt, tapioca
Beans and lentils	kidney beans, mung beans, soy (cheese, sauce), tur dal, urad dal	adzuki beans, black-eyed peas, chickpeas (garbanzo beans), lentils (brown, Puy, red), navy beans, pinto beans, soybeans, tempeh, tofu, white beans
Nuts	almonds, Brazil nuts, cashews, charoli nuts, hazelnuts, macadamia nuts, peanuts, pecans, pine nuts, pistachios, walnuts	
Seeds	poppy, psyllium, pumpkin, safflower, sesame, sunflower	
Dairy	butter, buttermilk, cheese (hard and soft), ghee, milk (cow's, goat's), sour cream, yogurt (fresh or store-bought)	
Animal protein	beef, buffalo, chicken (dark meat), duck, eggs, fish (fresh- and saltwater), shrimp, turkey (dark meat)	chicken (white meat), lamb, mutton, pork, rabbit, turkey (white meat), venison
Fats	almond oil, avocado oil, castor oil, ghee, mustard oil, olive oil, peanut oil, safflower oil, sesame oil, sunflower oil	corn oil, soybean oil

	Balancing	Unbalancing
Sweeteners	barley malt, date sugar, fructose, honey, jaggery (palm sugar), low-glycemic, maple syrup, molasses, rice syrup, Sucanat, turbinado, unrefined	white sugar
Herbs, spices and flavorings	ajwain, allspice, anise, asafoetida (hing), basil, bay leaf, black pepper, caraway, cardamom, cayenne pepper, chives, cilantro/coriander, cinnamon, cloves, cumin, dill, fennel, fenugreek, garlic, ginger (dry and fresh), horseradish, mace, marjoram, mint, miso, mustard, nutmeg, oregano, paprika, parsley, rock salt, rosemary, rose water, saffron, savory, sea salt, tarragon, turmeric, vanilla	chocolate, neem
Snacks	guacamole, nuts, tahini Endive with Honeyed Goat Cheese (page 274) Go-to-Sleep Nutmeg Milk (page 321) Vata Breakfast Banana (page 119) Vata Pitta Coconut Chai Shake (page 324) Vata Pitta Vitality Drink (page 320) Tridoshic Carrot (with a Kick) Spread (page 287) Tridoshic Zucchini Hummus (page 283) Zucchini Trail Bread (page 295)	chocolate, corn chips, crackers, energy bars, popcorn, potato chips, rice cakes, sweets with refined white sugar or high-glycemic index
Meals	meat broth soups (beef, buffalo, dark chicken meat), pasta with pesto (basil or arugula), soups, stews Beet Sweet Potato Soup (variation, page 185) Bison Meatloaf with Maple Tamarind Sauce (page 174) Broiled Salmon in Maple Lime Marinade (page 163) Dashi Clear Broth soups (pages 178, 183, 193, 200) Fennel-Crusted Paneer with Balsamic Reduction (page 161) Ginger-Braised Fennel and Sweet Potato (page 224) Gujarati Wedding Dal (page 128) Marco's Porcini Risotto (page 152) Mung Dal Cilantro Soup (page 195) Okra with Ginger Lemongrass Sauce (page 214) Spanish Chicken (page 168) Thai Lemongrass Vermicelli Soup (page 198) Urad Dal with Tamarind (page 127)	beans heavy combinations, raw dishes, salads

	Balancing	Unbalancing
Exercise and lifestyle	Exercise should be short-duration, low-intensity (minimal, if any, sweating) and mindful: walking, easy bike rides, gentle yoga combined with ujjayi pranayama (standing poses and forward bends are most grounding),* alternate nostril pranayama and meditation.* Lifestyles that help ground vata include slowing down, staying hydrated, keeping to a routine, getting plenty of rest, morning self-massage with sesame oil (leave on for 15–20 minutes, then shower with warm water). *__Caution:__ To avoid injury, seek the guidance of a qualified yoga instructor.	Exercise that will aggravate vata include high-intensity (heavy sweating), depleting exercises, such as running, salsa dancing and tennis. If you partake in these exercises, replenish/balance vata by getting adequate rest, eating grounding oily foods and drinking water and Vata Pitta Vitality Drink (page 320). Avoid caffeine (too much stimulation) and alcohol (too much ether/air quality).

Source: Appendix A is derived from the "Qualities of Food Substances" table in *Ayurvedic Cooking for Self-Healing* by Dr. Vasant Lad (The Ayurvedic Press, Albuquerque, NM: 1994). All rights reserved.

Pitta Balancing Aids

Signs and Symptoms of Imbalance

- anger
- bleeding disorders (such as bloodshot eyes or a bleeding rectum or gums)
- controlling behavior
- depression
- diarrhea
- dizziness
- fever
- fierce competitiveness
- hateful feelings
- heartburn
- indigestion
- inflammation
- jaundice
- migraines
- mistrust
- nausea
- rashes
- sour taste in mouth
- suicidal thoughts
- tendency to be judgmental and critical
- ulcers

Causes of Imbalance

- excess external heat (summertime, sunshine)
- excess hot, spicy, oily foods
- fermented foods
- inflated ego (sense of self)
- prolonged fasting
- repressed anger
- running
- salty foods
- sour foods

Balancing and Unbalancing Choices

	Balancing	Unbalancing
Tastes	astringent, bitter, sweet	pungent, salty, sour
Qualities	cold, dense, dry, heavy, slow/dull	fleshy smell, hot, light, liquid, oily, penetrating, spreading
Fruits	apples, avocados, berries (sweet), bitter melon, cherries (sweet), coconut, dates, figs, grapes (red), limes, melons, pears, pomegranate, prunes (soaked), raisins, watermelon	apricots, bananas, berries (sour), cherries (sour), cranberries, grapefruit, grapes (green), kiwifruit, lemons, olives (black), papayas, peaches, persimmons, pineapple, plums, rhubarb, tamarind
Vegetables	arugula, asparagus, beet greens, bell peppers, broccoli, Brussels sprouts, burdock root, cabbage, carrots (cooked), cauliflower, celery, chicory (endive, frisée), cucumbers, dandelion greens, fennel, green beans, greens, jicama, kale, leeks (cooked), lettuce, mizuna, parsnips, potatoes, radicchio, rutabaga, spinach (raw), sprouts, squash (winter and summer), sweet potatoes, zucchini	beets, carrots (raw), chile peppers, corn, eggplant, kohlrabi, mustard greens, onions (raw), radishes, spinach (cooked), tomatoes, turnips
Grains	amaranth, barley, Durham flour, oat bran, oats, pasta (wheat), quinoa, rice (basmati, white), rice cakes, sago, seitan, soy flour and powder, spelt, tapioca, wheat	buckwheat, corn, millet, rice (brown), rye
Beans and lentils	adzuki beans, black-eyed peas, chickpeas (garbanzo beans), kidney beans, lentils (brown, red), mung beans, navy beans, pinto beans, soybeans, tempeh, tofu, white beans	tur dal, urad dal
Nuts	almonds (soaked and peeled), charoli nuts	almonds (with skin), Brazil nuts, cashews, hazelnuts, macadamia nuts, peanuts, pecans, pine nuts, pistachios, walnuts
Seeds	psyllium, safflower, sunflower	pumpkin, sesame
Dairy	butter, cheese (soft), cottage cheese, ghee, milk (cow's, goat's), yogurt (fresh, not store-bought)	cheese (hard), sour cream, yogurt (store-bought)
Animal protein	buffalo, chicken (white meat), egg whites, rabbit, shrimp, turkey (white meat), venison	beef, chicken (dark meat), duck, egg yolks, fish (fresh- and saltwater), lamb, mutton, pork, turkey (dark meat)
Fats	avocado oil, castor oil, coconut oil, ghee, olive oil, soybean oil, sunflower oil	almond oil, corn oil, mustard oil, peanut oil, safflower oil, sesame oil

	Balancing	Unbalancing
Sweeteners	barley malt, date sugar, fructose, maple syrup, rice syrup, Sucanat, sugar (white), turbinado	honey, jaggery (palm sugar), molasses
Herbs, spices and flavorings	cilantro/coriander, cumin, dill, fennel, mint, rose water, saffron, salt (rock), tarragon, turmeric, vanilla	ajwain, allspice, anise, asafoetida (hing), basil, bay leaf, black pepper, caraway, cayenne pepper, cloves, ginger (ground), fenugreek, horseradish, mace, marjoram, miso, mustard, nutmeg, oregano, paprika, poppy seeds, rosemary, salt (sea), soy sauce
Snacks	almonds (peeled/soaked), artichoke dip or pesto, coconut water, ice cream, spirulina energy bars, sweet fruits Endive with Honeyed Goat Cheese (page 274) Go-to-Sleep Nutmeg Milk (page 321) Jicama Lime Sticks (page 275) Lemony Cannellini Bean Spread (page 285) Mexican Black Bean Spread (page 286) Pitta-Cooling Coriander Milk (page 320) Pitta-Refreshing Aloe Lime Drink (page 318) Pitta-Soothing Mint Rose Water Drink (page 317) Sweet Potato Fries (page 225) Tridoshic Zucchini Hummus (page 283) Vata Pitta Coconut Chai Shake (page 324)	aged Cheddar cheese, bananas, buffalo wings, chocolate (too acidic), corn chips and salsa, nuts (except almonds and charoli), popcorn, potato chips, salt and vinegar flavoring
Meals	egg white omelets with cilantro and fennel, Puy lentils, salads, steamed green leafy vegetables, turkey meatloaf Amaranth Porridge with Pear Juice, Currants and Almonds (page 105) Baked Falafel Balls (page 136) Barley Sauté with Sweet Potato, Asparagus and Burdock (page 140) Brazilian Black Bean Stew (page 210) Brussels Sprout and Sweet Potato Sauté (page 223) Caribbean Adzuki Bean Stew (page 209) Chilled Avocado Soup (page 184) Chilled Carrot Soup with Avocado (page 186) Coconut Cranberry Quinoa Porridge (page 106) Dashi Clear Broth (page 178) Escarole with Pomegranate and Sweet Balsamic Dressing (page 212)	chilis, fried foods, instant soup and packaged foods (due to high sodium), pasta with tomato sauce, sauerkraut, spicy Mexican/Asian foods, tomato-based dishes

	Balancing	Unbalancing
Meals (continued)	Fennel-Crusted Paneer with Balsamic Reduction (page 161) Ginger-Braised Fennel and Sweet Potato (page 224) Gujarati Wedding Dal (page 128) Kapha Pitta Barley Kale Soup (page 197) Kelp Noodles with Almond Sauce (page 234) Lime Tarragon Sweet Potato Breakfast Patties (page 114) Moroccan Veggie Burgers with Tangy Tamarind Sauce (page 135) Mung Dal Cilantro Soup (page 195) Pitta-Cooling Summer Mung Dal (page 123) Pitta Kapha Cannellini, Kale and Artichoke Sauté (page 131) Puy Lentil Soup with Pork Sausage (page 201) Puréed Potato-Leek Soup with Asparagus and Lemon (page 190) Rabbit Coconut Fenugreek Stew (page 176) Red Quinoa with Endive and Cranberries (page 150) Roasted Turkey Breast with Tarragon Cream Sauce (page 170) Rosemary-Infused Heirloom Scarlet Runners (page 134) Simple Red Dal and Lime (page 130)	
Exercise and lifestyle	Exercise should be cooling and moderate in duration and intensity: swimming, yoga asana (slow-flowing postures that emphasize the stomach, forward bends and twists),* pranayama (alternate nostril breathing, shitali).* Lifestyles that help cool pitta include spending time in nature (especially around calm water and with mellow friends), getting to bed before 10 p.m., meditating, "chilling out," morning self-massage with coconut oil (leave on for 15 minutes, then shower with warm water). *__Caution:__ To avoid injury, seek the guidance of a qualified yoga instructor.	Exercise and lifestyles that will aggravate pitta include running, excessive hours at the office, excessive debating/arguing, excessive time in the hot sun. Pitta should avoid coffee due to its stimulating and acidic qualities, or should add a pinch of cardamom or cinnamon to offset some of the effects. Try Teeccino mixed with coffee as a substitute. The antidote to burning the midnight oil is Pitta-Cooling Coriander Milk (page 320).

Source: Appendix B is derived from the "Qualities of Food Substances" table in *Ayurvedic Cooking for Self-Healing* by Dr. Vasant Lad (The Ayurvedic Press, Albuquerque, NM: 1994). All rights reserved.

Kapha Balancing Aids

Signs and Symptoms of Imbalance

- attachment (to possessions and relationships)
- colds
- congestion
- cysts
- depression
- diabetes
- excess salivation
- greed
- high cholesterol
- lethargy
- lipomas (benign tumors composed of fatty tissue)
- moodiness
- mucus
- obesity
- phlegm
- selfishness
- stubbornness
- swelling/water retention
- tumors
- weight gain (from emotional eating)

Causes of Imbalance

- cold drinks
- daytime sleeping
- eating for pleasure (without hunger)
- hydrophilic substances (such as salt)
- inadequate vigorous physical activity
- not enough variation in routine
- not feeling loved
- rich, heavy, oily foods
- winter and spring

Balancing and Unbalancing Choices

	Balancing	Unbalancing
Tastes	astringent, bitter, pungent	salty, sour, sweet
Qualities	light, mobile, sharp, warm	cool, heavy, liquid, oily, salty, slimy, slow, soft, stable, sweet, thick
Fruits	apples, apricots, berries, bitter melon, cherries, cranberries, peaches, pears, persimmons, pomegranates, prunes (soaked), raisins	avocados, bananas, coconut, dates, figs, grapefruit, grapes (green), kiwifruit, lemons, limes, melons, olives (black), plums, rhubarb, tamarind, watermelon
Vegetables	artichokes, arugula, asparagus, beet greens, beets, bell peppers, broccoli, Brussels sprouts, burdock root, cabbage, carrots, cauliflower, celery, chicory (endive, frisée), chile peppers, corn, dandelion greens, eggplant, fennel, green beans, green onions, kale, kohlrabi, leeks (cooked), lettuce, mizuna, mushrooms, mustard greens, okra, onions, peas, potatoes, radicchio, radishes, rutabagas, spinach, sprouts, turnips, winter squash	cucumbers, parsnips, sweet potatoes, tomatoes
Grains	amaranth, barley, buckwheat, corn, millet, oat bran, oats (dry), quinoa, rice (basmati), rice cakes, rye, sago, seitan, tapioca	Durham flour, oats (cooked), pasta (wheat), rice (brown, white), soy flour and powder, spelt, wheat
Beans and lentils	adzuki beans, black-eyed peas, chickpeas (garbanzo beans), lentils (brown, Puy, red, toor dal), navy beans, pinto beans, tempeh, white beans	kidney beans, soybeans, urad dal
Nuts	charoli nuts	almonds, Brazil nuts, cashews, hazelnuts, macadamia nuts, peanuts, pecans, pine nuts, pistachios, walnuts
Seeds	flax, mustard, psyllium, pumpkin, safflower, sunflower	sesame
Dairy	cottage cheese (paneer), ghee, goat's milk	butter, buttermilk, cheese, sour cream, yogurt (fresh or store-bought)
Animal protein	chicken (white meat), egg whites, rabbit, shrimp, turkey (white meat), venison	beef, buffalo, chicken (dark meat), duck, egg yolks, fish (fresh- and saltwater), lamb, mutton, pork, turkey (dark meat)
Fats	corn oil, ghee, mustard oil, sunflower oil	almond oil, avocado oil, castor oil, coconut oil, olive oil, peanut oil, safflower oil, sesame oil, soybean oil

	Balancing	Unbalancing
Sweeteners	honey (because it is heating and scrapes fat)	barley malt, date sugar, fructose, jaggery (palm sugar), maple syrup, molasses, rice syrup, Sucanat, sugar (white), turbinado
Herbs, spices and flavorings	ajwain, allspice, anise, asafoetida (hing), basil, bay leaf, black pepper, caraway, cardamom, cayenne pepper, chives, cilantro/coriander, cinnamon, cloves, cumin, dill, fennel, fenugreek, garlic, ginger, horseradish, mace, marjoram, mint, miso, mustard, neem, nutmeg, oregano, paprika, parsley, poppy seeds, rosemary, rose water, salt (rock), saffron, turmeric, vanilla, wasabi	chocolate, salt (sea), savory, tarragon
Snacks	apples, unsalted corn chips and salsa (page 290), unsalted popcorn, rice cakes with pesto, sweet berries Lemony Cannellini Bean Spread (page 285) Mexican Black Bean Spread (page 286) Mushroom Almond Pâté (page 288) Traditional Mexican Salsa (page 290)	bananas, candy, cheese, chocolate, ice cream, nuts
Meals	Baked Falafel Balls (page 136) Barley Sauté with Sweet Potato, Asparagus and Burdock (page 140) Borscht Lentil Soup (page 194) Cinnamon Lotus Edamame Sauté (page 228) Creamy Corn Soup (page 187) Escarole with Pomegranate and Sweet Balsamic Dressing (page 212) Fluffy Cinnamon Currant Millet (page 143) French Lentil Salad with Lemon Dressing (page 242) Kapha Broiled Polenta Slices (page 227) Kapha Mushroom and Artichoke Pesto Pizzettes (page 155) Kapha Pitta Barley Kale Soup (page 197) Millet Breakfast Patties (page 116) Millet with Wild Mushroom Vegetable Ragoût (page 144) Moroccan-Spiced Chickpea Stew (page 207) Moroccan Veggie Burgers with Tangy Tamarind Sauce (page 135) Mushroom Tarragon Purée (page 188)	

	Balancing	Unbalancing
Meals (continued)	Pitta Kapha Cannellini, Kale and Artichoke Sauté (page 131) Polenta with Minted Shiitake Sauce (page 146) Puréed Lemon Chickpea Soup (page 196) Quinoa Tabbouleh (page 149) Rabbit Coconut Fenugreek Stew (page 176) Red Quinoa with Endive and Cranberries (page 150) Roasted Turkey Breast with Tarragon Cream Sauce (page 170) Rosemary-Infused Heirloom Scarlet Runners (page 134)	beef, bean and cheese burritos, cheese tortillas, grilled cheese sandwiches, meatloaf and mashed potatoes, peanut butter sandwiches, Philly cheesesteak sub, pizza, steak with hollandaise sauce
Exercise and lifestyle	Exercise should be daily and can include vigorous, sweaty, long-duration workouts; running (unless overweight, due to impact on knees); cycling; swimming; salsa dancing; vinyasa yoga (sun salutations, abdominals, twists, arm balances and back bending)*; pranayama (bhastrika, kapalabhati).* Lifestyles that keep kapha from stagnating include lots of group activities, new adventures and varying daily routines. *Caution: To avoid injury, seek the guidance of a qualified yoga instructor.	Lifestyles that will aggravate kapha include daytime napping, an unvaried routine, lack of variety in life, lack of a social network, lack of love/close friendships.

Source: Appendix C is derived from the "Qualities of Food Substances" table in *Ayurvedic Cooking for Self-Healing* by Dr. Vasant Lad (The Ayurvedic Press, Albuquerque, NM: 1994). All rights reserved.

References

Annapoorani A, Anilakumar KR, Khanum F, et al. Studies on the physicochemical characteristics of heated honey, honey mixed with ghee and their food consumption pattern by rats. *Ayu*, 2010 Apr; 31 (2): 141–46. doi: 10.4103/0974-8520.72363.

Canadian Organic Growers. "Consumers & the Standards." Available at www.cog.ca/index.php?page=consumers-and-standards. Published 2011.

Environmental Working Group. "EWG's 2015 Shopper's Guide to Pesticides in Produce." Available at www.ewg.org/foodnews/summary.php. Accessed June 2015.

GM Watch. "GM Crops — Just the Science: Research Documenting the Limitations, Risks, and Alternatives." 2009.

Hallberg L. Does calcium interfere with iron absorption? *American Journal of Clinical Nutrition*, 1998; 68: 3–4.

Kristof Nicholas D. (OpEd columnist). "Cancer from the Kitchen?" *The New York Times*, December 5, 2009.

Lad, Dr. Vasant. *Ayurvedic Cooking for Self-Healing*. The Ayurvedic Press, Albuquerque, NM: 1994.

Lad, Vasant. *Textbook of Ayurveda: A Complete Guide to Clinical Assessment*, Vol. 2. The Ayurvedic Press, Albuquerque, NM: 2006.

Myhill, Sarah. "Digestive Enzymes are Necessary to Digest Food." Available at www.drmyhill.co.uk/wiki/Digestive_enzymes_are_necessary_to_digest_food. Last modified: February 7, 2015.

Nummer, Brian A. National Center for Home Food Preservation. "Fermenting Yogurt at Home." Available at: http://nchfp.uga.edu/publications/nchfp/factsheets/yogurt.html. Published October 2002.

Pavlov, Ivan. "Physiology of Digestion." From Nobel Lectures, *Physiology or Medicine 1901–1921*, Elsevier Publishing Company, Amsterdam, 1967. Available at www.nobelprize.org/nobel_prizes/medicine/laureates/1904/pavlov-lecture.html. Accessed April 18, 2013.

Sharma S, Kulkarni SK, Chopra K. "Curcumin, the active principle of turmeric (*Curcuma longa*), ameliorates diabetic nephropathy in rats." *Clinical and Experimental Pharmacology and Physiology*, 2006 Oct; 33 (10): 940–45.

Smith, Erik. "Choosing Healthy Cookware." *The Educated Vegetable*. Available at www.docstoc.com/docs/95647327/Choosing-Healthy-Cookware. Published September 2007.

United States Department of Agriculture. USDA National Organic Program/Agricultural Marketing Service. "Labeling Organic Products." Available at http://www.ams.usda.gov/AMSv1.0/getfile?dDocName=STELDEV3004446. Published October 2012.

U.S. Government Publishing Office. "Electronic Code of Federal Regulations." Available at www.ecfr.gov/cgi-bin/text-idx?c=ecfr&SID=9874504b6f1025eb0e6b67cadf9d3b40&rgn=div6&view=text&node=7:3.1.1.9.32.7&idno=7. Accessed June 2015.

Van Loon, Gabriel. *Charaka Samhita: Handbook on Ayurveda*, Vol. 1 (eBook). Lulu Press, 2013.

Weil, Andrew, "Cooking with Grains: Millet." *Weil Lifestyle*. Available at www.drweil.com/drw/u/ART03185/Cooking-With-Grains-Millet.html.

Index

P

palm sugar, 79
paneer
  Endive with Honeyed Goat
    Cheese, 274
  Escarole with Pomegranate
    and Sweet Balsamic
    Dressing (variation), 212
  Fennel-Crusted Paneer with
    Balsamic Reduction, 161
  Paneer, 160
  Tridoshic Red Lentil
    Hummus (variation), 284
  Zucchini Lasagna with
    Mary's Gravy (variation),
    156
parsley. See also herbs, fresh
  Lime Tarragon Sweet Potato
    Breakfast Patties, 114
  Mushroom Almond Pâté,
    288
  Red Quinoa with Endive and
    Cranberries (variation),
    150
  Vata Lemon Cashew Cream
    Sauce, 262
parsnips
  Puréed Parsnips with Thyme,
    215
  Rosemary Roasted Root
    Vegetables, 219
  Vegetable Broth (variation),
    182
peas (green). See also chickpeas
  Rabbit Coconut Fenugreek
    Stew, 176
  Soba Noodle Salad, 245
pepitas. See pumpkin seeds
peppers (chile)
  Bangalore Toor Dal
    Sambhar, 126
  Barley Sauté with Sweet
    Potato, Asparagus and
    Burdock (DM), 140
  Black Bean Avocado Salad,
    243
  Gujurati Wedding Dal, 128
  Kelp Noodles with Almond
    Sauce, 234
  Kerala-Inspired Toor Dal,
    124
  Masala Dosas (DM), 112
  Masala Spice Mix (variation),
    271
  Mexican Rice, 230
  Mexican Salsa, Traditional,
    290
  Okra with Ginger
    Lemongrass Sauce, 214

Quinoa Tabbouleh
  (variation), 149
Quinoa with Spinach Pesto
  "Cream" Sauce (variation),
  148
Soba Noodle Salad (DM),
  245
Thai Lemongrass Vermicelli
  Soup, 198
Urad Dal with Tamarind
  (DM), 127
Vata Sweet Onion Chutney,
  267
pitta, 24–25, 26, 53–54
  balancing aids, 332–35
  churna (spice blend) for, 272
  colors of, 27
  drinks and juices for, 314,
    323
  physical characteristics, 24,
    29–30
  salads and dressings for, 247,
    248
  tastes and, 35–39
pitta recipes
  Kapha Pitta Barley Kale
    Soup, 197
  Pitta-Cooling Coriander
    Milk, 320
  Pitta-Cooling Date Chutney,
    265
  Pitta-Cooling Summer
    Mung Dal, 123
  Pitta Green Tonic, 319
  Pitta Kapha Cannellini,
    Kale and Artichoke Sauté,
    131
  Pitta Kapha Pomegranate
    Vinaigrette, 253
  Pitta Pomegranate Lime
    Mocktail, 316
  Pitta-Refreshing Aloe Lime
    Drink, 318
  Pitta-Soothing Mint Rose
    Water Drink, 317
  Vata Pitta Avocado
    Cucumber Salad, 238
  Vata Pitta Coconut Chai
    Shake, 324
  Vata Pitta Ginger Tea, 326
  Vata Pitta Vitality Drink,
    320
Poached Eggs for Vata, 108
poha (flattened rice), 113
polenta, 70. See also cornmeal
  Kapha Broiled Polenta Slices,
    227
  Polenta with Minted Shiitake
    Sauce, 146

pomegranate. See also
  pomegranate syrup
  Escarole with Pomegranate
    and Sweet Balsamic
    Dressing, 212
  Iron-Boosting Pomegranate
    Lamb Soup, 204
pomegranate syrup (molasses),
  80
  Amaranth Crêpes with
    Pomegranate Syrup, 110
  Pitta Kapha Pomegranate
    Vinaigrette, 253
  Pitta Pomegranate Lime
    Mocktail, 316
  Pomegranate Orange Chip
    Bars, 306
  Tridoshic Pomegranate
    Orange Reduction Sauce,
    257
potatoes
  Bangalore Toor Dal
    Sambhar, 126
  Creamy Corn Soup, 187
  Ginger Almond Squash Pie,
    221
  Ginger-Braised Fennel and
    Sweet Potato (DM), 224
  Kapha Pitta Barley Kale
    Soup, 197
  Masala Potatoes, 226
  Minted Fingerling Potato
    Frittata, 109
  Mushroom Tarragon Purée,
    188
  Puréed Parsnips with Thyme
    (DM), 215
  Puréed Potato-Leek Soup
    with Asparagus and
    Lemon, 190
  Puy Lentils and Artichokes
    in Puff Pastry (variation),
    132
  Rosemary Roasted Root
    Vegetables, 219
  Summer Vegetable Soup, 192
  Tridoshic Carrot (with a
    Kick) Spread, 287
poultry, 90. See also chicken;
  turkey
prakruti (balance starting
  point), 23, 28, 29–32
protein, 41, 44. See also specific
  proteins
pumpkin. See also squash
  Ginger Pumpkin Soup, 189
  Red Quinoa with Endive and
    Cranberries (variation),
    150

squash. *See also* pumpkin; squash, summer
    Autumn Wild Rice Salad, 246
    Caribbean Adzuki Bean Stew, 209
    Citrus Spice Glass Noodle Stir-Fry, 154
    Ginger Almond Squash Pie, 221
    Kabocha Caramel Custard, 310
    Kabocha Cranberry Bread, 296
    Lemon Farro Cannellini Stew, 208
    Masala Potatoes (variation), 226
    Millet with Wild Mushroom Vegetable Ragoût (variation), 144
    Moroccan-Spiced Chickpea Stew, 207
    Roasted Kabocha Squash, 220
    Rosemary-Infused Heirloom Scarlet Runners (variation), 134
squash, summer. *See also* zucchini
    Spanish Chicken, 168
    Summer Squash Pasta, 217
    Thai Lemongrass Vermicelli Soup (variation), 198
stews, 176, 206–10
Summer Israeli Couscous Salad, 244
Summer Squash Pasta, 217
Summer Vegetable Soup, 192
sunflower oil, 79
sunflower seeds, 74. *See also* seeds
sweeteners, 79–80. *See also specific sweeteners*
sweet potatoes, 129. *See also* yams
    Autumn Wild Rice Salad (variation), 246
    Barley Sauté with Sweet Potato, Asparagus and Burdock, 140
    Brazilian Black Bean Stew, 210
    Brussels Sprout and Sweet Potato Sauté, 223
    Caribbean Adzuki Bean Stew, 209
    Creamy Beet Leek Soup (variation), 185
    Ginger Almond Squash Pie, 221
    Ginger-Braised Fennel and Sweet Potato, 224

Ginger Pumpkin Soup, 189
Kapha Pitta Barley Kale Soup (DM), 197
Lime Tarragon Sweet Potato Breakfast Patties, 114
Millet Breakfast Patties, 116
Minted Apricot Couscous (variation), 139
Rabbit Coconut Fenugreek Stew, 176
Red Quinoa with Endive and Cranberries (variation), 150
Rosemary Roasted Root Vegetables, 219
Sweet Potato Fries, 225
sweet tastes, 35–36

T

tahini
    Basic Tahini, 261
    Lemony Hummus, 282
    Tridoshic Zucchini Hummus, 283
    Turkish Halva, 304
tamari, 75–76
    Lime Ginger Tofu, 137
    Tridoshic Asian Lime Vinaigrette, 249
    Tridoshic Asian Tamari Dressing, 250
tamarind paste, 76
    Bison Meatloaf with Maple Tamarind Sauce, 174
    Cool Coconut Chutney, 264
    Moroccan Veggie Burgers with Tangy Tamarind Sauce, 135
    Tangy Tamarind Sauce, 258
    Urad Dal with Tamarind, 127
    Vata Tamarind Honey Dressing, 253
tarragon
    Lime Tarragon Sweet Potato Breakfast Patties, 114
    Mushroom Tarragon Purée, 188
    Roasted Turkey Breast with Tarragon Cream Sauce, 170
tastes, 34–39
teas, 325–27
Thai Lemongrass Vermicelli Soup, 198
thyroid disease, 69
tofu, 95
    Dry-Fried Tofu, 137
    Fennel-Crusted Paneer with Balsamic Reduction (variation), 161
    Lime Ginger Tofu, 137

Thai Lemongrass Vermicelli Soup (variation), 198
Tofu Marsala, 138
tomatoes. *See also* vegetables
    Bangalore Toor Dal Sambhar, 126
    Brazilian Black Bean Stew, 210
    Chicken Tikka Masala, 166
    Kerala-Inspired Toor Dal, 124
    Mary's Gravy, 158
    Mexican Rice, 230
    Mexican Salsa, Traditional, 290
    Moroccan-Spiced Chickpea Stew, 207
    Pitta Kapha Cannellini, Kale and Artichoke Sauté, 131
    Puy Lentils and Artichokes in Puff Pastry, 132
    Quinoa Tabbouleh, 149
    Stuffed Grape Leaves, Marinela's, 276
    Tridoshic Mediterranean Salad Plate, 241
toor dal, 66
    Bangalore Toor Dal Sambhar, 126
    Gujurati Wedding Dal (variation), 128
    Kerala-Inspired Toor Dal, 124
tororo-kombu, 178
Traditional Mexican Salsa, 290
Trail Mix, 278
Truffles, 309
turkey. *See also* chicken
    Bison Meatloaf with Maple Tamarind Sauce (variation), 174
    Lemon Rosemary Turkey Sausages, 169
    Roasted Turkey Breast with Tarragon Cream Sauce, 170
    Turkey Cilantro Meatballs, 172
Turkish Halva, 304
turmeric, 60
    Red Lentil Winter Stew with Turmeric Root and Kale, 206
    Turmeric Milk, 321
turnips
    Rosemary Roasted Root Vegetables, 219
    Vegetable Broth (variation), 182
Tzatziki, 260

Leonhardi, Lois A.,1963-, author
    The essential ayurvedic cookbook : 200 recipes for wellness / Lois A. Leonhardi.

Includes index.
ISBN 978-0-7788-0513-7 (paperback)

    1. Vegetarian cooking. 2. Medicine, Ayurvedic. 3. Cookbooks. I. Title.

TX837.L465 2015   641.5'636   C2015-904813-3